# ORGANIZATIONAL PSYCHOLOGY
## an experiential approach

David A. Kolb | Irwin M. Rubin | James M. McIntyre

*Case Western
Reserve University*

*Situation Management
Systems, Inc.*

*Development Research
Associates, Inc.*

PRENTICE-HALL, INC., Englewood Cliffs, New Jersey 07632

*Library of Congress Cataloging in Publication Data*

Kolb, David A 1939–
  Organizational psychology.

  (Prentice-Hall behavioral science in business series)
  Includes bibliographical references.
  1.–Psychology, Industrial.  I.–Rubin, Irwin M.,
1939– joint author.  II.–McIntyre, James, 1935–
joint author.  III.–Title.
HF5548.8.K552 1979      158.7      78-27786
ISBN 0-13-641258-0

Editorial/production supervision by Esther S. Koehn
Interior and cover design by Christine E. Gadekar
Manufacturing buyer: Harry P. Baisley


Prentice-Hall Behavioral Science in Business Series,
Herbert A. Simon, Editor

Printed in the United States of America
10  9  8  7  6  5  4  3  2  1




Prentice-Hall International, Inc., *London*
Prentice-Hall of Australia Pty. Limited, *Sydney*
Prentice-Hall of Canada, Ltd., *Toronto*
Prentice-Hall of India Private Limited, *New Delhi*
Prentice-Hall of Japan, Inc., *Tokyo*
Prentice-Hall of Southeast Asia Pte. Ltd., *Singapore*
Whitehall Books Limited, *Wellington, New Zealand*

*To Jonathon*

*Beth, Steven, Corey*

*Jimmy, Kerry, Jon, Tom*

# contents

v

# foreword

This book—or better, the body of experiences it proposes—seeks to communicate some knowledge of general psychological principles, and some skill in applying that knowledge to social and organizational situations. Science tries to illuminate concrete reality by disclosing the general laws and principles that make the reality what it is. The generalization gives meaning to the concrete instance, but the instance carries the generalization into the real world—makes it usable. Experiencing social situations and then analyzing that experience brings generalization and concrete reality into effective union.

In teaching undergraduate and graduate management courses, I have frequently encountered students who hold a magical belief in a real world, somehow entirely different from any world they had hitherto experienced, and different, too, from the world of their textbooks. In teaching experienced executives, I have as frequently encountered men who balked at the proposal to apply general psychological principles to the concrete experiences of their everyday world. If there are skeptics of either variety in a group that undertakes one of these exercises, they can conduct their own tests of the relevance of theory to experience and vice versa. That is what the exercises are about.

But are the exercises themselves "real"? Can you really simulate social or organizational phenomena in a laboratory? The answer hangs on what we know of people—of their readiness to take roles, or, more accurately, their *inability not* to take roles when they find themselves in appropriate social situations, but this in itself is a psychological generalization: Man is a role taker. Like any generalization, it should be tested empirically; and the exercises do just that. Each participant can be his own witness to the reality—or lack of it—of what has gone on.

But the purpose of the exercises is not just to increase understanding of principles, or understanding of concrete situations in terms of principles. They can be useful also as a means of developing skills for group situations: skills of observing, skills of self-insight, skills of understanding the behaviors and motives of others, skills of adapting behavior to the requirements of a task and the needs of groups and persons.

There is no magic to it. Learning here, like all learning, derives from time and attention directed to relevant material. The exercises provide the material. The time, attention, and active participation must be supplied by those who take part in them.

*Herbert A. Simon*

# preface

This book is intended for students, managers, and behavioral scientists who wish to explore the personal relevance and conceptual bases of the phenomena of organizational psychology. This book was designed with a focus on exercises, games, and role plays to make the insights of behavioral science meaningful and relevant to practicing managers and students of organizational behavior. After several years of experimentation with the classic educational methodologies—lectures, seminars, research project teams, and some newer approaches such as sensitivity training—we discovered for ourselves the power of the experience-based learning model (others had made similar discoveries long before). As we began to experiment seriously with this model, within the university and in our outside consulting activities, we saw that it is possible to design an educational intervention that facilitates each stage of the experience-based learning process. Exercises and simulations can be designed to produce experiences that create the phenomena of organizational psychology. Observation schemes and methods can be introduced to facilitate understanding of these experiences. Theories and models can be added to aid in forming generalizations. And finally, the intervention can be structured in a way that encourages the learner to experiment with what he has learned in new experiences related to his personal life. The seventeen units in this book represent our attempts to apply this approach to key concepts in organizational psychology.

There is also to be a companion book, *Readings in Organizational Psychology*, published by Prentice-Hall, Inc. Many footnotes in this volume make reference to articles which have been reprinted there. That these articles appear in our readings book will be denoted by *"Readings"* at the end of the footnote entry.

Our feelings of pride in the product are tempered by the great indebtedness we feel to many others whose ideas and insights preceded ours. It is a tribute to the spirit of collaboration that pervades our field that the origin of many of the exercises recorded here is unknown. We have tried throughout the manuscript to trace the origins of those exercises we know about and in the process we may in many areas fall short of the original insight. For that we can only apologize. The major unnamed contributors are our students. In a very real sense, this book could never have been completed without their active participation in our explorations.

The more immediate sources of indebtedness are easily identified—the friends and colleagues who helped in the creation of this manuscript. Dick Beckhard, Warren Bennis, Dave Berlew, Mason Haire, Frank Friedlander, the late Don Marquis, Ed Schein and Suresh Srivastva helped greatly in the design, testing, and evaluation of various exercises in the book. Their work did much to improve the quality of the manuscript, but we, of course, must remain responsible for its final form. A special word of thanks goes to Margaret Fox who collaborated with us in the creation of the Yellow Pages of Learning Experiences for the second edition. David Wilder of Prentice-Hall must also be mentioned for his part in the design and execution of the Yellow Pages.

*D. K.*
*I. R.*
*J. M.*

# introduction

*Photo by Sybil Shelton*

"I hear and I forget
I see and I remember
I do and I understand"
    Confucius

As teachers responsible for helping persons learn about the field of organizational psychology, we have grappled continuously with a number of basic dilemmas. Some revolve around the issue of how to teach the subject. The key concepts in organizational psychology (indeed, behavioral science in general) are rather abstract, and thus it is difficult to bring them to life and make them meaningful through the lecture method. Other problems concern issues of what to teach since the field of organizational psychology is large and continues to grow. Relevant concepts and theories come from a variety of disciplines, and no single course could begin to scratch the surface.

Central to these dilemmas is the problem of control. Who should be in control of the learning process? Who should decide what material is important to learn? Who should decide the pace at which learning should occur? Indeed, who should decide what constitutes learning? Our resolution of these and related dilemmas is contained within this book. It represents a relatively new approach to the teaching and learning of organizational psychology, in which primary emphasis is placed upon learning from your own experience. Each of the seventeen learning units begins with an introduction formulated to raise key questions and to provide a framework for your experiences in the unit. The core of each unit is an action-oriented behavioral simulation. The purpose of this approach is to have you generate your own data about each of the key concepts to be studied. A format is provided to facilitate your ability to observe and share the personal reactions you have experienced, while the summaries at the end of each unit help integrate the unit experiences and stimulate further questions and issues to be explored.

One place to begin exploring these questions and issues is in the Yellow Pages of Learning Experiences at the back of the book. It is intended as a guide for continuing the learning experiences you have started with the units, a way of continuing through the learning cycle on your own. By using both the units and the directory of learning experiences, you should begin to identify your own learning goals in a much clearer way, taking responsibility for your own learning. If there is an overriding objective of the book, it is that you learn how to learn from all your experiences.

## *Learning About Organizational Psychology*

It has been over ten years since we first began developing and testing the feasibility of experiential learning methods for teaching organizational psychology. Our initial attempts to substitute exercise games and role plays for the more traditional educational approaches were met in many quarters by polite skepticism and subtle resistance. Today experiential learning approaches are an integral part of management school curricula and management training programs everywhere.

During these ten years the subject matter of organizational psychology has undergone much change as well. Some of this change has been subtle and quiet, involving the consolidation and implementation of trends that began years ago. Other changes have been more dramatic. New vital perspectives have come alive, reorganizing and redirecting research, theory, and teaching in the field. Still other trends loom on the horizon as yet underdeveloped, pointing the way toward the future shape of the field.

As we began to work on this third edition we felt it was time to take stock of these changes so that we might faithfully, in new selection of topics and experiential exercises, portray the field of organizational psychology as it is today — a complex of vital themes enduring from the past, alive in the present, and emerging in the future. Such a stocktaking is difficult to achieve objectively. Organizational psychology is a vast field with indefinite boundaries overlapping sister disciplines of social psychology, sociology, and anthropology and management fields such as operations research, business policy, and industrial relations. One could convincingly argue that any patterns one sees in such diversity and complexity lie more in the eye of the beholder than in objective reality. At the very least where one stands in defining organizational psychology is greatly influenced by where one sits, by one's particular experience and orientation to the field. Recognizing that any organization of the field is constructed from a combination of objective reality and subjective preference, we nonetheless felt that there is value in making explicit our view of the field, since it was on the basis of that view that choices of topics and exercises were made. By understanding our view, you, as learners, may be better able to articulate your own agreements and disagreements, thereby helping to sort the actual state of the field from our individual viewpoints.

In Table 1 are summarized the changes we have seen in the field in the last ten years in six general areas — the way organizational psychology is defined, the way management education is conducted, the field's perspective on the nature of persons, its view as to how human resources are to be managed, its perspective on organizations, and the nature of the change/improvement process. In each of these areas there are three kinds of trends: *realized trends*, previous historical developments that are now widely influential in shaping the field; *active trends*, new foci of research and development which seem to be capturing the excitement and imagination of scholars and practitioners; and *emerging trends*, new issues and concerns which seem destined to shape the future of organizational psychology in research and practice.

### Definition of the Field

Organizational psychology began as an offshoot and integration of industrial psychology and social psychology and, as such, early scholars in the field maintained primary loyalty to their basic discipline. Organizational behavior departments were housed administratively in business schools, but in general they maintained their separate identity from the profession of management. The last decade

## Table 1. Thematic Trends in the Study of Organizations In the Last Decade

| | Realized Trends | | Active Trends | | Emerging Trends | |
|---|---|---|---|---|---|---|
| 1. Definition of the field | Behavioral science discipline orientation | to Professional orientation | Industrial/business focus | to Management focus | Psychological, social psychological emphasis | to Sociological, political, systems focus |
| 2. Management education | Academic | to Experiential | Creating awareness | to Skill building | Performance orientation | to Learning to learn orientation |
| 3. Perspective on persons | Tender (communication, intimacy, growth) | to Tough (power and influence) | Socio-emotional factors | to Cognitive problem-solving factors | Deficiency orientation (adjustment) | to Appreciation orientation (development) |
| 4. Human resource management | Human relations | to Human resources | Management of people | to Management of work | Organization development | to Career development |
| 5. Perspective on organizations | Job satisfaction, human fulfillment | to Organization productivity | Internal organizational functioning | to Organization, environment adaptation | Organizations as the dominant stable structures | to Relationship among professional careers, institutions, and organizations |
| 6. Change processes | Expert, content consultation | to Process consultation | Change created by change agents | to Management of change by the system | Change via intervention (action research) | to Change via organizational analysis (research action) |
| | | | Simple, global technologies | to Highly differentiated problem-specific techniques | | |

has seen major changes in this orientation as organizational behavior departments have become more integrated units within professional business schools. Most new faculty today have Ph.D.s in management as opposed to basic disciplines, and interdisciplinary research around the managerial task has burgeoned. Concepts are now more often defined in managerial terms (e.g., work team development) as opposed to behavioral science terms (group dynamics).

The most active developments in organizational psychology today involve the expansion of the field from an industrial, business focus to a wider application of behavioral science knowledge in other professional fields—health care management, law, public administration, education, and international development. Perhaps because of this expansion into more complex social and political institutions, an emerging trend is toward a focus on sociological and political concepts which increase our understanding of management in complex organizational environments.

## Management Education

From the beginning, organizational psychologists have been concerned with educational innovations, particularly those aimed at communicating abstract academic knowledge in a way that is helpful and meaningful to pragmatically oriented professional managers and management students. The two dominant innovative traditions in this respect have been the development of the case method, particularly at the Harvard Business School, and the experiential learning approaches which have grown from Kurt Lewins' early work on group dynamics and the sensitivity training movement that followed. Both of these traditions have developed educational technologies that are more and more sophisticated in their application of theory to practice. Today, most management schools offer a mix of educational approaches—the traditional lecture, the case discussion, and experiential exercises—sometimes combining them in new and innovative ways, such as in computer-based business simulations. With these new educational technologies, management educators have begun to raise their aspirations from increasing student awareness and understanding to actually improving skills in interpersonal relations, decision making, managing change, and other key managerial functions. These new aspirations create new challenges for the design of management education and training programs, where the criteria for success are based on performance rather than cognitive comprehension. Yet the future poses an even greater challenge. The rapid growth of knowledge and increasing rate of social and technological change are making specific skill training more and more vulnerable to obsolescence. The answer seems to lie not in learning new skills, but in learning how to learn and adapt throughout one's career. An emerging concern in management education and research is, therefore, how individuals and organizations learn; that is, the basic processes and adaptive competencies that facilitate effective adaptation to a changing world.

## Perspective on Persons

In their perspective on persons and human personality, organizational psychologists in the last decade have added an emphasis on power and influence processes to an earlier concern with the more "tender" aspects of socio-emotional behavior (e.g., communication, intimacy, and human growth). These concerns with the social/motivational aspects of human behavior are currently being expanded by many researchers to consider cognitive processes—learning, problem solving, decision making, and planning—thus contributing to a more holistic view of human behavior. A most promising future perspective on human functioning is emerging from the work of adult development psychologists in personality development, ego development, moral development, and cognitive development. Researchers in these fields are providing frameworks for human functioning in organizations that emphasize developmental/appreciative processes as opposed to the deficiency/adjustment perspective that has dominated much work on human behavior in organizations in the past.

### Human Resource Management

The changes in perspectives on the person that we have discussed above have been mirrored in changes in philosophy about how human beings are to be managed. From our current historical vantage point, early approaches to management in organizational psychology seem defensive and vaguely paternalistic. People were involved in work decisions and attention was paid to "human relations" to keep workers happy and to avoid resistance to change initiated by management. In the past decade, participative management has come to be viewed more as a positive tool for improving organizational functioning. People are involved in decision making not only to make them feel more satisfied, but also because the improved information and problem-solving capability resulting from a participative process is more productive and effective.

Current research takes a more systematic approach to human resource management, shifting the perspective from management of people and the social/motivational techniques of management style, organizational climate, management by objectives (MBO), and so on, to a management of work perspective. This perspective considers the whole person as he or she adapts to the work environment. Work is seen as a socio-technical system, considering the content of jobs as well as the management process. Managing work involves designing technological systems, organizational arrangements, and jobs themselves in order to obtain effective organizational adaptation to the environment *and* maximum utilization of human resources and talents.

An important emerging trend in human resource management involves the addition of a career development perspective to the organization development perspective we have outlined. A host of trends are occurring in the labor market, including an older population, a more balanced male/female work force, a more culturally/racially diverse work force, and increasing career mobility and change among workers through their work life. These, coupled with rapid changes in organizations themselves that require new skills and talents and render others obsolete, are increasing the need for systems to manage the career development of employees at all levels.

### Perspective on Organizations

As we have seen, early work in organizational psychology took a somewhat limited view of organizations, being primarily concerned with job satisfaction and human fulfillment in work. The recent past has included much research aimed at organizational productivity as well. But until recently, the primary focus on the study of organizations has been on internal functioning. Perhaps the most vital research activity in the field today stems from what is known as the open-systems view of organizations. This view states that since organizations, to survive, must adapt to their environment, organizational functioning cannot be understood without examining organization/environment relationships. This led to the contingency theory of organizations, which states that there is no one best way to organize and manage; it depends on the environmental demands and corresponding tasks for the organization.

The open-systems view of organizations leads to an important emerging trend in the study of organizations. In most research to date, the organization is the focal point of study, conceived as the dominant stable structure around which the environment revolves. Yet in many cases, the organization is but a part of a more pervasive and dominant institutional or professional career structure. Utilities, for example, cannot be understood without understanding the impact of their relationship with governmental regulatory institutions; and medical organizations such as hospitals are dominated by the medical profession as a whole and particularly by the socialization and training of M.D.s. Improvements in the effectiveness of these organizations can be achieved only by consideration of the system of relationships among the organization and the institutions and professions that shape it.

### Change Processes

Concern with change and organization improvement has been central to organizational psychology from its inception. Kurt Lewin's action research methodology has been a dominant approach to integrating knowledge generation and practical application following his dictum: "If you want to understand something, try to change it." In the last decade the specialized field of organization development (OD) has emerged from the Lewinian tradition as a powerful practical approach for using behavioral science knowledge to improve organizational effectiveness and human fulfillment in work. A major contribution of OD has been an understanding of the process of introducing change. Process consultation, an approach that helps the organization to solve its own problems by improving the problem-solving, communication, and relationship processes in the organization, has emerged as an alternative to expert consultation, the approach where outside consultants generate problem solutions and present them for consideration by the organization. Currently, the technologies for introducing and managing change are expanding and becoming more sophisticated and problem-specific as OD programs are being initiated in organizations of all types. As change becomes a way of life in most organizations, there is a shift of focus from change as something created and managed by external consultants to a concern with the manager as change agent, managing the change process as part of his job function. As a result, there is less concern today with training OD professionals and greater concern with improving managers' OD skills.

With greater change and complexity in organizational systems, the dialectic in Lewin's action research model seems to be shifting from an emphasis on action to an emphasis on research. Policy development and strategy planning techniques are being developed to assist organizations in their adaptation to increasingly complex and turbulent environments. These approaches seem to be reversing Lewin's dictum — "If you want to change something, try to understand it."

### *The Plan of This Book*

In choosing topics and exercises for this book, we have attempted to represent all of the current trends in organizational psychology: those that are mature and established, those that are the focus of current research excitement, and new ideas that suggest the future shape of the field. The first part of the book focuses on the basic human processes that shape human behavior in organizations: organizational socialization, learning and problem solving, motivation, perception, communication, and group dynamics. In Part II, these processes are examined as they apply to the basic leadership functions of management. Units in this part examine managerial decision making, supervision and employee development, the effective exercise of power and influence, work-team effectiveness, and the management of conflict among groups. Part III is concerned with organization as a whole, with the process of organization design, and with the organization as an open system transacting with its environment. Part IV focuses on development and change, on organization development and planned change processes, and on personal growth and career development.

### *Your Role as a Learner*

You will find as you work with this book that a new role is being asked of you as a learner. Whereas in many of your prior learning experiences you were in the role of a passive recipient, you will now find the opportunity to become an active creator of your own learning. This is an opportunity for you to develop new and different relationships with faculty members responsible for this course. As you may already have sensed, the experiential learning approach provides numerous opportunities for shared leadership in the learning process.

Initial reactions to this approach are varied. Almost everyone experiences some sense of anxiety; this is a method that asks you to experiment with new behavior and share reactions and feelings. This initial anxiety is often accompanied by an early feeling of confusion until one becomes accustomed to the format of the units. These initial anxieties disappear for most people and they find this course to be an exciting, demanding, challenging, and worthwhile educational experience. However, this will not occur automatically or immediately. You and your fellow learners will struggle very hard to deal with the new learning roles being asked of you. As you work to become an effective learning organization, you will experience *firsthand* virtually every relevant concept in the field of organizational psychology.

We have struggled with the problem of finding ways to effectively communicate the essence of this course so that participants would be better prepared to interpret their experiences. Herewith is a graduate management student's description of his reaction to the first group meeting. Perhaps better than anything else, it conveys some sense of what this course can mean to you.

No one was telling me what I was supposed to learn from this first class after three hours of meeting, discussing, questioning, etc. In fact, the whole three hours seemed totally useless. "I haven't gotten anything out of this," I said to myself.

"Are there any more questions?" the professor asked.

I raised my hand. "What was the central purpose of this first class?"

"What is the statement behind that question?" was the essence of the response.

In later thinking about my question, the response, and the process of analysis which the response initiated within me, I began to understand what those three hours were all about.

What were my learning objectives for this course? Was I willing to participate actively in the setting of those objectives and in their attainment? No course I had ever taken had asked me these questions. I have since realized that that is what the first three hours were all about. Though in retrospect these questions seem very important, I was wholly unprepared to answer them; in fact, as queries they made no sense to me. I was so conditioned by my previous experiences—entering organizations wherein on the first day I would listen to and accept objectives—that when I was asked during those three hours to participate actively in objective setting, I was unprepared to respond in any meaningful way.

My question at the end of class was a reflection of my unwillingness to accept an *active* role in objective setting. The statement behind my question was, of course, that these three hours seemed purposeless. Rather than face that statement squarely and examine it in light of what had transpired (an active process), I converted the statement into a question, thus attempting to retain a *passive* role while putting the professor in the position of having to set objectives for those three hours. Through later analysis of this interaction, I began to understand what the active learning process was.

Out of the confusion of those first three hours, two very important elements of a psychological contract between myself and the organization (the course including professors and learning groups) emerged. The elements directly concerned the learning process in which I would engage in this course.

First, this is to be an active learning experience. This sounds almost trivial, but it is the basis of the psychological contract between myself and the group and furthermore is fundamental to learning within the course. It means that I will learn about interpersonal interactions in organizational behavior by actively experiencing those interactions. I must scrutinize the functioning of the group of which I am a member, observe important interactions, make hypotheses about these interactions, and actively test these hypotheses within the group in order to learn.

Second, I am to be responsible for setting the learning objectives of this experience. (This almost directly follows from the first element.) These objectives are not given and thus cannot constrain or limit in any way the scope of learning which can be obtained.

The ramifications for the learning process of these two elements taken together are enormous. The most significant of these is the fact that now the scope of learning has no bounds other than those set by the student. This situation compares very favorably with the more traditional passive learning process where course objectives essentially place certain bounds on the learning process. Furthermore, when the student sets his own objectives, he has a vested interest in accomplishing them since they are his objectives and are not externally imposed. In the very process of setting these objectives, the student becomes committed to their attainment.

In combination, these two elements lead to a higher motivation to learn, and make a broader scope of learning possible. In point of fact, both my attitude toward learning and my behavior in learning have begun to reflect these effects. I am more inquisitive, more committed to learning, and, in short, more involved in the learning process than I have ever been. It is my judgment that this involvement will ultimately result in large rewards.

It is interesting to note that I have made little or no mention of grades, as they affect the learning process. It has become apparent to me that grades can and do interfere with the learning process. Grades represent another form of constraining objectives set by the professor (organization) in the traditional (passive) learning process. Grades represent an artificial and artificially allocated reward system which comes to replace learning. The objective of study is the attainment of the greatest artificial reward rather than the greatest participation and involvement in the learning process. Attempting to gain the greatest reward generally interferes directly with the process of participation in a learning experience.

As an example of this interference, I have just finished a short paper for another course. Looking back at my efforts, I can see that one of my prime concerns was whether or not the conclusions which I was drawing would be in direct conflict with those that the professor might have drawn, and thus, whether or not I was doomed to getting a failing grade on the paper because of my extreme stance. This concern definitely affected and otherwise interfered with what should have been my prime concern — i.e., expressing and supporting my views and research findings on the topic.

This type of interference has not hindered me in the process of writing this paper, since in writing it I am accomplishing real learning objectives which I have set for myself. In writing this paper, I have made explicit, via verbalization, some of the things which I learned during the first session of this course and some of the things I would like to learn in future sessions. By making them explicit, they have become much clearer and more reasonable to me. Writing this paper has thus been an essential part of the learning process initiated in the first session.

It is interesting to note that the writing of this paper is an active process. For the first time in my academic career, writing a paper has been a pleasure.

# PART

## I

## BASIC
## HUMAN
## PROCESSES

# chapter 1

## organizational socialization

*Photo courtesy of Case Western Reserve University, Cleveland, Ohio*

## I. OBJECTIVES

A. To introduce the concept of the psychological contract.

B. To articulate and share expectations (faculty and student) relevant to the organization (this learning group) you are about to join.

C. To identify problem areas based on conflicting expectations and to take steps to resolve any such conflict.

## II. PREMEETING PREPARATION

Read the Introduction.

## III. INTRODUCTION

A psychological contract is implicitly formed between the individual and the organizations of which he is a member. This contract, like others, deals with the organization's expectations of the individual and his contributions to meet them. It also deals with the individual's expectations of the organization and its contribution to meet his expectations. The psychological contract is unlike a legal contract in that it defines a dynamic, changing relationship that is continually being renegotiated. Often important aspects of the contract are not formally agreed upon—key organizational and individual expectations are sometimes unstated, as well as implicit premises about the relationship.

Organizational contributions, such as a sense of challenge in one's job and individual contributions such as loyalty to the company, are expected but often not consciously weighed. Yet this contract is a reality that has a great many implications for productivity and individual satisfaction. A company staffed by "cheated" individuals who expect far more than they get is headed for trouble. The rebel who refuses to meet key company expectations becomes a stumbling block to production. On the other hand, individual creativity is likely to be stifled in a company that demands total compliance to peripheral norms such as manner of dress.

The dynamic quality of the psychological contract means that individual and company expectations and individual and company contributions mutually influence one another. High expectations on the part of the company can produce increased individual contributions, and great contributions will likewise raise expectations. From the company's point of view, the questions become: How can we manage our human resources so that we can maximize individual contributions? How can we socialize our members to accept our expectations and norms as legitimate? For the individual, the questions are: How can I get the satisfaction and rewards that I want from this organization? How can I manage my own career so that my socialization takes place in organizational settings that encourage my personal growth and development?

A growing body of research evidence demonstrates the importance of early organizational experiences to future performance. Berlew and Hall,[1] in a study of managerial performance in a large public utility, report a very strong and consistent relationship between the company's *initial* expectations of the manager (during the first year on the job) and his future performance. Company expectations focused upon the type and quality of contributions expected of the manager, and performance was measured by rate of salary growth. In other words, the individuals for whom the organization had high initial job expectations were among the highest performers five years later.[2]

Support for the importance of the psychological contract between an individual and an organization comes from a number of other sources. Rosenthal's[3] findings on experimenter effects in behavioral research are particularly impressive and can be viewed as empirical verification of the power of the self-fulfilling prophecy. Taking the case of a classroom organization, for example, the prediction (and verified findings) are that if a teacher *thinks* students are less intelligent, capable, and motivated, they will, in fact, act that way. The critical variable in the example is the *teacher's expectation:* higher expectations were associated with higher learning.

Zimbardo's research on life in prisons provides further confirmation of the power of the self-fulfilling prophecy.[4] A mock prison was set up on the campus of Stanford University. A group of 10 "prisoners" and 11 "guards" was selected from a group of 75 volunteers because they were judged to be emotionally stable, physically healthy, mature law-abiding citizens.

---

[1] David E. Berlew and Douglas T. Hall, "The Socialization of Managers: The Effects of Expectations on Performance," *Administrative Science Quarterly*, Vol. 11, No. 2 (September 1966), pp. 207–223. *Readings.*

[2] An alternative explanation would be that better performers were given more challenging first assignments. A wealth of biographical, personality, and intelligence data were available only to the researchers. These data were not available to the organization, so matching would have been extremely difficult to accomplish.

[3] Robert Rosenthal, *Experimenter Effects in Behavioral Research* (New York: Appleton-Century-Crofts, 1966).

[4] Phillip Zimbardo, "A Pirondellian Prison," *The New York Times Magazine*, April 8, 1973.

The experiment, which was scheduled to continue for two weeks, had to be called off after six days. Everyone involved began to act in accordance with the expectations of their respective roles. "Prisoners" expected guards to be inhuman, insensitive, brutal, and so on. Guards expected prisoners to be surly, obdurate, plan rebellions and escapes, and so on. In a matter of hours, these expectations began to become reality and, once begun, the cycle fed upon itself and the experimental nature of the venture was lost. The emotional risks of continuing were too high.

Lest we try anxiously to wriggle away from the implications of his research too quickly, Zimbardo points out:

> For the most disturbing implication of our research comes from the parallels between what occurred in that basement mock prison and daily experiences in our own lives — and we presume yours. The physical institution of prison is but a concrete and steel metaphor for the existence of more pervasive, albeit less obvious, institutions of the mind that all of us daily create, populate, and perpetuate.
>
> To what extent do we allow ourselves to become imprisoned by docilely accepting the roles others assign to us or, indeed, choose to remain prisoners because being passive and dependent frees us from the need to act and be responsible for our actions?[5]

### A Model for Managing Psychological Contracts

Sherwood and Glidewell have developed a simple but powerful model which (1) describes the dynamic quality of psychological contracts and (2) suggests ways of minimizing the potentially dysfunctional consequences of shifting expectations (Figure 1-1).

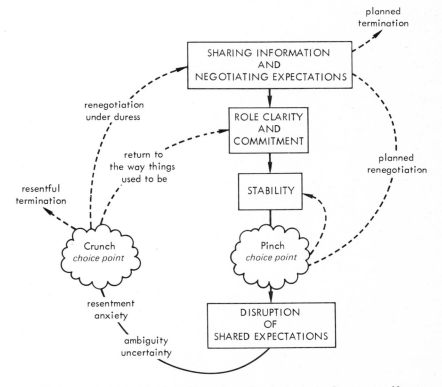

**Figure 1-1** Model for Managing Psychological Contracts (from J. J. Sherwood and J.C. Glidewell. Used with permission.

[5] Zimbardo, "A Pirodellian Prison," p. 60.

The first stage of any relationship between two individuals and/or an individual and an organization is characterized by a sharing of information and a negotiating of expectations. Suppose that an organization informed potential new employees that everyone was expected to work 9 A.M.–12 noon on Saturdays. The potential new employee expects to work only Monday through Friday. If this difference in expectations cannot be resolved at this point, the two will part ways. They have found out immediately that they have an irresolvable mismatch.

Assuming that both parties hear enough of what they expect to hear from the other, they make a joint commitment. The employee and employer both expect to move into a period of stability and productivity. It is time to get down to work.

Even with the best of intentions, assuming full sharing of initial expectations (which, given prior research, is unlikely), changes are likely to occur over time. These changes can and do take a variety of forms but the consequence is the same — there is a disruption of shared expectations.

Since the "rules" that were agreed to initially have been upset, one or both parties experience heightened uncertainty which invariably results in heightened anxiety. Human nature being what it is, energy is thus invested in reducing this anxiety. Typically, what happens at this point is an effort to return to the way things used to be. The parties apologize for the misunderstanding, smooth over the conflict, and renew their commitment to one another. To the extent that two parties remain unsatisfied in this cycle, the result is invariably some form of termination — psychological (apathy: "I'll be darned if I'm going to do any more than I'm required to") or physical.

At the point of anxiety, it is much more productive to cycle back to the starting point and test whether or not any new information is now available. Given the dynamic, changing nature of most relationships, it is very likely that a new psychological contract is appropriate and realistic. If it is discovered that new, changed expectations cannot be successfully negotiated, termination is still a possibility. The critical difference, however, in this condition is that the termination is an agreed-upon joint decision versus a unilateral decision based upon untested assumptions.

Sherwood and Glidewell point out that there is also a natural tendency to ignore a host of early warning signs ("pinches") which signal a potentially disruptive situation. "I don't have time to test this issue with him." "If I raise this issue with my boss, she'll think I'm just complaining so I'll ignore it." Dealing with pinches allows one to conduct the renegotiation process in a planned manner without the heat of emotion that can accompany a disruption. (It's like an automatic safety valve on a boiler.)

The purpose of this unit is to introduce you to the concept of the psychological contract as it exists in the learning organization you are about to enter. In this way you will be able to move as quickly as possible to a period of stability and productivity (learning) and set in motion the machinery needed to deal with any subsequent "pinches" that may develop.

## IV. PROCEDURE FOR GROUP MEETING

### A. Instructor Interviews Participants — Preparation

The goal in this part of the exercise is for the instructor to learn from the group members *their* expectations for the course: what they hope to learn, where they see these learnings as being useful. In addition, the instructor will try to learn what members feel they can contribute to the achievement of their expectations, how they can make these contributions, and what members feel they as learners can contribute to the learning process. In this part, the instructor will interview participants in the course via representatives.

*Step 1.* The total group should divide into small discussion groups, four or five people per group.

*Step 2.* Each group should elect a representative to the team that will be interviewed by the instructor.

*Step 3.* Using the guide provided on page 17 (Instructor's Interview of Participants: A Question Guide), each group should discuss the general question areas in which the instructor will pose specific questions to the representative team during the interview.

*Note:* The instructor may add at this point any specific issues of concern not covered in the Instructor's Interview of Participants: A Question Guide.

*Step 4.* All representatives must understand their group's position on each of these questions so that they can accurately represent their views in response to the questions the instructor will pose during the interview. (You may want to jot these down on the guide provided.)

(Time allotted for steps 1–4: 30 minutes)

## INSTRUCTOR'S INTERVIEW OF PARTICIPANTS: A QUESTION GUIDE

Few instructors ask group members to articulate their expectations for a class. During the ensuing interview, the instructor will try to gain an understanding of your views in the following general areas:

1. What are your goals for this course? To learn theories, to get a grade, to practice new behaviors? Personal change versus intellectual knowledge?

2. In what ways do you feel the instructor can best help you achieve your goals? Lecture, give examinations, lead seminar discussions? Let you work on your own? How do you feel about active, experiential learning?

3. What, if anything, have you heard about this textbook and/or this course from others?

4. What's the "best" thing that could happen in this course? What is the worst thing?

5. What are the class members' resources for this course? (Prior work experience, other courses in psychology, etc.)

*Notes*

## B. Instructor Interviews Participants

*Step 5.* The representatives, one from each team, meet with the instructor. The instructor will interview them (using Instructor's Interview of Participants: A Question Guide) in order to understand their expectations for the course.

*Step 6.* The remainder of the class act as observers, paying particular attention to the instructor's questions and the areas that seem most salient. You might find it helpful to jot down on the Participants' Interview of Instructor: A Suggested Question Guide (p. 21) the observations that you feel will help you to prepare for the second round of interviewing.

(Time allotted for steps 5 and 6: 20 minutes)

## C. Participants' Interview of Instructor — Preparation

The goal in this part of the exercise is for the course participants to find out what the instructor's expectations are for the course. What does the instructor hope they will learn from the course? What can the instructor contribute to the learning process? In this part, the participants will interview the instructor via representatives.

*Step 7.* The class should form into the same small discussion groups used in part A.

*Step 8.* Each group should elect a member (other than the person they elected in step 2) as their representative to the team that will interview the instructor.

*Step 9.* Using the guide provided as a starting point (Participants' Interview of Instructor: A Suggested Question Guide), each group should discuss any questions which they would like their representative to pose to the instructor.

*Step 10.* Representatives should make certain that they understand the group's concerns so that they can accurately translate these concerns into questions to be posed to the instructor. (You may want to jot these down on the guide provided.)

(Time alloted for steps 7-10: 30 minutes)

# PARTICIPANTS' INTERVIEW OF INSTRUCTOR: A SUGGESTED QUESTION GUIDE

You will have the opportunity to ask the instructor any questions you feel are relevant to effective learning during this term. (*Note:* It is important that you ask the questions that are of real concern to you at this point. Only in this way can potentially important problems or conflicts be identified and be dealt with.) You probably have many ideas of your own and the questions asked by the instructor during the first interview should suggest others to you.

Some areas you may want to discuss are the following:

1. The instructor's theory of learning (i.e., how do people learn).
2. The instructor's feelings on the question of evaluation.
3. The instructor's role in the class.
4. Any stereotypes the instructor may hold about you.
5. Anything else you think is important.

Be sure to ask specific questions. Think about the assumptions that may underlie some of your questions — i.e., why you feel this is an important question. Test these assumptions by asking the instructor's opinion if you feel it will be helpful.

*Notes*

D. Participants' Interview of Instructor (Time Allotted: 30 Minutes)

*Step 11.* Representatives interview instructor in order to understand the instructor's expectations for them and the course.

*Step 12.* The remainder of the group acts as observers, paying particular attention to the following areas:

    a. In what ways do your (groups') expectations agree/disagree with the contributions the instructor feels s/he can make?

    b. In what way do the instructor's expectations agree/disagree with the contributions you feel you can make?

    c. In what way do you feel that you can contribute to the achievement of your own expectations?

    d. In looking back over your group discussions, how much diversity was there within the group concerning expectations?

E. Comparison of Interviews and Identification of Potential Pinches
(Time Allotted: 30–40 Minutes)

*Step 13.* The total group should develop a list of (1) areas of difference which became apparent during the previous two interviews and (2) possible future conflicts — pinches — that will be important to watch for.

    a. To the extent possible, differences that will influence the learning process should be discussed further, with an eye toward a mutually acceptable negotiated resolution.

    b. With respect to potential future pinches, the group should discuss their expectations concerning:

        1. Whose responsibility it will be/should be to raise a pinch if/when it develops.

        2. The mechanisms to be used for raising pinches (e.g., written comments, informal discussions at the end of meetings, etc.).

*Step 14.* Instructor and participants should discuss their feelings and assessment of the value of this way of beginning a new course.

## V. SUMMARY

Although we do not often view the processes in the same terms, entering a classroom environment the first time is very much like the first day on a new job. The typical orientation program in a company is usually very one-sided. Most company communication flows from the organization to the individual, "These are our policies, procedures, expectations."

One effect of this one-sided process is to cause "new employees" to feel that the organization is much more powerful than they are as individuals. This feeling of powerlessness often creates a situation in which new employees, when asked their expectations, try to second-guess the company's expectations. Instead of trying to formulate and articulate their own expectations, the new employees (participants) often repeat what they *think* the organization (instructor) wants to hear. Another effect is the organization's tendency to oversocialize new members. The new employee's feeling of powerlessness often results in more passivity than might ordinarily be felt appropriate in the situation.

Recall your last job interview. Remember how you tried to "look good" to the organization — to guess what it wanted, on what qualities it was evaluating you. How much time did you spend telling the interviewer what your expectations were and asking what the organization could contribute to your needs? Probably very little and then very cautiously. Our studies of individuals' entries into organizations and our work with orientation and training programs has led to the conclusion that in entering an organization nearly everyone experiences a feeling of helplessness and dependency on the organization. From a functional point of view this dependency seems necessary so that the organization can begin to socialize the incoming member to meet its norms and values, its way of doing things. Yet our observations have led us to conclude that most organizations overdo this—they tend to over-socialize their members. The phase of entry into an organization seems to be a critical period for the new members. Individuals who are overpowered and overcontrolled by organizational constraints become listless, passive members. Those who are challenged by the tasks they face and encouraged toward responsibility can move toward success and mastery of their organizational life.

The organization often reads passivity as a sign that new employees want and need more direction and control—they want to be told exactly what to do. This situation can create a feedback cycle that, in the long run, operates to the detriment of both the individual and the organization. The organization needs people who are innovative, creative, and independent thinkers in order to survive and remain productive in a rapidly changing environment. Individual growth and satisfaction also demand these same kinds of behavior. Often, however, the new employee's (participant's) first contact with the organization sets in motion a cycle that acts directly counter to these long-range goals and needs.

There is another way in which we can view the process of organizational socialization and the notion of the psychological contract. In approaching any new organization, an individual makes two classes of decisions: a decision to join and a decision to participate.[6] In some cases, the individual has no control over his/her decision to join, perhaps in the military or in a required course. When this condition exists, the organization often reacts by tightly controlling the socialization process and the psychological contract becomes extremely structured (in the sense of policies, rules, and the like) and limiting in the sense that legitimate behavior on the part of the organization members is clearly spelled out.[7]

There are many cases, however, in which individuals do have control over their decision to join. One often finds, however, that the factors people use to help make the decision to join are unrelated to longer-run, higher-order goals they may have. For example, when interviewing a company for a job, most people ask questions about pay, fringe benefits, insurance plans, vacations, and the like. Few ask about the specific nature of their first job or the opportunities for personal growth and development. In the case of a class, most people, when given the chance, ask about the grading scheme, the amount of reading, the length of the required term paper, and the like. Few ask about the value of the course to them as individuals or about what they can expect to learn.

The process by which we join an organization has implications for the second class of decisions—the decision to participate. The focus here is on what happens after the individual has decided to join (voluntarily or otherwise) and has to do with the manner in which the person interacts with the organization on a day-to-day basis. In companies many people find that the job they are doing fails to meet many of their needs for challenge, responsibility, individual initiative, and so on. They become frustrated and dissatisfied and often leave after a few months.[8] Note, however, that these are expectations that they did not make explicit at the entry point—their decision to join.

In the classroom people often find a course dull, boring, and unexciting, and feel that they are wasting their time. They sit passively in class every week (if they bother to keep attending), uninvolved in their own learning, and work to meet the organization's expectations in order to get a grade. Their

[6] See J. G. March and H. A. Simon, *Organization* (New York: John Wiley & Sons, Inc., 1963), especially Chapter 4, for a fuller discussion of this conceptual scheme.

[7] Edgar H. Schein, "How to Break in the College Graduate," *Harvard Business Review*, November–December 1964, pp. 68–76.

[8] A more complete description of the psychological contract may be found in Chapter 4 of Edgar H. Schein, *Organizational Psychology* (Englewood Cliffs, N.J.: Prentice-Hall, Inc., 1965).

own expectations for learning, involvement, and stimulation go unsatisfied, in large measure because they never made such expectations explicit.

You may have experienced some of these dilemmas during this unit. Learners often are unused to bearing much responsibility for their own learning. They are much more accustomed to the instructor's assuming full responsibility. Thus, when confronted with a genuine opportunity to participate in the learning process, they often become confused ("What kind of way is this to start a class?") and suspicious ("I wonder what the instructor has got up his sleeve?")

When asked to articulate expectations, learners tend to be very vague and general, frustrating to all involved. Expectations are much more likely to be satisfied when a set of realistic, concrete goals can be developed. Instructors must realize that learners who are unused to controlling their own education will have to learn to accept that responsibility. The point is that *both* participants and instructor have a share of the responsibility for the learning process.

This point is an important one to reemphasize. A confusion often develops, as a result of this initial contracting session, of the form: "Why all this talk about our expectations and stuff? You (the instructor) already have the course laid out, the syllabus typed, and the schedule planned!" As is true in any organization, the general thrust or goals are given. This is not a course in art or home economics. It is a course in organizational psychology, but there are many areas of flexibility: what *specific* goals you as a participating learner set within the general objectives; how you relate to peers and staff; who takes what responsibility for *how* goals are achieved. Differences will exist around those issues and they need to be explored during the initial socialization process.

Clearly, within the context of a first class session of a few hours, all the possible conflicts that can arise will not be anticipated nor can all those anticipated be solved. More important than any concrete conclusions that may come out of this contract-setting exercise is a series of norms for dealing with conflicts. As a result of this contract exploration process, the legitimacy of conflict or difference can be established, the right to question each other and particularly the instructor can be demonstrated, and a decision-making process of shared responsibility to resolve conflicts can be introduced.

# VI. SELF-EVALUATION AND COMPLETING THE LEARNING LOOP

A. What questions do you now have as a result of your learning experiences from this unit? Jot these down below.

B. From these questions, what *key concepts* can you extrapolate for further learning? Write these concepts below.

C. How can you now go about finding answers to the questions you raised above? Below are some suggested ways to continue your learning process by beginning new learning loops:

1. Look up the key concepts from your questions above in the Yellow Pages of Learning Experiences at the back of the book. Find a few suggested readings or exercises to facilitate the learning of these key concepts.

2. If you don't find the key concepts in the Yellow Pages related specifically to your questions, perhaps there are other concepts listed in the index that might lead you to relevant learning resources at this time. Look for concepts similar to those you identified in B above.

3. In the event that you don't find the Yellow Pages directory useful for your present learning goals, discuss your questions with other students, faculty, or persons outside your learning environment. Discuss further learning possibilities with them.

# chapter 2

## learning and problem solving

*Photo by Sybil Shelton*

## I. OBJECTIVES

A. To describe the characteristics of the process of learning and problem solving.

B. To identify individual learning styles.

C. To identify and analyze personal approaches to problem solving.

D. To ensure the effective operation of this learning organization by sharing:

1. Learning objectives.

2. Available resources for learning.

3. Learning environment preferences.

## II. PREMEETING PREPARATION (TIME ALLOTTED: 1 HOUR)

A. Complete the Learning Style Inventory.

B. Complete a Personal Problem Solving Analysis for two problems of your choice.

C. Score the Learning Style Inventory and record your scores on the two normative profiles.

D. Read the entire unit *after* completing A, B, and C.

# LEARNING STYLE INVENTORY

**Instructions**

There are nine sets of four words listed below. Rank-order the words in each set by assigning a *4* to the word that best characterizes your learning style, a *3* to the word that next best characterizes your learning style, a *2* to the next most characteristic word, and a *1* to the word that is least characteristic of you as a learner.

You may find it hard to choose the words that best characterize your learning style. Nevertheless, keep in mind that there are no right or wrong answers — all the choices are equally acceptable. The aim of the inventory is to describe how you learn, not to evaluate your learning ability.

*Be sure to assign a different rank number to each of the four words in each set; do not make ties.*

1. ____discriminating  ____tentative  ____involved  ____practical
2. ____receptive  ____relevant  ____analytical  ____impartial
3. ____feeling  ____watching  ____thinking  ____doing
4. ____accepting  ____risk-taker  ____evaluative  ____aware
5. ____intuitive  ____productive  ____logical  ____questioning
6. ____abstract  ____observing  ____concrete  ____active
7. ____present-oriented  ____reflecting  ____future-oriented  ____pragmatic
8. ____experience  ____observation  ____conceptualization  ____experimentation
9. ____intense  ____reserved  ____rational  ____responsible

**Scoring**

The four columns of words above correspond to the four learning style scales: CE, RO, AC, and AE. To compute your scale scores, write your rank numbers in the boxes below only for the designated items. For example, in the third column (AC), you would fill in the rank numbers you have assigned to items 2, 3, 4, 5, 8, and 9. Compute your scale scores by adding the rank numbers for each set of boxes.

Score items:
2 3 4 5 7 8
☐☐☐☐☐☐
CE = ____

Score items:
1 3 6 7 8 9
☐☐☐☐☐☐
RO = ____

Score items:
2 3 4 5 8 9
☐☐☐☐☐☐
AC = ____

Score items:
1 3 6 7 8 9
☐☐☐☐☐☐
AE = ____

To compute the two combination scores, subtract *CE* from *AC* and subtract *RO* from *AE*. Preserve negative signs if they appear.

AC–CE: AC ☐ – CE ☐ =          AE – RO: AE ☐ – RO ☐ =

## PERSONAL PROBLEM-SOLVING ANALYSIS

Imagine that you face two of the problems described below and describe how you would go about dealing with each of them by recording your approach on the Personal Problem-Solving Process Worksheets that follow. Try to describe in outline form what you would do from start to finish, from your first involvement to the final resolution of the problem. Try to pick problems that seem real to you, that you can imagine yourself dealing with. Instead of picking problems listed here you may want to redefine them or choose similar problems from your own experience, i.e., problems you have faced or are currently dealing with.

### PROBLEM LIST

1. Someone has given you $100,000 to invest for them. How would you go about it?
2. You want to buy a new car (or other major purchase). How would you proceed?
3. You want to start your own business.
4. You are a middle manager supervising a group of about 12 people. You want to increase their morale and productivity.

## PERSONAL PROBLEM-SOLVING PROCESS WORKSHEET

Problem 1 (briefly state the problem) _____
    Outline below as specifically as possible how you would go about dealing with this problem from start to finish.

Problem 2 (briefly state the problem) _____
    Outline below as specifically as possible how you would go about dealing with this problem from start to finish.

## III. INTRODUCTION

For most of us, the first associations we have to the word "learning" are teacher, classroom, and textbook. These associations belie some implicit assumptions that we tend to make about the nature of the learning process. Our years in school have trained us to think that the primary responsibility for learning lies with teachers. Their training and experience make them experts; we are more passive participants in the learning process. As students, our job is to observe, read, and memorize what the teacher assigns, and then to repeat "what we have learned" in examinations. Teachers have the responsibility of evaluating our performance and telling us what we should learn next. They set requirements and objectives for learning since it is often assumed that students do not yet have the experience to know what is best for themselves.

The textbook symbolizes the assumption that learning is primarily concerned with abstract ideas and concepts. Learning is the process of acquiring and remembering ideas and concepts. The more remembered, the more you have learned. The relevance and application of these concepts to your own job will come later. Concepts come before experience.

The classroom symbolizes the assumption that learning is a special activity cut off from the real world and unrelated to one's life. Learning and doing are separate and antithetical activities. Many students at graduation feel, "Now I am finished with learning, I can begin living." The belief that learning occurs only in the classroom is so strong that academic credentials are assigned great importance in hiring and promotions, in spite of the fact that psychological research has had little success in establishing correlations between performance in the classroom (grades) and success in later life.

As a result of these assumptions, the concept of learning seldom seems relevant to us in our daily lives and work. And yet a moment of deeper reflection says that this cannot be so. In a world where the rate of change is increasing rapidly every year, in a time when few will end their careers in the same jobs or even the same occupations that they started in, the ability to learn seems an important, if not the most important, skill.

The concept of problem solving, on the other hand, evokes some associations that are opposite to those of the concept of learning. We tend to think of problem solving as an active, rather than a passive, process. Although we have a word for someone who directs the learning process (teacher), we have no similar word for the problem-solving process. The responsibility for problem solving rests with the problem solver. He must experiment, take risks, and come to grips with the problem. Usually no external sources of evaluation are needed. He knows when the problem is solved.

Although general principles can emerge from the solution to a specific problem, problems are usually specific rather than general, concrete rather than abstract. Problem solving is not separate from the life of the problem solver. The focus of the problem solving is on a specific problem felt to be relevant to the problem solver; it is, in fact, his involvement in the problem that makes it a problem.

### A Model of the Learning/Problem-Solving Process

By combining these characteristics of learning and problem solving and conceiving of them as a single process, we can come closer to understanding how it is that people generate from their experience concepts, rules, and principles to guide their behavior in new situations, and how they modify these concepts in order to improve their effectiveness. This process is both active and passive, concrete and abstract. It can be conceived of as a four-stage cycle: (1) concrete experience is followed by (2) observation and reflection, which leads to (3) the formation of abstract concepts and generalizations, which lead to (4) hypotheses to be tested in future action, which in turn leads to new experiences. There are several observations to be made about this model of the learning process. First, this learning cycle is continuously recurring. We continuously test our concepts in experience and modify them as a result of our observation of the experience. In a very important sense, all learning is relearning and all education is reeducation.

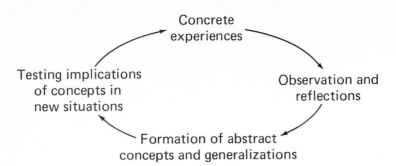

Second, the direction that learning takes is governed by one's felt needs and goals. We seek experiences that are related to our goals, interpret them in the light of our goals, and form concepts and test implications of these concepts that are relevant to our felt needs and goals. The implication of this fact is that the process of learning is erratic and inefficient when objectives are not clear.

Third, since the learning process is directed by individual needs and goals, learning styles become highly individual in both direction and process. For example, a mathematician may come to place great emphasis on abstract concepts, whereas a poet may value concrete experience more highly. A manager may be primarily concerned with active application of concepts, whereas a naturalist may develop observational skills highly. Each of us in a more personal way develops a learning style that has some weak points and strong points. We may jump into experiences but fail to observe the lessons to be derived from these experiences; we may form concepts but fail to test their validity. In some areas our objectives and needs may be clear guides to learning; in others, we wander aimlessly.

*Interpretation of Your Scores on the Learning Style Inventory*

The Learning Style Inventory (LSI)[1] is a simple self-description test, based on experiential learning theory, that is designed to measure your strengths and weaknesses as a learner in the four stages of the learning process. Effective learners rely on four different learning modes: *concrete experience* (CE), *reflective observation* (RO), *abstract conceptualization* (AC), and *active experimentation* (AE). That is, they must be able to involve themselves fully, openly, and without bias in new experiences (CE), they must be able to reflect on and observe these experiences from many perspectives (RO), they must be able to create concepts that integrate their observations into logically sound theories (AC), and they must be able to use these theories to make decisions and solve problems (AE).

The LSI measures your relative emphasis on the four learning modes by asking you to rank-order a series of four words that describe these different abilities. For example, one set of four words is *feeling, watching, thinking, doing*, which reflects CE, RO, AC, and AE respectively. Combination scores indicate the extent to which you emphasize abstractness over concreteness (AC–CE) and the extent to which you emphasize active experimentation over reflection (AE–RO).

One way to better understand the meaning of your scores on the LSI is to compare them with the scores of others. The "target" in Figure 2–1 gives norms on the four basic scales (CE, RO, AC, AE) for 1,933 adults ranging from 18 to 60 years of age. About two-thirds of the group are men and the group as a whole is highly educated (two-thirds have college degrees or higher). A wide range of occupations and educational backgrounds are represented, including teachers, counselors, engineers, salespersons, managers, doctors, and lawyers.

The raw scores for each of the four basic scales are listed on the crossed lines of the target. By circling your raw scores on the four scales and connecting them with straight lines you can create a graphic representation of your learning style profile. The concentric circles on the target represent

---

[1] The Learning Style Inventory is copyrighted by David A. Kolb (1976) and distributed by McBer and Co. 137 Newbury St., Boston, Mass. 02116. Further information on theory, construction, reliability, and validity of the inventory is reported in *The Learning Style Inventory: Technical Manual*, available from McBer and Co.

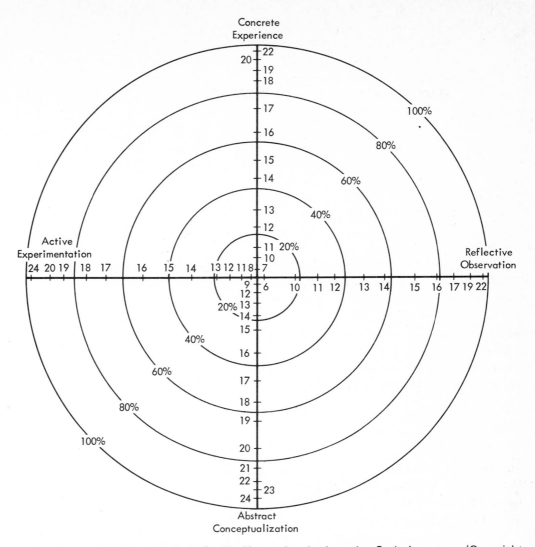

**Figure 2-1** The Learning Style Profile Norms for the Learning Style Inventory (Copyright 1976 by David A. Kolb)

percentile scores for the normative group. For example, if your raw score on *concrete experience* was 15, you scored higher on this scale than about 55 percent of the people in the normative group. If your CE score was 22 or higher, you scored higher than 99 percent of the normative group. Therefore, in comparison to the normative group, the shape of your profile indicates which of the four basic modes you tend to emphasize and which are less emphasized.

The Learning Style Inventory was designed as an aid for helping you identify your own learning style. The four learning modes—concrete experience, reflective observation, abstract conceptualization, and active experimentation—represent the four stages of the learning process. The inventory is designed to assess the relative importance of each of these stages to you so that you can get some indication of which learning modes you tend to emphasize. No individual mode is better or worse than any other. Even a totally balanced profile is not necessarily best. The key to effective learning is being competent in each mode when it is appropriate. A high score on one mode may mean a tendency to overemphasize that aspect of the learning process at the expense of others. A low score on a mode may indicate a tendency to avoid that aspect of the learning process.

A high score on *concrete experience* represents a receptive, experience-based approach to learning that relies heavily on feeling-based judgments. High CE individuals tend to be empathetic and "people-oriented." They generally find theoretical approaches to be unhelpful and prefer to treat each situation as a unique case. They learn best from specific examples in which they can become involved. Individuals who emphasize *concrete experience* tend to be oriented more toward peers and less toward authority in their approach to learning, and benefit most from feedback and discussion with fellow CE learners.

A high score on *abstract conceptualization* indicates an analytical, conceptual approach to learning that relies heavily on logical thinking and rational evaluation. High-AC individuals tend to be oriented more toward things and symbols and less toward other people. They learn best in authority-directed, impersonal learning situations that emphasize theory and systematic analysis. They are often frustrated and benefit little from unstructured "discovery" learning approaches such as exercises and simulations.

A high score on *active experimentation* indicates an active, "doing" orientation to learning that relies heavily on experimentation. High-AE individuals learn best when they can engage in such things as projects, homework, or small group discussions. They dislike passive learning situations such as lectures. These individuals tend to be extroverts.

A high score on *reflective observation* indicates a tentative, impartial, and reflective approach to learning. High-RO individuals rely heavily on careful observation in making judgments, and prefer learning situations such as lectures that allow them to take the role of impartial objective observers. These individuals tend to be introverts.

It should be emphasized that the LSI does not measure your learning style with 100 percent accuracy. Rather it is only an indication of how you see yourself as a learner. You will need data from other sources if you wish to pinpoint your learning style more exactly (e.g., how you make decisions on the job, how others see you, and what kinds of problems you solve best).

*Identifying Your Learning Style Type*

It is unlikely that your learning style will be described accurately by just one of the four preceding paragraphs. This is because each person's learning style is a combination of the four basic learning modes. It is therefore more meaningful to describe your learning style by a single data point that combines your scores on the four basic modes. This is accomplished by using the two combination scores, AC-CE and AE-RO. These scales indicate the degree to which you emphasize abstractness over concreteness and action over reflection, respectively.

The grid shown in Figure 2-2 has the raw scores for these two scales on the crossed lines (AC-CE on the vertical and AE-RO on the horizontal) and percentile scores based on the normative group on the sides. By marking your raw scores on the two lines and plotting their point of interception, you can find which of the four learning style quadrants you fall into. These four quadrants, labeled *accommodator*, *diverger*, *converger*, and *assimilator*, represent the four dominant learning styles. If your AC-CE score were -4 and your AE-RO score were +8, you would fall strongly in the accommodator quadrant. An AC-CE score of +4 and an AE-RO score of +3 would put you only slightly in the converger quadrant. The closer your data point is to the point where the lines cross, the more balanced is your learning style. If your data point is close to any of the four corners, this indicates that you rely heavily on one particular learning style.

The following summary of the four basic learning style types is based on both research and clinical observation of these patterns of LSI scores.

The *converger's* dominant learning abilities are abstract conceptualization (AC) and active experimentation (AE). This person's greatest strength lies in the practical application of such ideas. A person with this style seems to do best in those situations, such as conventional intelligence tests, where there is a single correct answer or solution to a question or problem. This person's knowledge is organized in such a way that through hypothetical-deductive reasoning the person can focus it on specific problems. Research on this style of learning shows that convergers are relatively unemotional, preferring to deal with things rather than people. They tend to have narrow technical interests and choose to specialize in the physical sciences. This learning style is characteristic of many engineers.

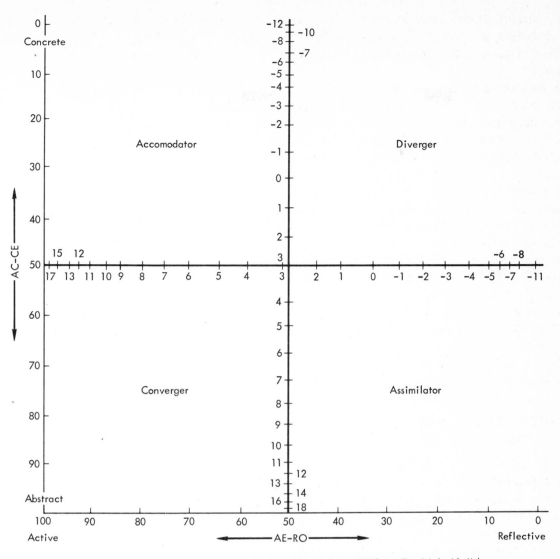

**Figure 2-2**   Learning Style Type Grid (Copyright 1976 by David A. Kolb)

The *diverger* has the opposite learning strengths of the converger. This person is best at concrete experience (CE) and reflective observation (RO). This person's greatest strength lies in imaginative ability. This person excels in the ability to view concrete situations from many perspectives. We have labeled this style "diverger" because a person with this style performs better in situations that call for the generation of ideas, such as a "brainstorming" idea session. Research shows that divergers are interested in people and tend to be imaginative and emotional. They have broad cultural interests and tend to specialize in the arts. This style is characteristic of individuals from humanities and liberal arts backgrounds. Counselors, organization development specialists, and personnel managers tend to be characterized by this learning style.

The *assimilator's* dominant learning abilities are abstract conceptualization (AC) and reflective observation (RO). This person's greatest strength lies in the ability to create theoretical models. This person excels in inductive reasoning and in assimilating disparate observations into an integrated explanation. This person, like the converger, is less interested in people and more concerned with abstract concepts, but is less concerned with the practical use of theories. For this person it is more important that the theory be logically sound and precise; in a situation where a theory or plan does not fit the "facts," the assimilator would be likely to disregard or reexamine the facts. As a result, this learning style is more characteristic of the basic sciences and mathematics rather than the applied sciences. In organizations this learning style is found most often in the research and planning departments.

The *accommodator* has the opposite learning strengths of the assimilator. This person is best at concrete experience (CE) and active experimentation (AE). This person's greatest strength lies in doing things—in carrying out plans and experiments—and involving oneself in new experiences. This person tends to be more of a risk taker than people with the other three learning styles. We have labeled this person "accommodator" because this person tends to excel in those situations where one must adapt oneself to specific immediate circumstances. In situations where a theory or plan does not fit the "facts," this person will most likely discard the plan or theory. This person tends to solve problems in an intuitive trial-and-error manner, relying heavily on other people for information rather than on one's own analytic ability. The accommodator is at ease with people but is sometimes seen as impatient and "pushy." This person's educational background is often in technical or practical fields such as business. In organizations people with this learning style are found in "action-oriented" jobs, often in marketing or sales.

**MISS PEACH**                                                                    **By Mell Lazarus**

*Reprinted courtesy of Mell Lazarus and Field Newspaper Syndicate*

## IV. PROCEDURE FOR GROUP MEETING

### A. Sharing Individual Learning Styles, Objectives, and Resources (Time Allotted: 1 Hour)

The Learning Style Inventory scores for each member of the group should be recorded on the blackboard in a form similar to that shown on the Group Summary of Individual Learning Styles sheet (p. 43). An average learning profile for the group should also be computed to determine whether the group is balanced or weighted heavily toward a particular learning style.

When this is completed, all members of the group, in turn, should share with the group their thoughts on the following four topics. (The questions listed under these topics are suggestions only. Each person should speak about what he or she thinks is relevant.)

Topic 1. *Individual Learning Style.* Do your learning profile scores seem valid to you? How do you characterize the way you learn? What do you think is your greatest strength as a learner? What is your greatest weakness?

Topic 2. *Personal Learning Goals.* What do you want to achieve in this course? What do you want to know about behavioral science? In what ways do you want to improve your managerial skills? Are you seeking knowledge about yourself? What changes would you like to make in your learning style?

| GROUP SUMMARY OF INDIVIDUAL LEARNING STYLES | | | | | |
|---|---|---|---|---|---|
| Name | Concrete Experience | Reflective Observation | Abstract Conceptualization | Active Experimentation | Learning Style Type |
| 1. | | | | | |
| 2. | | | | | |
| 3. | | | | | |
| 4. | | | | | |
| 5. | | | | | |
| 6. | | | | | |
| 7. | | | | | |
| 8. | | | | | |
| 9. | | | | | |
| 10. | | | | | |
| 11. | | | | | |
| 12. | | | | | |
| 13. | | | | | |
| 14. | | | | | |
| 15. | | | | | |
| 16. | | | | | |
| 17. | | | | | |
| 18. | | | | | |
| 19. | | | | | |
| 20. | | | | | |
| Total | | | | | |
| Average | | | | | |

Topic 3. *Resources for Learning.* What experiences have you had that may help other group members attain their learning objectives? Have you had other relevant courses in psychology or been in other management development programs? What work experiences can you draw on to provide examples and specific problems for the group to learn from?

Topic 4. *Preferred Learning Environment.* What kinds of learning situations help you learn best? What makes it difficult for you to learn? What can the instructor and other group members do to make this the best learning experience for you?

Other members of the group may ask questions as each person speaks; however, the group should budget its time so that everyone gets a chance to share their thoughts on these questions. If the group is large, it may want to divide into smaller subgroups for this discussion.

B. Understanding Personal Approaches to Problem Solving (Time Allotted: 1 Hour)

As we have seen, learning and problem solving are activities that emphasize different aspects of a single adaptive process described by the experiential learning cycle. Thus, we might expect some relationship between an individual's learning style and the way that person goes about solving problems in work and personal life. The purpose of this portion of the session is to help participants analyze their personal problem-solving process and thereby to deepen their understanding of their learning/problem-solving style.

*Step 1.* The group should divide into two four-person groups of homogeneous learning style types. For example, if there are six convergers, they should form two groups, four divergers should form a single group, and so on. Individuals whose LSI scores are balanced should choose the group they think fits them best.

*Step 2.* The small groups should review the following section describing relationships between learning styles and problem-solving process and then score both of each member's descriptions of the problem-solving process using the Guide for Analysis of Personal Problem-Solving Process (p. 48). To do the scoring, each person in turn should read one of his or her problem process descriptions and other group members together should score the description following the instructions on the Guide. The person who read the problem should then record these scores on his or her copy of the Guide. When the first problem of each member is scored, then the group should repeat the process for the second problem.

*Step 3.* Each group should record the total individual scores of its group members on accommodation, divergence, assimilation, and convergence on a flip chart or blackboard.

(Time allotted for steps 1–3: 30 minutes)

*Step 4.* Total group discussion (time allotted: 30 minutes). Using the small group data as a starting point, the group should address the following questions:

a. Are there relationships between learning style as measured by the LSI and personal approaches to problem solving?

b. Are individuals relatively balanced in their use of different problem-solving activities or are there distinctive personal styles that emphasize some activities over others?

c. Do approaches to problem-solving vary as a function of the problem that is chosen or the way the problem is defined? For example, do "people" problems tend to be approached via divergence and accommodation activities while technical problems are approached by assimilation and convergence activities?

d. How do you think differences in managerial problem-solving styles influence organizational functioning?

*Using the Experiential Learning Model to Analyze Personal Approaches to Problem Solving*

Figure 2–3 overlays a model of the problem-solving process on the experiential learning cycle and identifies problem-solving activities that characterize different stages of the cycle. In this figure we can see that the stages in a problem-solving sequence generally correspond with the learning style strengths of the four major learning styles described earlier. The accommodator's problem-solving strengths lie in executing solutions and in initiating problem finding based on some goal or model about how things should be. The diverger's problem-solving strengths lie in identifying the multitude of possible problems and opportunities that exist in reality ("compare model with reality" and "identify differences"). The assimilator excels in the abstract model building that is necessary to choose a priority problem and alternative solutions. The converger's strengths lie in the evaluation of solution consequences and solution selection.

**Figure 2–3**   Comparison of the Experiential Learning Model and the Problem-solving Process

Let us briefly examine two organizational studies to illustrate the practical implications of this theoretical model. The first study[2] was conducted in the Trust Department of a large U.S. bank. One aim of this study was to discover how the learning styles of investment portfolio managers affected their problem solving and decision making in the management of the assets in their portfolios. While the study involved only 31 managers, there was a strong correspondence between the type of decisions these managers faced and their learning styles. More specifically, nearly all the managers in the Investment Advisory section of the department, a high-risk, high-pressure job (as indicated by a large percentage of holdings in common stock, a large percentage of discretionary accounts, and a high performance and risk orientation on the part of clients), had accommodative learning styles (scoring very high on the AE and CE LSI scales). On the other hand, the men in the Personal Trust section, where risk and performance orientation were low and where there were few discretionary accounts and fewer holdings in common stock, scored highest on reflective observation. This finding supports the view that high-pressure management jobs select and develop active experimentation learning skills and inhibit reflective observation learning skills.

The study also attempted to study differences on the basis of their LSI scores, in the way managers went about making investment decisions. The research focused on differences between managers with concrete experience (CE) learning skills and abstract conceptualization (AC) learning skills. Managers were asked to evaluate the importance of the information sources that they used in making decisions. CE managers cited more people as important sources (e.g., colleagues, brokers, and traders), while the AC managers listed more analytically oriented printed material as sources (e.g., economic analyses, industry and company reviews). In addition, it seemed that CE managers sought services that would give them a specific recommendation that they could accept or reject (e.g., a potential list), while the AC managers sought information that they could analyze themselves in order to choose an investment. This analytic orientation of the AC managers is further illustrated by the fact that they tended to use more information sources in their decisions than the CE managers. These data fit well with the learning/problem-solving model. The concrete managers prefer go/no-go implementation decisions based on personal recommendations, while the abstract managers prefer to consider and evaluate alternative solutions themselves.

The second study of the relationship between learning styles and managerial problem solving was a laboratory computer simulation of a production "trouble-shooting" problem where the problem solver had to determine which specific type of "widget" was failure-prone.[3] This experiment was conducted with 22 middle-level managers at the Massachusetts Institute of Technology's Sloan Fellows program. The study focused on the different types of problem-solving strategies that assimilators and accommodators would use to solve this problem. It was predicted that the accommodators would use a strategy that called for little complexity in use and interpretation, little inference from the data, and little cognitive strain in assimilating information, while assimilators would prefer a strategy that had the opposite characteristics—more complex use and interpretation, and more assimilation strain and required inference. The former strategy, called successive scanning, was simply a process whereby the problem solver scans the data base of widgets for a direct test of his current hypothesis. It requires little conceptual analysis, since the current hypothesis is either validated or not in each trial. The latter strategy, called simultaneous scanning, is in a sense an "optimal" strategy in that each data point is used to eliminate the maximum number of data points still possible. This strategy requires considerable conceptual analysis since the problem solver must keep several hypotheses in his head at the same time and deduce the optimal widget to examine in order to test these hypotheses. The results of the experiment confirmed the hypothesis that accommodators would use successive scanning, while assimilators would use the more analytical simultaneous scanning strategy. It was further found that managers with accommodative learning styles tended to show more inconsistency in their use of strategies,

[2] Charles Stabell, "The Impact of a Conventional Computer System on Human Problem-Solving Behavior" (unpublished Working Paper, Sloan School of Management, Massachusetts Institute of Technology, 1973).
[3] Jerrold Grochow, "Cognitive Style as a Factor in the Design of Interactive Decision-Support Systems" (Ph.D. thesis, Sloan School of Management, Massachusetts Institute of Technology, 1973).

while the assimilative managers were quite consistent in their use of the simultaneous scanning strategy. The accommodative managers seemed to be taking a more intuitive approach, switching strategies as they gathered more data during the experiment. Interestingly enough, the study found no differences between accommodative and assimilative managers in the amount of time it took them to solve the problem. Although the two groups used very different styles in this problem, they performed equally well.

The Guide for Analysis of Personal Problem-Solving Process that follows identifies more specifically the types of problem-solving activities that characterize the different phases of the learning/problem-solving process. Its purpose is to assist you in the analysis of problem situations and how you approach them in a manner similar to that used in the experiments described above. Activities that characterize the four learning style types are grouped together under the four type headings so you can assess your stylistic emphasis in the problem-solving processes you reported.

### GUIDE FOR ANALYSIS OF PERSONAL PROBLEM-SOLVING PROCESS

*Instructions:* Score *2* points for each activity listed below that represents a major portion of your problem-solving process description. Score *1* point for activities that are a minor portion of the process description. Score *0* for activities not mentioned at all. Sum the points under each type for the total score for the four types.

|  | | *Problem 1* | *Problem 2* |
|---|---|---|---|
| Accommodation | Total | ☐ | ☐ |
| — Implementing plans/accomplishing tasks | | ___ | ___ |
| — Getting involved/committed to goals | | ___ | ___ |
| — Exploring opportunities | | ___ | ___ |
| — Dealing with people | | ___ | ___ |
| — Trying things out | | ___ | ___ |
| | | | |
| Divergence | Total | ☐ | ☐ |
| — Identifying problems/opportunities | | ___ | ___ |
| — Creative thinking | | ___ | ___ |
| — Generating alternatives/ideas | | ___ | ___ |
| — Sensing values or feelings | | ___ | ___ |
| — Information collection/seeking advice | | ___ | ___ |
| | | | |
| Assimilation | Total | ☐ | ☐ |
| — Defining the problem | | ___ | ___ |
| — Planning | | ___ | ___ |
| — Establishing evaluation criteria | | ___ | ___ |
| — Quantitative analysis | | ___ | ___ |
| — Formulating and using models/theory | | ___ | ___ |
| | | | |
| Convergence | Total | ☐ | ☐ |
| — Data interpretation | | ___ | ___ |
| — Evaluation/measurement | | ___ | ___ |
| — Decision making | | ___ | ___ |
| — Design of experiments | | ___ | ___ |
| — Setting priorities/goals | | ___ | ___ |

## V. SUMMARY

Today's highly successful managers and administrators are distinguished not so much by any single set of knowledge or skills but by their ability to adapt to and master the changing demands of their job and career, i.e., by their ability to *learn*. The same is true for successful organizations. Continuing success in a changing world requires an ability to explore new opportunities and learn from past successes and failures. So stated, these ideas are neither new nor particularly controversial. Yet it is surprising that this ability to learn, which is so widely regarded as important, receives little explicit attention by managers and their organizations. There is a kind of fatalism about learning: one either learns or one does not. The ability to consciously control and manage the learning process is usually limited to such schoolboy maxims as "Study hard" and "Do your homework."

Part of the reason for this fatalism lies in a lack of understanding about the learning process itself. If managers and administrators had a model about how individuals and organizations learn, they would better be able to enhance their own and their organization's ability to learn. This unit described such a model and attempted to show some of the ways in which the learning process and individual learning styles affect management education, managerial decision making and problem solving, and organizational learning.

### Learning Styles and Management Education

Differences in learning styles need to be managed in management education. For example, managers who come to the university for midcareer education experience something of a "culture shock." Fresh from a world of time deadlines and concrete specific problems that they must solve, they are suddenly immersed in a strange slow-paced world of generalities where the elegant solution to problems is sought even when workable solutions have been found. One gets rewarded here for reflection and analysis rather than concrete goal-directed action. Managers who "act before they think — if they ever think" meet the scientists who "think before they act — if they ever act." Research on learning styles has shown that managers on the whole are distinguished by very strong active experimentation skills and are very weak on reflective observation skills. Business school faculty members usually have the reverse profile. To bridge this gap in learning styles, the management educator must somehow respond to pragmatic demands for relevance and the application of knowledge, while encouraging the reflective examination of experience that is necessary to refine old theories and to build new ones. In encouraging reflective observation, the teacher often is seen as an interrupter of action — as a passive "ivory-tower" thinker. Indeed, this is a critical role to be played in the learning process. Yet if the reflective observer role is not internalized by the students themselves, the learning process can degenerate into a value conflict between teacher and student, each maintaining that theirs is the right perspective for learning.

Neither the faculty nor student perspective alone is valid. Managerial education will not be improved by eliminating theoretical analysis *or* relevant case problems. Improvement will come through the *integration* of the scholarly and practical learning styles. One approach to achieving this integration is to apply the experiential learning model directly in the classroom. This workbook provides games, role plays, and exercises (concrete experiences) that focus on central concepts in organizational psychology. These simulations provide a common experiential starting point for participants and faculty to explore the relevance of psychological concepts for their work. In traditional management education methods, the conflict between scholar and practitioner learning styles is exaggerated because the material to be taught is filtered through the learning style of faculty members in their lectures or presentation and analysis of cases. Students are "one down" in their own analysis because the data are secondhand and already biased. In the experiential learning approach, this filtering process does not take place because both teacher and student are observers of immediate experiences which they both interpret according to their own learning style. In this approach to learning, the teachers' role is that of facilitator of a learning process that is basically self-directed. They help students to experience in a personal and immediate way the phenomena in their field of specialization. They provide observational schemes and perspectives from which to observe these experiences. They stand ready with alternative theories and concepts as students attempt to assimilate their observations into their own conception of reality. They assist in deducing the implications of the student's concepts and in designing new "experiments" to test these implications through practical "real-world" experience.

There are two goals in the experiential learning process. One is to learn the specifics of a particular subject matter. The other goal is to learn about one's own strengths and weaknesses as a learner—i.e., learning how to learn from experience. When the process works well, participants finish their educational experience not only with new intellectual insights, but also with an understanding of their own learning style. This understanding of learning strengths and weaknesses helps in the back-home application of what has been learned and provides a framework for continuing learning on the job. Day-to-day experience becomes a focus for testing and exploring new ideas. Learning is no longer a special activity reserved for the classroom, but becomes an integral and explicit part of work itself.

### The Organization as a Learning System

Like individuals, organizations learn and develop distinctive learning styles. They, like individuals, do so through their transactions with the environment and through their choice of how to relate to that environment. This has come to be known as the open-systems view of organizations. Since many organizations are large and complex, the environment they relate to becomes highly differentiated and diverse. The way the organization adapts to this external environment is to differentiate itself into units each of which deals with just one part of the firm's external conditions. Marketing and sales face problems associated with the market, customers, and competitors; research deals with the academic and technological worlds; production deals with production equipment and raw materials sources; personnel and labor relations deal with the labor market; and so on.

Because of this need to relate to different aspects of the environment, the different units of the firm develop characteristic ways of thinking and working together—different styles of decision making and problem solving. These units select and shape managers to solve problems and make decisions in the way their environment demands. In fact, Lawrence and Lorsch define organizational differentiation as "the difference in cognitive and emotional orientation among managers in different functional departments."[4]

If the organization is thought of as a learning system, each of the differentiated units that is charged with adapting to the challenges of one segment of the environment can be thought of as having a characteristic learning style that is best suited to meet those environmental demands. The Learning Style Inventory (LSI) should be a useful tool for measuring this organizational differentiation among the functional units of a firm. To test this we studied about 20 managers from each of five functional groups in a midwestern division of a large American industrial corporation.[5] The five functional groups are described below, followed by our hypothesis about the learning style that should characterize each group given the environments to which they relate.

1. Marketing ($n = 20$). This group is made up primarily of former salespersons. They have a nonquantitative "intuitive" approach to their work. Because of their practical sales orientation in meeting customer demands, they should have accommodative learning styles—i.e., concrete and active.

[4] Paul Lawrence and Jay Lorsch, *Organization and Environment* (Boston: Division of Research, Graduate School of Business Administration, Harvard University, 1967).
[5] These data were collected by Frank Weisner as part of his Sloan School of Management M.S. thesis (1971). We have reanalyzed his data for presentation here.

2. Research ($n = 22$). The work of this group is split about 50/50 between pioneer research and applied research projects. The emphasis is on basic research. Researchers should be the most assimilative group — i.e., abstract and reflective, a style fitted to the world of knowledge and ideas.

3. Personnel/labor relations ($n = 20$). In this company, workers from this department serve two primary functions, interpreting personnel policy and promoting interaction among groups to reduce conflict and disagreement. Because of their "people orientation," these people should be predominantly divergers, concrete and reflective.

4. Engineering ($n = 18$). This group is made up primarily of design engineers who are quite production-oriented. They should be the most convergent subgroup — i.e., abstract and active, although they should be less abstract than the research group. They represent a bridge between thought and action.

4. Finance ($n = 20$). This group has a strong computer information systems bias. Financial personnel, given their orientation toward the mathematical task of information system design, should be highly abstract. Their crucial role in organizational survival should produce an active orientation. Thus, finance group members should have convergent learning styles.

Figure 2-4 shows the average scores on the active/reflective (AE–RO) and abstract/concrete (AC–CE) learning dimensions for the five functional groups. These results are consistent with the predictions above with the exception of the finance group, whose scores are less active than predicted and thus fall between the assimilative and convergent quadrants. The LSI clearly differentiates the learning styles that characterize the functional units of at least this one company. Managers in each of these units apparently use very different styles in doing their jobs.

But differentiation is only part of the story of organizational adaptation and effectiveness. The result of the differentiation necessary to adapt to the external environment is the creation of a corresponding internal need to integrate and coordinate the different units. This necessitates resolving in some way the conflicts inherent in these different learning styles. In actual practice this conflict gets resolved in many ways. Sometimes it is resolved through confrontation and integration of the different learning styles. More often, however, it is resolved through dominance by one unit over the other units, resulting in an unbalanced organizational learning style. We all know of organizations that are controlled by the marketing department or are heavily engineering oriented, and so on. This imbalance can be effective if it matches environmental demands in a stable environment; but it can be costly if the organization is called upon to learn to respond to changing environmental demands and opportunities.

One important question concerns the extent to which the integrative conflict between units is a function of managers' learning styles rather than merely a matter of conflicting job and role demands. To get at this question we asked the managers in each of the five functional units in the study above to rate how difficult they found it to communicate with each of the other four units. If integrative communication is a function of learning style, there should be a correspondence between how similar two units are in their learning style and how easy they find it to communicate. When the average communication difficulty ratings among the five units are compared with differences in unit learning styles, we find that in most cases this hypothesis is confirmed — i.e., those units that are most different in learning style have most difficulty communicating with one another. To test this notion more rigorously we did a more intensive study of communication between the two units who were most different in learning styles, marketing and research. To ascertain whether it was the managers' learning style itself that accounted for communication difficulty, we divided managers in the marketing unit into two groups. One group had learning styles that were similar to those managers in research (i.e., assimilators), while the other group had accommodative learning styles typical of the marketing function. The research group was divided similarly. The results of this analysis showed that when

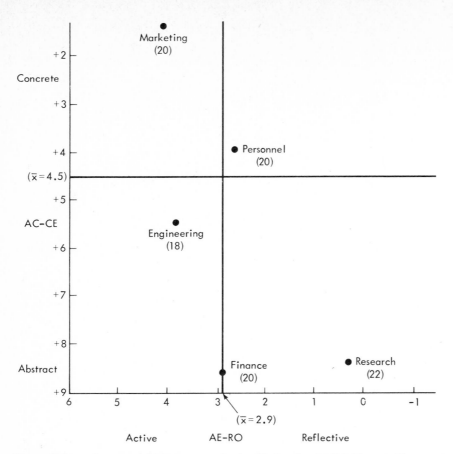

**Figure 2-4**    Average LSI Scores on Active/Reflective (AE-RO) and Abstract/ Concrete (AC-CE) by Organizational Function

managers have learning styles similar to another group, they have little trouble communicating with that group. When style differences are great, communication difficulty rises. These results suggest that managers learning styles are an important factor to consider in achieving integration among functional units.

*Managing the Learning Process*

To conclude, let us examine how managers and organizations can explicitly manage their learning process. We have seen that the experiential learning model is useful not only for examining the educational process but also for understanding managerial problem solving and organizational adaptation. But how can an awareness of the experiential learning model and our own individual learning style help improve individual and organizational learning? Two recommendations seem important.

First, learning should be an explicit objective that is pursued as consciously and deliberately as profit or productivity. Managers and organizations should budget time to specifically learn from their experiences. When important meetings are held or important decisions are made, time should be set aside to critique and learn from these events. All too few organizations have a climate that allows for free exploration of such questions as: "What have we learned from this venture?" Usually, active experimentation norms dictate: "We don't have time, let's move on."

This leads to the second recommendation. The nature of the learning process is such that opposing perspectives, action and reflection, concrete involvement and analytical detachment, are all essential for optimal learning. When one perspective comes to dominate others, learning effectiveness is reduced. From this we can conclude that the most effective learning systems are those that can tolerate differences in perspective. This point can be illustrated by the case of an electronics firm that we have worked with over the years. The firm was started by a group of engineers with a unique product. For several years they had no competitors and when some competition entered the market, they continued to dominate and do well because of their superior engineering quality. Today it is a different story. They are now faced with stiff competition in their original product area, and, in addition, their very success has caused new problems. They are no longer a small intimate company but a large organization with several plants in the United States and Europe. The company has had great difficulty in responding to these changes because it still responds to problems primarily from an engineering point of view. Most of the top executives in the company are former engineers with no formal management training. Many of the specialists in marketing, finance, and personnel who have been brought in to help the organization solve its new problems feel like "second-class citizens." Their ideas just don't seem to carry much weight. What was once the organization's strength, its engineering expertise, has become to some extent its weakness. Because engineering has flourished at the expense of the development of other organizational functions such as marketing and the management of human resources, the firm is today struggling with, rather than mastering, its environment.

## VI. SELF-EVALUATION AND COMPLETING THE LEARNING LOOP

A. What questions do you now have as a result of your learning experiences from this unit? Jot these down below.

B. From these questions, what *key concepts* can you extrapolate for further learning? Write these concepts below.

C. How can you now go about finding answers to the questions you raised above? Below are some suggested ways to continue your learning process by beginning new learning loops:

1. Look up the key concepts from your questions above in the Yellow Pages of Learning Experiences at the back of the book. Find a few suggested readings or exercises to facilitate the learning of these key concepts.

2. If you don't find the key concepts in the Yellow Pages related specifically to your questions, perhaps there are other concepts listed in the index that might lead you to relevant learning resources at this time. Look for concepts similar to those you identified in B above.

3. In the event that you don't find the Yellow Pages directory useful for your present learning goals, discuss your questions with other students, faculty, or persons outside your learning environment. Discuss further learning possibilities with them.

# chapter 3

## individual motivation and behavior

*Photo by Sybil Shelton*

## I. OBJECTIVES

A. To learn about three basic social motives and how they are defined.

B. To gain insight into your own motive patterns.

C. To explore the relationship between individual motivation and behavior.

## II. PREMEETING PREPARATION

A. Read the Instructions for the Test of Imagination.[1]

B. Write stories on *four* pictures of your choice on the pages following those pictures.

C. Do not take more than 5 minutes per story.

D. Do this before reading further in this unit.

E. Then read the Introduction and the Procedure for Group Meeting, part A (pp. 71–73).

---

[1] This test is a variation of the standard six-picture Thematic Apperception Test cited in John Atkinson (ed.), *Motives in Fantasy, Action, and Society* (Princeton, N.J.: D. Van Nostrand Co., Inc., 1958).

# TEST OF IMAGINATION

Name _____ Date _____
            Last                        First

Age _____ Sex _____

PLEASE READ THE FOLLOWING INSTRUCTIONS CAREFULLY BEFORE TURNING THE PAGE.

An important asset in the world is imagination. This test gives you an opportunity to use your imagination, to show how you can create ideas and situations by yourself. In other words, instead of presenting you with already made answers from which you choose one, it gives you the chance to show how you can think things up on your own.

On the following pages, write out some brief stories that you make up on your own. In order to help you get started, there is a series of pictures that you can interpret and around which you can build your stories. When you have finished reading these instructions, turn the page, look at the first picture briefly, then turn the page again and write a story suggested by the picture. To help you cover all the elements of a story plot in the time allowed, you will find four questions spaced out over the page:

1. What is happening? Who are the people?
2. What has led up to this situation? That is, what has happened in the past?
3. What is being thought? What is wanted? By whom?
4. What will happen? What will be done?

Please remember that the questions are only guides for your thinking, and need not be answered specifically in so many words. That is, *your story should be continuous and not just a set of answers to these questions.* Do not take more than five minutes per story. You should complete the whole test thirty minutes after you begin, although you may finish in less time if you like.

There are no right or wrong stories. In fact, any kind of story is all right. You have a chance to show how quickly you can imagine and write a story on your own. Do not simply describe the pictures; write a story about them. They are vague and suggestive of many things on purpose, and are just to help give you an idea to write about.

Try to make your stories interesting and dramatic. Show that you have an understanding of people and can make up stories about human relationships.

If you have read these instructions carefully and understand them, turn the page, look at the picture, and then write your story. Do not take more than five minutes. Then turn the page, look at the next picture briefly, write out the story it suggests, and so on through the booklet.

JUST LOOK AT THE PICTURE BRIEFLY (10-15 SECONDS),
TURN THE PAGE, AND WRITE THE STORY IT SUGGESTS.

**WORK RAPIDLY. DO NOT SPEND OVER FIVE MINUTES ON THIS STORY.**

1.  What is happening? Who are the people?

2.  What has led up to this situation? That is, what has happened in the past?

3.  What is being thought? What is wanted? By whom?

4.  What will happen? What will be done?

*When you have finished your story or your time is up, turn to the next picture. If you have not finished, go on anyway. You may return at the end to complete this story.*

JUST LOOK AT THE PICTURE BRIEFLY (10–15 SECONDS),
TURN THE PAGE, AND WRITE THE STORY IT SUGGESTS.

WORK RAPIDLY. DO NOT SPEND OVER 5 MINUTES ON THIS STORY.

1. What is happening? Who are the people?

2. What has led up to this situation? That is, what has happened in the past?

3. What is being thought? What is wanted? By whom?

4. What will happen? What will be done?

*When you have finished your story or your time is up, turn to the next picture. If you have not finished, go on anyway. You may return at the end to complete this story.*

JUST LOOK AT THE PICTURE BRIEFLY (10–15 SECONDS),
TURN THE PAGE, AND WRITE THE STORY IT SUGGESTS.

**WORK RAPIDLY. DO NOT SPEND OVER 5 MINUTES ON THIS STORY.**

1. What is happening? Who are the people?

2. What has led up to this situation? That is, what has happened in the past?

3. What is being thought? What is wanted? By whom?

4. What will happen? What will be done?

*When you have finished your story or your time is up, turn to the next picture. If you have not finished, go on anyway. You may return at the end to complete this story.*

JUST LOOK AT THE PICTURE BRIEFLY (10–15 SECONDS),
TURN THE PAGE, AND WRITE THE STORY IT SUGGESTS.

**WORK RAPIDLY. DO NOT SPEND OVER 5 MINUTES ON THIS STORY.**

1. What is happening? Who are the people?

2. What has led up to this situation? That is, what has happened in the past?

3. What is being thought? What is wanted? By whom?

4. What will happen? What will be done?

*When you have finished your story or your time is up, turn to the next picture. If you have not finished, go on anyway. You may return at the end to complete this story.*

JUST LOOK AT THE PICTURE BRIEFLY (10-15 SECONDS),
TURN THE PAGE, AND WRITE THE STORY IT SUGGESTS.

**WORK RAPIDLY. DO NOT SPEND OVER 5 MINUTES ON THIS STORY.**

1. What is happening? Who are the people?

2. What has led up to this situation? That is, what has happened in the past?

3. What is being thought? What is wanted? By whom?

4. What will happen? What will be done?

*When you have finished your story or your time is up, turn to the next picture. If you have not finished, go on anyway. You may return at the end to complete this story.*

JUST LOOK AT THE PICTURE BRIEFLY (10-15 SECONDS),
TURN THE PAGE, AND WRITE THE STORY IT SUGGESTS.

**WORK RAPIDLY. DO NOT SPEND OVER 5 MINUTES ON THIS STORY.**

1. What is happening? Who are the people?

2. What has led up to this situation? That is, what has happened in the past?

3. What is being thought? What is wanted? By whom?

4. What will happen? What will be done?

*When you have finished your story or your time is up, turn to the next picture. If you have not finished, go on anyway. You may return at the end to complete this story.*

## III. INTRODUCTION

*Motive* is a word often used in mystery stories and among actors. All of us have some intuitive understanding of the meaning of the term in those contexts. The detective, for instance, in looking for the culprit, will always seek someone with a "motive," a *reason* for committing the murder. An actor or actress, in a like manner, wants to understand the motivation of some character. In both instances the search for motive is the search for a process of thinking and feeling that causes a person to act in specific ways.

Our understanding of human motivation has increased substantially over the past few decades. Simplistic theories which argued that people worked primarily for money or primarily for social gratification have been replaced with more complex theories of human nature.[2] Maslow's work, for example, provided two important postulates concerning human motivation. One is that human needs can be viewed in an hierarchical fashion. Lower-order needs — needs for physical safety and security — must be satisfied to some extent before higher-order needs — needs for self-esteem and self-actualization — become activated. Second is the notion that a satisfied need is no longer a motivator of behavior. Insights such as these can help us understand why it is that a salary increase may be of marginal motivational value. Individuals are at different levels in the motivational hierarchy at different times, causing different needs to be aroused. Herzberg suggests a two-factor theory of motivation based on Maslow's hierarchy. Hygiene factors — things like attractiveness of physical facilities, good salaries, and so on — create dissatisfaction if they do not exist. Their presence, however, does not create positive motivation. A second set of factors — motivation factors such as challenge, responsibility, and so on — are necessary to stimulate positive motivation. Once we have met a person's hygiene needs, "more of the same" yields marginal benefits.

Psychologists, most notably David McClelland of Harvard, have made a great deal of progress over the past 20 years in scientifically measuring and defining human motives.[3] McClelland began by looking not at external action but at the way a person thinks. He used the Thematic Apperception Test (TAT), which you have taken in preparation for today, to record thought samples that could then be studied and grouped according to the dominant concerns, or themes, expressed in the stories. He and his co-workers were able to group the responses into three broad categories, each representing an identifiable human motive. The need for affiliation (n-Aff), the need for power (n-Pow), and the need to achieve (n-Ach).

Most people, McClelland found, have a degree of each of these motives in their thoughts, but seldom in the same strength. A person may be high in the need for affiliation (n-Aff), low in the need for achievement (n-Ach), and moderate in the need for power (n-Pow). Such people would tend to think more about friendship than about doing a good job or controlling others. Their motivation to work will be of a different order than that of the employee who is high in achievement motivation and low in affiliation and power motivations. The needs identified in McClelland's framework are similar to Maslow' higher-order needs and Herzberg's motivation factors.

## IV. PROCEDURE FOR GROUP MEETING

A. Motive Analysis and Scoring (Time Allotted: 1¼ Hours)

The purpose of this exercise is to help you identify (but not score in detail) the motivational themes you expressed in your TAT stories.

[2] For a more complete discussion of various theories of motivation, see Edgar H. Schein, *Organizational Psychology* (Englewood Cliffs, N.J.: Prentice-Hall, Inc., 1965).
[3] See John Atkinson, *Motives in Fantasy, Action, and Society* (Princeton, N.J.: D. Van Nostrand Co., Inc., 1958), and David C. McClelland, *The Achieving Society* (Princeton, N.J.: D. Van Nostrand Co., Inc., 1961).

Divide the group into trios for the scoring and have one trio member read their first story to the other two. Using the criteria listed forthwith, score the story and enter it on the Individual Scoring Form on page 75. Repeat until all stories of each trio member have been scored and entered.

The following criteria, taken from the empirical scoring systems, will help you decide which of the three motives, *if any*, is present in your stories. Record on the form provided those motives present in each story plus any other motivational concerns that you and your group may notice. It is possible for a story to contain none or all three of these motives, as well as other motivational concerns, such as sex, aggression, hunger, or security.

In approaching the task, you should keep several things in mind. The TAT pictures and your responses are meant to be stimuli for reflection and discussion, not necessarily an absolute measure of your motives. In addition, you are not expected to become expert scorers, but to become familiar with general patterns. Finally, be wary of the pressure to reach consensus in your trio meetings. Each listener will, in fact, hear another's story through their own (the listener's) motivational filter. For example, a person high in the need for affiliation may well "see" considerable affiliation imagery in someone else's story.

An essential point of this exercise is that people *do* have different needs and they *do* consequently see the world in different ways. The managerial task is to become aware of and effectively integrate these real differences.

*Achievement motivation is present in a story when any one of the following three things occurs:*

1.  Someone in the story is concerned about a *standard of excellence*. They want to win or to do well in a competition. They have self-imposed standards for a good performance; or they are emotionally involved in attaining an achievement goal. Standards of excellence can be inferred by the use of words such as *good* or *better* or similar words when used to evaluate performance.

2.  Someone in the story is involved in a unique accomplishment, such as an invention or an artistic creation. Here the standard of excellence can be inferred and need not be explicitly stated.

3.  Someone in the story is involved in a *long-term goal*, such as an invention or an artistic creation. Here the standard of excellence can be inferred and need not be explicitly stated.

*Power motivation is present in a story when any one of the following three things occurs:*

1.  Someone in the story is affected or *emotionally concerned about getting or maintaining control of the means of influencing a person*. Wanting to win a point, to show dominance, to convince someone, or to gain a position of control, as well as wanting to avoid weakness or humiliation, are obvious examples. However, weaker statements, such as wanting to teach or inspire another person, should also be scored. If the teaching or advice is solicited, then imagery should not be scored unless there is additional evidence of power concern.

2.  *Someone is actually doing something to get or keep control of the means of influence,* such as arguing, demanding or forcing, giving a command, trying to convince, or punishing. Theoretically, any activity could be scored here, as long as it is oriented toward control of the means to influence. Physical power could be scored as power imagery, but not if it were only an expression of hostility.

3.  There is a statement of an interpersonal *relationship that is culturally defined as one*

*in which a superior has control of the means of influencing a subordinate.* The relationship must not only be mentioned but also carried out in activity. If a boss-worker story goes on to elaborate an affiliative bond, power imagery would not be scored. Furthermore, either the subordinate must be mentioned or the effect on the person must be clear. The parent-child relationship, in and of itself, is not scored as a power relationship.

*Affiliation motivation is present when any of the following three things occurs:*

1. Someone in the story is concerned about establishing, maintaining, or restoring a *positive emotional relationship* with another person. Friendship is the most basic kind of positive emotional relationship, and to mention that two characters in the story are friends would be a minimum basis for scoring imagery. Other relationships, such as father-son, or lover-lover, should be scored *only* if they have the warm, compassionate quality implied in the definition given.

2. Statements that *one person likes or wants to be liked* by someone else, or that someone has some similar feeling about another. Moreover, if a close interpersonal relationship has been disrupted or broken, imagery can be scored if someone feels sorrow or grief or takes action to restore the relationship.

3. Also, score if the story mentions such *affiliative activities* as parties, reunions, visits, or relaxed small talk as in a bull session. However, if the affiliative nature of the situation is explicitly denied in the story, such as by describing it as a business meeting or an angry debate, imagery is not scored. Friendly actions such as consoling or being concerned about the well-being or happiness of another person are scored, except where these actions are culturally prescribed by the relationship — e.g., father-son. In other words, there must be evidence that the nurturant activity is not motivated solely by a sense of obligation.

## Discussion of Motive Scores

When a trio has finished scoring their stories, they should join with another trio and discuss the following questions:

1. How much similarity/difference was there in your group concerning the dominant motivational concerns expressed in the stories? Of what significance is this similarity/difference?

2. In what ways did the motivational concerns you expressed in the stories agree/disagree with the image you held of yourself *before* you took the test? Of what significance are any differences?

3. What kinds of things cause one person to express affiliation concerns, another person to express power concerns, and a third to express achievement concerns in response to the *same* picture? Consider immediate (e.g., "He hadn't had anything to eat all day") as well as historical (e.g., "She flunked math in high school") factors.

4. Were there any particular reasons that you chose the four pictures you did? In other words, you chose not to respond to two pictures in particular — Why? Did others choose the same pictures as you?

5. What motives do you think are relevant/important within the context of a job?

6. Of what value, if any, do you feel are projective techniques such as the TAT in assessing human motivation? What other alternatives might be feasible or better?

# INDIVIDUAL SCORING FORM FOR TEST OF IMAGINATION

Circle the motives present in each story and indicate other motivational concerns in the space provided.

| | Primary Social Motives | Other Motives Present in Story |
|---|---|---|
| Story 1 | Achievement<br>Power<br>Affiliation | |
| Story 2 | Achievement<br>Power<br>Affiliation | |
| Story 3 | Achievement<br>Power<br>Affiliation | |
| Story 4 | Achievement<br>Power<br>Affiliation | |
| Story 5 | Achievement<br>Power<br>Affiliation | |
| Story 6 | Achievement<br>Power<br>Affiliation | |
| Summary | Number of stories with<br><br>Achievement___<br>Power___<br>Affiliation ___ | Other major concerns: |

B. Individual Motives and Behavior (Time Allotted: 1¼ Hours)

The focus in this part of the class is on the relationship between individual motives and behavior. The exercise has been designed to focus primarily upon the behavioral manifestations of n-Power, n-Affiliation, and n-Achievement.

The Money Auction (Time Allotted: 90 Minutes)

*Step 1.* The first step in this exercise[4] is for the total group to divide into groups of three. If there are one or two individuals remaining after the trios are formed, they should join a trio as observers.

Each trio is made of *one auctioneer* and *two bidders*. This exercise will continue for three rounds, giving each member of the trio a chance to be the auctioneer. *During the exercise no talking is allowed except for stating bids.*

*Step 2.* In the exercise itself the auctioneer should be considered the dispenser of funds. *It is not his/her money.* Auctioneers will offer for auction to the two bidders seven imaginary nickels, one at a time. Each nickel will be sold to the highest bidder. There is nothing special about these nickels (e.g., they are not rare coins). The opportunity for the first bid will alternate between the two bidders during the seven trials. Bidder 1 will bid first on the first trial, bidder 2 bids first on the second, and so on. Bids must be made alternatively between bidders in at least 1-cent units. Players should record the process of the auction on the Money Auction Record Form on page 79. *Remember that it is helpful if you do no talking except to state bids until all three rounds are completed.*

*Step 3.* *Individual reflection.* When all three rounds have been completed, each individual should take 10–15 minutes of alone time to record personal reactions to the questions that follow:

1. a. What was your goal in the nickel auction when you were a bidder?

   b. What strategy did you follow to reach your goal?

   c. Did you maintain the same goal and strategy throughout the exercise? If you changed, what caused you to do so?

2. What thoughts did you have before/during the exercise you just completed which you would say were reflective of the three motives under examination?

   a. n-Ach thoughts:

   b. n-Pow thoughts:

   c. n-Aff thoughts:

3. In what ways was your behavior, in your view, reflective of each of the three motives under examination? Jot down some specific examples:

   a. n-Ach behavior I exhibited:

   b. n-Pow behavior I exhibited:

   c. n-Aff behavior I exhibited:

4. In what ways did other members of your trio behave which you would say were reflective of each of the three motives under examination? Jot down some specific examples:

   a. n-Ach behavior others exhibited:

[4] This game is a modification of an exercise introduced to us by Edgar H. Schein.

b. n-Pow behavior others exhibited:

c. n-Aff behavior others exhibited:

Step 4. *Trio discussion.* Each member of the trio should share their individual responses to the questions raised above. The following will help to guide and focus this discussion:

a. How did n-Achievement, n-Power, and n-Affiliation behavior exhibited by individuals influence each other and interact — for example, what happened when one person was exhibiting n-Affiliation while another was exhibiting n-Power?

b. What differences, if any, did you notice between the first, second, and third rounds of the auction? To what do you attribute these differences?

Step 5. After you have finished discussing these points, read the next section (pp. 78–81), join another trio, and continue your discussion.

## Typical Patterns in Money Auction

The average person ends up breaking even in the Money Auction Game — i.e., no profit, no loss. A few people make a little money — 2–5 cents after seven trials. Many people *lose* money (as much as $2!) by bidding considerably more than 5 cents for a nickel! It is possible for each bidder to make as much as 28 cents in each of their two rounds. This can happen only under the following conditions:

1. Bidder 2 passes after an opening bid of 1 cent by bidder 1. (How many people even open the bidding at 1 cent?)

2. Bidder 1 then passes after bidder 2's opening bid of 1 cent, and so on.

To achieve this solution, one member must take the first step (risk) and *trust* the other to see that they are trying to *collaborate* and not to compete. Sometimes one person tries this strategy (trusting the other) and invariably is betrayed. The other (B) thinks, "Have I got a sucker here!" But, "once burned, twice shy," and A says, "I'm no fool," and the result is that neither makes any more money. B often comes away feeling as if he won. Did he? It depends on one's definition of the situation and the goals each is pursuing — achievement goals, such as winning money; power goals, such as getting the nickels from the other person at any cost; or affiliation goals, such as cooperation and sharing with the other person.

People often ask, "Are you saying affiliation and cooperation are the answer and that power and competition are no good?" The answer is yes; under certain conditions, competition has destructive effects. For example, competition between two departments in the same organization can hurt overall company achievement, whereas competition between two companies can be healthy.

It is important to note that n-Achievement has different behavioral manifestations than either n-Power or n-Affiliation in terms of the individual's relationships with people. N-Power and n-Affiliation are interpersonally-oriented needs. Implicit in their definitions is the existence of other human beings who the n-Power- and n-Affiliation-motivated individual can influence and control or be friends with. N-Achievement, on the other hand, is a more individualized need. N-Achievement-motivated individuals may need other people to help them reach achievement goals, but the nature of their relationship with others and their strategies for dealing with other people will be determined by needs other than achievement.

*The key point is this:* We often define a situation as being a "zero-sum" power game (you win; ergo, I must lose). Our definition causes us to behave in a certain way — e.g., to compete instead of to collaborate in order to achieve our goals. This behavior on our part elicits comparable behavior from others — e.g., the person who starts out collaborating (trusting) but is taken advantage of immediately

## THE MONEY AUCTION RECORD FORM

Indicate how much the winner of each trial paid for each nickel and subtract from five to get profit or loss for that round.

### Round One

Auctioneer _____

| Bidder 1 _____ | Bidder 2 _____ |
|---|---|
| Nickel 1  5¢ – _____ = _____ | 5¢ – _____ = _____ |
| Nickel 2  5¢ – _____ = _____ | 5¢ – _____ = _____ |
| Nickel 3  5¢ – _____ = _____ | 5¢ – _____ = _____ |
| Nickel 4  5¢ – _____ = _____ | 5¢ – _____ = _____ |
| Nickel 5  5¢ – _____ = _____ | 5¢ – _____ = _____ |
| Nickel 6  5¢ – _____ = _____ | 5¢ – _____ = _____ |
| Nickel 7  5¢ – _____ = _____ | 5¢ – _____ = _____ |
| Total Earnings _____ | Total Earnings _____ |

### Round Two

Auctioneer _____

| Bidder 1 _____ | Bidder 2 _____ |
|---|---|
| Nickel 1  5¢ – _____ = _____ | 5¢ – _____ = _____ |
| Nickel 2  5¢ – _____ = _____ | 5¢ – _____ = _____ |
| Nickel 3  5¢ – _____ = _____ | 5¢ – _____ = _____ |
| Nickel 4  5¢ – _____ = _____ | 5¢ – _____ = _____ |
| Nickel 5  5¢ – _____ = _____ | 5¢ – _____ = _____ |
| Nickel 6  5¢ – _____ = _____ | 5¢ – _____ = _____ |
| Nickel 7  5¢ – _____ = _____ | 5¢ – _____ = _____ |
| Total Earnings _____ | Total Earnings _____ |

### Round Three

Auctioneer _____

| Bidder 1 _____ | Bidder 2 _____ |
|---|---|
| Nickel 1  5¢ – _____ = _____ | 5¢ – _____ = _____ |
| Nickel 2  5¢ – _____ = _____ | 5¢ – _____ = _____ |
| Nickel 3  5¢ – _____ = _____ | 5¢ – _____ = _____ |
| Nickel 4  5¢ – _____ = _____ | 5¢ – _____ = _____ |
| Nickel 5  5¢ – _____ = _____ | 5¢ – _____ = _____ |
| Nickel 6  5¢ – _____ = _____ | 5¢ – _____ = _____ |
| Nickel 7  5¢ – _____ = _____ | 5¢ – _____ = _____ |
| Total Earnings _____ | Total Earnings _____ |

begins to compete. A circle of events, a self-fulfilling prophecy, has begun that is extremely difficult to break!

The critical element in the point above is the crucial role played by our own definition of the situation — our goals/objectives. Two trio groups should now address the following questions:

1. The goals/objectives that people had for the money auction game (or might have had) can be categorized as primarily related to one of the three primary motives.
   a. What were/would have been examples of n-Achievement-oriented goals/objectives (e.g., to maximize profit)?
   b. What were/would have been examples of n-Power-oriented objectives (e.g., to beat the other person)?
   c. What were/would have been examples of n-Affiliation-oriented objectives (e.g., not to make the other person look bad)?

2. After each person defined a goal/objective for the game, s/he presumably then began to behave in a certain way to reach that goal/objective.
   a. What were/would have been examples of n-Achievement-oriented behaviors or strategies?
   b. What were/would have been examples of n-Power-oriented behaviors or strategies?
   c. What were/would have been examples of n-Affiliation-oriented behaviors or strategies?

3. In what ways can you see new/clearer connections between your own TAT results and your behavior in this game? In what ways did the structure of the game and/or your partner's behavior induce you to behave in a way different from that which your personal motive pattern might suggest? Did your motives remain constant throughout the exercise or did events arouse different motives at different times?

*Reprinted by permission of the Chicago Tribune-New York News Syndicate*

## V. SUMMARY

It is easy to conclude from the Money Auction Game that competitive behavior, resulting from high n-Power, is bad and that collaborative behavior, resulting from high n-Affiliation, is good. The simplicity of such a conclusion should make clear its invalidity. The salient issues are:

1. Under what conditions are the two forms of behavior — competitive versus collaborative — appropriate?

2. What kinds of factors cause us to misread a given situation and what are the consequences?

The reward structure existing in any social situation provides the key to whether it is logically a competitive or a collaborative situation. If there is only a limited amount of reward available, such that if one person wins, another must lose, the situation can be defined as competitive. If, on the other hand, it is possible for all participants to achieve their goals, and goal achievement by one person involves or leads to goal achievement by another, the situation is collaborative.

It is not difficult to think of examples of pure competitive and collaborative situations. A serious poker game or the interaction between a buyer and a used car dealer are purely competitive situations. An army squad in combat or several people working on a joint research project are examples of collaborative situations.

The behaviors most appropriate and effective in a competitive situation are quite different from, and often directly opposite to, behaviors that are most adaptive in a collaborative situation. The following is a partial list of behaviors or strategies appropriate and effective in each type of situation.[5]

| *Effective Competitive Behavior* | *Effective Collaborative Behavior* |
|---|---|
| 1. Behavior is directed toward achieving personal goals. | 1. Behavior is directed toward goals held in common. |
| 2. Secrecy. | 2. Openness. |
| 3. Accurate personal understanding of own needs, but they are either hidden or misrepresented. If others do not know just what you want and how much you want it, they do not know how much you are willing to give up to get it. | 3. Accurate personal understanding of own needs, and accurate representation of them. |
| 4. Unpredictable, mixed strategies utilizing the element of surprise. | 4. Predictable. Although flexible behavior is appropriate, it is not designed to take the other party by surprise. |
| 5. Threats and bluffs. | 5. Threats and bluffs are not used. |
| 6. Logical, nonrational, and irrational arguments are used to defend a position to which you are strategically committed. | 6. Logical and innovative processes are used to defend your views, if you are convinced of their validity, or to find solutions to problems. |
| 7. Where teams, committees, or organizations are involved, communicating bad stereotypes of the other, ignoring his/her logic, impugning his/her motives, and arousing in-group hostility. This tends to strengthen in-group loyalty, increase motivation, and convince others you mean business. | 7. Success demands that stereotypes be dropped, that ideas be given consideration on their merit regardless of source, and that good working relationships be maintained. Positive feelings about others are both a cause and an effect of collaboration. |

[5] This list and parts of the following discussion are reproduced from Richard Walton's paper, "How to Choose Between Strategies of Conflict and Collaboration," in R. Golembrewski and R. Blumberg (eds.) *Sensitivity Training and the Laboratory Approach* (Itasca, Ill.: F. E. Peacock Publishers, Inc., 1970).

The use of competitive strategies, particularly, has some effects that often go unrecognized. These effects are probably functional if the persons or groups interact only under purely competitive conditions. However, they will make any subsequent attempt at joint problem solving much more difficult. Three such consequences of the use of competitive strategies are:

1. *The development of a competitive, win–lose climate that emphasizes the separateness of "we" and "they."* We are superior — they are inferior. Individual factions or groups under competitive pressure invariably rate themselves above average in both cohesion and ability.

2. *Distortions in judgment.* Individuals or groups under competitive pressure invariably evaluate their own contributions as best, and fall into downgrading the efforts of others.

3. *Distortions in perception.* Experiments demonstrate that under competitive pressure persons perceive that they understand the other's proposal when, in fact, they do not. Consequently, shared areas are likely to go unrecognized.

Unfortunately, most of the social situations we find ourselves in are neither purely competitive nor purely collaborative. One complication is that we frequently have to play the competitive and the collaborative games simultaneously, such as when we are trying to problem-solve with the same persons with whom we are competing for promotion, or when two work groups or departments that are trying to be "best" have to work together to complete a job.

A second complication arises from the fact that we frequently cannot accurately diagnose a situation as competitive or collaborative until we know how the other participants are viewing the situation and we have some expectations concerning how they will behave. In real-life situations, when asked why they do not collaborate in what logically appears to be a collaborative situation, people will respond that they do not behave collaboratively because they cannot trust the other participants to do the same. This is a common dilemma, and a very real one. But there is a possible alternative to simply relying on competitive strategies: It lies in the possibility of influencing the behavior of the other parties in the situation through communication and trust building.

Some people may approach every situation as if it were a competitive game; e.g., they will transform every discussion into a debate. Another person will approach every situation as if it were a collaborative game. Another will tend to see the objective reality of the situation, and choose approaches that are appropriate. The first type can be called *cynical*, the second *naive*, and the third *realistic*.

The common problem in industry today is cynicism — we characteristically approach situations as if they are competitive even when they are not. Similarly, the early decades of union–management relations were conducted in a strictly win–lose manner, as if the entire process were competitive bargaining — what labor gains, management must lose, and vice versa. However, attitudes changed over a period of time, and parties began to wonder if the game might have some collaborative aspects. Note the key role of attitude change in permitting collaborative behavior to substitute for competitive. The important thing is that the parties begin to know each other and have some trust in each other (if not positive feeling). They can begin to reexamine the situation to find the collaborative aspects that will facilitate the goal achievement of both parties.

## VI. SELF-EVALUATION AND COMPLETING THE LEARNING LOOP

A. What questions do you now have as a result of your learning experiences from this unit? Jot these down below.

B. From these questions, what *key concepts* can you extrapolate for further learning? Write these concepts below.

C. How can you now go about finding answers to the questions you raised above? Below are some suggested ways to continue your learning process by beginning new learning loops:

1. Look up the key concepts from your questions above in the Yellow Pages of Learning Experiences at the back of the book. Find a few suggested readings or exercises to facilitate the learning of these key concepts.

2. If you don't find the key concepts in the Yellow Pages related specifically to your questions, perhaps there are other concepts listed in the index that might lead you to relevant learning resources at this time. Look for concepts similar to those you identified in B above.

3. In the event that you don't find the Yellow Pages directory useful for your present learning goals now, discuss your questions with other students, faculty, or persons outside your learning environment. Discuss further learning possibilities with them.

# chapter 4

## motivation and work

*Photo by Sybil Shelton*

## I. OBJECTIVES

    A. To explore sources of motive satisfaction in work.

    B. To design ways of creating work situations that stimulate achievement motivation and productivity.

    C. To identify the kind of work situation that you personally find most satisfying.

## II. PREMEETING PREPARATION

    A. Read the Introduction.

    B. Using the sheets provided at the end of this unit, learn to fold the Moon Tent and the Shallow-Water Cargo Carrier.

# III. INTRODUCTION

Much of the psychological research on motivation leaves the practicing manager with a number of questions about the practical utility of such knowledge when dealing with a work force that seems generally "unmotivated." The question becomes: "How can I increase their motivation to work at our task?" The motivation to work may be seen as a function of the situation in which workers find themselves, situations that are variously motivating or demotivating according to a number of factors. The intrinsic motivation of the employee is, of course, important, but changes in the situation are often needed in order to tap that motivation and turn it to productive ends.

It is helpful to look at some of the situational variables that people with a high need to achieve tend to want from their work environment as a way of beginning to think about situational factors that lead to productivity. People with a high need to achieve tend to want:

1. *Immediate, concrete feedback.* They want to know as soon as possible how well they are doing. If they are not doing well, they also want to know that so that they may adjust their performance to meet their personal and/or organizational goals.

2. *Moderate risk-taking situations.* They like the kind of situation that is a personal challenge, but not one that is going to be left to fate. They operate best in the area where the probability of success at a task and its incentive value are about equal. A task that is too simple will not offer enough of a challenge, and will not capture their interest for very long, unless it is a component of a more challenging goal. In short, they like situations in which they can be successful most of the time, as long as they give it their best shot.

3. *Personal responsibility for their own success or failure.* This is an outgrowth of both of the above. When high achievement-motivated people fail at a task, they want to know why, not alibi. They learn from facing the data squarely so as not to repeat their mistakes.[1]

Although the characteristics above are those exhibited by a rather special group of people, the high achievers, we can learn something about structuring work situations to ensure productivity from the way these highly productive people like their work situations designed. Litwin and Stringer, for instance, created three mock companies in the same business and varied them only by style of the manager and the climate he created. At the end of the 2-week experiment, the company that had been run on the achievement principles had outperformed the other two on most dimensions (the other two had been organized on "authoritarian" and "friendly" principles).[2] McIntyre has demonstrated a similar effect with fifth-grade mathematics students, raising performance and learning levels by changing the classroom structure to emphasize personal responsibility, feedback, and moderate risk taking.[3]

The work of Frederick Herzberg has been helpful in learning what it is about a work situation that increases satisfaction and productivity. Herzberg has differentiated between factors in a work situation that are motivating to the employee, and those that we often assume are motivators but are really "hygiene factors."[4] A motivator is a condition of the way the work is done that keeps satisfac-

---

[1] David C. McClelland, *The Achieving Society* (Princeton, N.J.: D. Van Nostrand Co., 1961).
[2] George H. Litwin, "Climate and Motivation: An Experimental Study," in Renato Tagiuri and George H. Litwin (eds.), *Organizational Climate: Explorations of a Concept* (Boston: Harvard University, 1968), pp. 169–190. *Readings.*
[3] J. McIntyre, "The Math Game" (Cambridge Mass.: Harvard Graduate School of Education Working Paper, 1966).
[4] F. Herzberg, *Work and the Nature of Man* (Cleveland: World Publishing Company, 1966).

tion and productivity high. A hygiene factor is never a motivator, but will decrease motivation if it is not present or if it is present in inadequate ways. Salary seldom motivates a person positively, but a salary seen as inadequate will tend to decrease performance.

Examples of motivating factors in the work setting, according to Herzberg, are:

1. *The work itself.* If the work is challenging enough and is structured in such a way as to provide feedback on performance, it is more likely to be a satisfier.
2. *Relationships.* The opportunity to develop positive relationships with other workers on the job is likely to lead to job satisfaction when combined with challenging work.
3. *Autonomy.* The latitude to make decisions about the "how" of the work is also a motivator. Management should communicate production goals, for instance, but the process by which they are met is motiving only insofar as that decision is made by involving the people who implement it.

In all these approaches, the emphasis is on the person, not the technology the person works with. But in most instances the employee is working with a specific technology in order to produce for the organization, and that technology affects the social system (people) to some extent. The use of large machines that require one operator is going to create a different social system than an assembly line will. An ad agency, with its "image" technology, will be vastly different in social interaction from a production unit in an oil refinery. Technology will help or hinder the development of relationships and will determine many of the areas of latitude for employee decision making. Similarly, paid workers will experience vastly different responsibilities in an assembling operation and driving a truck. The crucial factors in work motivation are therefore often limited by the "sociotechnical" system operant in the organization. Successful changes in work design must address both the technology and the social system.

The exercise that follows is designed to allow you to experiment with a sociotechnical system of your own creation. You will be asked to divide into teams of five to seven members and consider yourselves manufacturing companies. During the first round you will work in assembly-line fashion, followed by a second round in which you may organize as you wish. By keeping productivity records as well as satisfaction indices from the questionnaire provided, you will be able to examine the factors that influence work motivation and productivity.

## IV. PROCEDURE FOR GROUP MEETING

*Step 1.* *Company formation and organization* (10 minutes). Organize the class into groups of five to seven people, each group becoming a company that will make Moon Tents and Shallow-Water Cargo Carriers. Name your company and announce it. Choose two members of your group to be managers. One will be the General Manager (GM), in charge of making purchasing and production decisions and organizing the work force. The other is the Assistant General Manager (AGM), in charge of quality control and sales. Other group members will be assembly line workers.

*Step 2.* *Preparation for production of the Moon Tent* (10 minutes). The GM should organize the production line and make decisions about production goals and materials to purchase following the steps in Moon Tent Production Forms beginning on page 93. Workers should practice building Moon Tents under the direction of the AGM, who should also establish quality control procedures.

*Step 3.* *Production of the Moon Tent* (30 minutes). The GM should conduct the timed practice run (number 4 on the Moon Tent Form), make final production decisions, and then direct a 6-minute production run as specified on the Moon Tent Form. Following production, the instructor should buy those products of acceptable quality from each company's AGM. Companies should compute their profit/loss and each person should complete the Moon Tent Questionnaire on page 97.

## DIRECTIONS FOR MAKING THE MOON TENT

The following are directions for making a Moon Tent. For each step there is a picture showing you what to do and another picture showing how it should then look. Check this before going on to the next step. There are 14 steps.

1. You should have a piece of paper that is blank on one side and looks like this on the other side:

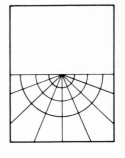

2. Turn the paper over so that the *blank side* is facing up and the pattern is nearest you.

printed pattern at this end

YOU

3. Fold AB to CD.

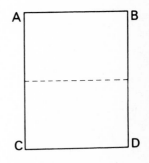

It should look like this:

4. Fold G to F.

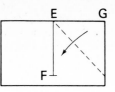

It should now look like this:

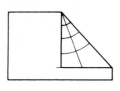

5. Bend down H to F.

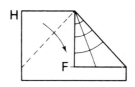

It should now look like this:

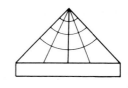

6. Fold one layer of paper (up direction) along JK.

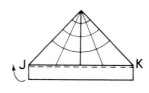

It should now look like this:

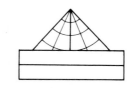

7. Turn the moon tent over to the other side. It should now look like this:

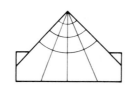

8. Fold (up direction) along LM.

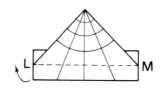

It should now look like this:

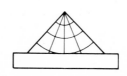

9. Tuck section N (just the top layer of paper) back around the edge of the tent, so it is between the back of the tent and the back layer of paper.

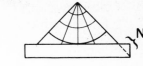

Fold section O (back piece) toward you over the edge of the tent and press flat.

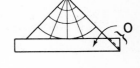

It should now look like this:

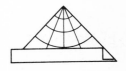

10. Do the same thing to the *left end* (don't turn it over). It should look like this:

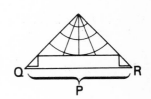

11. Pick up the tent and hold it in your hands with open side (P) down.
Open up P with your fingers and keep pulling it apart until points Q and R meet.

Turn the paper so that Q is facing up and R is underneath. It should look like this:

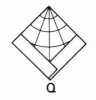

12. Fold up Q along ST.

It should now look like this:

13. Turn over so that R is facing up.
Fold up on UV.

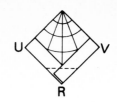

It should now look like this:

14. Open up W and stand up your Moon Tent!

For "quality control" make sure Q & R stay up along the tent.

Passes Quality Control →   Q   R

Not Good   →   Q   R

**QUALITY CONTROL POINTS FOR THE MOON TENT**

1. The top of the tent must come to a point.
2. The printing must be on the outside of the tent.
3. The turned-up points at the base of the tent must lie flat against the tent sides.

## STEPS IN MOON TENT PRODUCTION*

Cost and profit information for the Moon Tent, as well as typical assembly times for one unit, are given below.

### 1. Cost and Profit Information for the Moon Tent

| Number of Sets Purchased | Total Cost | Total Selling Price | Total Profit |
|---|---|---|---|
| 3 | $147,900 | $150,000 | $ 2,100 |
| 4 | 195,000 | 200,000 | 5,000 |
| 5 | 240,000 | 250,000 | 10,000 |
| 6 | 279,900 | 300,000 | 20,100 |
| 7 | 319,900 | 350,000 | 30,100 |
| 8 | 360,000 | 400,000 | 40,000 |
| 9 | 400,000 | 450,000 | 50,000 |
| 10 | 440,000 | 500,000 | 60,000 |
| 11 | 474,000 | 550,000 | 76,000 |
| 12 | 519,600 | 600,000 | 80,400 |
| 13 | 559,650 | 650,000 | 90,350 |
| 14 | 599,900 | 700,000 | 100,100 |
| $14 + n$ | $499,900 + 40,250n$ | $700,000 + 50,000n$ | $100,100 + 9,750n$ |

### 2. Assembly Times for One Moon Tent

This table gives assembly times for one Moon Tent based on the actual *individual* performance of people who have assembled them.

- Fast assembly time (top 10%)    35–45 seconds
- Average assembly time            45–55 seconds
- Slow assembly time (low 10%)    over 55 seconds

### 3. Tentative Decision

After building your model and inspecting the information given, make a tentative decision about the number of units you wish to buy for production in a six-minute period. Record the number here_____ .

### 4. Final Decision and Production

Now that you have made your tentative decision, prepare for a timed practice trial. When you are ready, take a timed practice assembly and record the construction time for the group here_____ .

*The instructor or a nonparticipant should record original bids, final bids, products accepted, and profit/loss on a chalkboard or newsprint so that all may see the bids of all companies. The instructor should also act as the buyer and final approver of product quality.

## 5. Profit Reduction Resulting from Change of Decision

Having taken the time trial, you may wish to change your decision about the number of Moon Tents you can produce in six minutes. Production decision changes invariably cost money. The following table tells how much this change will cost.

| Change | Profit Reduction |
|---|---|
| 1 more or 1 less | $1,500 |
| 2 more or 2 less | 2,500 |
| 3 more or 3 less | 3,600 |
| 4 more or 4 less | 4,800 |
| 5 more or 5 less | 6,100 |
| 6 more or 6 less | 7,500 |

## 6. Production Decision

After making your final decision, record here the number of sets you decided to produce_____.

## 7. Maximum Potential Profit

Your maximum potential profit can be computed in the following manner:

a.  From the information provided in the cost/profit table (step 1), you can determine the profit associated with reaching your *final* production decision (step 6). Enter the total profit here:

$$a = \underline{\hspace{1cm}}$$

b.  If your *final* production decision (Step 6), is *different* from your *tentative* production decision (step 3), you must subtract from the profit entered in (a) the correct profit reduction indicated in the table provided in step 5. Enter that amount here:

$$b = \underline{\hspace{1cm}}$$

c.  Enter your maximum potential profit here; subtract (b) from (a):

$$c = \underline{\hspace{1cm}}$$

Production of the Moon Tent: You now have six minutes to produce the number of Moon Tents for which you purchased materials. Only units that meet quality control specifications will be accepted for sale.

## 8. Post-Production Inspection

Carefully inspect the units you have produced for quality and record the acceptable number of completed products here_____. (Wait for the leader or inspector to inspect your products.)

## 9. Actual Profit Earned

To determine the actual amount of your net profit (or loss, if negative):

a. Enter here the total selling price (see cost and profit table) for the number of products of satisfactory quality you have completed:

$$a = \underline{\hspace{1cm}}$$

*Note:* You cannot sell more products than your final production decision (item 6).

b. Enter here the total costs (item 1) for the final number of products you decided to produce (item 6).

$$b = \underline{\hspace{1cm}}$$

c. If your final production decision (item 6) was different from your tentative production decision (item 3), enter here the correct profit reduction as indicated in the table provided in item 5:

$$c = \underline{\hspace{1cm}}$$

d. Your actual net profit or loss can then be computed in the following manner:

$$\text{Net profit or loss} = a - (b + c) = \underline{\hspace{3cm}}$$

## 10. Possible Profit Ratio

Your percentage of possible profit earned is the ratio between net profit (9d) and maximum potential profit (7c). Enter that ratio here _____.

## 11. Each person should fill out the Moon Tent Questionnaire (p. 97).

Company (Team) Name_____

**MOON TENT QUESTIONNAIRE**

1.  How satisfied were you with your company's performance in the Moon Tent Pro-
    duction?

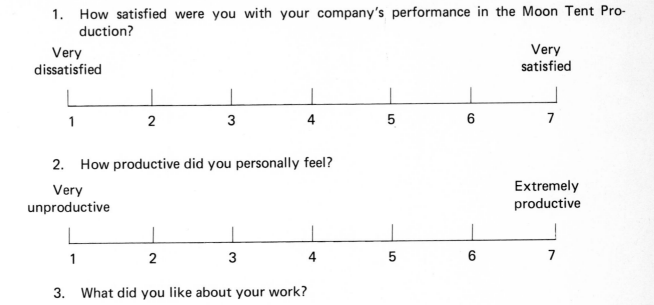

Very
dissatisfied

Very
satisfied

|_____|_____|_____|_____|_____|_____|

1       2       3       4       5       6       7

2.  How productive did you personally feel?

Very
unproductive

Extremely
productive

|_____|_____|_____|_____|_____|_____|

1       2       3       4       5       6       7

3.  What did you like about your work?

4.  What did you dislike?

*Step 4.*    *Production of Shallow-Water Cargo Carrier* (40 minutes). In this round, you will proceed exactly as in the Moon Tent production (practice, bid, time trial, rebid, produce), but your company may organize in any way and establish whatever work procedures it wishes. You may find the data from the Moon Test Questionnaire useful in planning to produce the Shallow-Water Cargo Carrier in the next round.

## DIRECTIONS FOR MAKING THE SHALLOW-WATER CARGO CARRIER

These are directions for making a Shallow-Water Cargo Carrier. The first 9 steps are the same as for the Moon Tent. For each step there is a picture showing what to do, and another picture showing what it should then look like. There are 14 steps.

1. Hold the sheet of paper so the printing on it is facing up, the letters SWCC nearest you are upside down (SWCC).

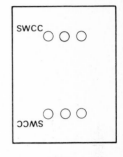

   It should look like this:

2. Fold AB to CD.

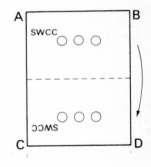

   It should now look like this:

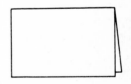

3. Fold in along JG and JH so that E and F meet at point K.

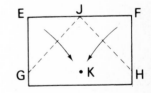

   It should now look like this:

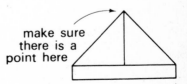

make sure there is a point here

4. Fold *one layer* of paper (up direction) along LM.

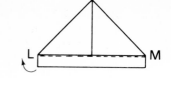

It should now look like this:

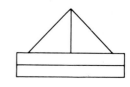

5. Turn your Shallow-Water Cargo Carrier over to the other side. It should look like this:

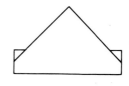

6. Fold (up direction) along NP.

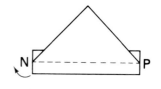

It should look like this:

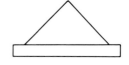

7. Tuck section Q (just the top layer of paper) back around the edge of the carrier, so it is between the back of the carrier and the back layer of paper.

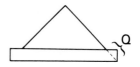

Fold section Q (back piece) toward you over the edge of the carrier and press flat.

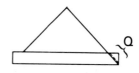

It should now look like this:

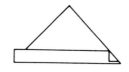

8. Do the same thing to the *left end* (*don't turn it over*). It should now look like this:

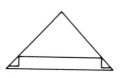

9.  Pick up the Shallow-Water Cargo Carrier and hold it in your hands with the open side (R) down. Open up R with your fingers and keep pulling it apart until points S and T meet.

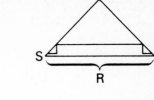

Turn the paper so that S is facing up and T is underneath. It should now look like this:

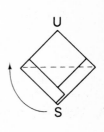

10. Fold up S to U.

It should now look like this:

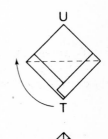

11. Turn over so that T is facing up (side without printing on it). Fold up T to U.

It should now look like this:

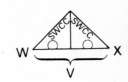

12. Pick up the carrier and hold it in your hands, with the open side, V, down. Open V with your fingers and keep pulling it apart until points W and X meet. Turn the paper so that W is facing up and X is underneath. It should look like the diagram shown here:

13. Fold W to A and then *bring W back down* again to its original position. There should now be a crease at BC.

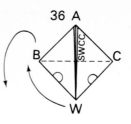

Turn over so that X is facing up. Fold X to A and then *bring X down* again to its original position. There should now be a crease at DE.

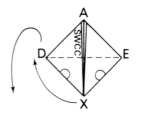

Grab Y (front and back at the top left point) with left hand, and Z (front and back at the top right point) with right hand and pull apart as far as it will go.

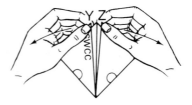

It should now look like this:

14. Stand it up. You have finished making your Shallow-Water Cargo Carrier!

## QUALITY CONTROL POINTS FOR THE SHALLOW-WATER CARGO CARRIER

1. The lettering SWCC must appear on the outside of the boat.
2. The middle point must be a point, not a curve.
3. The middle point must come even with or above the sides of the boat.

# STEPS IN SHALLOW-WATER CARGO CARRIER PRODUCTION

Cost and profit information for the Shallow-Water Cargo Carrier (SWCC), as well as typical assembly times for one unit, are given below.

### 1. Cost and Profit Information for the Shallow-Water Cargo Carrier

| Number of Sets Purchased | Total Cost | Total Selling Price | Total Profit |
|---|---|---|---|
| 3 | $267,000 | $ 270,000 | $ 3,000 |
| 4 | 352,000 | 360,000 | 8,000 |
| 5 | 420,000 | 450,000 | 30,000 |
| 6 | 450,000 | 540,000 | 90,000 |
| 7 | 483,000 | 630,000 | 147,000 |
| 8 | 512,000 | 720,000 | 208,000 |
| 9 | 540,000 | 810,000 | 270,000 |
| 10 | 570,000 | 900,000 | 330,000 |
| 11 | 605,000 | 990,000 | 385,000 |
| 12 | 636,000 | 1,080,000 | 444,000 |
| 13 | 663,000 | 1,170,000 | 507,000 |
| 14 | 700,000 | 1,260,000 | 560,000 |
| $14 + n$ | $700,000 + 37,000n$ | $1,260,000 + 10,000n$ | $560,000 + 53,000n$ |

### 2. Assembly Times for One Shallow-Water Cargo Carrier

This table gives assembly times for one SWCC based on the actual performance of people who have produced them.

- Fast assembly time (top 10%)    40–50 seconds
- Average assembly time    50–60 seconds
- Slow assembly time (low 10%)  over 60 seconds

### 3. Tentative Decision

After building your model and inspecting the information given, make a tentative decision about the number of units you wish to buy for production in a six-minute period. Record that number here____ .

### 4. Final Decision and Production

Now that you have made your tentative production decision, prepare for a timed practice trial. When you are ready, take a timed practice assembly and record the construction time here_____ .

### 5. Profit Reduction Resulting from Change of Decision

Having taken the time trial, you may wish to change your decision about the number of SWCCs you can produce in six minutes. Production decision changes invariably cost money. The following table tells how much this change will cost.

| Change | Profit Reduction |
|---|---|
| 1 more or 1 less | $12,000 |
| 2 more or 2 less | 19,000 |
| 3 more or 3 less | 27,000 |
| 4 more or 4 less | 36,000 |
| 5 more or 5 less | 46,000 |
| 6 more or 6 less | 57,000 |

## 6. Production Decision

After making your final decision, record here the number of sets you decided to produce_____ .

## 7. Maximum Potential Profit

Your maximum potential profit can be computed in the following manner.

a.  From the information provided in the cost/profit table (item 1), you can determine the profit associated with reaching your final production decision (item 6). Enter that total profit here:

$$a = \text{\_\_\_\_\_}$$

b.  If your final production decision (item 6) is different from your tentative production decision (item 3), you must subtract from the profit entered in (a) the correct profit reduction indicated in the table provided in item 5. Enter that amount here:

$$b = \text{\_\_\_\_\_}$$

c.  Enter your maximum potential profit here; subtract (b) from (a):

$$c = \text{\_\_\_\_\_}$$

Production of the Shallow-Water Cargo Carrier: You now have six minutes to produce the number of SWCCs for which you purchased materials. Only units that meet quality control specifications will be accepted for sale.

## 8. Post-Production Inspection

Carefully inspect the units you have produced for quality and record the acceptable number of completed products here_____ . (If you are working in a group, wait for the leader to inspect your products.)

## 9. Actual Profit Earned

To determine the actual amount of your net profit (or loss, if negative):

a.  Enter here the total selling price (see table, item 1) for the number of products of satisfactory quality you have completed:

$$a = \text{\_\_\_\_\_}$$

*Note:* You cannot sell more products than your final production decision (step 6).

b.  Enter here the total costs (item 1) for the final number of products you decided to produce (item 6):

$$b = \underline{\hphantom{XXXX}}$$

c.  If your final production decision (item 6) was different from your tentative production decision (item 3), enter here the correct profit reduction as indicated in the table provided in item 5:

$$c = \underline{\hphantom{XXXX}}$$

d.  Your actual net profit or loss can then be computed in the following manner:

$$\text{Net profit or loss} = a - (b + c) = \underline{\hphantom{XXXXXX}}$$

**10. Possible Profit Ratio**

Your percentage of possible profit earned is the ratio between net profit (9d) and maximum potential profit (7c). Enter that ratio here \_\_\_\_\_ .

**11. Each person should fill out the Shallow-Water Cargo Carrier Questionnaire (p. 109).**

**SHALLOW-WATER CARGO CARRIER QUESTIONNAIRE**

1. How satisfied were you with your group's performance in the SWCC production?

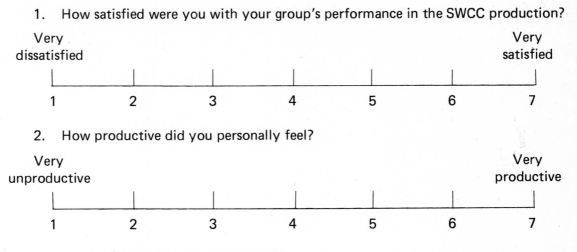

Very
dissatisfied

Very
satisfied

1    2    3    4    5    6    7

2. How productive did you personally feel?

Very
unproductive

Very
productive

1    2    3    4    5    6    7

3. What did you like about your work?

4. What did you dislike?

*Step 5.* *Work and motivation discussion* (30 minutes; entire group). Tabulate the data from the two questionnaires by teams and display them on chalkboard or newsprint. The discussion should explore the following questions:

1. What were the most dramatic data differences between the first and second rounds? In which teams did they occur?

2. Have the teams with the greatest differences discussed the reasons for them? Did similar things happen in other teams? List them.

3. In general, what were the factors that led to satisfaction and productivity in the first round? In the second round?

4. If you had to continue working in this kind of production, which arrangement of work would you prefer? Why?

5. What conclusions can you now come to about improving the quality of work life in organizations? What kinds of things are helpful in sustaining interest and motivation?

6. Had there been a different technology and task, what would the effect have been on the way you went about the work?

7. How might you redesign the jobs you had to increase productivity? Satisfaction?

## V. SUMMARY

You have just finished a simulation designed to allow you to create your own work situation and try it out. You have probably drawn some conclusions about how work of this type can be best organized to maximize productivity and employee satisfaction, and quite probably your conclusions differ from those of some others in the class. In that regard you are not much different from other managers and the behavioral scientists who have worked in the area of motivation. Just about everything conceivable has been tried to improve employee motivation and productivity, from incentive plans to piped-in music, all with some success, but also some failures.[5]

A number of experiments have been conducted, however, that are aimed at allowing employees to work on higher-order needs (achievement, self-esteem, self-actualization) while working toward organization goals. Assuming that lower-level needs are met (safety, security), a motivating climate would have a number of factors:

1. *The work itself* must allow opportunities for employees to satisfy their higher-order needs.

2. *The employee must be involved* in determining what needs are important and what will be done to satisfy those needs.

3. *The immediate work context* must be supportive of these efforts at improvement.

Given these factors, three major types of intervention have been applied to work situations in attempting to improve them:

1. *Data feedback* methods, in which information about the state of the organization is collected from employees, organized, and fed back to them as a basis for collaborative problem solving.

2. *Job enrichment* methods, which attempt to change the nature of the job by broadening

[5] See W. A. Pasmore, "Turning People on to Work," in *Readings,* for a more complete exposition.

responsibilities, giving more autonomy for decision making, creating client systems, and generally enlarging the scopes of jobs.

3. *Sociotechnical system* interventions, which attempt to match the necessary technology of the job with the social needs of the employees.

All these interventions have achieved success in many instances and in some others have not been as successful. The deficiencies have tended to be due to a lack of attention to one or more of the above-mentioned factors of a motivating work climate. Productivity does not necessarily follow from improved employee satisfaction alone, nor is the reverse true. Improving productivity takes attention to the technology, the work environment, and the social system in which the employee operates.

Future efforts to improve satisfaction and productivity will most probably move in the direction of a combination of feedback, job enrichment, and sociotechnical interventions. Contemporary projects on the "Quality of Work Life," often joint ventures of management and organized labor, are but a first indication of this kind of integrated emphasis on motivation and work.

## VI. SELF-EVALUATION AND COMPLETING THE LEARNING LOOP

A.  What questions do you now have as a result of your learning experiences from this unit? Jot these down below.

B.  From these questions, what *key concepts* can you extrapolate for further learning? Write these concepts below.

C.  How can you now go about finding answers to the questions you raised above? Below are some suggested ways to continue your learning process by beginning new learning loops:

1.  Look up the key concepts from your questions above in the Yellow Pages of Learning Experiences at the back of the book. Find a few suggested readings or exercises to facilitate the learning of these key concepts.

2.  If you don't find the key concepts in the Yellow Pages related specifically to your questions, perhaps there are other concepts listed in the index that might lead you to relevant learning resources at this time. Look for concepts similar to those you identified in B above.

3.  In the event that you don't find the Yellow Pages directory useful for your present learning goals, discuss your questions with other students, faculty, or persons outside your learning environment. Discuss further learning possibilities with them.

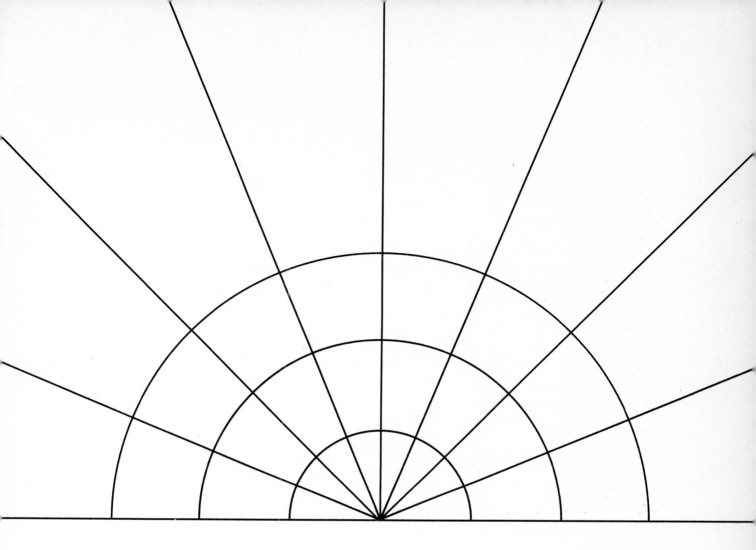

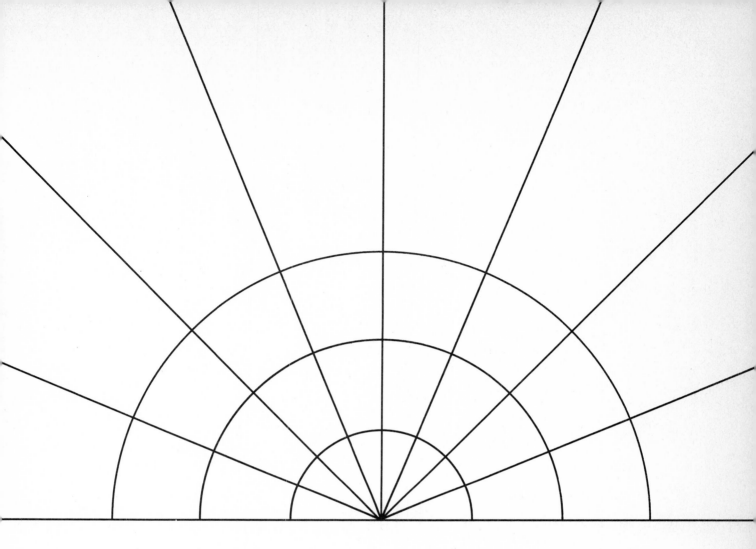

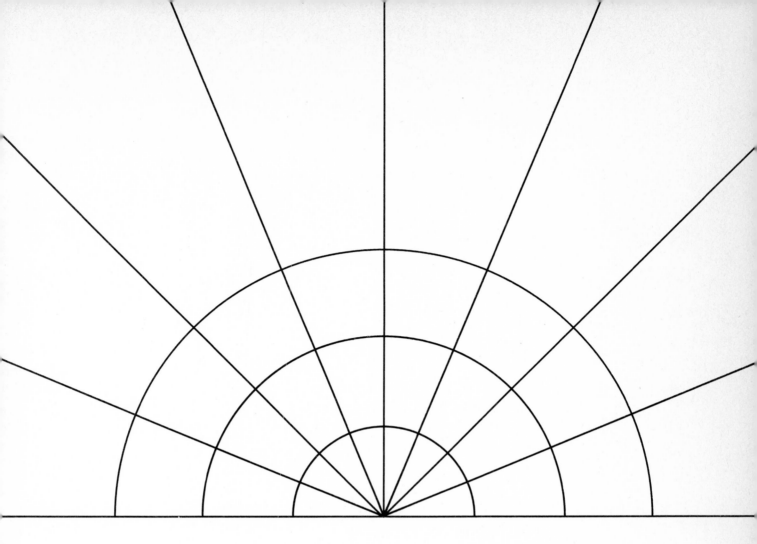

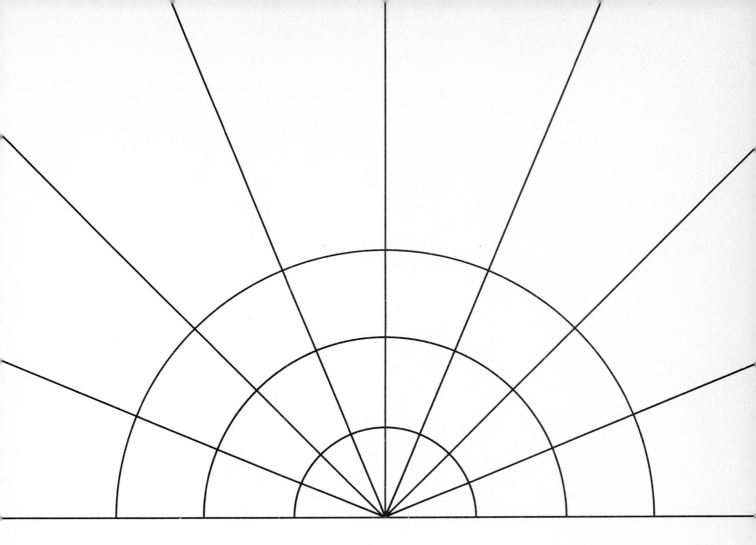

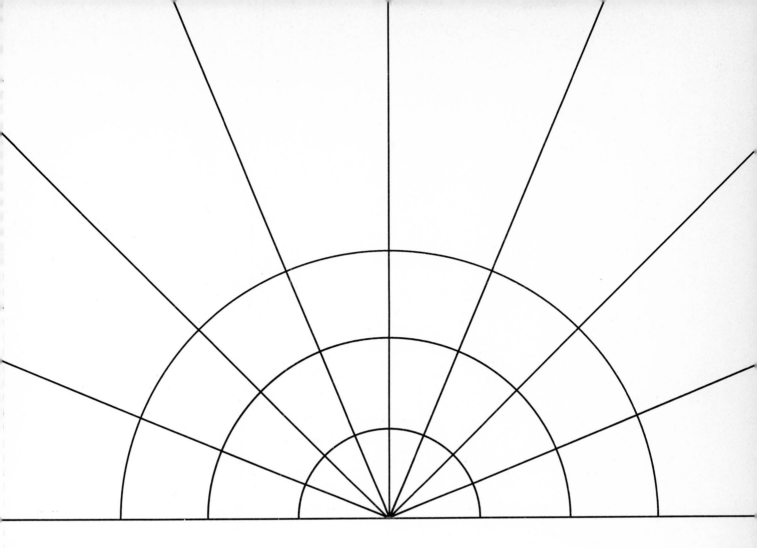

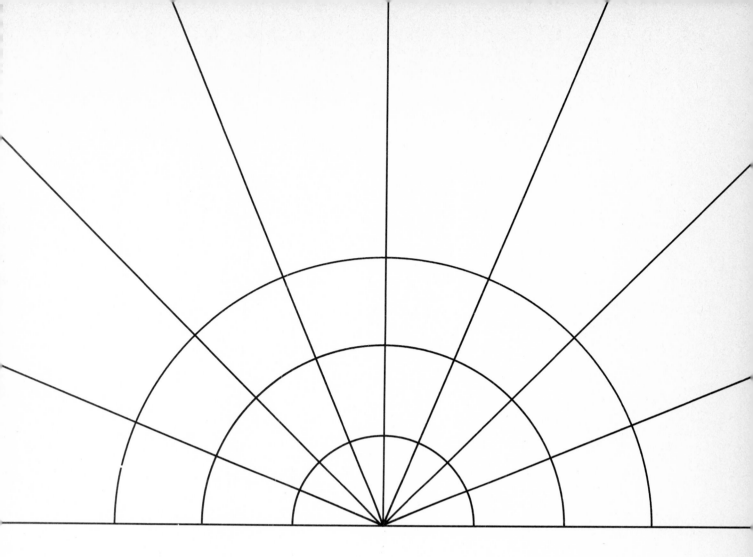

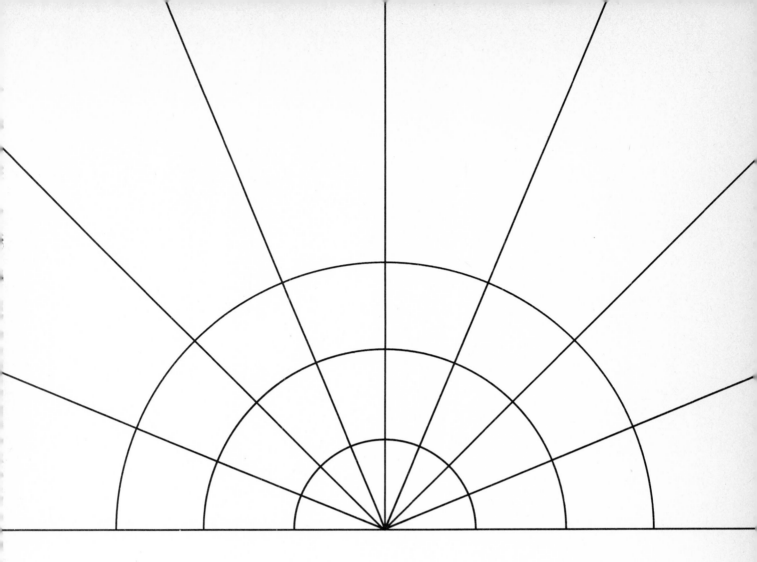

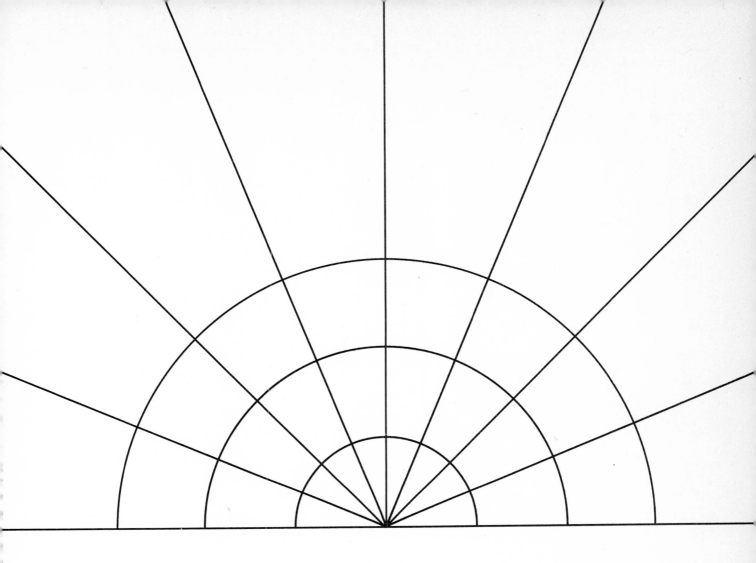

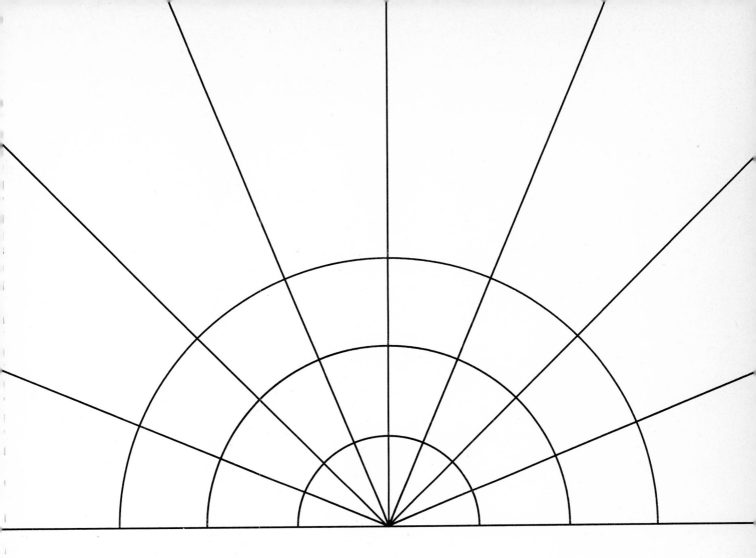

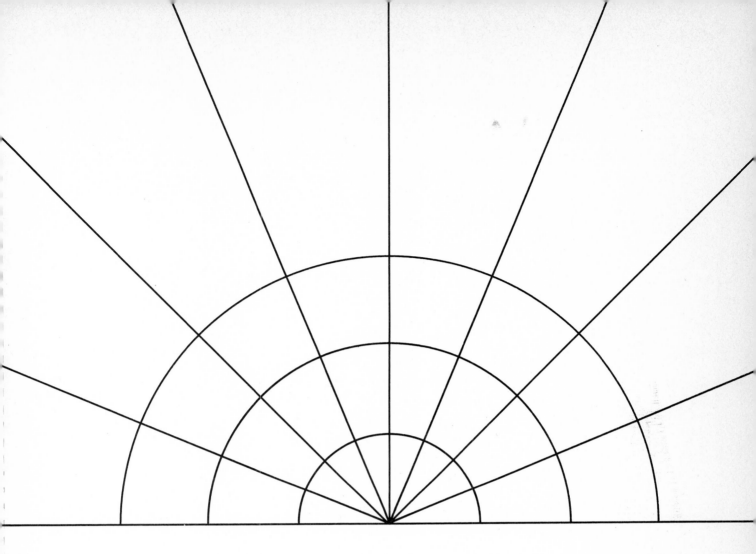

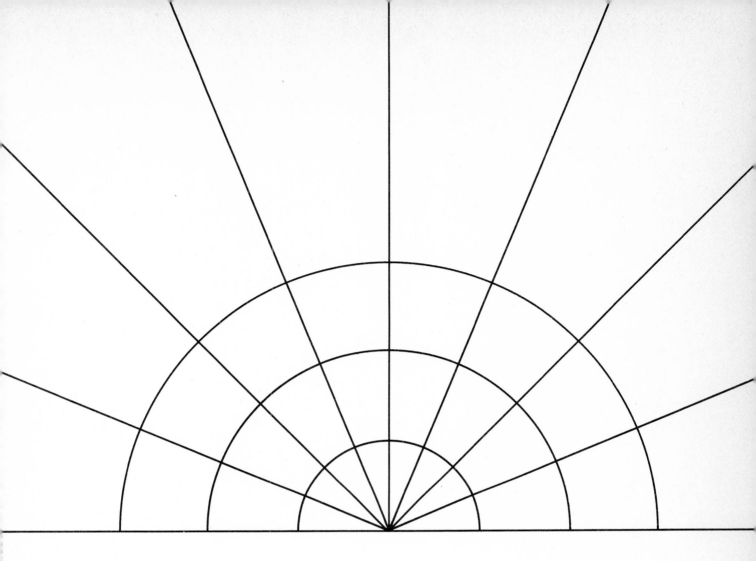

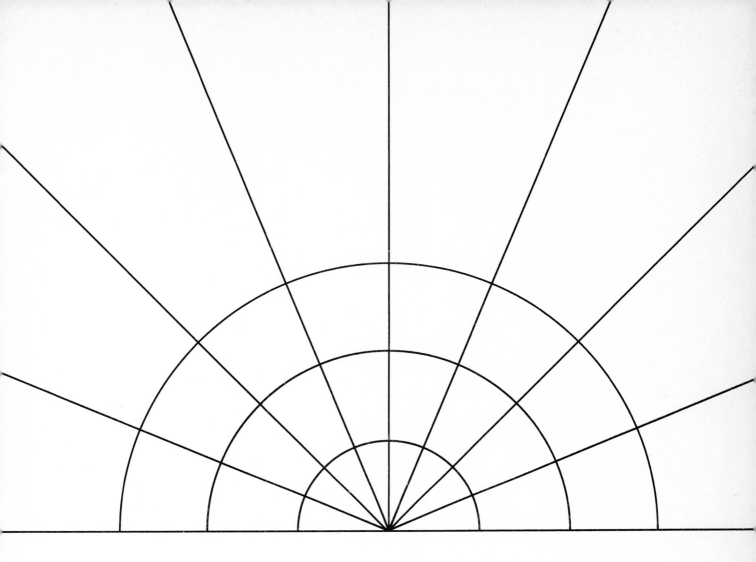

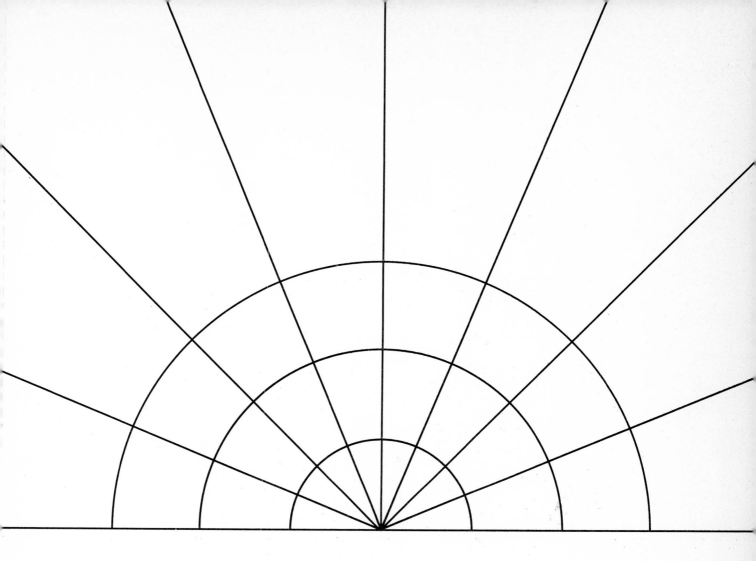

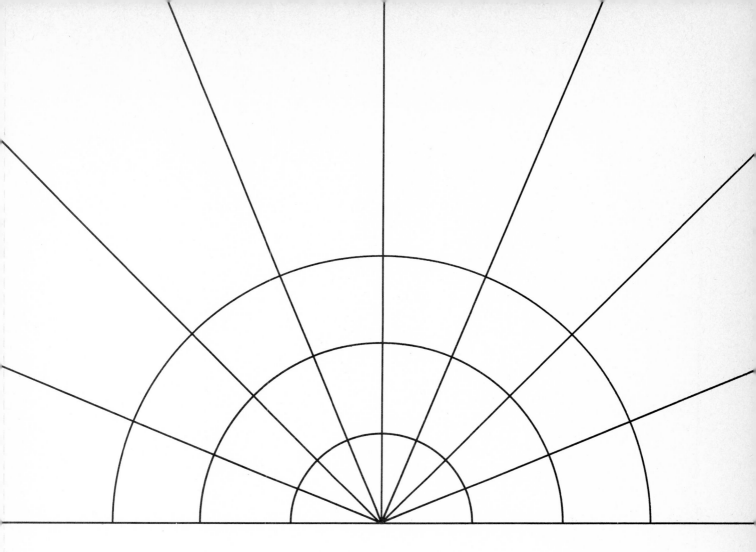

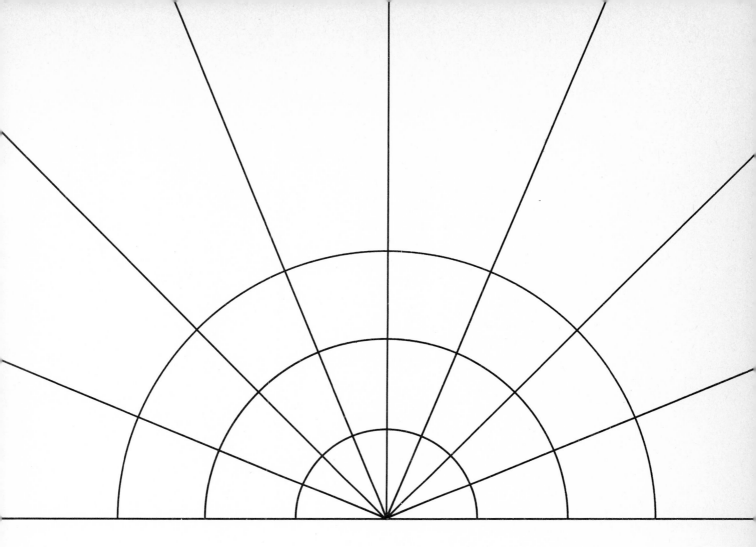

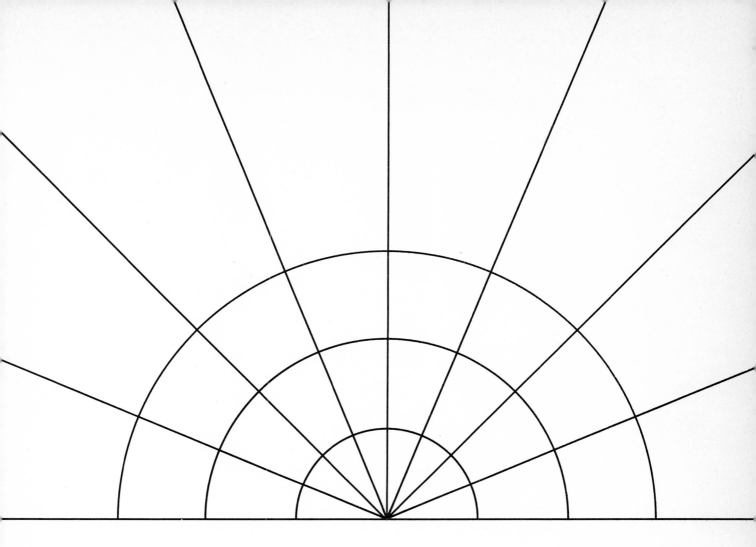

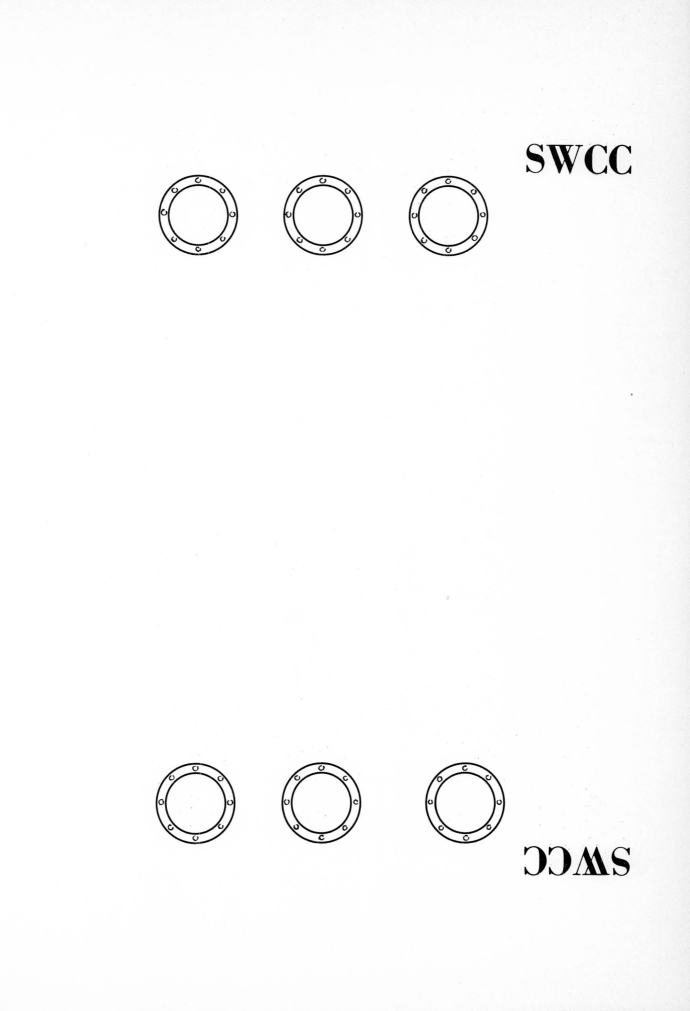

SWCC

SWCC

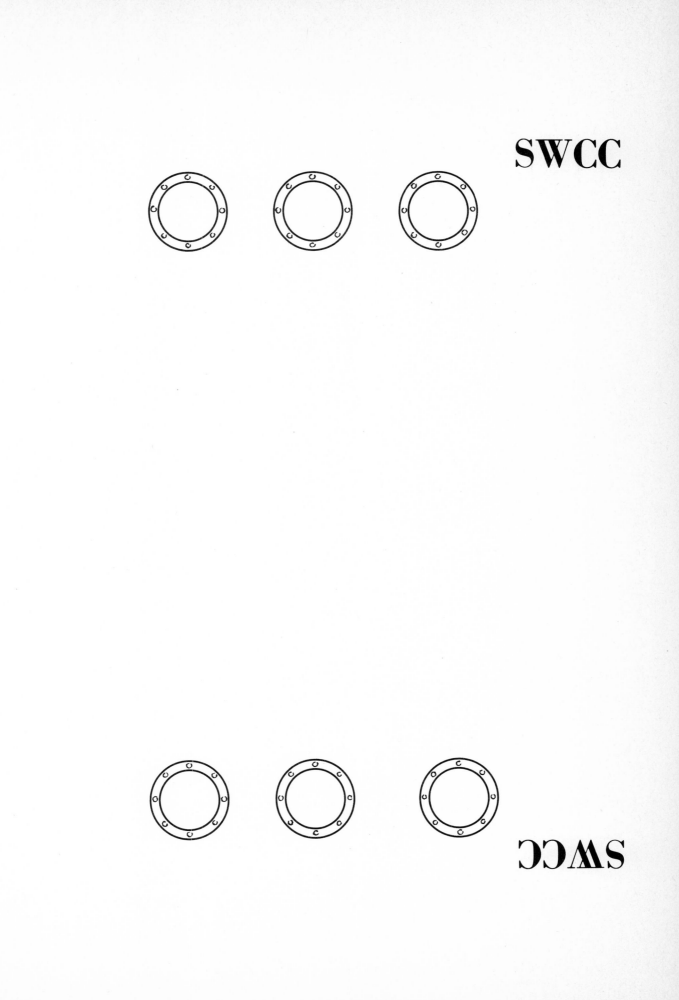

SWCC

SWCC

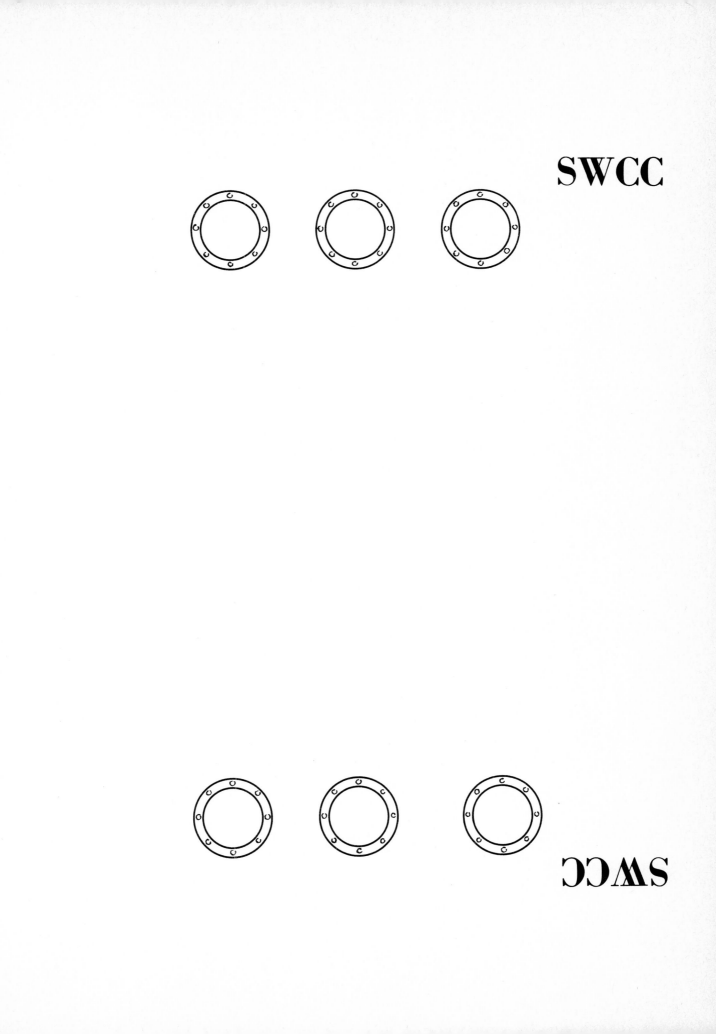

SWCC

SWCC

SWCC

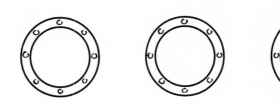

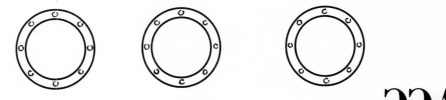

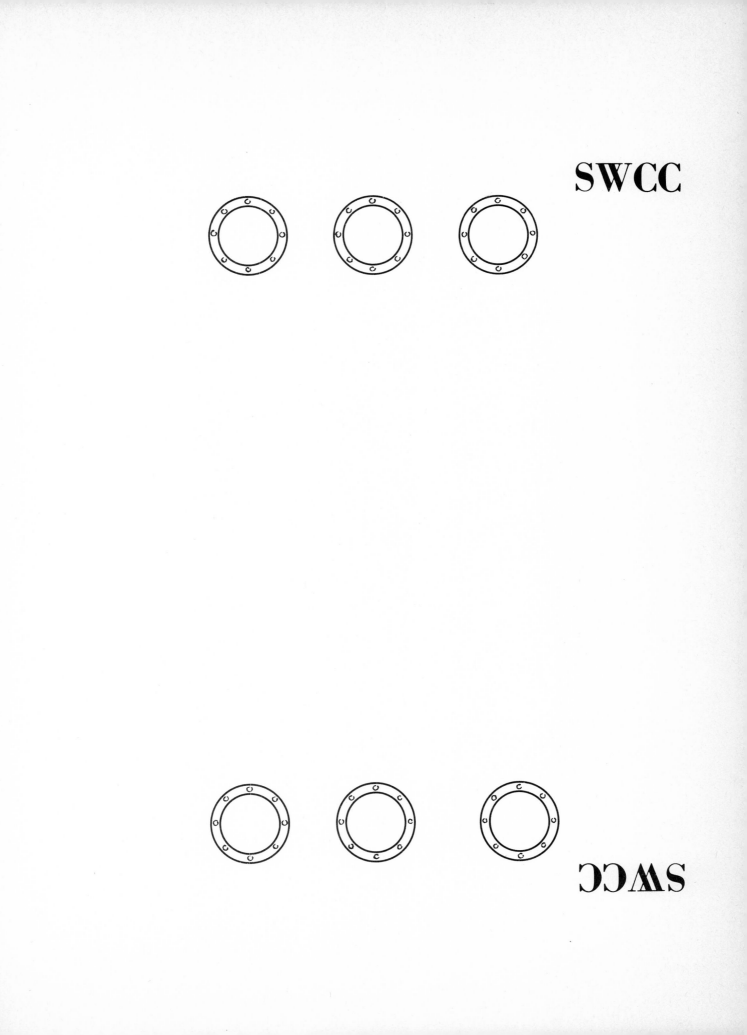

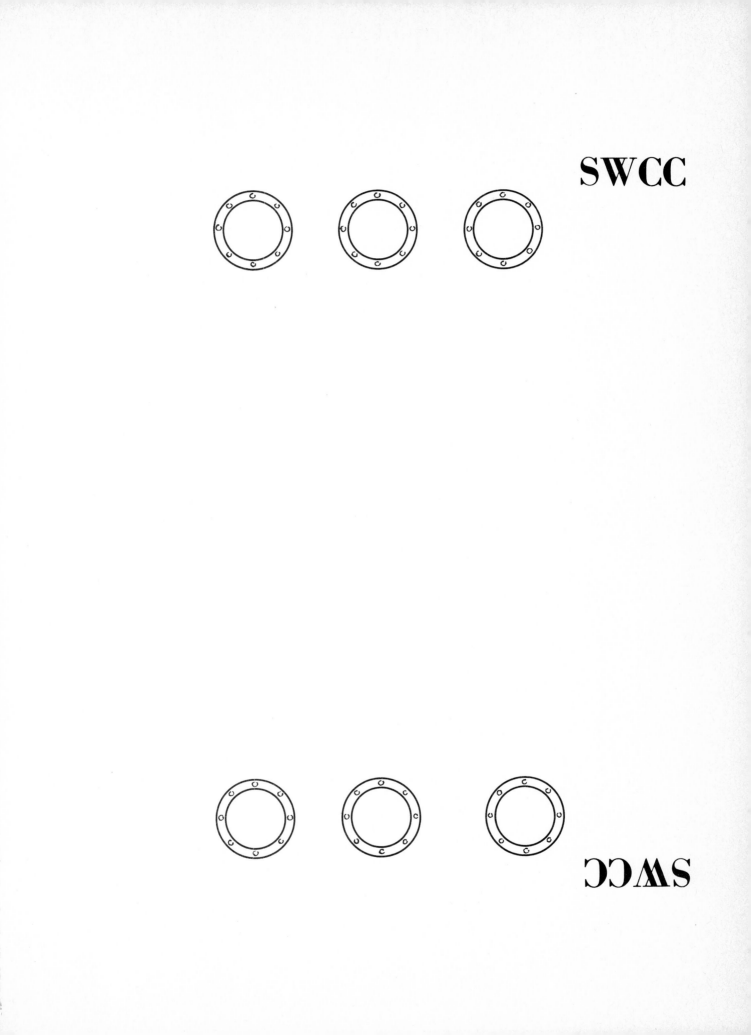

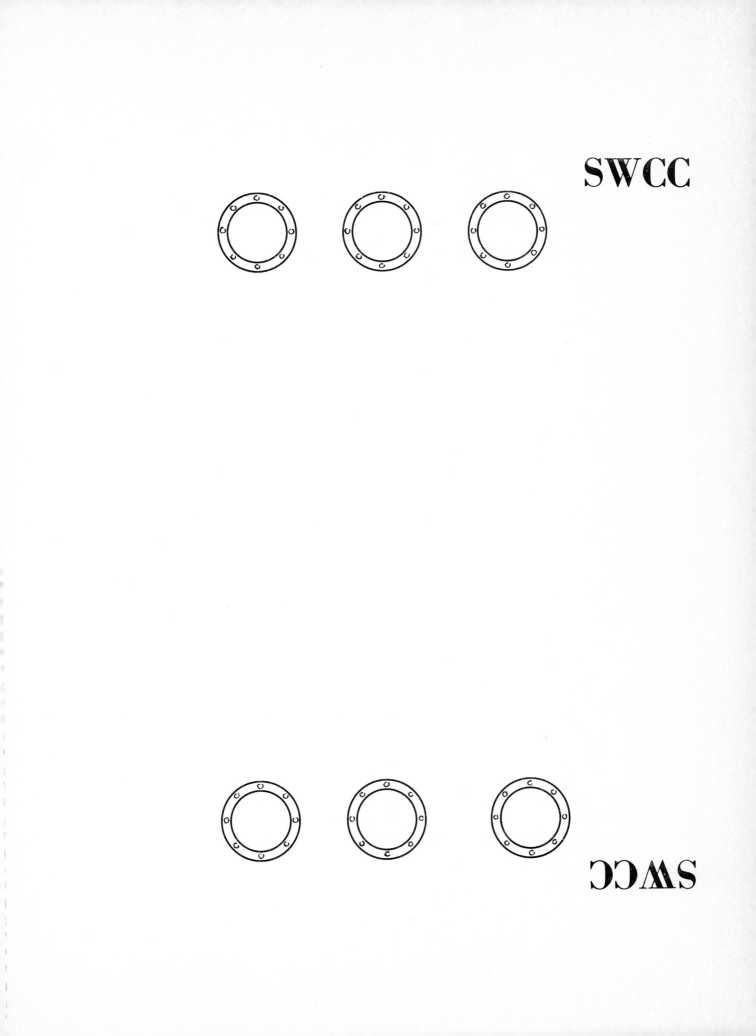

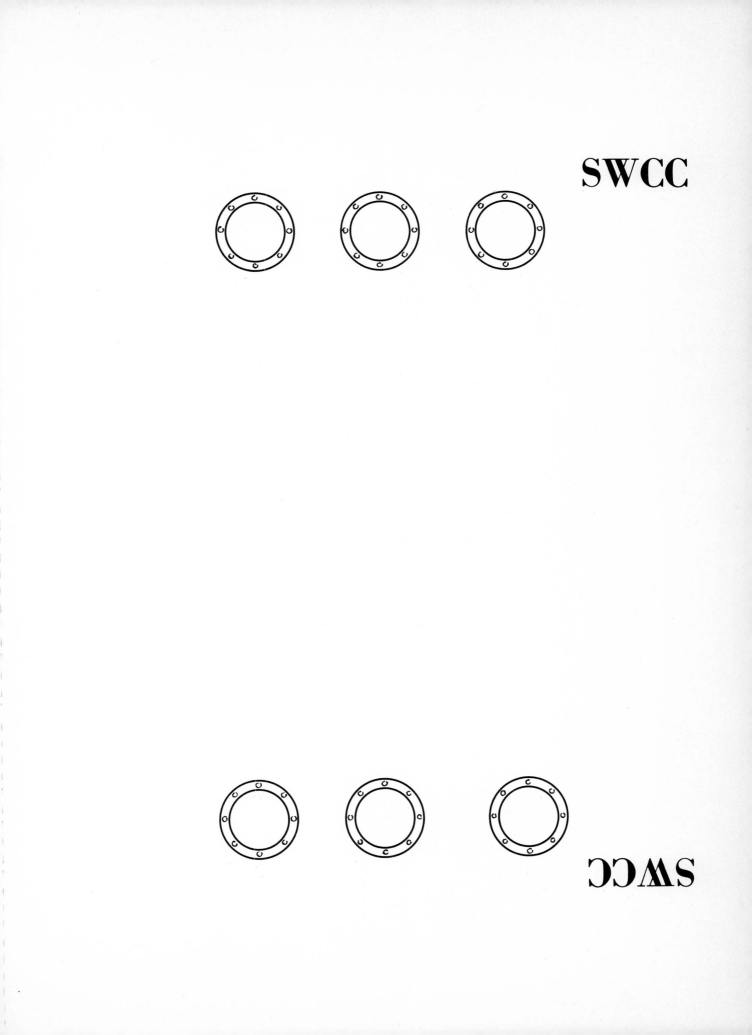

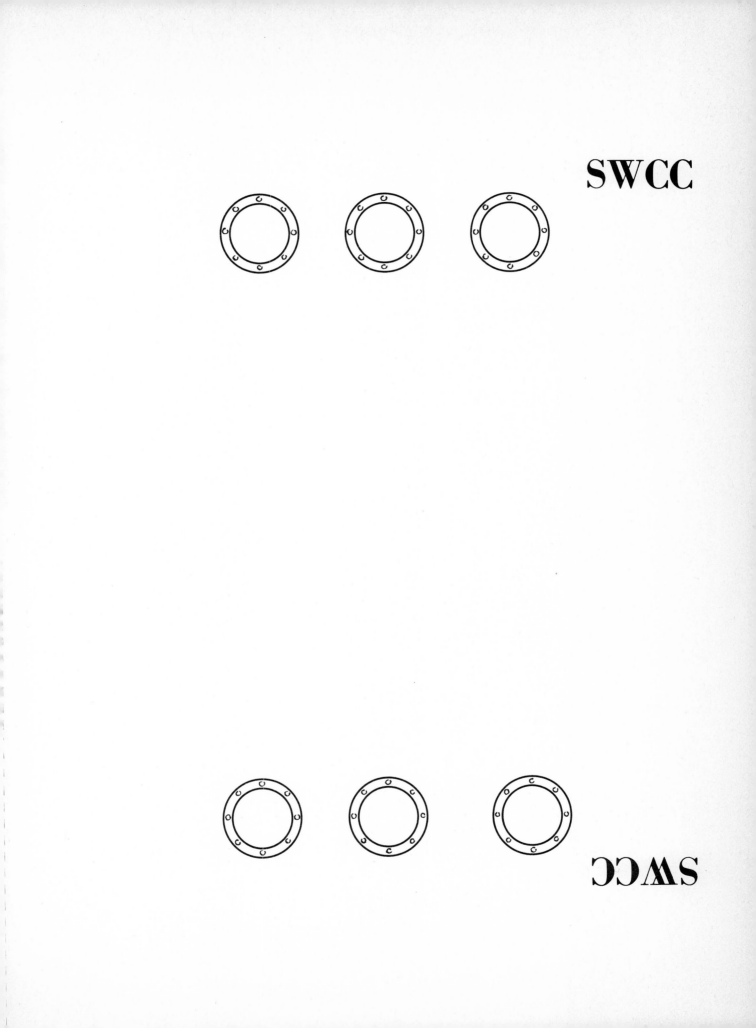

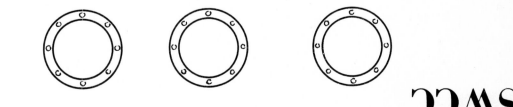

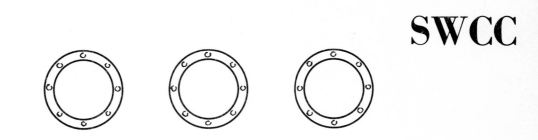

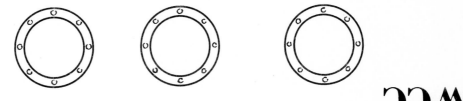

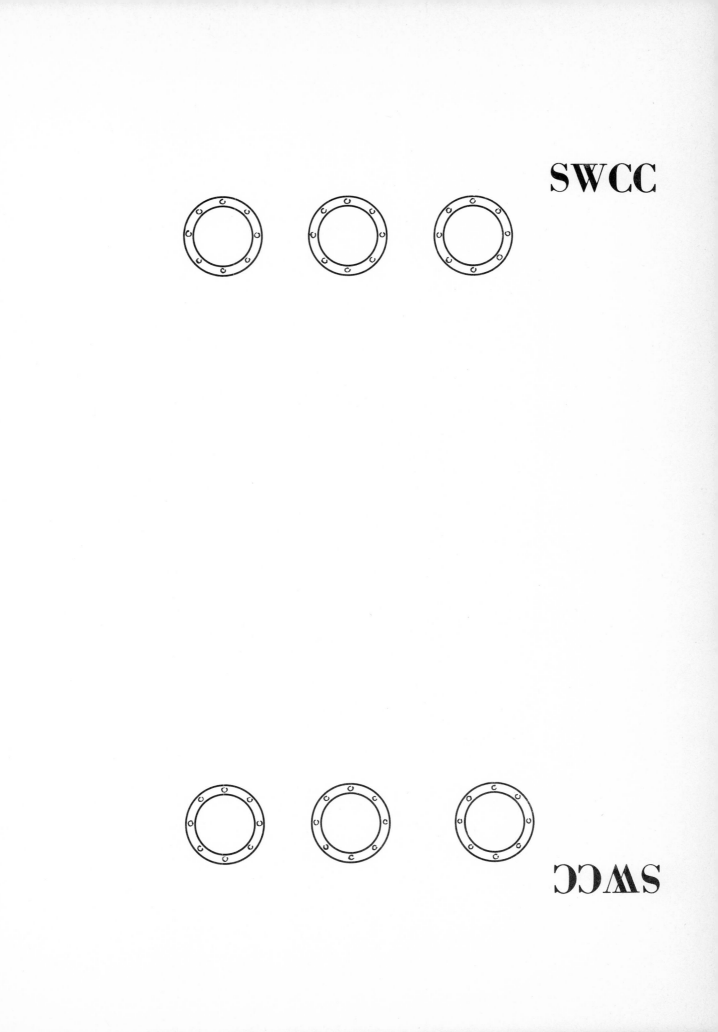

SWCC

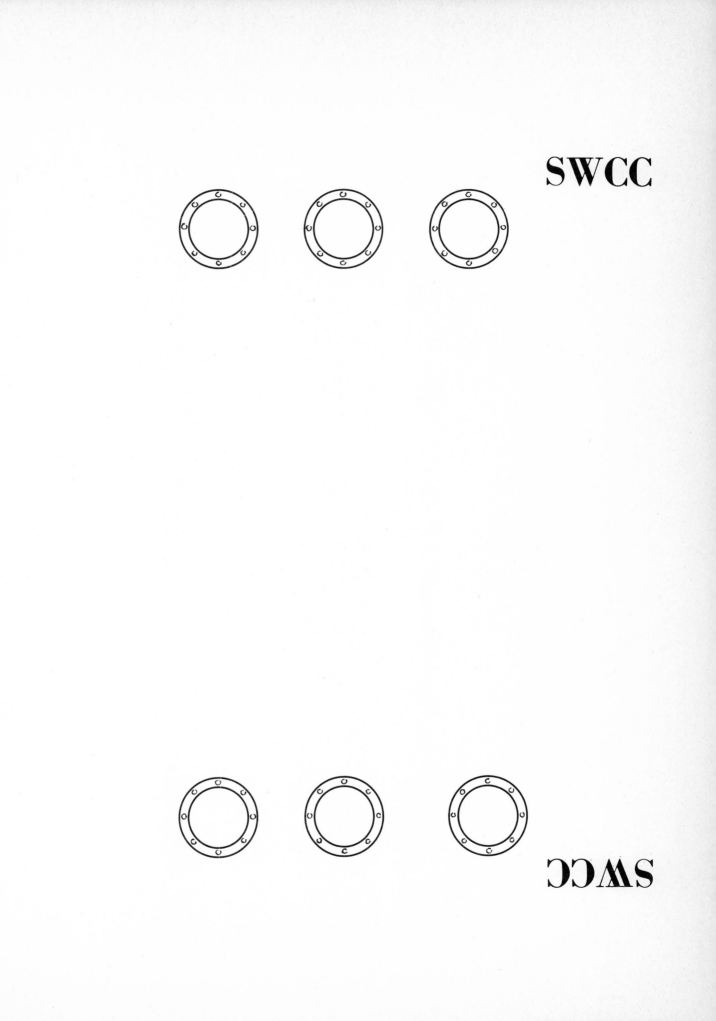

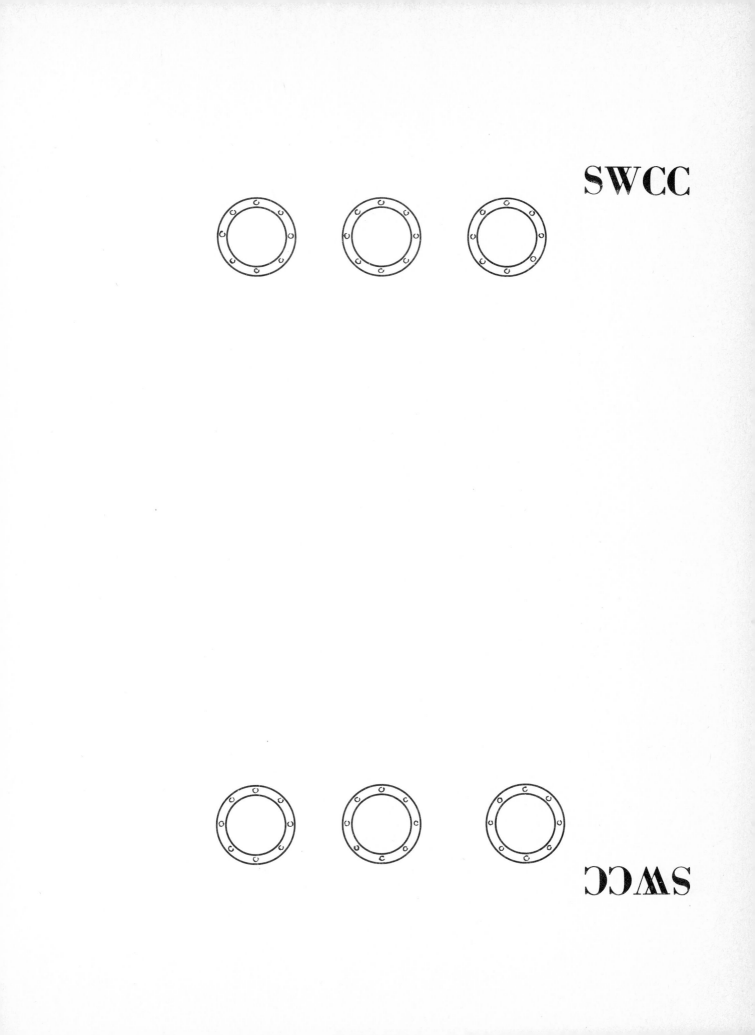

SWCC

SWCC

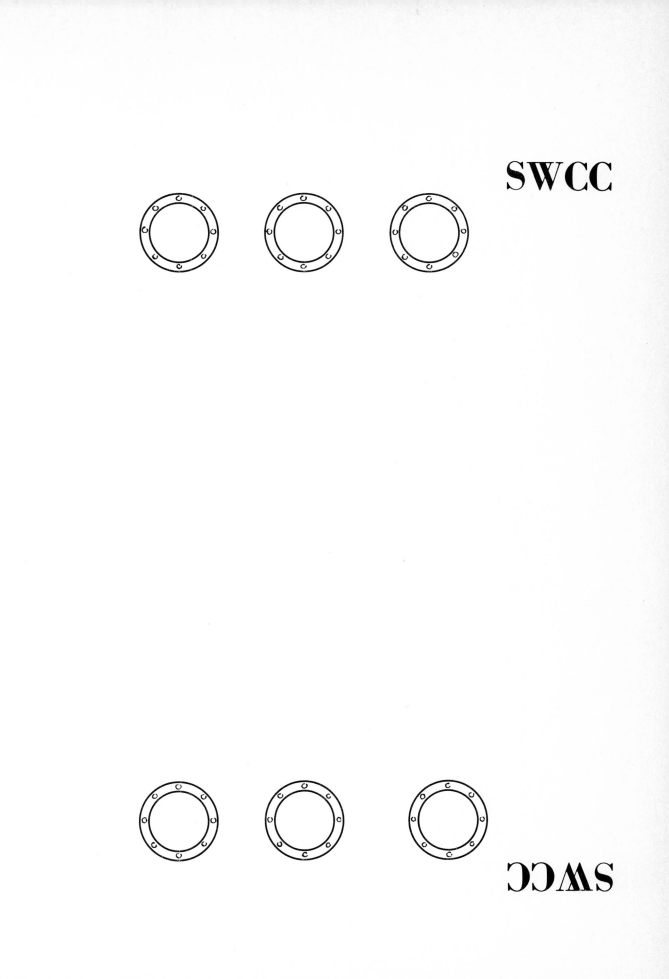

SWCC

SWCC

# chapter 5

## motivation and organization climate

*Photo by Mike Sands, courtesy of Case Western Reserve University*

## I. OBJECTIVES

A.  To explore the relationship between individual motives and the psychological climate of an organization.

B.  To understand the relationship between psychological climate and individual behavior.

C.  To assess the psychological climate of the "classroom organization."

## II. PREMEETING PREPARATION

A.  Read the G.B.A. Construction Company case and prepare individual analyses.

B.  Read the Introduction.

# THE G.B.A. CONSTRUCTION COMPANY

## Introduction

The G.B.A. Construction Company was started in the early 1930s by Mr. G. B. A., Sr. His son, G. B. A., Jr., took over as president in 1946. G. B. A., Sr. passed away a few years later. There are two major stockholders at present: G. B. A., Jr., who owns 65 percent of the stock, and Mr. H., who owns 35 percent. Mr. H. started the business with G. B. A., Sr.

The following thumbnail sketches provide a brief view of G. B. A., Jr. and the business history of the G.B.A. Co.

## G. B. A., Jr. — A Snapshot

G. B. A., Jr., as mentioned, took over as president of the company in 1946. He is a seemingly tireless worker and through his many years of experience has become a businessman *par excellence.*

Under his leadership the company has developed a reputation for excellence — highest-quality work, on-time delivery, and within-budget estimates. G. B. A., Jr.'s personal reputation has done much to build the company. While very knowledgeable in all aspects of the construction business, he is particularly skilled in financial matters.

His managerial style can best be described as that of a benevolent autocrat. He is used to making most, if not all, of the major decisions by himself. As he put it, "It's my company, so why shouldn't I make the decisions?"

The benevolent part of his style manifests itself in a somewhat paternal attitude toward employees. For example, he recently instituted a program wherein key employees received company pins with diamonds to signify their length of service to the organization. G. B. A., Jr. felt that rewarding people in this manner would motivate employees. According to the grapevine, however, many recipients felt these pins (and other similar awards) were "mickey mouse."

His relationships with his key officers are rather aloof; "he's not the kind of guy you can get very close to." The climate of the organization is very much influenced by his personal style. Secrecy is high (lots of closed files) and people maintain JIC files (*just in case* the boss asks). As is characteristic of benevolent autocrats, people fear and respect him at the same time.

He is presently in his mid-fifties and in good physical condition. While not concerned overtly with his own personal health, he is somewhat concerned that his partner and other colleagues in the industry are increasingly suffering heart attacks, for example.

He and his wife do some traveling and he looks forward to the time when he can relax more and travel, play tennis, and so on. His son has just entered an Ivy League school but shows few signs of being interested in coming into the business. His daughter is a budding commercial artist and is presently unmarried.

## Business History

For the purposes of this case, considerable detail on the quantitative history of the G.B.A. Co. (e.g., 10-year sales figures) will not be needed.

The history of the company has been solid and profitable. When the entire construction industry had lean years, the G.B.A. Co. continued to do as well or better than comparable companies in the field. Their main business is in the area of shopping centers, office buildings, hotels, motels, and the like. Several recent trends are important.

Volume in 1973 was $200 million and is predicted to be $300 million in 1974, and $400–$500 million in 1975. Although no one expects this rapid rate of growth to continue at its present/projected pace, the long-range goal is to grow at about 15-20 percent per year in both volume and profit.

Job or project size has increased to the point at which the "average" job is now about $5 million per job. The company expects this trend to continue. The company expects, in other words, to be in a position to take on and successfully manage larger projects of longer duration rather than a lot of small projects.

Increasingly, the company was finding itself in the position, and indeed was seeking such situations, in which it was brought in at the early planning stages of a project. In this way, the company worked directly with architects and planners, under a negotiated overall cost and fee, and was in a position to significantly influence design and specifications.

Although the company is always looking for ways to improve and grow, there is no expectation that the nature of its basic business will change substantially in the future, e.g., to go into the construction of nuclear power plants. They know their business, know they can do it well, and plan to continue in this vein.

**Organization Structure**

The company is organized into four divisions and a central office as follows:

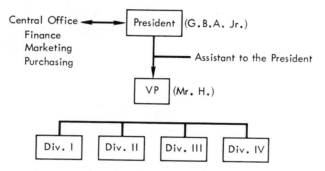

Geographically, most of the business is in the South, Southeast, Midwest, and West of the United States. Division II is located in the same city as the corporate central offices.

**The Problem**

Early in 1973, G. B. A., Jr. contacted a Boston-based consulting firm. He had seen a seminar flyer which described this consulting company's capability as being in the general area of the "human side of enterprise." He believed this group might be able to help him with some of his concerns. Discussions with G. B. A., Jr. and his top management group led to the specification of two major problem areas — succession and continuity of management.

G. B. A., Jr. recognized that the time would soon come when he could not or would not want to be as involved in the day-to-day problems of the company. The G.B.A. Co. would need a new president sometime soon and he ought to be planning for it now.

From his viewpoint and that of his top management group as well, it was very undesirable to go outside for a new president. Most felt that this would be taken as a sign in the industry that the G.B.A. Co. did not have the back-up strength or the internal capability to "grow their own new chief executive." An outsider, in addition, would find it hard to break into the organization and quickly develop the necessary relationships with other key executives.

The candidates from within the organization were essentially four: the Assistant to the President,

Division Manager I, Division Manager II, and Division Manager III.* A thumbnail sketch of each of these men follows.

### Assistant to the President — Mr. W.

Mr. W. is a man in his mid-forties who has worked for the company about ten years. He holds a B.S. in engineering. Prior to coming to work for G.B.A. Co., he worked as the equivalent of a division manager with a comparable company.

His main responsibilities have been to work with G. B. A., Jr. in the design and implementation of corporate policies and procedures. In this capacity he has become exposed to some of the modern thinking in the areas of recruitment, executive compensation, and so on. His technical skills in construction and his prior experiences have enabled him to be a "back-up division manager." In other words, when the need arose, he has been more than able to step in and manage business as do the existing division managers.

He is very soft spoken, less overtly aggressive than his officer colleagues, and believes very strongly in loyalty as a motivation of people. He is very loyal to G. B. A., Jr. and the company — "They have treated me very well and I'll do anything I'm asked to do." His willingness to stay in the very difficult position of Assistant to the President, with all its attendant home office/field office conflicts, is an example of his loyalty. His compensation is lower than that of the division managers because he is not as directly tied in to profits as they are.

In spite of the conflicts of his job, he gets along reasonably well with the key officers. They and he recognize that the problems encountered are a function of the role and not a function of Mr. W's personality per se.

### Manager I

Manager I is the youngest of the division managers — late thirties. He graduated from a prestigious southern engineering school and came into the company about six years ago. He was hired to start a new division in the Southeast and worked closely with Mr. H., the vice president, to build this new division.

The first four-five years of this effort were very disappointing. His division was consistently the big loser. At officers' meetings when financial figures were reviewed, Manager I was always the target of digs and barbs from the others. That situation has changed dramatically and his division is now the biggest winner. In 1973 alone, his division will account for a substantial portion of the total volume and profits. He has progressed from being the black sheep to being the shining star.

Like G. B. A., Jr., Manager I can best be characterized as an autocratic leader. He is hard-driving, level-headed, and has a quiet charm and confidence that appeals to clients. He has a reputation of letting some details fall through the cracks; e.g., he never answers phone messages, misses planes, and is often the last to arrive (often late) at an officers' meeting. His rationale is that selling new business and taking care of clients are his primary jobs — anything else comes second.

### Manager II

Manager II is also relatively young — early forties — and a college graduate. He was hired eight years ago by G. B. A., Jr. to take over as manager of the Central Division. Prior to coming to the G.B.A. Co., he held a high-level position with a competitor.

*Division Manager IV was very new, young, and therefore not a candidate.

His division has been a solid producer under his leadership — not outstanding but clearly adequate. The fact that he is physically located in the same building as the corporate offices is, in the minds of some people, the reason for his success. In other words, some people believe that G. B. A., Jr. is responsible for a large percentage of the business that Manager II gets for the company. From his point of view, his physical proximity to G. B. A., Jr. does not interfere with his ability to "be his own man."

Of all the division managers, Manager II's style is the most participative. He is a good group builder and has the reputation for developing his younger people very well. He is more willing and able to delegate responsibility. He demonstrates, in much that he does, a concern for the human side of issues. During officers' meetings, for example, he would be most likely to support someone who was under attack.

**Manager III**

Manager III is the senior man among the managers (25 years), just a few years younger than G. B. A., Jr. himself. He is the only one of the division managers without a formal college education, having learned the business from the University of Hardknocks. His knowledge of the business is unquestioned and he is respected by all.

His division, the Western Division, has always been a high-variance division in terms of profit performance. From a volume perspective, it has always been high — "He'll take any job" was the comment often made. Profits, however, have never been as high as expected, and others attribute this in large measure to Manager III's style.

"He does everything his own way by himself" is the comment most often made. He calls *every* site several times a day, issues orders, and makes all the decisions by himself. Not one of his subordinates does anything without checking with him first. As could be expected, this style creates many home office/field office problems and conflicts. He resists most corporate policies and procedures and yields grudgingly only after direct intervention by G. B. A., Jr.; even then, there are some "special rules" for him, i.e., he is often allowed to ignore company policy.

As a group the candidates were "a bunch of supreme primadonnas," by their own admission. Each believed that he could handle the job of president. While they all "said" they could work under the others, it was very clear that the choice of one would have to be handled delicately. Whoever among them was chosen might have a period of some tension, jealousy, and covert (if not overt) conflict until he "proved his mettle."

In spite of this dilemma, it was not considered desirable, unless no other alternative existed, to bring in someone from the outside. However, G. B. A., Jr. was smart enough to realize that some other changes might also be necessary to deal with the second of his concerns — continuity of management. Simply selecting a new president might not be enough.

The concern over continuity of management comes from several sources. G. B. A., Jr. recognized that to a man, his key executives were in high demand. None of them would find it hard to switch jobs quickly and beneficially. Their individual compensations (with the exception of Mr. W., his assistant) were tied directly and heavily into their individual profit performance. In terms of both salary and bonus they all did very well, but they wanted "something" more.

The key executives had several concerns regarding continuity. What happened to the company if/ when G. B. A., Jr. died? How could they get security? What would happen to them? As they put it: "We, too, have put our sweat and blood into this company. Do we fall to the whims of some trustees? Your wife?"

G. B. A., Jr. recognized that he had been the central, dominant figure in the life of the company during the past 25 years. It was not clear whether, even if he remained president, the company could continue to be managed in the same way and cope with all the normal problems of rapid and continued growth. So, in addition to succession, he was concerned with making any changes required to ensure continuity of management.

**Your Task**

The concerns of succession and continuity are clearly complex problems, and many factors are involved in successfully dealing with such problems. For the purposes of this case, however, you are asked to take a somewhat limited perspective and consider these issues from a motivational framework.

The McClelland framework of n-Achievement, n-Power, n-Affiliation has considerable relevance for issues of leadership style, organizational climate, and organizational growth. You have been provided in this case with qualitative descriptions of G. B. A., Jr. and his key officers. The description of the company was *explicitly* nonquantitative. This is not to imply that quantitative issues are unimportant — they are critical. *For the purposes of this case discussion,* however, the only "quantitative data" you need appear below, indicating how each of the key people score in terms of McClelland's three motives (rank-ordered, where 1 = highest). By narrowing the focus, you will be able to sharpen your understanding of some critical nonquantitative aspects of organizations.

| | Pres. | Mgr. I | Mgr. II | Mgr. III | Assistant to the President |
|---|---|---|---|---|---|
| n Achievement | 1* | 1 | 1 | 1* | 2 |
| n Power | 1* | 2 | 3 | 1* | 3 |
| n Affiliation | 3 | 3 | 2 | 3 | 1 |

*Indicates equal motive strength.

In preparation for the upcoming class, you need to do the following:

1.  Rank the four main characters (Mgr. I, Mgr. II, Mgr. III, and Assistant to the President) in the order in which you would recommend they be considered as the new president of the G.B.A. Co.
2.  Be prepared to discuss your rank ordering with reference to the following issues:
    a. Where is the company today? Where is it going in the future?
    b. What kind of leadership style will be needed to help the company continue to grow and be profitable over the next 5 years? What are each candidate's strengths/weaknesses in this regard?
    c. In addition to a new president, what other changes should the G.B.A. Co. consider to provide for the continuity of management and organizational climate it will need in the future? New structures? New procedures? New reward systems? Why?

## III. INTRODUCTION

One of the most widely accepted and important insights of social psychologists is that behavior is a function of the person and his/her environment; $B = f(P \times E)$. In the terms we are using here, this means that behavior (achievement-, affiliation-, or power-related) is a function of people's motivational concerns *and* their perception of which of these concerns will be rewarded by the environment in which they find themselves. Let us examine two examples.

Suppose that the strength of a person's N-Aff were measurable on a scale of 0 to 100. Person A's motive strength (a person factor) is 75 (rather high). Put the person in a library, where all the environmental cues (be-quiet signs, stern-looking librarians, etc.) are nonaffiliative and their affiliation-oriented behavior is likely to be very low. Conversely, low-n-Aff persons (motive strength of 25) at a cocktail party will probably engage in social conversation i.e., act in an affiliation-oriented way.

Organization climate, therefore, is an important concept for the manager to understand. It is through the creation of an effective organization climate that the manager can "manage the motivation of employees. Organization effectiveness can be increased by creating an organization climate that satisfies members' needs while channeling their motivated behavior toward organizational goals.

### Dimensions of Organizational Climate

Litwin and Stringer[1] defined six key variables in organizational climate and tested them in a laboratory situation in which they set up three companies that would be engaged in similar production and development work over a two-week period. The top managers of the companies, chosen for their personal styles of management, were given instructions on how their companies should be run. One company was set up on highly authoritarian lines designed to arouse the power motive. Communication was in writing, jobs were well defined, all decisions were made by the president, and little room was left for individuals to show initiative. A second company was organized along friendly democratic lines, emphasizing warm, friendly working relationships more than task accomplishment or formal organization. People were encouraged to talk and play, and interpersonal issues were confronted in daily group meetings. The president was always available to all employees and encouraged them to bring their problems to him. The third company was designed for an achieving climate. The president formulated objectives in collaboration with other executives, allowed groups to establish their own procedures, established a reward system for productivity, and constantly communicated his expectation of high performance by showing approval of good work. He was interested in everything, but he trusted his employees to make decisions affecting their own work. He posted progress reports for all to see every time he received any data on sales or new-product acceptance.

Summarizing the data of Litwin and Stringer somewhat oversimplifies their study; nevertheless, job satisfaction was high in the achieving and friendly democratic climates, low in the authoritarian group. In terms of profits made, the achieving group far outstripped the other two, who were relatively even in profits. The achieving climate also completed the experiment with a greater number of new products developed and accepted than the other two companies. In terms of overall performance the achieving climate seemed far ahead, probably because it encouraged people to satisfy their achievement needs in the work situation, structuring the situation to stimulate that motive.

Many times the task of building an achieving climate in an organization is one of changing the concerns of management from power compliance ("Here is what needs doing, and here is how to do it") to one that offers warmth and support to each individual, communicating organizational goals and standards but not attempting to control the means of reaching those goals. In a classroom "organiza-

---

[1] George H. Litwin and Robert Stringer, "The Influence of Organizational Climate on Human Motivation" (Graduate School of Business Administration, Harvard University, May 1966). An expanded version of this article appears in *Organizational Psychology: A Book of Readings*, 2nd ed.

tion," Alschuler[2] gives another example of the effects of climate change on performance. An experienced typing teacher in a suburban Boston high school decided to stop prescribing goals for her pupils, to stop scheduling tests for all at the same time, and to stop enforcing behavior rules unrelated to typing skill (talking, gum chewing). She gave one speed test a week, at a time of the pupils' choosing, asked them to estimate their goals for the test in terms of speed and errors, and gave them as many tests as needed to reach their goals. When not taking the tests, pupils were free to practice as they wished, working on problems they felt most important. When they brought a record player and records to class, she merely asked them not to play it so loud that it would disturb other classes.

In this climate, which emphasized affiliation and achievement and deemphasized compliance with authority, the pupils improved their speed and accuracy to an extraordinary degree. Compared to a previous class almost perfectly matched in IQ and manual ability, every one in the experimental group tied or outscored the highest scorer in the more conventional classroom climate. Clearly, the difference in climate increased performance and satisfaction.

### The Motive Pattern of Managers

We can sharpen our understanding of the relationship between individual behavior and organizational climate by examining the motive patterns of some "typical" managers. The personal motivational concerns of an organization's top manager/top management often sets a tone for the climate in the wider organization.

### A. N-Power

Many top managers have a high need for power. Their effectiveness as creators of company climate depends not only on their need for power, but also on the other values they bring to their job.

John Andrews' study of two Mexican companies is striking in this regard.[3] Both companies had presidents who scored high in n-Power, but one firm was stagnating whereas the other was growing rapidly. The manager of the growing company, although high in n-Power, was also high in n-Achievement and was dedicated to letting others in the organization satisfy their own needs for achievement by introducing improvements and making decisions on their own. The stagnant company, although well capitalized and enjoying a favorable market, was constantly in turmoil and experienced a high rate of turnover, particularly among its executives. In this company, the president's high n-Power, coupled with highly authoritarian values, led him to make all the decisions himself, leaving no room for individual responsibility on the part of his personnel. A comparison of motivation scores of upper-level managers of the two companies showed that the dynamic company's managers were significantly higher in n-Achievement than those of the stagnant company, who tended to be more concerned with power and compliance than with individual responsibility and decision making.

The results of research have shown that a manager needs a reasonably high n-Power in order to function as a leader.[4] Whether he uses it well depends in large part on the other values and motives he holds. Being high in n-Power does not automatically make one autocratic or authoritarian. Good leadership may indeed be a function of the manager's ability to understand his/her need for power and to use it in creative, satisfying ways.[5]

[2] Alfred Alschuler, "How to Increase Motivation through Structure and Climate"(Achievement Motivation Development Project, Working Paper 10, Graduate School of Education, Harvard University, 1968).
[3] John D. W. Andrews, "The Achievement Motive in Two Types of Organizations," *Journal of Personality and Social Psychology*, Vol. 6 (1967), pp. 163–168.
[4] Herbert A. Wainer and Irwin M. Rubin, "Motivation of Research and Development Entrepreneurs: Determinants of Company Success," *Journal of Applied Psychology*, Vol. 53, No. 3 (1969), pp. 178–184. *Readings*.
[5] This issue will be addressed in more depth in the chapter, "Leadership: The Effective Exercise of Power and Influence."

## B. N-Affiliation

The person high in n-Affiliation alone, since their concerns are more with warm, friendly relationships, are more likely to be in supervisory jobs (if they are in industry at all), a job where maintaining relationships is more important than decision making. Kolb and Boyatzis[6] have shown that people high in n-Affiliation alone are seen as ineffective helpers, probably because they fear disrupting relationships by forthrightness and confrontation. They have also shown, however, that the people who are seen by others as effective helpers tend to have relatively even motive strengths across the three motives, not being extremely high or low on any of the three. Although strong n-Affiliation does not seem to be central to leadership and management performance, some concern with the feelings of others is necessary. Some concern with affiliation is important in understanding the needs of others and in generating a climate that takes those needs into consideration. Noujaim[7] has shown that high-n-Affiliation managers spend more time communicating than high-n-Achievement or high-n-Power managers. Communicating with others in warm, friendly ways is of real importance to the achievement of organizational goals particularly in achieving cooperation and effective coordination. When people can collaborate and communicate on task accomplishment, the climate of the organization is improved.

## C. N-Achievement

Whereas a high need for achievement seems absolutely necessary for the entrepreneur, it is not always functional for managers, as creators of an organization's climate, to be extremely high in this motive. Noujaim[7] has shown that executives high in n-Achievement tend to have fewer meetings than other executives and tend to want to work alone, despite the fact that many organizational problems would be better solved by collaborative effort. (For example, high-n-Achievement managers spend significantly more time doing personnel work alone.) As with executives high in n-Power, their effectiveness as managers depends more on their other values than on their motivation alone.

Persons high in n-Achievement want to take personal responsibility for their success or failure, like to take calculated (moderate) risks, and like situations in which they get immediate, concrete feedback on how well they are doing. Their need for feedback keeps them from getting too involved in open-ended exploratory situations with no concrete goal and no benchmarks along the way. Their sense of personal responsibility will keep them from delegating authority, unless they hold values that let them see developing a responsive organization as a legitimate achievement goal. They will be task-oriented, but the kind of climate they create in an organization will be healthier if their strong n-Achievement is balanced by moderate needs for power and affiliation and if they are committed to building an achievement-oriented organization that stimulates personal responsibility and calculated risks, getting feedback on how it is doing at each step along the way.

*Stages of Organization Growth*

Organizational growth poses a further complexity concerning the relationship between individual motivation and organizational climate. Organizations (like individuals) go through various stages of growth and development. The "best" or most appropriate combination of personal motivational concerns and characteristics of organizational climate can only be answered by addressing the questions: What stage of growth are we in now? Where are we trying to go? What kind of personal motivation and organizational climate will be needed to ensure that we can cope with our next stage of development? A simplified picture of the stages of organizational growth and development is shown

---

[6] David A. Kolb and Richard Boyatzis, "On the Dynamics of the Helping Relationship," *Journal of Applied Behavior Science*, (1970), *Readings.*

[7] Khalil Noujaim, "Some Motivational Determinants of Effort Allocation and Performance" (Ph.D. thesis, Sloan School of Management, Massachusetts Institute of Technology, 1968).

in Figure 5-1. Stage I is the typical start-up phase for the classical entrepreneur. It is often a very small show with a simple organization. The individual entrepreneur, high in n-Achievement, carries most of the weight with his or her energy, vision, and strong drive to succeed. Others get caught up in the excitement because they are in on the ground floor of a new venture.

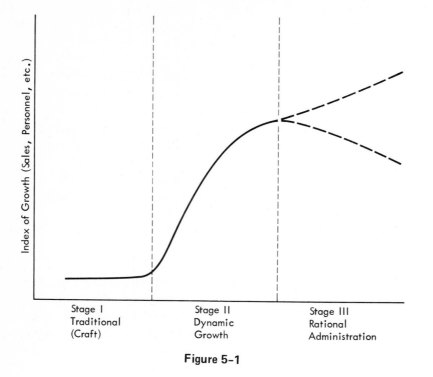

**Figure 5-1**

If the organization survives this stage (and many do not), it then moves into a period of rapid growth (stage II). The morale and excitement, so high in stage I, begin to show the signs of stress. That old feeling of personal contact, easy access to the boss, and so on, begins to wane as the organization grows in size. If this period of growth is not effectively managed, any of the following indicators will be experienced:

1. Lower morale due to loss of close family feeling.
2. Lack of coordination among functional departments (now the organization structure has become more complex).
3. Missed deadlines, overrun budgets, poor or uneven quality control (things are falling through the cracks).
4. Chief executive officer overload — "I'd like to let go but I don't dare."
5. Frequent reorganization (about every 6 months).

If these normal stresses and strains are not effectively managed, the organization may find itself on a sharp downward spiral. While the forces are undoubtedly many and complex in nature, a critical variable appears to be the organization's ability to reorganize and accept the fact that at different points in its life it needs different kinds of top management motivation/leadership and a different organizational climate. These transitional issues are particularly disconcerting to the entrepreneur/owner. The organization is his or her "baby" and letting go in certain areas and recognizing the need for more teamwork and group problem solving and conflict resolution, for example, is by no means easy.

These issues are all highlighted in the G.B.A. Construction Company case, which you will discuss and analyze in the upcoming class session.

## IV. PROCEDURE FOR GROUP MEETING

### A. The G.B.A. Construction Company Case (Time Allotted: 90 Minutes)

*Step 1.* Entire class should break up into groups of approximately 5 to 6 persons per group.

*Step 2.* Each group should prepare a 5-minute summary analysis of the G.B.A. case to share with the total class. (Time: 45 minutes.) This summary should touch on the following points:

a. Which candidate would you recommend as the new president of the G.B.A. Co.?

b. What is your rationale for this choice?

c. What do you see as the major strengths/weaknesses of the other three candidates?

d. What other changes would you recommend to help the new president create the kind of organizational climate needed by the G.B.A. Co. over the next five years?

*Note:* It is helpful if these points could be summarized on a piece of newsprint to facilitate the total group discussion during step 3.

*Step 3.* When the subgroups have completed their work in step 2, the entire class should reconvene for a summary discussion and analysis. (Time: 45 minutes.)

a. Each of the subgroups should share its analysis with the total class. Others should ask questions of clarification during the process to ensure understanding.

*Note:* The actual candidate who assumed the presidency is described in the Solutions section on page 465 and a summary of the rationale is given. While this is "what actually happened," there is no presumption that everyone in the class will/should agree with this choice. Any differences between the class's analysis and the actual outcome should be explored further to ensure that the points of differences are understood.

### B. Assessing the Climate in the Classroom Organization (Time Allotted: 60 Minutes)

You will have an opportunity during this part of the class to assess the organization climate *in your learning organization* — this course. To facilitate the analysis, a modified form of the organization climate dimensions developed by Litwin and Stringer[8] is presented on pages 193–194.

*Step 1.* Individuals should complete this questionnaire to show how they would ideally like the climate of the classroom to be and how they now see the actual climate. (Time: 5 minutes.)

---

[8] See Litwin and Stringer, "The Influence of Organizational Climate on Human Motivation."

*Note:* Completed questionnaires should be given to the instructor/coordinator of the session. The person should compute the group average on each dimension and transfer the real and ideal climate scores to a summary form like the one shown on page 195.

*Step 2.* While the total class scores are being computed, the class should break up into five- or six-person subgroups and discuss questions 1–4 on the Discussion Questions About Organization Climate sheet, which appears on page 197. (Time: 30 minutes.)

*Step 3.* When the total scores have been completed and summarized, the entire class should reconvene and discuss this climate profile of their own learning organization. (Time: 45 minutes.)

a. Questions 5–8 on the Discussion Questions About Organization Climate sheet (p. 197) should be addressed.

*Introduction*

For each of the seven organization climate dimensions described below place an (A) above the number that indicates your assessment of the organization's current position on that dimension and an (I) above the number that indicates your choice of where the organization should ideally be on this dimension.

1. *Conformity.* The feeling that there are many externally imposed constraints in the organization; the degree to which members feel that there are many rules, procedures, policies, and practices to which they have to conform rather than being able to do their work as they see fit.

Conformity is not charac-  1  2  3  4  5  6  7  8  9  10  Conformity is very characteristic of this organiza-                                   teristic of this organization.
tion.

2. *Responsibility.* Members of the organization are given personal responsibility to achieve their part of the organization's goals; the degree to which members feel that they can make decisions and solve problems without checking with superiors each step of the way.

No responsibility is given  1  2  3  4  5  6  7  8  9  10  There is a great emphasis on
in the organization.                                        personal responsibility in the
                                                            organization.

3. *Standards.* The emphasis the organization places on quality performance and outstanding production including the degree to which the member feels the organization is setting challenging goals for itself and communicating these goal commitments to members.

Standards are very low  1  2  3  4  5  6  7  8  9  10  High challenging standards
or nonexistent in the or-                               are set in the organization.
ganization.

4. *Rewards.* The degree to which members feel that they are being recognized and rewarded for good work rather than being ignored, criticized, or punished when something goes wrong.

Members are ignored,  1  2  3  4  5  6  7  8  9  10  Members are recognized and
punished, or criticized.                              rewarded positively.

5. *Organizational clarity.* The feeling among members that things are well-organized and goals are clearly defined rather than being disorderly, confused, or chaotic.

The organization is dis-  1  2  3  4  5  6  7  8  9  10  The organization is well-
orderly, confused, and                                  organized with clearly de-
chaotic.                                                fined goals.

6. *Warmth and support.* The feeling that friendliness is a valued norm in the organization; that members trust one another and offer support to one another. The feeling that good relationships prevail in the work environment.

| There is no warmth and support in the organization. | 1  2  3  4  5  6  7  8  9  10 | Warmth and support are very characteristic of the organization. |

7. *Leadership.* The willingness of organization members to accept leadership and direction from qualified others. As needs for leadership arise, members feel free to take leadership roles and are rewarded for successful leadership. Leadership is based on expertise. The organization is not dominated by, or dependent on, one or two individuals.

| Leadership is not re-warded; members are dominated or dependent and resist leadership attempts. | 1  2  3  4  5  6  7  8  9  10 | Members accept and reward leadership based on expertise. |

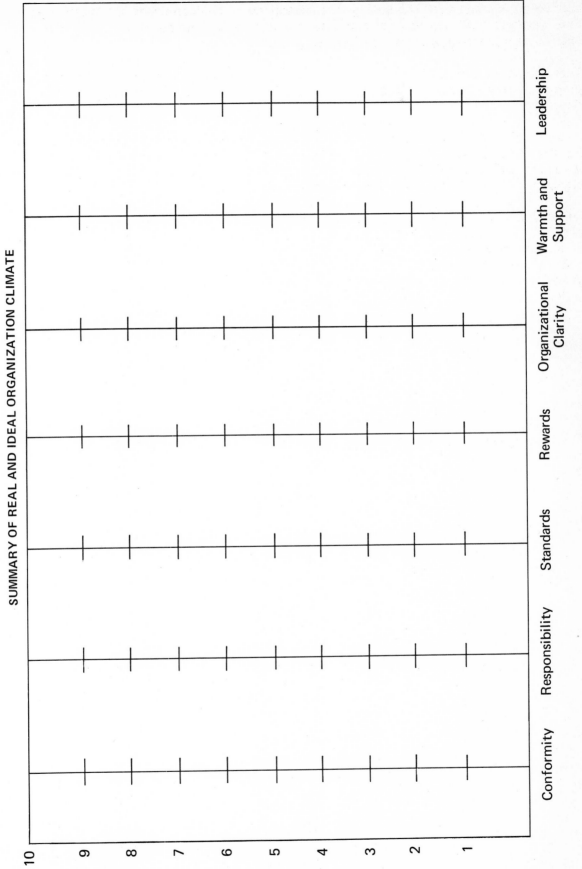

SUMMARY OF REAL AND IDEAL ORGANIZATION CLIMATE

Organization Climate Dimension

**DISCUSSION QUESTIONS ABOUT ORGANIZATION CLIMATE**

1. How did your motive pattern influence your choice of an ideal climate?

2. How did your perception of the organization's task influence your choice of an ideal climate?

3. Which climate dimensions in your opinion stimulate (or inhibit) n-Achievement? N-Power? N-Affiliation?

4. Which motives should be stimulated (or inhibited) to effectively accomplish the task of this learning organization?

5. How much agreement or disagreement was there in the group's choice of an ideal climate? In the perception of the actual climate?

6. What dimensions show the greatest discrepancy between real and ideal climate?

7. During the unit on organizational socialization, a psychological contract was formulated. To what extent is the climate supporting/inhibiting this contract?

8. What steps can be taken to change the climate in this classroom to enhance the realization of the psychological contract?

## V. SUMMARY

In choosing a management system and organization structure, an organization must consider the interaction among the following variables:

1. The *people* in the organization, their abilities and motives.
2. The *organization's tasks* and the kinds of behavior needed to accomplish that task most effectively.
3. The *organization's external environment* and the demands it makes on the organization for creativity, flexibility, quality, and so on.
4. The *organization climate* as determined by the leadership styles of management and the organization's structure.

Stated simply, the goal of organization design is to match people with tasks that require and inspire their motives and abilities and to design tasks that cope with environmental demands and opportunities. The most manageable variable of the four is organization climate. It can serve as an effective management tool for integrating individual motivation with the goals and tasks of the organization.

Let us examine several examples of the relationships among organizational structure, climate, and individual motivation. All complex organizations need standard operating procedures and policies to some degree. Given the issues raised in this unit, policies and procedures that appear to an employee to require arbitrary, non-work-related conformity would, it would be predicted, have the effect of reducing n-Achievement behavior and increasing n-Power behavior (i.e., behaviors aimed at beating the system/rules).

High-n-Achievement persons must be able to take moderate risks; get fresh, clear feedback on their actions; and see a direct link between their actions and desired rewards. Many organizational reward systems, goal-setting systems, and performance appraisal systems have the unanticipated effect of reducing n-Achievement behavior. Feedback is a once-per-year event, rewards are tied to seniority versus performance, and failure (an inevitable consequence of risk taking) is punished rather than treated as a learning event.

An example of how organization structure changes can produce improvements in organization climate and effectiveness occurred in the assembly division of an electronics company. The morale, productivity, and return rates on equipment were very bad in one group until management changed the physical structure of the group (of female assemblers) from a linear assembly line to a circle. When the women sat in a face-to-face group, their morale improved as their affiliation needs were met. This resulted in improved production, sharing of workloads, and better quality control resulting from a sense of team spirit. It is important to note in connection with this case that climate must be changed by giving consideration to both the individuals' motives and the job demand. Harris[9] highlights this point in his study of the interaction between the motives and organization climate of a research and development organization. He found that when all managers were considered together, there was a positive relationship between warmth and support and the effectiveness ratings. Yet, when he considered the effect of a warm and supporting climate only on those managers with high n-Affiliation, he found a negative relationship between the amount of warmth and support and the effectiveness ratings. The implication of this finding is that when high-n-Affiliation people are placed in a warm, supportive setting, they lose sight of any concerns about getting the job done. Thus, changes in climate must be attuned to the individual needs of managers as well as the task requirements.

[9] Henry H. Harris, "An Experimental Study of Organizational Climate and Motivation in Effective Management Teams" (Master's thesis, Sloan School of Management, Massachusetts Institute of Technology, 1969).

## VI. SELF-EVALUATION AND COMPLETING THE LEARNING LOOP

A. What questions do you now have as a result of your learning experiences from this unit? Jot these down below.

B. From these questions, what *key concepts* can you extrapolate for further learning? Write these concepts below.

C. How can you now go about finding answers to the questions you raised above? Below are some suggested ways to continue your learning process by beginning new learning loops:

1. Look up the key concepts from your questions above in the Yellow Pages of Learning Experiences at the back of the book. Find a few suggested readings or exercises to facilitate the learning of these key concepts.
2. If you don't find the key concepts in the Yellow Pages related specifically to your questions, perhaps there are other concepts listed in the index that might lead you to relevant learning resources at this time. Look for concepts similar to those you identified in B above.
3. In the event that you don't find the Yellow Pages directory useful for your present learning goals, discuss your questions with other students, faculty, or persons outside your learning environment. Discuss further learning possibilities with them.

# chapter 6
## interpersonal communication

*Photo by Mike Sands, courtesy of Case Western Reserve University*

## I. OBJECTIVES

A. To understand the barriers to effective communication and to explore ways of eliminating some of these barriers.

B. To increase the ability to listen and to understand another person.

C. To increase sensitivity to other than verbal modes of communication.

D. To give feedback to group members on their personal communication style.

## II. PREMEETING PREPARATION

Read the Introduction.

## III. INTRODUCTION

A rational mechanical view of the process of communication could be depicted in the following manner:

Person A ⟶ Person B

In other words, A says something to B and B hears what A said. In reality, however, communication is seldom this simple. Communication is much more than just the words that flow between people. *All behavior* conveys some message—it is a form of communication. In the broadest sense, when we study the concept of interpersonal communication we must examine interpersonal relationships in general.

In the example of the rational mechanical process depicted, person A brings to the interaction with person B much more than just the content of the message he wishes to convey. He brings himself as a person. Person A has an image of himself as a person and to varying degrees of specificity and intensity (it may be a first impression) he also has a set of attitudes and feelings toward person B. The message to person B, therefore, in addition to a certain content, may well contain some cues as to who A feels he is as a person (e.g., confident and secure versus tentative and wary), how A feels about B as a person (e.g., warm and receptive versus cold and uncaring), and how A expects B to react to his (A's) communication.

This picture becomes somewhat more complex when we realize that A may be only partially aware of all that he may be communicating to person B. This can create what Warren Bennis has called an "arc of distortion"[1]—A communicates something to B that he did not intend, B reacts to this unintended communication and confuses A, who may not understand why his intended communication was responded to so strangely. A common example of this is the boss, who, unaware of his threatening tone of voice, asks for his employees' honest opinion of his actions. He is surprised at his employees' lack of candor.

The focus thus far has been upon A—the sender of the communication. A mirror image is operating with respect to person B in terms of his self-image and his attitudes toward person A. All that A communicated (intended or otherwise) will be received by B through his set of perceptual filters. B's response to A will be partly a function of what B heard. Listening is a selective process—we hear what we want to hear and what we expect to hear.

In the case of interpersonal communication, one's very presence in the situation can have an impact on the nature of the interaction. Talking to a rock is a static process because a rock does not react; talking to another person is a dynamic process because the other person does react and that reaction influences our future reactions.

To successfully improve the ability to communicate with others, it is essential to understand the gaps in our communication with others. The most effective way to do this is for others to provide us with feedback about what they heard us say (both the words and feelings) and how it affected them (the impact it had). We can then compare the "intended versus the actual" consequences, and be in a better position to change our communication behavior. The crucial issue here is *not* that there is one right style of communicating, but one of *congruence:* Am I communicating what I want to be communicating? Are my words and actions consistent with my feelings or am I "managing" my communications in ways that I don't realize?

Feedback is one way of helping other people to consider changing their behavior. (Remember, all behavior conveys some message and is, therefore, a form of communication.) It is communication to a person (or group) which gives that person information about how he affects others. As in a guided missile system, feedback helps an individual to keep his behavior "on target" and thus to better achieve his goals. Feedback that can help another person improve has the following characteristics:[2]

---

[1] H. Baumgartel, Warren G. Bennis, and N. R. De (eds.), *Readings in Group Development for Managers and Trainers* (New York: Asia Publishing House, 1967), pp. 151–156.

[2] The following eight characteristics of helpful feedback are taken from an unpublished pamphlet from the

1. It is descriptive rather than evaluative. Describing one's own reaction leaves the other individual free to use it or not to use it as he sees fit. Avoiding evaluative language reduces the need for the other individual to react defensively.

2. It is specific rather than general. To be told that one is "domineering" will probably not be as useful as to be told "Just now, when we were deciding the issue, you did not listen to what others said and I felt forced to accept your arguments or face attack from you."

3. It takes into account the needs of both the receiver and giver of feedback. Feedback can be destructive when it serves only our needs and fails to consider the needs of the person on the receiving end.

4. It is directed toward behavior that the receiver can control. Frustration is increased when a person is reminded of some shortcoming over which s/he has no control.

5. It is solicited, rather than imposed. Feedback is most useful when the receiver has asked for it.

6. It is well timed. In general, feedback is most useful at the earliest opportunity after the given behavior (depending, of course, on the person's readiness to hear it, on support available from others, and so on).

7. It is checked to ensure clear communication. One way of doing this is to have the receiver try to rephrase the feedback he has received to see if it corresponds to what the sender had in mind.

8. When feedback is given in a group, both giver and receiver have opportunity to check with others in the group on the accuracy of the feedback. Is this one person's impression or an impression shared by others?

Feedback, then, is a way of giving help; it is a corrective mechanism for individuals who want to learn how well their behavior matches their intentions — i.e., to better understand the gaps in communication with others.

The following exercise is meant to help you get feedback on your own style of communicating. The process of giving and receiving feedback demands the most in communications skills to be effective.

## IV. PROCEDURE FOR GROUP MEETING

A. Communications Exercise (Time Allotted: 60 Minutes)

For this exercise, the class should split into groups of four. (If there are extra individuals, groups of five should be formed with two observers.)

*Step 1.* One member of the group is selected as an observer.

*Step 2.* Place three chairs in a line in front of the observer and the other three members each take a seat. These chairs should be close together. The group now looks as follows:

NTL Institute for Applied Behavioral Sciences. See also Richard E. Boyatzis and David A. Kolb, "Feedback and Self-Directed Behavior Change" (Working Paper 344-69, Sloan School of Management, Massachusetts Institute of Technology, 1969) for research comparing the impact of different kinds of feedback.

*Step 3.*   A and C are supposed to *ignore the fact that the other exists;* as far as C is concerned, only he and B are seated there.

*Step 4.*   A and C are to try and get B's *undivided* attention in a conversation *as best they can.* A should guard against answering C's questions to B and the same for C to A because, to repeat, *A is to ignore C's presence* and *C is to ignore A's presence.* The observer should help to enforce this rule if necessary. (Time: 5 minutes.)

*Step 5.*   Observer should record observations on Observer Recording Form provided on page 205.

*Step 6.*   Repeat steps 1–5 until everyone has had a chance to be in each position—i.e., do the exercise four times.

*Step 7.*   *Discussion.* Two quartets should get together (i.e., to form groups of eight) to discuss their reactions to the exercise (from both the position of observers and participants) with particular focus on how it felt to be in each position. The focus should be on the *process* (how, with what feelings, etc.) of what was communicated, not so much the substance (the topic) of what was communicated.

Clearly, this situation is extreme and highly exaggerated. Try to draw out concepts and analogies that have wider relevance than this admittedly unique situation.

*Variations on Discussion Process*

There are several techniques you can try during these eight-man discussions that will highlight some frequent barriers to effective communication.

1.   *Listening.* Few of us ever really try to listen to what another person is saying. More often, we hear only part of what another person said and then immediately begin to form our own response, counterargument, or rebuttal. Sometimes we are so anxious to make our own point that we do not hear anything anyone else has said. Frequently, we hear and respond to just words but not the feelings another person was communicating. Then there is the "but, but," or "motorboat phenomenon," most frequently manifested by "yeah, but. . . ." Generally speaking, when a person begins by saying, "Yeah, but . . ." you can be reasonably sure he has not really heard what the preceding speaker said.

# INTERPERSONAL COMMUNICATION OBSERVER RECORDING FORM

Your role during this part of the exercise is important since one goal for today's unit is that individuals get feedback on their styles of interpersonal communication. In giving feedback during the discussion, try to follow the guidelines that were outlined in the Introduction. A few suggested dimensions to focus upon are listed here.

1. Who was more aggressive? Passive?

2. What methods (verbal, physical) were used by A and C to get B's attention? What methods seemed most successful?

3. Did B try to satisfy both A and C equally? What did B do in response to their efforts?

4. How did A or C react to being ignored? How did they seem to feel in their position? Upon what basis did you decide they felt that way?

5. How did B seem to feel about his position — enjoying the power, concerned about keeping A and C happy, withdrawn?

6. What kinds of nonverbal communication were exhibited by each of the three parties? With what effects?

7. What kinds of motivation did each exhibit? What did they do that made you feel that way?

*Notes*

*Exercise* — Before a person (A) can respond to another (B) or begin a new topic, A must repeat what B just said (both words and feelings) to B's satisfaction — i.e., A cannot make her point until B is satisfied that A heard her. Merely parroting what another person has said does not convey *understanding.* Restate the other's position in your own words.

If any other person in the group thinks B communicated something (verbally or nonverbally) that A did not hear or has a different interpretation of what A said, she should check this with B — i.e., tell B what she heard to see if this is what B meant to communicate.

2. *Clarity of expression.* Many of us often become involved in our own communications to the extent that we make it very difficult for others to listen to and understand what we are saying. Others, for a variety of reasons, are very reluctant, once they get the floor, to give it up. They make long speeches when short answers would suffice.

*Exercise* — The Telegram Game: Assume that you can verbally send a 10-word message for free, but that every word after 10 words costs $5 per word to transmit. Try, in other words, to communicate in sets of "10 words or less." You may, of course, say more than 10 words (at no cost) during the course of the *total discussion,* but any more than *10 words at one time* carries the $5 per word charge.

3. *Restricted communication.* Much communication today takes place by written memo or telephone. In order to simulate some of the issues raised by this form of communication, you can carry on part of your discussion with your eyes closed. The entire group can try it together, any pair of communicators, or any individual. After this exercise, try carrying on the discussion for another few minutes using only numbers. One person may begin for instance, by saying, "15, 31, 6,341, 18." Another could respond to what she felt the first person was trying to say with numbers of her own. This will require the group to concentrate on the nonverbal aspects of spoken communication — vocal inflection and body movement. Discuss the differences between the two experiences.

4. Other variations, ideas, and innovations may come to you that may help to highlight barriers to effective communication. You are encouraged to introduce and try any such innovations on your own.

B. Fishbowl Exercise (Time Allotted: 60 Minutes)

For this part of the exercise, we will make use of what has become known as a "fishbowl."

*Step 1.* The class should form two groups (A and B) of equal size (possibly the eight-person groups that met during the discussions in Part I).

*Step 2.* The members of one group (A) should form a circle.

*Step 3.* The members of the other group (B) should form a circle *around* the circle formed by group A, making a "fishbowl."

*Step 4.* Each member of group B should pair off with someone in group A and *position herself so as to observe her partner's interaction.*

### Task for the Inner Group

The inner group should discuss (using the following Time Schedule) what they learned from Part I of the exercise. Considerations should be given to the following factors:

1. What did I learn about my own style of communicating (or more generally, relating) with another person?

2. How do I feel about the process of communication that took place in the discussion (i.e., eight-person groups) after the exercise and/or the communication process in this class in general?
   a. Was I comfortable saying what I really felt? What might have made me feel more comfortable? What kinds of behavior made me feel less comfortable?
   b. Did people seem to be really listening to what I had to say? How could I tell if they were or were not?
   c. Did others try to help me clarify and better understand my feelings during the exercise? How did I react? Did I show my reactions?
   d. Did others make it easy or difficult for me to get into the conversation? How did it feel? Did I try to help others share their ideas and feelings? Was I effective?

### Task for the Outer Group

Your task is to observe carefully (outer group should be silent except during feedback sessions) your partner in group A while she and the rest of her group discuss the first part of today's exercise. You should pay particular attention to the kinds of things (verbal and nonverbal) your partner does (or does not do) that appear to influence (positive or negative) her ability to communicate with others (and they with her). Try to focus on the things your partner does of which she may not be aware (e.g., cutting others off). You will have an opportunity to feed your observations back during the exercise.

### Time Schedule

1. Inner group discuss; outer group observe. (Time: 15 minutes.)
2. Partners get together and observer feeds back the observations she feels will help her partner improve her communication skills. (Time: 5 minutes.)

3.  Inner group returns to discussion; outer group observes. (Time: 10 minutes.) *Switch roles (outer group becomes inner group) and repeat steps 1–3.*


Any remaining time should be spent in pairs (the partners), sharing observations aimed at helping each other improve their own communications skills.


## V. SUMMARY


If one were to ask the question, "How can people improve their ability to communicate?" the answers would probably be of the form, "Speak more clearly, articulate the words more carefully, think about what you want to say, don't use unfamiliar, technical jargon." There is no doubt that these will serve to improve one's ability to communicate, yet communication is also influenced by interpersonal factors. We have already mentioned some of these factors:


1.  Communication is much more than just the words that flow between people; *all behavior* conveys some message — it is a form of communication — words as well as feelings, nonverbal as well as verbal cues.
2.  People spend a good deal of energy "managing their communications" — i.e., not saying what they really mean or feel.
3.  Listening is a selective process — i.e., we hear what we want to hear.
4.  Communication (and interpersonal relationships in general) is *not* a static process — rather, it is a dynamic process.


One simple but powerful model for analyzing the dynamic process of interpersonal communication is transactional analysis (TA).[3] TA begins from the premise that within each personality there are elements of the Parent, the Adult, and the Child. Clues that the Parent in us is operating are the use of such words as "always," "never," "should," "ought"; global evaluative feedback (e.g., "What a stupid person you are!") vs. specific descriptive feedback (e.g., "When you leave your clothes on the floor, it upsets me"); guilt-inducing statements (e.g., "If you respected me, you would never___"; and physical cues (such as pointing an accusing finger at somebody). In the exercise of power, the Parent in us is very likely to use threats (e.g., the withholding of affection) and resolve conflicts by forcing ("I'm boss; we'll do it my way").

The use of such words as "I wish," "I guess," "I don't care" (baby talk); comparative statements coming from the "Mine is better than yours" game; and physical cues such as slouching or looking away or down are indicators of the Child in us. The Child is likely to lead us to behave like "pawns," to be dependent, to be competitive (e.g., sibling rivalry), and to approach conflict resolution through avoidance or smoothing.

The Adult in us, by contrast, shows itself in a variety of ways: in such phrases as "I see," "I think," "It is my opinion"; in an emphasis on data collection — e.g., why, what, where, when, who, how; and in an emphasis on data processing and problem solving.

Interpersonal transactions can be analyzed in terms of whether the communications between two people are complementary (congruent) or crossed (incongruent). Let us look at an example:

[3] Thomas A. Harris, *I'm OK — You're OK* (New York: Harper & Row, Publishers, 1969). Also, M. James and D. Jorgewood, *Born to Win* (Reading, Mass.: Addison-Wesley Publishing Co., Inc., 1971).

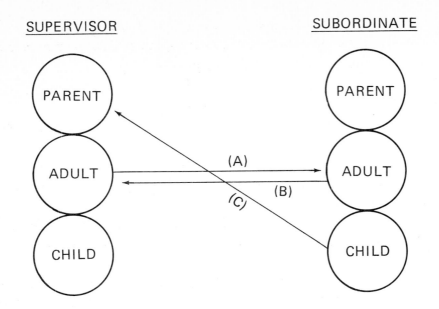

SUPERVISOR                                    SUBORDINATE

PARENT                                        PARENT

ADULT        (A)                              ADULT
             (B)
             (C)

CHILD                                         CHILD

(A)  Supervisor to subordinate: "I need last month's production reports. Do you know
     where they are?"
(B)  Subordinate to supervisor: "In the file" or "I don't know, but I'll help you look."
(C)  Subordinate to supervisor: "Where you left them!"

Using TA to examine this potential series of interactions, we would conclude the following:

1.  The (A)–(B) interaction is a congruent, Adult-to-Adult interaction. The supervisor (A)
    is an Adult seeking information. The subordinate (B) is an Adult giving direct in-
    formation.

2.  The (A)–(C) interaction, by contrast, is a crossed or incongruent transaction. The sub-
    ordinate (C) responds *as if* he were a Child talking to a Parent. You can imagine in your
    own minds the variety of ways in which this interaction might proceed and the pitfalls
    that can develop. When stimulus and response cross (are incongruent), in terms of the
    Parent/Adult/Child framework, continuing communication either stops or becomes
    defensive and distorted.

There are direct analogies between family dynamics — upon which TA is based — and communication in organizations. A manager, for example, who assumes that people are immature and irresponsible (childish) may well behave like a Parent. A Parent-like posture could also lead to conflict resolution
by forcing and the utilization of fear (threat of punishment) in the exercise of power. It is important
to emphasize that the concept of a transaction highlights the dual responsibility of *both* parties in
the interaction. *Without followership there can be no leadership.* By how they initiate *and* how they
respond, superiors and subordinates can have a significant impact on the nature and quality of the
communication transaction.

Although cookbook-like statements about how to be an effective communicator would do an
injustice to the dynamic nature of the communication process, it seems appropriate here to consider
some characteristics of a relationship between two or more people in which all parties would be capable of improving the effectiveness of their interpersonal communications.

1.  An awareness that I am a person with feelings and that I can live with the fact that my
    feelings influence me and my communication.

2. A tolerance of other people's feelings and an awareness that their feelings, which may be different from mine, affect their sending and receiving communications.

3. The intention as sender to build feelings of security in the receiver.

4. The intention, as a receiver, to listen from the sender's point of view rather than to evaluate the communication from mine.

5. The willingness to take more than half the responsibility for the effectiveness of communication whether as sender or receiver.

6. The conscious effort to build feedback into all communications.

7. The ability to resist acting on and reacting to my assumptions about another person's reasons behind a particular communication.

8. A recognition that communications are at best imperfect and the avoidance of undue cynicism resulting from difficulties or failures to communicate.

Improving one's communication with others requires commitment to such a process. This process requires a climate that is trusting and supportive in order that the feedback, so essential to improving our ability to communicate, can be given and received in a way that encourages listening and acceptance rather than increased defensiveness.

# VI. SELF-EVALUATION AND COMPLETING THE LEARNING LOOP

A. What questions do you now have as a result of your learning experiences from this unit? Jot these down below.

B. From these questions, what *key concepts* can you extrapolate for further learning? Write these concepts below.

C. How can you now go about finding answers to the questions you raised above? Below are some suggested ways to continue your learning process by beginning new learning loops:

1. Look up the key concepts from your questions above in the Yellow Pages of Learning Experiences at the back of the book. Find a few suggested readings or exercises to facilitate the learning of these key concepts.

2. If you don't find the key concepts in the Yellow Pages related specifically to your questions, perhaps there are other concepts listed in the index that might lead you to relevant learning resources at this time. Look for concepts similar to those you identified in B above.

3. In the event that you don't find the Yellow Pages directory useful for your present learning goals, discuss your questions with other students, faculty, or persons outside your learning environment. Discuss further learning possibilities with them.

# chapter 7
## interpersonal
## perception

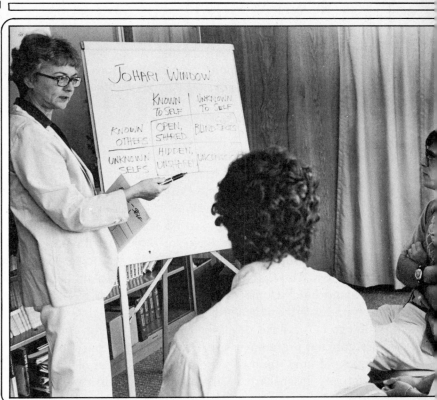

*Photo by Sybil Shelton*

## I. OBJECTIVES

A.  To understand the factors that influence our perception of other people.

B.  To understand the manner in which perceptions of other people, particularly first impressions, influence interpersonal relationships.

C.  To explore methods for giving and receiving feedback by sharing the perceptions group members hold of each other.

## II. PREMEETING PREPARATION

Read the Introduction.

## III. INTRODUCTION

We are not cameras or tape recorders. We do not take in, with our eyes, exactly what is "out there." We constantly respond to cues that have meaning for us. We see what we want or need to see to define ourselves or to advance our aims. We do not see people as they are, we see them for what they mean to us.

Consider how we understand the world we live in, particularly those parts of it concerning ourselves and our relations with other people.[1] First, we organize the world according to *concepts*, or categories. We say that things are warm or cold; good or bad; simple or complex. Each of these concepts may be considered a dimension along which we can place events in the world, some closer to one end of the dimension, some closer to the other.

Any time we consider the qualities of ourselves, other persons, or events in the inanimate world, we have to use these concepts to do it. We are dependent for our understanding of the world on the concepts and categories we have for organizing our experiences. If we lack a concept for something that occurs in the world, we have to invent one or we cannot respond to the event in an organized fashion. How, for example, would a person explain his own and others' behavior without the concepts of love and hate? Consider how much behavior would simply puzzle or confuse a person or, perhaps, just go on by without really being perceived at all, for lack of this one dimension.

Most of us have developed our own set of concepts that we use to interpret others' behavior. These concept preferences are often related to our motivation. People with high affiliation motivation, for example, may tend to see the world in terms of love and hate, acceptance and rejection. They may be relatively insensitive to issues of leadership or excellence. Thus, an administrator who is overly sensitive to whether or not subordinates are friendly may, as a result, be in a poor position to judge other important aspects of subordinates' performance. The ability to develop differentiated perceptions of others is related to leadership effectiveness. Fiedler[2] has reported some research where he found that effective leaders, in contrast to ineffective leaders, were able to differentiate among their followers on a variety of dimensions. For example, whereas the captain of a losing basketball team tends to distinguish among his players only in terms of their overall ability, the captain of a winning team tends to be aware of who dribbles well, who passes well, who shoots well, who plays well under pressure, and so on. In other words, effective managers seem to have a large number of concepts in their conceptual schemes and tend to perceive differences among their subordinates along these dimensions.

Concepts do not exist in isolation; they are connected to one another by a network of relationships. Taken together, the concepts we use to understand a situation, plus the relationships among the concepts, are called a *conceptual system*. For example, we may say, "People who are warm and friendly are usually trusting, and hence they are often deceived by others." Here we have a conceptual system linking the concepts of *friendliness*, *warmth*, *trust in others*, and *proneness to deception*. Because concepts are linked to one another, the location of an event in one concept usually indicates where that event is located in each of a whole network of concepts. Thus, it is almost impossible to take in a small bit of information about a characteristic of a person or event without a host of implications about other characteristics.

Images and stereotypes operate this way. When we discover that a person is black, or a union leader, a social scientist, or a wife, the information on these concepts immediately calls up an entire network of expectations about other characteristics of the person. In the case of stereotypes, these expectations may even be so strong that we do not check to find out whether our conceptual system worked accurately this time, but go to the other extreme of ignoring or distorting information that

---

[1] See O. J. Harvey, D. E. Hunt, and H. M. Schroder, *Conceptual Systems and Personality Organization* (New York: W. W. Norton & Company, Inc., 1955).

[2] F. E. Fiedler, *Leader Attitudes and Group Effectiveness* (Urbana, Ill.: University of Illinois Press, 1958). Also, Irwin M. Rubin and M. Goldman, "An Open System Model of Leadership Performance," *Organizational Behavior and Human Performance*, Vol. 3, No. 2 (May 1968), pp. 143–156.

does not fit the conceptual system, so that the system may remain quite unaffected by contradictory experiences.

In other words, these concepts (or sets of dimensions) enable us to organize the multitude of experiences we have each day. Without them we would be in a continuous state of chaos, so, to this extent, they are functional and necessary parts of the human personality. The fact that we are so dependent on our conceptual system means that we are sometimes hesitant to accept any information that does not fit into it.

To protect ourselves from disconfirming experiences, we have at our disposal a host of perceptual defenses. These defenses[3] act like a screen or filter, blocking out that which we do not want to see and letting through that which we wish to see. The closer we get to conceptual systems concerned with our *self-perceptions* (self-image) and our relationships with important others, the more likely we are to call upon these defensive screens.[4]

These defensive screens help to create self-fulfilling or circular perceptual processes. Let us examine how these circular processes can (and often do) function with a few examples.

*Example 1: The Stereotypical Female*

1. As a woman, I believe that men prefer women who are passive and unassertive.
2. Since I would like to develop meaningful relationships with men, I behave in a passive and unassertive manner.

3. I tend to develop relationships with men who themselves expect women to be passive and unassertive.

3. I do not approach and/or am not approached by men who expect a woman to be active and assertive.

4. I am confirmed in my belief that men prefer women who are passive and unassertive.

4. I do not have the opportunity to develop my own assertiveness.

*Example 2: A Managerial Dilemma*

1. As a manager, I believe that subordinates are basically lazy and dislike work.
2. I assume, therefore, that to get the most out of subordinates, I must watch over their every move.
3. I behave in a strict manner, delegating little responsibility and demanding that everything be cleared through me first.
4. My subordinates react to this parent-like stance by acting like rebellious teenagers. I have to lean on them all the time or they'll never do what I tell them.
5. Consequently, my original belief is confirmed; subordinates are basically lazy and dislike work.

The underlying pattern in these processes is one of (a) assumption/belief, (b) leading to behavior that is congruent with the assumption, followed by (c) observation of consequences which, to the ex-

[3] There are a large number of relevant sources here, some of which are:
(a) Mason Haire and W. F. Grunes, "Perceptual Defenses: Processes Protecting an Organized Perception of Another Personality," *Human Relations*, Vol. 3 (1950), pp. 403–412.
(b) M. Rokeach, *The Open and Closed Mind* (New York: Basic Books, Inc., 1960).
[4] For two excellent collections of material relevant to this point, see:
(a) Warren G. Bennis et al., *Interpersonal Dynamics*, rev. ed. (Homewood, Ill.: Dorsey Press, 1968).
(b) R. Wylie, *The Self Concept* (Lincoln, Neb.: University of Nebraska Press, 1965).

tent that selective perception is occurring, leads to (d) confirmation of the original assumption/belief. Testing the validity or desirability of this conceptual pattern is difficult, for several reasons.

One important reason is that normal social interaction is basically conservative—social norms operate to preserve existing interaction patterns and perceptions. Sociologist Erving Goffman[5] has described the tendency of people to preserve the "face" that others present to them. When someone acts "out of character," social pressures are mobilized to force them back into their role. In social situations we tend to act in such a way that we maintain our own self-image and the self-image we see others presenting. We resist telling someone that they have egg on their chin because we assume that this is not part of the image they want to present and we do not want them to "lose face" and be embarrassed. This conservative interaction norm tends to decrease the accuracy of interpersonal perception by relinquishing opportunities to test the accuracy of our perceptions of ourselves and others. The norm dictates that we cannot frankly tell others our impressions of them if these impressions differ from the face they are presenting. It also acts as an obstacle to our testing with others whether or not we are projecting the kind of self-image we think we are. "Do you see me the way I see myself?" If someone presents himself/herself as a leader, it is hard to tell him/her that you do not feel like following. Thus, we are denied information about others' true thoughts and feelings by the face we present.

A theoretical conceptualization of this process can be depicted in the following manner, called the Johari Window, named after Joe Luft and Harry Ingram, its creators.

|  | Known to Self | Not known to Self |
| --- | --- | --- |
| Known to Others | Open Area | Blind Area |
| Not Known to Others | Hidden Area | Unknown Area |

*Open Area.* This cell includes all the factors upon which I and others have mutually shared perceptions; i.e., people see me the way I see myself (e.g., I feel confident and people see me as confident).

*Unknown Area.* In this cell are factors that I do not see in myself nor do others see them in me.

*Hidden Area.* In this cell are factors that I see in myself but that I hide from others (e.g., I feel insecure, but I strive to project the image of a very secure person)—i.e., people see a "false me" and I must always be on guard not to let them see the "real me."

*Blind Area.* In this cell are factors that other people perceive in me but that I do not see in myself (e.g., others see my anxiety reducing my effectiveness but I do not see—or will not admit to myself—that I am anxious); i.e., people know certain things about me but they don't tell me ("Even your best friends won't tell you").

To move from the hidden to the open area requires a sufficient level of trust and psychological safety to enable me to share my self-perceptions with another. To move from the blind to the open area requires that people give me feedback as to how they see me. The conditions of trust and psychological safety are again critical—so that people will risk telling me and so I will not react defensively to what they say. It is only as we move from the hidden and blind areas into the open area that true sharing of perceptions and understanding between people can develop.

---

[5] E. Goffman, "On Face-Work: An Analysis of Ritual Elements in Social Interaction," *Psychiatry*, Vol. 18 (1955), pp. 213–231.

# IV. PROCEDURE FOR GROUP MEETING

A. Self-Perceptions: Individual Work (Time Allotted: 30–40 Minutes)

The first part of this unit is designed to help you sharpen your understanding of the image/ perceptions you believe you communicate to others. During the second part of this unit, you will have the opportunity to explore how others believe they see you.

Step 1.    As you think about the *image you have of yourself*, list, in the appropriate spaces provided below:

a. The first five or six words that come to your mind.

b. An animal.

c. A musical instrument.

d. A food.

*It is important that you work quickly. Let your first thought be the one you record.*

### HOW I SEE MYSELF

| | |
|---|---|
| 5-6 Words | |
| Animal | |
| Musical instrument | |
| Food | |

Step 2.    The words you listed above are, at best, simplified cues or indicators of important elements of how you see yourself — your self-image. It is your own interpretation of what these words mean to you that contributes to your self-image. In this step you are asked to (a) interpret the meaning of those words and (b) decide whether or not each element of your self-image (known to self) is a part of your Open Area or your Hidden Area. Use the space provided below to record these points.

a. Elements of my self-image that I believe are in my *Open Area* (i.e., known to me and known to others).

b. Elements of my self-image that I believe are in my *Hidden Area* (i.e., known to me but not known to others).

*Step 3.* Each of us *behaves* in ways designed to allow various aspects of our self-image (known to self) to be known to others—an Open Area. Similarly, we behave in ways to keep various aspects of our self-image in our Hidden Area (not known to others).

   a. In the space below, jot down examples of how you communicate to others important elements of your Open Area. (For example, if you feel confident and believe people see you as confident, how do you behave to communicate confidence?)

   b. In the space below, jot down examples of how you behave in order to keep elements of your self-image (known to self) in the Hidden Area. (For example, if you feel insecure, but try to project an image of confidence, how do you behave to "cover" your feelings of insecurity?)

B. Testing Self Perceptions: Small-Group Sharing (Time Allotted: 60–90 Minutes)

In this part of the unit, you will have the opportunity to get a glimpse of how others see you. This will be a real test of your interpersonal skills. Giving and receiving feedback in a productive manner is difficult but important.

*Step 1.* Class should form into groups of four or five members. Join people with whom you feel some degree of comfort and who have seen enough of your behavior to be in a position to share their impressions.

*Step 2.* As soon as the groups are formed, each individual should fill out the Perception Matrix form on page 221 for others in the group.

*It is important in filling out the Perception Matrix that you work quickly. Let your first thought be the one you record. It is helpful if there is no communication during this step.*

Step 3.   *Individual Reading Prior to Group Sharing.* The sharing process you are about to begin will not be an easy task. As was pointed out in the Introduction, normal social interaction is basically conservative — social norms operate to preserve existing interaction patterns and perceptions. During this sharing process, you are, in effect, being asked to operate with an atypical set of social norms — to share and discuss your impressions of one another.

# PERCEPTION MATRIX

*Own Perceptions*

| Member / Category | How You See Yourself* | How You See A | How You See B | How You See C | How You See D |
|---|---|---|---|---|---|
| 5-6 Words | | | | | |
| Animal | | | | | |
| Musical Instrument | | | | | |
| Food | | | | | |

*These are the self-perceptions you recorded in step 1 of your Individual Work.

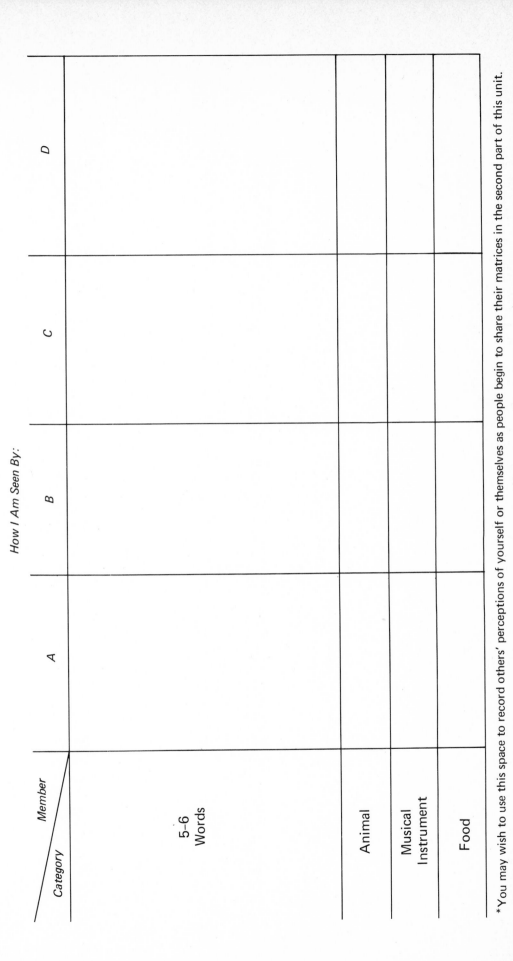

**PERCEPTION MATRIX**

*Others' Perceptions* *

*How I Am Seen By:*

| Category \ Member | A | B | C | D |
|---|---|---|---|---|
| 5–6 Words | | | | |
| Animal | | | | |
| Musical Instrument | | | | |
| Food | | | | |

*You may wish to use this space to record others' perceptions of yourself or themselves as people begin to share their matrices in the second part of this unit.

In the discussions you have, it is important to remember that there is no one reality or truth. You have perceptions of yourself. Others have perceptions of you. Some of these perceptions will be shared—held in common. Others will be different. The issue is *not* whose perception is right or whose is wrong.

If I have a perception of someone and they do not share that perception of themselves, this discrepancy can serve as an important learning opportunity for *both of us.*

1. If I am the one being perceived, I may learn something about my Blind Area. I may learn about behavior that serves to move elements from my Hidden Area to my Open Area.

2. If I am the perceiver, I may learn something about the perceptual filters I use; e.g., I assume all big people are confident. I may learn that I tend to see in others elements of how I see myself.

All of us can learn something more about our own inevitably circular self-fulfilling perceptual processes. This awareness is only a first step. Whether or not a person chooses to alter these perceptual patterns is clearly a matter of individual choice.

*Step 4.* People should share the perceptions they have of each other as recorded on their Perception Matrix.

*Step 5.* Groups should now discuss their perceptions using the following suggestions to guide their discussions.

a. What can you infer about the concepts in your cognitive map (the concepts or categories you most often use in perceiving other people) from the words you listed for each person in your group?

1. Did you list mostly adjectives (which tend to be evaluative or difference-oriented—e.g., good versus bad, big versus small) or nouns (which tend to be neutral or non-difference-oriented—e.g., man, student) or verbs (which are behavior-oriented as opposed to trait or characteristic-oriented)?

2. Did your lists of words differ for each person or did your lists reflect similar concepts for each person? What does this tell you about the breadth versus narrowness of your conceptual system; the degree to which the major concepts in your system are separate or highly interconnected?

b. Was your perception of some people generally closer to the ways they saw themselves than was true of your perception of other people? To what do you attribute any differences? Do some people project clearer self-images? Length of time/context within which you knew the person? Similarity to yourself?

c. Where two or more people saw the same person in substantially different ways, they should try to understand how these differences arise.

d. Based on the Individual Work you did in the beginning of this unit, some of you may have found:

1. Elements you thought were in your Open Area were not known to others (i.e., they were in your Hidden Area).

2. Elements you thought were in your Hidden Area were known to others (i.e., they are in your Open Area).

3. New perceptions which were in your Blind Area.

*In exploring these "surprises" it is most important that you listen to and understand others' descriptions of how you behave, which leads them to form the impressions they have.*

    e. It is very likely that you will uncover some typical circular perceptual processes such as those discussed in the Introduction. The group may want to outline a few of their own such processes.

       1. What does a person gain/achieve through the pattern?

       2. What costs are incurred/opportunities forgone by maintaining the pattern?

       3. What steps could be taken to change the nature of these circular patterns?

    f. Finally, each of you chose, on some basis, to join this particular small group. What, if anything, have you learned during this exercise that might help to explain that choice process and its consequences?

## V. SUMMARY

It is as difficult for human beings to understand the impact of their own conceptual system as it is for a fish to understand the concept of water. Yet, our conceptual maps and the fish's water are equally important for survival. Without a conceptual system to simplify and order our experiences we would become overwhelmed, helpless victims of our environment. Yet failure to recognize that our perceptions are to some extent our own creation can leave one closed, defensive, and unable to profit from new experiences. In the following analysis by an engineer of his reactions to the perception unit, we see one individual's struggle to understand his own way of perceiving others.

Again it seems I am going to write a paper about myself rather than the suggested topic. Whenever I reflect on the subject matter we study, I can directly relate it to myself. I have always considered myself "free of hang-ups"; however, there are many things I do that I do not completely understand. Previously I have never taken the time to question myself, but now, being forced to think about a concept, I can see how I have been influenced by that concept and can attempt to explain, but not always justify, the way I feel toward many things. Well, here goes!

I am the perfect example of a person blinded by his own perception of the world. Not all of the time, mind you, but mainly in one case — the case being when I become "snowed" by a girl. I'll begin by relating my current project in this area — at least I think the project is current, although I'm not sure as of this moment because of a possible misperception on my part. Being alone in a new city, I engaged in the well-known game of mixer this autumn in the hope of meeting someone interesting. I accomplished my goal without any difficulties, and here is where my problem began — I committed my unpardonable sin of becoming snowed.

I do not have many difficulties with first perceptions. I think I am pretty objective and usually make good judgments. First impressions are almost solely objective! As long as I do not become emotionally involved, that is, as long as there is no filter between what I see and how I perceive what I have seen, I am quite able to understand what is communicated. However, once I am personally involved with the reason behind the attempted communication, my vision of what is actually happening is, I believe, distorted.

This weekend, for example, I did not take Mary [a fictitious name] out because of our last date and a phone call I made after the date. Even though I wanted to take her out, I didn't; consequently, I have been asking myself all weekend what motivated me not to ask her out; and I do not have a specific answer — but I know it stems from how I perceived how she feels. However, this is what I think she feels, which just might not be what she does feel, and I do not let myself comprehend that there may be a difference between these two versions of the same feelings. I guess I feel that my logical reasoning of what a particular look or remark means necessarily is the correct idea. I completely leave out the possibility that everyone does not (thankfully) think about everything the same way I do.

Zalkind and Costello, in their article on perception, give five reasons of how a person misperceives. These are:

1.   You are influenced by cues below your own threshold — i.e., the cues you don't know you perceived.

2.   You respond to irrelevant cues to arrive at a judgment.

3.   You are influenced by emotional factors — i.e., what is liked is perceived as correct.

4.   You weigh perceptual evidence heavily if it comes from a respectable source.

5.   You are not able to identify all factors — i.e., not realizing how much weight is given to a single item.

I feel I am guilty, if one can be "guilty," of most of the mentioned means of misperception. However, I feel that rather than imposing a perceptual defense upon myself, I project a perceptual offense, and this greatly compounds my misperception. Rather than looking for favorable acts of communication and not allowing unfavorable perceptions, I am forever (when I become emotionally involved with a girl) on the lookout for any signs of displeasure. And at the slightest hint, my mind begins to work on such questions as "What if that means . . .?"

For example, to the question, "Did you have a good time?," I got the reply, "Yeah, I guess so." This was not perceived favorably. My perceptual offense was quickly in play and I have since been analyzing that statement. I don't know Mary well enough to say what anything she says really means, but because I was afraid the reply meant "I had a bad time," that is what I have convinced myself that she meant (although nothing else that was said even hinted at that idea; and to the friend who doubled with me, the opposite was obviously true). I didn't ask her out this weekend for reasons mainly based on this one perception of how she feels about dating me. Looking back on my action, I see I have committed three of the Zalkind–Costello means of misperception.:

• No. 2 — I may have responded to an irrelevant cue — her remark probably just came out and didn't really have any deep meaning behind it.

• No. 3 — I was influenced by a (negative) emotional factor — I am so worried that she was not enjoying herself, with the repercussions that would have to my emotional happiness, that my perception might have been distorted.

• No. 5 — I did not realize how heavily I weighted this single cue.

Being apprehensive of how she felt, I ended up analyzing every little remark made. I do not take time to think that my ways of comprehending a perception may be inaccurate — the thought never seems to enter my mind. The handout on perception states, "These defenses act like a screen or filter . . . blocking out that which we don't want to see and letting through that which we wish to see." I, however, feel that I block out that which I want to see and let in that which I don't want to see. This is a definite problem, but one that I never thought of before. And to compound matters, the perceptions I let in are my own personal version of what is perceived and may be the opposite of what is being communicated.

I do not have this problem until I begin to like a girl. Trained as an engineer, I think I am able to cope with objective matters; but when I try to understand another person, I seem to fail—especially when there are present emotional filters through which my perceptions are received. To take a statement *out* of context, Zalkind and Costello say: "A little learning encourages the perceiver to respond with increased sensitivity to individual differences without making it possible for him to gauge the real meaning of what he has seen." Well, I have had only a little learning about perception, and their statement applies to me perfectly. I try to play psychologist without knowing the first thing about what I am looking for. This is a habit I have gotten myself addicted to, and one I will have to break down in order to have a better understanding of the people around me. Right now the unknown (i.e., the human unknown—what people are thinking) confronts me and I am frustrated by it. In response to this frustration, I set up a perceptual defense (I guess my perceptual offense is nothing but a type of perceptual defense—there is an old football theory that the best offense is a good defense, which only adds to my frustration). Thus, in order to move from the unknown to perceptual understanding, I must first realize that I am reacting defensively to what is being communicated to me.

It seems I am now coming back to what seems to be a familiar theme in all the topics we have covered so far. Zalkind and Costello say, "The person who accepts himself is more likely to be able to see favorable aspects of other people." I feel this is especially true of myself. If I stop and realize that my date is probably thinking of the same things that I am (at the initial stages of human relations, most of the time is spent in the unconscious, hidden, and blind areas of perception), then I may prevent my perceptual defense from operating at the level it is now operating. If I continually look at weak points, and never strong points, and do not realize that I am doing such, I am not really aware of myself and therefore not aware of how others perceive me.

I feel I can improve myself in a number of ways. First, I must accept my own feelings and not worry or analyze them. As is stated in the pamphlet: "Each of us has both his tender and tough emotions." Second, I should stop analyzing everything logically—it's hard for me to accept the fact that all of my world is not logical. Third, I should experiment more in the giving and receiving of perceptual feedback. I spend too much time analyzing a date's behavior and not enough giving her feedback, thus blocking the understanding between us. Finally, the fourth area of improvement, and the factor that this paper has led me to explore, is increasing my own awareness and understanding of the causes of emotion. These steps of improvement exactly parallel those given in the pamphlet on how to use our emotional resources effectively. I hope I can put them to use; and once they are in use, build on them.

## VI. SELF-EVALUATION AND COMPLETING THE LEARNING LOOP

A. What questions do you now have as a result of your learning experiences from this unit? Jot these down below.

B. From these questions, what *key concepts* can you extrapolate for further learning? Write these concepts below.

C. How can you now go about finding answers to the questions you raised above? Below are some suggested ways to continue your learning process by beginning new learning loops:

1. Look up the key concepts from your questions above in the Yellow Pages of Learning Experiences at the back of the book. Find a few suggested readings or exercises to facilitate the learning of these key concepts.

2. If you don't find the key concepts in the Yellow Pages related specifically to your questions, perhaps there are other concepts listed in the index that might lead you to relevant learning resources at this time. Look for concepts similar to those you identified in B above.

3. In the event that you don't find the Yellow Pages directory useful for your present learning goals, discuss your questions with other students, faculty, or persons outside your learning environment. Discuss further learning possibilities with them.

# chapter 8

## group
## dynamics

*Photo by Sybil Shelton*

## I. OBJECTIVES

A.  To increase understanding of interpersonal processes that facilitate or hinder a group's ability to function effectively.

B.  To sharpen ability to observe and diagnose these process factors.

C.  To practice trying to combine the role of a participant in task accomplishment with the role of an observer.

## II. PREMEETING PREPARATION

Read the Introduction.

## III. INTRODUCTION

"A camel is a horse put together by a committee." "Group-think." These two clichés are often applied to group decision making. Most people believe that working in groups is inevitably less efficient, more time consuming, and very frustrating, and that it creates conformity in thinking. Many of these deeply help beliefs are simply unsubstantiated or found to be less generally true than was originally believed. Stoner's work,[1] for example, on the riskiness of group versus individual decisions is a case in point. Although the reasons are not yet fully understood[2] it is clear that, contrary to popular belief, under certain conditions groups make more *risky* decisions than do individuals.

All of us have participated in groups of various sorts, family, gang, team, work group, and the like, but rarely have we taken the time to observe what was going on in the group or why the members were behaving in the way they were.[3] In thinking about groups, few people realize that in any group there are at least two classes of issues operating at any given point. One is the reason for the group's existence in the first place—e.g., to solve a particular problem. These are called *content* or *task issues*. A second, and equally important, set of issues concerns elements of how the group is going about achieving its formal task. These are called *process issues.*[4]

### Content Versus Process

When we observe what a group is talking about, we are focusing on the *content*. When we try to observe how the group is handling its communication—i.e, who talks how much or who talks to whom, we are focusing on group *process*. The content of the conversation is often a good clue as to what process issue may be on people's minds when they find it difficult to confront the issue directly. It often seems that groups spend considerable time talking about things that, on the surface, have nothing to do with the task at hand. Discussing the worthlessness of their previous PTA meetings may mean that members are not satisfied with the performance of their present group. The assumption is that it is less threatening to talk about how we feel about PTA meetings (there and then) than it is to talk about our feelings about these (here-and-now) meetings.

### Communication

One of the easiest aspects of group process to observe is the pattern of communication:

1.  Who talks? For how long? How often?
2.  Whom do people look at when they talk?
    a. Individuals, possibly potential supporters.
    b. The group.
    c. Nobody.
3.  Who talks after whom, or who interrupts whom?

---

[1] James A. F. Stoner, "Risky and Cautious Shifts in Group Decisions: The Influence of Widely Held Values" (Working Paper, Sloan School of Management, Massachusetts Institute of Technology, October 1967).

[2] Roger Brown, "Group Dynamics," in *Social Psychology* (New York: Free Press, 1967).

[3] The literature on group dynamics has grown to enormous proportions. See: (a) D. Cartwright and A. Zander (eds.), *Group Dynamics—Research and Theory*, 3rd ed. (New York: Harper & Row, Publishers, 1968). (b) B. E. Collins and H. Guetzkow, *A Social Psychology of Group Processes for Decision-Making* (New York: John Wiley & Sons, Inc., 1964).

[4] For a discussion of the differences between content and process issues, see Edgar H. Schein, *Process Consultation: Its Role in Organizational Development* (Reading, Mass.: Addison-Wesley Publishing Co., Inc., 1969).

4. What style of communication is used (assertions, questions, tone of voice, gesture, etc.)?

The kind of observations we make gives us clues to other important things that may be going on in the group, such as who leads whom and who influences whom.

*Decision-Making Procedures*[5]

Whether we are aware of it or not, groups are making decisions all the time, some of them consciously and in reference to the major tasks at hand, some of them without much awareness and in reference to group procedures or standards of operation. It is important to observe how decisions are made in a group, to assess the appropriateness of the decision to the matter being decided on and to assess whether the consequences of given methods are really what the group members bargained for.

Reprinted by permission of the Chicago Tribune-New York News Syndicate

Group decisions are notoriously hard to undo.[6] When someone says, "Well, we decided to do it, didn't we?", any budding opposition is quickly immobilized. We can undo the decision only if we reconstruct and understand how we made it and test whether this method was appropriate or not.

Some methods by which groups make decisions:[7]

1. The *plop:* "I think we should appoint a chairperson.". . . Silence.
2. The *self-authorized agenda:* "I think we should introduce ourselves. My name is Joe Smith. . . ."
3. The *handclasp:* Person A: "I wonder if it would be helpful to introduce ourselves?" Person B: "I think it would; my name is Pete Jones."
4. The *minority decision:* "Does anyone object?" or "We all agree."
5. *Majority–minority voting.*
6. *Polling:* "Let's see where everyone stands. What do you think?"

---

[5] Much of the following material has appeared in a variety of places and is a standard input into many training programs, such as those conducted by the National Training Laboratory. This particular material was abridged, with permission of the author, from an unpublished paper by Edgar H. Schein, "What to Observe in Groups." The Collins and Guetzkow book, *A Social Psychology of Group Processes for Decision-Making,* is also very relevant here.

[6] Literature on group conformity is relevant to this point. For a summary, see E. L. Walker and R. W. Heyns, *An Anatomy for Conformity* (Englewood Cliffs, N.J.: Prentice-Hall, Inc., 1962).

[7] This typology was developed by Robert R. Blake.

7. *Consensus testing:* Genuine exploration to test for opposition and to determine whether opposition feels strongly enough to refuse to implement decision; not necessarily unanimity but essential agreement by all. Consensus does *not* involve pseudo "listening" ("Let's hear Joe out") and then doing what we were going to do in the first place ("OK, now that everyone has had a chance to talk, let's go ahead with the original decision").

*Task, Maintenance, and Self-Oriented Behavior*[8]

Behavior in the group can be viewed in terms of what its purpose or function seems to be. When a member says something, is the intent primarily to get the group task accomplished (task) or to improve or patch up some relationship among members (maintenance), or is the behavior primarily meeting a personal need or goal without regard to the group's problems (self-oriented)?

As the group grows and members' needs become integrated with group goals, there will be less self-oriented behavior and more task or maintenance behavior. Types of behavior relevant to the group's fulfillment of its *task:*

1. *Initiating.* For any group to function, some person(s) must be willing to take some initiative. These can be seemingly trivial statements like "Let's build an agenda," or "It's time we moved on to the next item," but without them, little task-related activity would occur in a group. People would either sit in silence and/or side conversations would develop.

2/3. *Seeking/giving information or openness.* The clear and efficient flow of information, facts, and opinions is essential to any task accomplishment. Giving-type statements— "I have some information that may be relevant," or "My own opinion in this matter is . . ." are important to ensure decisions based on full information. Information-seeking statements not only help the seeker but the entire group.

4. *Clarifying and elaborating.* Many useful inputs into group work get lost if this task-related behavior is missing. "Let me give an example that will clarify the point just made" and "Let me elaborate and build upon that idea" are examples of positive behaviors in this regard. They communicate a listening and collaborative stance.

5. *Summarizing.* At various points during a group's work, it is very helpful if someone takes a moment to summarize the group's discussion. This gives the entire group an opportunity to pause for a moment, step back, see how far they have come, where they are, and how much further they must go to complete their work.

6. *Consensus testing.* Many times a group's work must result in a consensus decision.[9] At various points in the meeting, the statement "Have we made a decision on that point?" can be very helpful. Even if the group is not yet ready to commit to a decision, it serves to remind everyone that a decision needs to be made and, as such, it adds positive work tension into the group.

Following are types of behavior relevant to the group's remaining in good working order, with a

---

[8] K. D. Benne and P. Sheats, "Functional Roles of Group Members," *Journal of Social Issues*, 2 (1948), 42–47.

[9] Not all decisions can/should be made by group consensus. For more details on this issue, see Chapter 9 "Leadership and Decision Making" and Victor H. Vroom and P. Yetton, *Leadership and Decision Making* (Pittsburgh, Pa.: University of Pittsburgh Press, 1973).

good climate for task work and good relationships that permit maximum use of member resources—i.e., *group maintenance:*

1. *Gatekeeping.* Gatekeeping is an essential maintenance function in a group. Without it, information gets lost, multiple conversations develop, and less assertive people get cut off and drop out of the meeting. "Let's give Joe a chance to finish his thought" and "If people would talk one at a time, I'd find it easier to listen and add to our discussion" are examples in this regard.

2. *Encouraging.* Encouraging also ensures that all the potentially relevant information the group needs is shared, listened to, and considered. "I know you haven't had a chance to work it through in your mind but keep thinking out loud and we'll try to help." "Before we close this off, Mary, do you have anything to add?"

3. *Harmonizing/compromising.* These two functions are very important but tricky because their overuse or inappropriate use can serve to reduce a group's effectiveness. If smoothing over issues (harmonizing) and each party giving in a bit (compromise) serve to mask important underlying issues, creative solutions to problems will be fewer in number and commitment to decisions taken will be reduced.

4. *Standard setting and testing.* This category of behavior acts as a kind of overall maintenance function. Its focus is how well the group's needs for task-oriented behavior and maintenance-oriented behaviors are being met. All groups will reach a point where "something is going wrong" or "something doesn't feel right." At such points, effective groups stop the music, test their own process, and set new standards where they are required. "I'm losing track of the conversation. If other people are willing, maybe it would help if someone could summarize the last 10 minutes."

For a group to be effective, both task-oriented behavior and maintenance-oriented behavior is needed.

*Emotional Issues: Causes of Self-Oriented Emotional Behavior*[10]

The processes described so far deal with the group's attempt to work and the work-facilitating functions of task and maintenance. But there are many forces active in groups that disturb work, that represent a kind of emotional underground or undercurrent in the stream of group life. These underlying emotional issues produce a variety of self-oriented behaviors that interfere with or are destructive to effective group functioning. They cannot be ignored or wished away, however. Rather, they must be recognized, their causes must be understood, and as the group develops, conditions must be created that permit these same emotional energies to be channeled in the direction of group effort. What are these issues or basic causes?

1. The problem of identity: Who am I here? How am I to present myself to others? What role should I play in the group?

2. The problem of control and power: Who has the power in the situation? How much power, control, and influence do I have in the situation? How much do I need?

3. The problem of goals: Which of my needs and goals can this group fulfill? Can any of my needs be met here? To which of the group's goals can I attach myself?

[10] This section is based on Schein's *Process Consultation.*

4. The problem of acceptance and intimacy: Am I accepted by the others? Do I accept them? Do they like me? Do I like them? How close to others do I want to become?

Self-oriented behaviors tend to be more prevalent in a group at certain points in the group's life. Early in the life of a new group one can expect to see many examples of self-oriented behaviors. Members are new to one another and a certain amount of "feeling out" is to be expected. Sometimes this takes place in after-hours social situations—"Why don't we get together after work for a drink?" On a less intense scale, the same phenomenon can be observed at the start of a group meeting with an old, established group. Side conversations and social chatter characterize the first few minutes while people catch up on where they have been since the last meeting.

A third point in a group's life when self-oriented behaviors can be observed is when a newcomer joins an already-established group. It is not unlike the dynamics that develop when a new sibling arrives in a family. Everyone else may be sincerely happy with the newcomer ("We really need her resources"); nonetheless, this is now a "new" group. The old equilibrium has been changed and a new one must take its place.

None of the above sounds particularly like an undercurrent, an emotional underground, which could be potentially destructive to effective group functioning. While all these issues can be observed in a group, their potential destructiveness is highest at that time when the group most needs to be maximally effective—under stress. In that sense, they are akin to regressive individual behaviors: in times of stress, individuals will regress to an earlier stage of development. Different individuals handle their anxiety in different ways, thus generating many different kinds of reactions in groups.

Following are types of emotional behavior that result from tension and from the attempt to resolve underlying problems:[11]

1. Tough emotions: anger, hostility, self-assertiveness
   a. Fighting with others
   b. Punishing others
   c. Controlling others
   d. Counterdependency
2. Tender emotions: love, sympathy, desire to help, need for affiliation with others
   a. Supporting and helping others
   b. Depending on others
   c. Pairing up or affiliating with others
3. Denial of all emotion
   a. Withdrawing from others
   b. Falling back on logic or reason

Individuals have different styles of reducing tension and expressing emotion. Three "pure types" have been identified:

1. The "friendly helper" orientation: acceptance of tender emotions, denial of tough emotions—"Let's not fight, let's help each other;" can give and receive affection but cannot tolerate hostility and fight.

[11] For another view of emotional behavior in groups, see William C. Schutz, "Interpersonal Underworld," *Harvard Business Review*, Vol. 36, No. 4 (July–August 1958), 123–125.

2.  The "tough battler" orientation: acceptance of tough emotions and denial of tender emotions — "Let's fight it out;" can deal with hostility but not with love, support, and affiliation.

3.  The "logical thinker" orientation: denial of all emotion — "Let's reason this thing out;" cannot deal with tender or tough emotions, hence shuts eyes and ears to much going on around him.

*But:*

Friendly Helpers will achieve their world of warmth and intimacy *only* by allowing conflicts and differences to be raised and resolved. They find that they can become close with people *only* if they can accept what is dissimilar as well as what is similar in their behavior.

Tough Battlers will achieve their world of toughness and conflict *only* if they can create a climate of warmth and trust in which these will be allowed to develop.

Logical Thinkers will achieve their world of understanding and logic *only* if they can accept that their feelings and the feelings of others (both tough and tender) are also facts and contribute importantly toward our ability to understand interpersonal situations (see Table 1).

These three, as described, are clearly pure types; the average person has some elements of each. What varies is emphasis or the most characteristic style. The three styles can be depicted as corners of an equilateral triangle:

*Group Norms*

There is one final issue that must be addressed with respect to group functioning — group norms. A norm in a group is like an individual habit. It is an unwritten, often implicit, rule which defines what attitudes and behaviors constitute being a "good" group member versus a "bad" group member.

All groups create norms as they develop and mature. In and of themselves, norms are neither good nor bad. The important point is whether or not the norms that do exist support the group's work or act to reduce effectiveness.

Let us examine an example. Many groups operate under the norm: "You argue rigorously with everyone's ideas and proposals . . . except the boss's!" In addition to the norm, the group also develops, often in very subtle ways, reward-and-punishment mechanisms to keep violators of the norm in line, e.g., the "Dutch uncle" talk after the meeting, which starts off: "Let me tell you something for your own benefit." Now, if the boss's ideas are always better than anyone else's, this norm probably saves the group time and energy. If this were not true it is not hard to see how the group's work can begin to suffer (both in terms of quality and individual commitment).

There is one instance in which a norm always had a bad effect, however. This is when the unspoken rule says, "In this group, no one ever dares to question or suggest we examine our norms." With respect to the maintenance behaviors discussed earlier, there is an absence of standard setting and testing and an implied punishment for anyone who engages in such behavior. Such a "Catch 22" norm is unlikely to facilitate an effectively functioning group.

| 1. Friendly Helper | 2. Tough Battler | 3. Logical Thinker |
|---|---|---|
| A world of mutual love, affection, tenderness, sympathy | A world of conflict, fight, power, assertiveness | A world of understanding, logic, systems, knowledge |

*Task Maintenance Behavior*

| | | |
|---|---|---|
| Harmonizing<br>Compromising<br>Gatekeeping by concern<br>Encouraging<br>Expressing warmth | Initiating<br>Coordinating<br>Pressing for results<br>Pressing for consensus<br>Exploring differences<br>Gatekeeping by command | Gathering information<br>Clarifying ideas and words<br>Systematizing<br>Procedures<br>Evaluating the logic of proposals |

*Constructs Used in Evaluating Others*

| | | |
|---|---|---|
| Who is warm and who is hostile?<br>Who helps and who hurts others? | Who is strong and who is weak?<br>Who is winning and who is losing? | Who is bright and who is stupid?<br>Who is accurate and who is inaccurate?<br>Who thinks clearly and who is fuzzy? |

*Methods of Influence*

| | | |
|---|---|---|
| Appeasing<br>Appealing to pity | Giving orders<br>Offering challenges<br>Threatening | Appealing to rules and regulations<br>Appealing to logic<br>Referring to "facts" and overwhelming knowledge |

*Personal Threats*

| | | |
|---|---|---|
| That s/he will not be loved<br>That s/he will be overwhelmed by feelings of hostility | That s/he will lose her/his ability to fight (power)<br>That s/he will become "soft" and "sentimental | That his/her world is not ordered<br>That s/he will be overwhelmed by love or hate |

## IV. PROCEDURE FOR GROUP MEETING

A. Group Dynamics Simulation Exercise

The purpose of the following exercise is to sharpen skills both in observing how a group goes about solving a task (diagnosing process) and in participating in the task. An effective group member is one who can function well at both of these levels—s/he is a *participant-observer*. This unit has four major elements:

1. One half of a group will be involved in a decision-making exercise (participants) while the other half (observers) attempts to develop a better understanding of the group process.
2. Observers will provide individual feedback to their participant partner.
3. Observers and participants switch roles.
4. All discuss the exercise.

*Step 1.* The entire class should form into pairs (plus one trio if necessary).

*Step 2.* One half of each pair will participate in the first round of the decision-making exercises. These people should seat themselves in a small circle. Their partners will be observers for the first round. Observers should seat themselves around the outside of the decision-making group so as to be able to observe their partners.

*Note:* If the class if very large, two separate fishbowls should be created.

*Step 3.* The inner group will have *30 minutes* to complete a given task, which will involve coming to a consensus decision (see Task A, page 243). Observers should view the group's process in general and their partner's behavior in particular using the Observer Rating Form on page 241. Observers should remain silent.

*Step 4.* Observers meet and give feedback to their participant partner using the observations recorded on the Observer Rating Form as a beginning. (Time: 10 minutes.)

*Groups should then switch positions and repeat steps 3 and 4 above except that the second decision-making group begins with task B, pages 245–246.*

B. Discussion of Group Dynamics Simulation (Time Allotted: 40–60 Minutes)

*Step 1.* (30 minutes) The discussion of this exercise is probably best conducted within two equal subgroups of the total class. Each subgroup should be made up of several of the originally formed pairs of participant–observers.

The following points should help to guide this discussion:

a. What task-oriented behaviors/maintenance-oriented behaviors seemed most frequently used? Least frequently used?
b. In what ways, if any, did the group's work suffer because certain task/maintenance functions were underutilized?
c. How did "friendly helpers," "tough battlers," and "logical thinkers" interact with and influence each other? What impact did these styles have on group functioning?
d. Tasks A and B were designed to be different along a dimension of potential personal involvement and value implications; e.g., task B often engages significant personal values.
   1. Did certain TOBs/MOBs/SOBs arise more frequently around task A vs. task B? With what consequence?
   2. What kinds of TOBs/MOBs are particularly critical in highly charged task situations? In more neutral situations?

e. The second group to move into the inner circle often exhibits some form of intergroup competition ("They never finished and/or did a poor job. Let's do better!") Did any such competition develop? If so, how did it influence the group's process?

*Step 2.* (10 minutes) This final discussion is still another live example of a group trying to accomplish a task. To what extent during the discussion have you been able to function as both a participant and an observer—i.e., to what extent has this group concerned itself with process issues that might have arisen as the group discussed the earlier exercise? Discuss your process over the last 20 minutes.

# OBSERVER RATING FORM

| Examples of:<br>Process Dimension/Category | Impact on Group Functioning |
|---|---|
| 1. Task-oriented behaviors | |
| 2. Maintenance-oriented behaviors | |
| 3. Self-oriented behaviors | |
| 4. Group norms observed | |
| 5. Communication patterns | |
| 6. Decision-making patterns | |

1.  The group should develop a consensus ranking of the following items in terms of their importance for improving the effectiveness of organizations. Place number 1 by the most important item, number 2 by the next most important item, and so on down to 10, which represents the least important consideration. Make your rankings in terms of organizations in general.

- Create conditions where employees can participate in making decisions that vitally affect them.
- Develop early retirement programs to weed out people in the older age categories who are nonproductive.
- Give craft, technical, or social skill training to improve skills at all levels.
- Expand personal contact between top management and the rest of the organization.
- Fill jobs on qualifications rather than by seniority.
- Improve incentive system for nonsupervisory personnel.
- Institute regular replacement hiring program.
- Discharge all poor performance personnel, including supervisors.
- Stress feedback in communication programs.
- Put key categories of employees on merit salary.

*Note:* If first decision-making group should finish the above before their time is up, they should begin same process with Task 2 below.

2.  The group should develop a consensus ranking of the following items in terms of their importance in selecting a middle manager, like department head, who is effective in making and carrying out decisions. Place number 1 by the most important item, number 2 by the next most important item, and so on down to 10, which represents the least important consideration.

- Able to grasp the structure of the organization quickly and to use it effectively.
- Able to give clear-cut instructions.
- Keeps all parties who are concerned with a decision fully informed on progress and final actions taken.
- Able to change his own conclusions when they prove to be wrong.
- Goes about decision making by developing a range of alternatives before coming to a final verdict.
- Able to grasp instructions and to act appropriately in terms of them.
- Capable of making fast decisions under time and other pressures.
- Able to delegate effectively.
- Capable of seeing appropriate relations among a variety of items.
- Able to resist shaping an opinion before all the facts are in.

## TASK B

Below you will find two situations described involving a difficult personal choice. The group should develop a consensus choice for situation 1. If the group should finish situation 1 before their 30 minutes have elapsed, they should move on to situation 2.

### Situation 1

Mr. A., a 45-year-old concert pianist with two children in high school, has recently been informed by his physician that he has a partially plugged artery (sclerosis) in his right arm. The condition causes continuous and severe pain, but he is able to carry on his career with no reduction in skill. The physician informs Mr. A that there is a new surgical operation, which, if successful, would completely relieve the condition. If the operation failed, his hand would be left useless, and it would be impossible for him to go on with his work as a pianist.

*Imagine that your group is Mr. A.* Listed below are several probabilities or odds that the operation will prove successful. *Please check the lowest probability that your group would consider acceptable for the operation to be performed.*

—— The chances are 0 in 10 that the operation will be a success (i.e., the operation is certain to be a failure).

—— The chances are 1 in 10 that the operation will be a success.

—— The chances are 2 in 10 that the operation will be a success.

—— The chances are 3 in 10 that the operation will be a success.

—— The chances are 4 in 10 that the operation will be a success.

—— The chances are 5 in 10 that the operation will be a success.

—— The chances are 6 in 10 that the operation will be a success.

—— The chances are 7 in 10 that the operation will be a success.

—— The chances are 8 in 10 that the operation will be a success.

—— The chances are 9 in 10 that the operation will be a success.

—— The chances are 10 in 10 that the operation will be a success (i.e., the operation is certain to be a success).

### Situation 2

Mr. and Mrs. H., a childless couple, have been attempting to have a child for a number of years. Mrs. H. is now pregnant, but a complication has arisen. The doctor has advised Mr. and Mrs. H. that if the pregnancy is allowed to progress, Mrs. H.'s life will be in danger. If further complications do develop, the doctor will not be able to save the child and may not be able to save Mrs. H. If the pregnancy is terminated at this time, it will be impossible for Mrs. H. to become pregnant again.

Imagine that your group is advising Mr. and Mrs. H. Listed below are several probabilities that *no* further complications will occur during Mrs. H.'s pregnancy. *Please check the lowest probability of the occurrence of no additional complications that your group would consider acceptable for Mr. and Mrs. H. to allow the pregnancy to progress.*

—— The chances are 0 in 10 that further complications *will not* arise (i.e., it is certain that further complications *will* arise).

—— The chances are 1 in 10 that further complications will *not* arise.

—— The chances are 2 in 10 that further complications will *not* arise.

—— The chances are 3 in 10 that further complications will *not* arise.

—— The chances are 4 in 10 that further complications will *not* arise.

—— The chances are 5 in 10 that further complications will *not* arise.

—— The chances are 6 in 10 that further complications will *not* arise.

—— The chances are 7 in 10 that further complications will *not* arise.

—— The chances are 8 in 10 that further complications will *not* arise.

—— The chances are 9 in 10 that further complications will *not* arise.

—— The chances are 10 in 10 that further complications will *not* arise (i.e., it is certain that further complications *will not* arise).

## V. SUMMARY

As society becomes more complex and we continue to make major advances in our technological capability, more and more of organizational life will revolve around a team or group structure. The "information explosion" will guarantee that no one person can expect to have all the facts necessary to make many decisions. The notion of a "temporary system" in which a group of people join for a short-term task and then disperse to form new and different task groups to tackle other problems will become more prevalent.[12] Groups play an important part in organizational life today, and every indication points toward increased importance in the future.

The distinction made in this exercise between task issues, maintenance issues, and self-oriented issues can be important in understanding how groups function. Most of us assume that if a group of people is called together to perform a task, nothing but the task is important or relevant. This assumption rests upon the belief that it is not only feasible but essential that we separate our emotional self (needs, wants, motives) from our intellectual, rational, problem-solving self. This is impossible. When people enter a group situation, they bring their total selves, the emotional as well as the intellectual. In fact, certain aspects of our emotional selves will become more salient because we are in a group situation. Attempts to bury, wish away, or ignore the interpersonal aspects of group interaction is much like sweeping dirt under the rug—sooner or later the pile gets big enough that someone will trip over it.

In some ways, the appointment of a chairperson or moderator reflects recognition of the fact that groups do not always "stay on the track." While this is often useful, there are two potential problems with this approach. First, seldom does the group spend any time discussing why they are "off the track." More often the chairman will say something like "We're getting off the main track, let's get back to it!" and that's all that happens. It is extremely important to realize that if people are having difficulty staying on the track, there are reasons for the behavior and simply saying "Let's get back to it" does nothing to eliminate the basic causes. Worse than that, this kind of behavior ("Let's quit wasting time and get to the task") may further accelerate the underlying reasons for lack of involvement and may make the situation worse.

Second, there is no inherent reason that only one person in a group should have the responsibility for worrying about how the group is progressing. Everyone can and should share this responsibility. To delegate this function or role to one individual is in some situations a highly inefficient utilization of resources. People can learn to be effective participant–observers at one and the same time. In such a group, *anyone* who feels something is not right can and should raise the issue for the total group to examine. Anyone who observes a need for a particular kind of task or maintenance behavior can help the group. In a well-functioning group (working on something other than a routine programmable task) an observer looking in from the outside might not be able to pick out the formal leadership. The "leadership function" could pass around according to the group's need at a particular point.

It is important, in other words, to distinguish between leaders as persons and leadership as a function. To provide a summary or gatekeeping when these are needed by the group is to engage in an important act of leadership. To see the need and fail to respond can be viewed as a failure to fulfill one's membership responsibilities as well. A group is in some ways just like a machine. In order for a machine to continue to produce a high-quality product, it must continually be maintained. The maintenance function in a group is equally important, for, again, people bring their whole selves to a group, not just that part of themselves having to do with the task.

It is often argued that "We haven't got the time to worry about people's feelings or to discuss how the group is working." Sometimes this is perfectly true, and under severe task pressure a different kind of process is necessary and legitimate. People can accept this, however, if they know from past

[12] M. B. Miles, "On Temporary Systems," in M. B. Miles, ed., *Innovation in Education* (New York: Teachers College, Columbia University Press, 1964), pp. 84-112. See also Warren G. Bennis and Philip E. Slater, *The Temporary Society* (New York: Harper & Row, Publishers, 1968).

experience that this situation is temporary. More often, however, lack of time is used as a defense mechanism to avoid the discussion completely. Furthermore, if a group really is under severe time pressure continually, some time ought to be spent examining the effectiveness of the group's planning procedures.

A group that ignores individual members' needs and its own process may well find that it meets several times to make the same set of decisions. The reason for this is that the effectiveness of many decisions is based on two factors[13] — logical soundness and the level of psychological commitment among the members to the decision made. These two dimensions are not independent; in fact, some people who are uncommitted (often because of process issues) may withhold, on a logical basis, information necessary to make the soundest decision. In any event, the best decision (on a task or logical level) forged at the expense of individual commitment is indeed not a very good decision at all.

Finally, what can be done to learn to use self-oriented emotional resources more appropriately? As a first step, it is important to accept our own feelings and to realize that everyone has both tender and tough emotions. Within American culture at least, businessmen (and males in general) are expected to be tough, hard, aggressive, and the like. Any sign of "tender emotions" (warmth, affection) is taken to be a sign of weakness and therefore unmasculine. But if we can accept the fact that feelings are a part of an individual's and therefore a group's reality, we can begin to explore ways of dealing with these realities rather than trying to clear them away. Given the opportunity to experiment with and get feedback on our emotional behavior (and a climate that supports such behavior), we can become more aware of when it is appropriate to be tough, tender, or neither.

The point here is that it is foolhardy to assume that simply because a group of people assemble to perform a task, they will somehow automatically know how to work together effectively.[14] A comparison between the behavior of a football team and the behavior of a management team highlights the essence of this paradox. The football team spends untold hours practicing teamwork in preparation for the 60 minutes each week that their performance as a team really counts. In contrast, most management teams do not spend 60 minutes per year practicing teamwork in spite of the fact that for 40 or more hours every week their behavior as a team really counts.

[13] This dichotomy of a decision's quality is analogous to issues raised during the discussion of the concept of psychological contract in the introduction to Chapter 1, "Organizational Socialization." In that case, the dichotomy was the decision to join versus the decision to participate. See also Chapter 9, "Leadership and Decision Making," for more detail on effective decision-making styles.

[14] One such process for learning how to work more effectively in groups is called broadly "laboratory training." For a full discussion of this and related educational techniques, see Edgar H. Schein and Warren G. Bennis, *Personal and Organizational Change Through Group Methods: The Laboratory Approach* (New York: John Wiley & Sons, Inc., 1965).

# VI. SELF-EVALUATION AND COMPLETING THE LEARNING LOOP

A. What questions do you now have as a result of your learning experiences from this unit? Jot these down below.

B. From these questions, what *key concepts* can you extrapolate for further learning? Write these concepts below.

C. How can you now go about finding answers to the questions you raised above? Below are some suggested ways to continue your learning process by beginning new learning loops:

1. Look up the key concepts from your questions above in the Yellow Pages of Learning Experiences at the back of the book. Find a few suggested readings or exercises to facilitate the learning of these key concepts.

2. If you don't find the key concepts in the Yellow Pages related specifically to your questions, perhaps there are other concepts listed in the index that might lead you to relevant learning resources at this time. Look for concepts similar to those you identified in B above.

3. In the event that you don't find the Yellow Pages directory useful for your present learning goals, discuss your questions with other students, faculty, or persons outside your learning environment. Discuss further learning possibilities with them.

# PART II

# LEADERSHIP AND MANAGEMENT

# chapter 9

## leadership and decision making

## I. OBJECTIVES

A.   To examine decision making in organizations as a social process.[1]

B.   To identify personal approaches to organizational decision making.

C.   To compare personal approaches with a formal model of organizational decision making.

D.   To practice using the formal model to analyze actual organizational decision situations.

## II. PREMEETING PREPARATION (TIME ALLOTTED: 30 MINUTES)

A.   Read the descriptions of decision-making alternatives for individual and group problems on the next page and then describe how you would handle each of the five decision-making cases that follow. Indicate whether the case describes an individual or group problem and which decision-making approach you would use.

B.   After completing A, read the Introduction and the Procedure for Group Meeting (pp. 267–273).

---

[1] This unit is based on the research of Victor Vroom and his colleagues. Cases are used with permission of the University of Pittsburgh Press (case 1, 3, 5 and the engineering case) and the American Institute for Decision Sciences (cases 2 and 4). Further information about training programs based on the model can be obtained from Kepner-Trego Associates, Inc.

# INDIVIDUAL PROBLEM

An individual problem (IP) involves a decision that will have potential effects on only one immediate subordinate. The problem is confined to that manager's area of responsibility.

## Decision-Making Alternatives For Individual Problems

AI    You solve the problem or make the decision yourself, using information available to you at that time.

AII    You obtain any necessary information from the subordinate, then decide on the solution to the problem yourself. You may or may not tell the subordinate what the probem is in getting the information from him. The role played by your subordinate in making the decision is clearly one of providing specific information that you request, rather than generating or evaluating alternative solutions.

CI    You share the problem with the relevant subordinate, getting his ideas and suggestions. Then you make the decision. This decision may or may not reflect your subordinate's influence.

GI    You share the problem with one of your subordinates, and together you analyze the problem and arrive at a mutually satisfactory solution in an atmosphere of free and open exchange of information and ideas. You both contribute to the resolution of the problem with the relative contribution of each being dependent on knowledge rather than formal authority.

DI    You delegate the problem to one of your subordinates, providing him with any relevant information that you possess, but giving him responsibility for solving the problem by himself. Any solution that the person reaches will receive your support.

# GROUP PROBLEM

In a group problem (GP), the decision adopted will have potential effects on all or some subgroup of immediate subordinates. The problem overlaps areas of at least some subordinates' responsibilities and/or expertise.

## Decision-Making Alternatives

AI    You solve the problem or make the decision yourself, using information available to you at that time.

AII    You obtain any necessary information from subordinates, then decide on the solution to the problem yourself. You may or may not tell subordinates what the problem is in getting the information from them. The role played by your subordinates in making the decision is clearly one of providing specific information that you request, rather than generating or evaluating solutions.

CI    You share the problem with the relevant subordinates individually, getting their ideas and suggestions without bringing them together as a group. Then *you* make the decision. This decision may or may not reflect your subordinates' influence.

CII    You share the problem with your subordinates in a group meeting. In this meeting you obtain their ideas and suggestions. Then, *you* make the decision, which may or may not reflect your subordinates' influence.

GII   You share the problem with your subordinates as a group. Together you generate and evaluate alternatives and attempt to reach agreement (consensus) on a solution. Your role is much like that of chairman, coordinating the discussion, keeping it focused on the problem, and making sure that the critical issues are discussed. You do not try to influence the group to adopt "your" solutions and are willing to accept and implement any solution that has the support of the entire group.

## CASE 1 – THE FINANCE CASE

You are the head of a staff unit reporting to the vice president of finance. He has asked you to provide a report on the firm's current portfolio to include recommendations for changes in the selection criteria currently employed. Doubts have been raised about the efficiency of the existing system in the current market conditions, and there is considerable dissatisfaction with prevailing rates of return.

You plan to write the report, but at the moment you are quite perplexed about the approach to take. Your own specialty is the bond market, and it is clear to you that detailed knowledge of the equity market, which you lack, would greatly enhance the value of the report. Fortunately, four members of your staff are specialists in different segments of the equity market. Together, they possess a vast amount of knowledge about the intricacies of investment. However, they seldom agree on the best way to achieve anything when it comes to investment philosophy and strategy.

You have six weeks before the report is due. You have already begun to familiarize yourself with the firm's current portfolio and have been provided by management with a specific set of constraints that any portfolio must satisfy. Your immediate problem is to come up with some alternatives to the firm's present practices and select the most promising for detailed analysis in your report.

How would you go about doing this?
Is it an individual or a group problem?
What decision-making method would you use?
(Circle the box that indicates the approach you would use in this case.)

| | | | | | |
|---|---|---|---|---|---|
| Individual | A1 | A11 | C1 | G1 | D1 |
| Group | A1 | A11 | C1 | C11 | G11 |

You are regional manager of an international management consulting company. You have a staff of six consultants reporting to you, each of whom enjoys a considerable amount of autonomy with clients in the field.

Yesterday you received a complaint from one of your major clients to the effect that the consultant whom you assigned to work on the contract with them was not doing his job effectively. They were not very explicit as to the nature of the problem, but it was clear that they were dissatisfied and that something would have to be done if you were to restore the client's faith in your company.

The consultant assigned to work on that contract has been with the company for six years. He is a systems analyst and is one of the best in that profession. For the first four or five years his performance was superb, and he was a model for the more junior consultants. However, recently he has seemed to have a "chip on his shoulder," and his previous identification with the company and its objectives has been replaced with indifference. His negative attitude has been noticed by other consultants, as well as by clients. This is not the first such complaint that you have had from a client this year about his performance. A previous client even reported to you that the consultant reported to work several times obviously suffering from a hangover and that he had been seen around town in the company of "fast" women.

It is important to get to the root of this problem quickly if that client is to be retained. The consultant obviously has the skill necessary to work with the clients effectively. If only he were willing to use it!

Is it an individual or a group problem?
How would you as regional manager deal with this problem?
(Circle the box that indicates the approach you would use in this case.)

| | | | | | |
|---|---|---|---|---|---|
| Individual | A1 | A11 | C1 | G1 | D1 |
| Group | A1 | A11 | C1 | C11 | G11 |

## CASE 3 — THE UNIVERSAL DATA SYSTEM

You are on the division manager's staff and work on a wide variety of problems of both an administrative and a technical nature. You have been given the assignment of developing a universal method to be used in each of the five plants in the division for manually reading equipment registers, recording the readings, and transmitting the scorings to a centralized information system. All plants are located in a relatively small geographical region.

Until now there has been a high error rate in the reading and/or transmittal of the data. Some locations have considerably higher error rates than others, and the methods used to record and transmit the data vary between plants. It is probable, therefore, that part of the error variance is a function of specific local conditions rather than anything else, and this will complicate the establishment of any system common to all plants. You have the information on error rates but no information on the local practices that generate these errors or on the local conditions that necessitate the different practices.

Everyone would benefit from an improvement in the quality of the data as it is used in a number of important decisions. Your contacts with the plants are through the quality control supervisors, who are responsible for collecting the data. They are a conscientious group committed to doing their jobs well but are highly sensitive to interference on the part of higher management in their own operations. Any solution that does not receive the active support of the various plant supervisors is unlikely to reduce the error rate significantly.

Is it an individual or a group problem?
How would you deal with this problem?
(Circle the box that indicates the approach you would use in this case.)

| | | | | | |
|---|---|---|---|---|---|
| Individual | A1 | A11 | C1 | G1 | D1 |
| Group | A1 | A11 | C1 | C11 | G11 |

# CASE 4 — THE PHARMACEUTICAL COMPANY

You are executive vice president for a small pharmaceutical manufacturer. You have the opportunity to bid on a contract for the Defense Department pertaining to biological warfare. The contract is outside the mainstream of your business; however, it could make economic sense, since you do have unused capacity in one of your plants, and the manufacturing processes are not dissimilar.

You have written the document to accompany the bid and now have the problem of determining the dollar value of the quotation which you think will win the job for your company. If the bid is too high, you will undoubtedly lose to one of your competitors; if it is too low, you would stand to lose money on the program.

There are many factors to be considered in making this decision, including the cost of the new raw materials and the additional administrative burden of relationships with a new client, not to speak of factors that are likely to influence the bids of your competitors, such as how much they *need* this particular contract. You have been busy assembling the necessary data to make this decision, but there remain several "unknowns," one of which involves the manager of the plant in which the new products will be manufactured. Of all your subordinates, only he is in the position to estimate the costs of adapting the present equipment to its new purpose, and his cooperation and support will be necessary in ensuring that the specifications of the contract will be met. However, in an initial discussion with him when you first learned of the possibility of the contract, he seemed adamantly opposed to the idea. His previous experience has not particularly equipped him with the ability to evaluate projects like this one, so you were not overly influenced by his opinions. From the nature of his arguments, you inferred that his opposition was ideological rather than economic. You recall that he was actively involved in a local "peace organization" and was one of the most vocal opponents in the company to the war in Vietnam.

Is it an individual or a group problem?
How will you go about determining the amount of the bid?
(Circle the box that indicates the approach you would use in this case.)

| | | | | | |
|---|---|---|---|---|---|
| Individual | A1 | A11 | C1 | G1 | D1 |
| Group | A1 | A11 | C1 | C11 | G11 |

**CASE 5 — THE OIL PIPELINE**

You are general foreman in charge of a large gang laying an oil pipeline. It is now necessary to estimate your expected rate of progress in order to schedule material deliveries to the next field site.

You know the nature of the terrain you will be traveling and have in your records the historical data needed to compute the mean and variance in the rate of speed over that type of terrain. Given these two variables it is a simple matter to calculate the earliest and latest times at which materials and support facilities will be needed at the next site. It is important that your estimate be reasonably accurate. Underestimates result in idle foremen and workers, and an overestimate results in tying up materials for a period of time before they are to be used.

Progress has been good, and your five foremen and other members of the gang stand to receive substantial bonuses if the project is completed ahead of schedule.

Is it an individual or a group problem?
How would you go about scheduling material deliveries?
(Circle the box that indicates the approach you would use in this case.)

| | | | | | |
|---|---|---|---|---|---|
| Individual | A1 | A11 | C1 | G1 | D1 |
| Group | A1 | A11 | C1 | C11 | G11 |

## III. INTRODUCTION

To a manager, executive, or administrator, no other job function encapsulates the frustrations and joys of leadership more dramatically than decision making. It is in making decisions that managers most acutely feel the responsibilities, the power, and the vulnerability of their jobs. This central focus of decision making in the experience of leadership is illustrated in the autobiographies of political leaders, who characteristically organize their life stories around major decision points they faced, the dilemmas and pressures they experienced, and how in the end the "buck" stopped on their desks, confronting them with lonely moments of decision. Harry Truman described his decision to fire General MacArthur and his decision to drop the atomic bomb in this way. Richard Nixon's "six crises" were phrased as major decision points that called for lonely soul searching and personal commitment to the right course of action. Although most of us in our life and work face decisions of less than presidential magnitude, nonetheless from time to time we share with them the existential loneliness of making an important decision.

Yet there are two things wrong with using this admittedly powerful subjective experience of decision making as the focus for analyzing and improving the decision-making process in organizations. First, this experience would suggest that decisions can be thought of as independent solitary events relatively unconnected to other decisions and the process that brought the decision point to a head. If there is anything to be learned from the Bay of Pigs fiasco or the Vietnam experience, it is that the organizational process of problem identification, information sharing, and problem solving, if mishandled, can undo the work of the finest, most logical, and experienced individual decision maker.

Second, the experience suggests that decision making is an individual process and that therefore the skills of logical analysis and problem solving (described in the Learning and Problem-Solving chapter) are sufficient to produce high-quality decisions. However, decision making in organizations is also a social process. Organizational functioning requires an unending stream of decisions great and small. These decisions are identified, made, and communicated by individuals throughout the organization. As a manager you depend on the decisions of others and the information they bring you. You also delegate decisions and share information with them. The sense that any decision is made alone in an organization is an illusion. There are those who feel that Richard Nixon's greatest failure was falling prey to this illusion. Those who knew him say that he was a brilliant analyst and individual problem solver. Yet he was done in by his inability to develop an effective social process of decision making that involved others in appropriate ways.

The focus of this unit is on managing the process of decision making, as opposed to the problem-solving skills of making a specific decision. It further focuses on the social aspects of that process and the alternative ways of making decisions with other people: the costs and benefits and the appropriate application of these decision-making methods in different situations.

To understand the decision-making *process*, we must first examine the nature of effective organizational decisions and the components of decision effectiveness. The effectiveness of a decision can be judged in terms of three outcomes:

1. The quality or rationality of the decision.
2. The acceptance or commitment on the part of subordinates to execute the decision effectively.
3. The amount of time required to make the decision.

The extent to which these three criteria of quality, acceptance, and efficiency are critical varies from one decision to another. For some decisions, particularly those you will implement yourself, acceptance is not critical but high quality may be absolutely essential, as for example in decisions about how to program the computer for inventory control. Other decisions have very little quality requirement but require great acceptance. The decision about how the secretarial pool will cover the phones at lunch time is an example of this type of decision. The solution devised here has little in the way of a logical requirement, but it must be acceptable to the people involved. Efficiency is usually an important consideration in everything we do in organizations, but other objectives, such as developing subordinates or learning, sometimes take priority.

It is therefore important to be able to diagnose decision situations in order to determine the quality, acceptance, and efficiency requirements and the method of decision making that will maximize these requirements. No single decision-making method or management style is appropriate for all jobs or even all decisions in a single job. For some situations the authoritative decision is best, for others the consultation style, and still others require a participative approach.

Victor Vroom and his associates[2] have developed a formal model that helps us to analyze specific decision situations and to determine the decision-making approach that is likely to be most effective. The model is constructed in the form of a decision tree based on ten rules derived from research on problem solving and decision making.[3] It poses eight questions for managers to ask about a decision:

A. Is there a quality requirement such that one solution is likely to be more rational than another?

B. Do I have sufficient information to make a high-quality decision?

C. Is the problem structured?

D. Is acceptance of decision by subordinates critical to effective implementation?

E. If I were to make the decision by myself, is it reasonably certain that it would be accepted by my subordinates?

F. Do subordinates share the organizational goals to be attained in solving this problem?

G. Is conflict among subordinates likely in preferred solutions? (This question is irrelevant to individual problems.)

H. Do subordinates have sufficient information to make a high-quality decision?

By answering these questions sequentially and tracing the answers through the model's decision tree (see Figure 9–1) the manager is led to a set of effective decision alternatives for the problem. There are 18 effective decision sets, one at the end of each branch of the decision tree. These are listed below the decision tree in Figure 9–1. The decision-making methods listed in the effective decision sets are those described at the beginning of the chapter. For group problems these are: A1, A11, C1, C11, and G11. For individual problems these are: A1, D1, A11, C1, and G1. The method listed first in a set indicates the approach that minimizes man-hours, i.e., is most efficient given quality and acceptance constraints. The method listed last is the approach that maximizes participation, given quality and acceptance constraints. Thus, the decision tree eliminates those decision-making methods that would jeopardize quality and acceptance requirements of a given problem. The manager can then choose from the methods remaining in the effective decision set depending on whether he aims to maximize efficiency or participation.

To summarize and understand how the model works, let us analyze an actual case problem using Vroom's model.

You are supervising the work of 12 engineers. Their formal training and work experience are very similar, permitting you to use them interchangeably on projects. Yesterday your

[2] Victor H. Vroom and P. Yetton, *Leadership and Decision Making* (Pittsburgh, Pa.: University of Pittsburgh Press, 1973).
[3] The details of these rules are spelled out in Victor H. Vroom and Arthur G. Jago, "Decision Making as a Social Process: Normative and Descriptive Models of Leader Behavior," *Decision Sciences*, Vol. 5 (1974). *Readings.*

A. Is there a quality requirement such that one solution is likely to be more rational than another?
B. Do I have sufficient info to make a high quality decision?
C. Is the problem structured?
D. Is acceptance of decision by subordinates critical to effective implementation?
E. If I were to make the decision by myself, is it reasonably certain that it would be accepted by my subordinates?
F. Do subordinates share the organizational goals to be attained in solving this problem?
G. Is conflict among subordinates likely in preferred solutions? (This question is irrelevant to individual problems.)
H. Do subordinates have sufficient info to make a high quality decision?

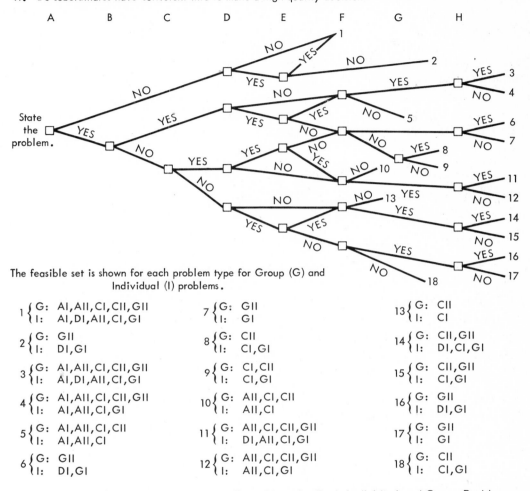

The feasible set is shown for each problem type for Group (G) and Individual (I) problems.

1 { G: AI,AII,CI,CII,GII
    I: AI,DI,AII,CI,GI

2 { G: GII
    I: DI,GI

3 { G: AI,AII,CI,CII,GII
    I: AI,DI,AII,CI,GI

4 { G: AI,AII,CI,CII,GII
    I: AI,AII,CI,GI

5 { G: AI,AII,CI,CII
    I: AI,AII,CI

6 { G: GII
    I: DI,GI

7 { G: GII
    I: GI

8 { G: CII
    I: CI,GI

9 { G: CI,CII
    I: CI,GI

10 { G: AII,CI,CII
     I: AII,CI

11 { G: AII,CI,CII,GII
     I: DI,AII,CI,GI

12 { G: AII,CI,CII,GII
     I: AII,CI,GI

13 { G: CII
     I: CI

14 { G: CII,GII
     I: DI,CI,GI

15 { G: CII,GII
     I: CI,GI

16 { G: GII
     I: DI,GI

17 { G: GII
     I: GI

18 { G: CII
     I: CI,GI

**Figure 9-1** Decision-Process Flow Chart for Both Individual and Group Problems

*Source:* Victor H. Vroom and Arthur G. Jago, "Decision Making as a Social Process: Normative and Descriptive Models of Leader Behavior," *Decision Sciences,* Vol. 5 (1974); by permission of the American Institute for Decision Sciences.

manager informed you that a request had been received from an overseas affiliate for four engineers to go abroad on extended loan for a period of six to eight months. For a number of reasons, he argued and you agreed that this request should be met from your group.

All your engineers are capable of handling this assignment, and from the standpoint of present and future projects there is no particular reason why any one should be retained over any other. The problem is somewhat complicated by the fact that the overseas assignment is in what is generally regarded in the company as an undesirable location.

First, we can see that this is a group problem, since it potentially affects at least a subgroup of subordinates. Then by answering the eight diagnostic questions and tracing them through the decision tree, we get:

- A (Quality) = No, the engineers have equal experience, are interchangeable, and all are capable of handling the assignment.
- D (Acceptance) = Yes, performance would suffer in such a job if the person were not committed.
- E (Probability of acceptance of leader decision) = No, the leader probably doesn't know individual circumstances and preferences. His decision is likely to be seen as arbitrary.

This leads then to feasible set 2, which has only one feasible decision method for this group problem — GII. Thus, the model recommends a group consensus decision in deciding which engineers should go to the field assignment.

## IV. PROCEDURE FOR GROUP MEETING

The purpose of the group exercise is to compare your individual approaches to the case problems in the premeeting preparation to the recommendations proposed by Vroom's model for these cases and to identify and discuss reasons for differences between what the model recommends and what you would do.

*Step 1.* The group should divide into subgroups of five or six people and record their answers to the five cases on the blackboard or flip chart so that all members can view one another's approach to the cases. The Case Analysis Record Form on page 271 provides a format for recording the data.

*Step 2.* The group should reread the introduction to the unit, with particular emphasis on Vroom's model and clarify with one another the procedure for using the model to analyze a case using the sample case in the introduction as a guide.

(Time for steps 1 and 2 = 30 minutes)

*Step 3.* The group should then analyze each of the five problems using Vroom's model and record their conclusion on the Model Recommendation line of the Case Analysis Record Form. Vroom's answers to the five cases are listed on page 466.

(Time for step 3 = 30 minutes)

## CASE ANALYSIS RECORD FORM

| Participant Names | Case 1 | Case 2 | Case 3 | Case 4 | Case 5 |
|---|---|---|---|---|---|
| | | | | | |
| | | | | | |
| | | | | | |
| | | | | | |
| | | | | | |
| | | | | | |
| | | | | | |
| | | | | | |
| Vroom Model Recommendation | | | | | |

*Step 4.* Comparison of individual responses and model recommendations. The group should compare the solutions provided by its members to the five cases with those recommended by the Vroom model. They should prepare a list on a flip chart or blackboard of reasons why a given group member differed from the model recommendation.

(Time for step 4 = 30 minutes)

*Step 5.* *Total group discussion.* The total group should reconvene, read the unit Summary, and discuss the lists created in step D by each of the subgroups.

(Time for step 5 = 30 minutes)

## V. SUMMARY

Research comparing the Vroom model with the actual behavior of managers has shown that there is a general correspondence between the model recommendations for a specific situation and a manager's behavior in that situation. Vroom and Jago report: "In approximately two-thirds of the problems, nevertheless, the behavior which the manager reported was within the feasible set of methods prescribed for that problem, and in about 40 percent of the cases it corresponded exactly to the minimum man-hours solution."[4] Thus, managers seem to be using an intuitive notion something like the Vroom model to manage the decision-making process in their organizations. In some ways, however, the *differences* between model recommendations and managerial behavior are more interesting, in that they shed light on the assumptions on which the model is based and on the particularly difficult issues in managing the decision-making process.

For example, when we have asked managers how they would solve the engineering department case described in the introduction to this unit, many of them chose an AI or AII decision. Most resisted strongly the idea of bringing the group together for decision making either in the CII or GII modes. The Vroom model GII solution brought cries of "No way!" or "It will never work!" Further discussion of differences between individual styles and the Vroom GII decision recommendations raised some interesting comments:

- "The group wouldn't be able to deal with a difficult problem like this."
- "I wouldn't know how to control the conflict this situation creates if it were made a group decision."
- "In most groups the members would expect the manager to make this decision and they would have to live with it."

These comments bring out some of the assumptions underlying Vroom's model and hence define some of the problems in its application. These assumptions are:

1. Managers are equally skilled in using the different decision-making alternatives.
2. Groups are equally skilled in their adaptation to these decision-making alternatives.
3. Organizational history and the resulting organizational climate have no impact on a single decision analyzed by the model.

What the model does is analyze a specific decision dispassionately in terms of its quality, acceptance, and efficiency requirements without regard to the preceding assumptions about managerial and

[4] Vroom and Jago, "Decision Making as a Social Process," p. 754.

group skill or organization climate. Yet in any specific situation, these issues must be considered to ensure that decisions are effective.

In conclusion, we suggest the following considerations in applying the Vroom model to actual managerial situations:

1. Intuitive managerial decision-making models are more simplified than the Vroom model. They do not account for some of the interactions among decision rules portrayed in Figure 9–1. This is supported by Vroom and Jago's research.

2. Managers tend to underemphasize the importance of acceptance and commitment components of decision effectiveness. This is also supported by Vroom and Jago's research.

3. Managers tend to use decision-making procedures they are skilled at and avoid procedures they feel uncomfortable with. For many this means avoiding the more difficult group decision-making procedures.

4. Organization history and climate will affect the decision-making method chosen, independent of the logical dictates of the situation. Organization climate affects decision making in several ways:

   a. Group members will adjust to norms about "the way things are decided around here" and may have little experience or skill in other methods, such as group consensus.

   b. Managers may use a particular decision-making method because their boss uses it and be constrained in their flexibility of decision making by the style dictated from above. If your boss is AI with you, you have nothing to be GII with your subordinates about.

   c. Answers to the eight diagnostic questions may be influenced inaccurately by organizational norms. For example, in the military, where obeying orders is a pivotal norm, managers may tend to believe wrongly that their authoritative decision will be accepted (question E).

These considerations suggest that the Vroom model is useful in determining how the decision-making process *should* be conducted, but the application of this ideal requires management development for skills in all of the decision-making methods, team development in the various forms of group decision making, and organizational development to create norms that value quality, acceptance, and efficiency as the primary criteria for effective decision making.

## VI. SELF-EVALUATION AND COMPLETING THE LEARNING LOOP

A. What questions do you now have as a result of your learning experiences from this unit? Jot these down below.

B. From these questions, what *key concepts* can you extrapolate for further learning? Write these concepts below.

C. How can you now go about finding answers to the questions you raised above? Below are some suggested ways to continue your learning process by beginning new learning loops:

1. Look up the key concepts from your questions above in the Yellow Pages of Learning Experiences at the back of the book. Find a few suggested readings or exercises to facilitate the learning of these key concepts.

2. If you don't find the key concepts in the Yellow Pages related specifically to your questions, perhaps there are other concepts listed in the index that might lead you to relevant learning resources at this time. Look for concepts similar to those you identified in B above.

3. In the event that you don't find the Yellow Pages directory useful for your present learning goals, discuss your questions with other students, faculty, or persons outside your learning environment. Discuss further learning possibilities with them.

# chapter 10

## leadership: supervision and employee development

*Photo by Sybil Shelton*

## I. OBJECTIVES

    A.   To increase understanding of leadership as a helping relationship.

    B.   To practice giving help.

    C.   To practice receiving help.

## II. PREMEETING PREPARATION

    A.   Read the Introduction.

    B.   Gather material. Each four-person group in the Tower Building Game will require the following materials:

        1. Two blindfolds.

        2. Approximately 30–40 toy building blocks. (If toy blocks are not available, sugar cubes may be used.)

## III. INTRODUCTION

There is an inherent mutuality in the leadership transaction which is clearly highlighted in the following anecdote about a production manager:

A new production manager decided it was important to establish himself as "boss" immediately. Upon arriving on the job, he walked out onto the shop floor and called over to the union steward. In "no uncertain terms," he communicated to the union steward (who was also his assistant) that he, the manager, was in charge of this department. He expected to have things done his way.

The union steward listened carefully, turned to the men on the shop floor, and gave a nonverbal signal with his hands. Work immediately stopped and the room became silent. He then turned to the manager, with a slight smile on his face, and said, "Okay, boss, it's *all* yours. Let's see you run this department!"

This naive production manager clearly did not realize that superiors and subordinates are dependent upon one another. While he assumed that his subordinates needed him — after all, he was their boss — he found out dramatically that he needed them as well. Without their acceptance of his power, he, in fact, had little power at all. As was pointed out earlier, without followership there is no leadership. Subordinates *always* have the choice of accepting or not accepting someone's attempt to provide leadership.

This situation of mutual dependence adds one further element to the already complex demands of the leadership transaction. In addition to the need to be personally flexible and adaptive, the effective leader must also be skilled as a helper and consultant. It is only with a recognition that the roles of leader and helper are substantially overlapping that managers will be able to help their subordinates help them (the managers) to be more effective.

The leadership role of helper and consultant, while an element of managerial behavior on a day-to-day basis, is perhaps most clear in two specific situations, performance appraisal and goal setting. Let us examine the performance-appraisal situation first.

While the specific mechanics of implementation will vary across organizations, the "ideal" performance-appraisal system is designed to achieve four basic objectives:

1. Provide feedback to subordinates to facilitate their ability to achieve organizational (and personal) goals.
2. Provide management with data to make salary and promotional decisions.
3. Identify improvement areas to facilitate employee career development.
4. Motivate employees to be more effective workers.

Depending on how this process gets implemented, managers often find themselves in a role conflict. On the one hand, they are asked to be helper/coaches in the feedback process, while on the other hand they serve as judges — linking performance assessment to salary and promotion decisions. Some research done in the performance-appraisal process points strongly to the need to separate these roles.[1]

With respect to goal setting, many organizations have adopted a process called *management by objectives* (MBO).[2] Again, while the specifics may vary, the fundamental steps of MBO are basically three in number:

[1] J. R. P. French, Jr., E. Kay, and H. H. Myer, "Split Roles in Performance Appraisal," *Harvard Business Review*, 43, No. 1 (January–February 1965).

[2] (a) Henry L. Tosi, Carroll Tosi, Jr., and J. Stephen, "Some Factors Affecting the Success of Management by Objectives," *Journal of Management Studies*, Vol. 7 (May 1970). (b) Steven Kerr, "Overcoming the Dysfunctions of MBO," *Management by Objectives*, Vol. 5, No. 1 (1976). *Readings.*

1.  Superior and subordinate set mutually acceptable performance goals for the subordinate for some time period.

2.  Periodic review sessions are held to measure progress against objectives with the supervisor providing feedback and counseling.

3.  The extent of goal attainment is used as a major input into promotion and salary decisions.

Here, again, the supervisor is put into the difficult position of being both helper and evaluator. While certain structural changes can help to alleviate this dilemma, the conflict is built into the very fiber of the leadership situation. The formal power to reward and punish cannot be wished away. Nor can the manager's responsibility to help subordinates grow and develop.

The inevitability of this dilemma means that effective managers need to understand the dynamics of the helping relationship. In the following section, a model of the helping relationship will be described. While most of the research on this issue has come from psychotherapy and counseling, the points have clear relevance and application to the dilemmas of supervision and employee development.

### The Helping Relationship: A Generic Model

The way to an effective helping relationship is fraught with many psychological difficulties that can either sidetrack or destroy the relationship. The process of sharing wealth, knowledge, or skill with one who happens to have less of these valuable commodities is far from being a simple exchange, easily accomplished.[3] Carl Rogers, in his classic article, "The Characteristics of a Helping Relationship," defines a helping relationship as one "in which at least one of the parties has the intent of promoting the growth, development, maturity, improved functioning, improved coping with life of the other."[4] This definition would include parent and child, teacher and students, manager and subordinates, therapist and patient, consultant and client, and many other less formally defined relationships.

Figure 10–1 depicts a model of the helping relationship that will serve as a focus for this class session. The model emphasizes five key elements in the helping relationship: (1) the task or problem around which the helping relationship develops; (2) the helpers with their motives (achievement motivation, power motivation, and affiliation motivation and self-image); (3) the receivers of help with their motives and self-image; (4) the environment and psychological climate in which the helping activities occur; and (5) the information feedback that occurs during the helping process.

### A. The Task

The tasks around which helping relationships develop are widely varied — they range from tying a shoe to changing attitudes about birth control to conducting a performance-appraisal review session to improving the effectiveness of an organization. It is possible to classify all tasks on a single dimension, namely, the extent to which it is required that the receiver of help be capable of accomplishing the task independently when the helper is no longer present. At one end of this dimension are tasks defined as assistance; situations in which there is no emphasis on the receiver's independent task performance. Giving a vagrant money for a cup of coffee is a good example of this end of the continuum. Many welfare and foreign-aid programs are close to this end of the dimension. The emphasis is on the solution of an immediate problem, with no provision for handling recurrences of that problem or similar problems. This type of assistance, aimed only at symptom relief, is likely to induce a depen-

---

[3] See G. C. Homans, *Social Behavior: Its Elementary Forms* (New York: Harcourt Brace Jovanovich, Inc., 1961), for a discussion of two very relevant concepts, exchange and reciprocity.
[4] Carl C. Rogers, *On Becoming a Person* (Boston: Houghton Mifflin Company, 1961), pp. 34–40.

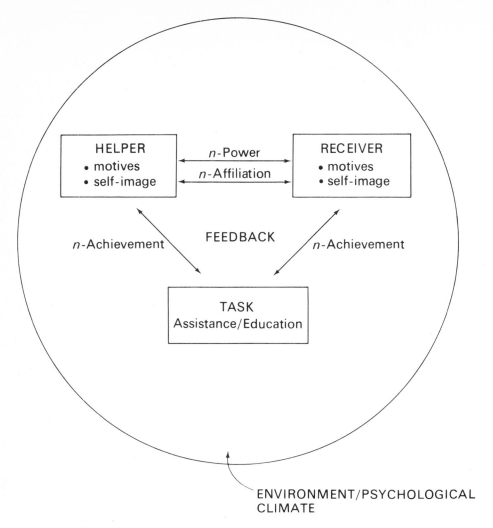

**Figure 10-1**　A Model for Analysis of the Helping Relationship

dency on the helper,[5] making termination of the helping interaction difficult. When the interaction has been concluded, the receiver may blame the helper for inadequate help if s/he cannot replicate a successful result.

At the other end of the continuum is education. Here the emphasis is on increasing the receivers' ecological wisdom — i.e., their ability to solve problems that are similar to the present one by developing their ability to make use of the resources of their natural environment. The helper avoids using the special knowledge, skills, or other resources she may command to relieve the receiver's immediate need, but instead works with persons in their frame of reference, to increase their problem-solving ability.

While the educational approach often holds the greatest potential for the receiver's long-term benefit, it can cause great frustration to a person with strong needs for symptom relief. In addition, the educational approach will frequently be seen by receivers as an intrusion on their privacy and an escalation of their problem. At the international level, for example, India was quite willing to receive assistance in the form of surplus food, but grew resentful at U.S. insistence that such assistance be coupled with an educational program to solve their basic problems of food production.

[5] Much of the present reactions of ghetto residents and the poor to welfare programs can be understood in these terms — a sense of dependency often leads to hostile responses.

## B. The Helper and Receiver of Help

The personal characteristics of the helper and receiver of help are major factors influencing the process and outcome of the helping relationship. Two types of characteristics are particularly important — the motives and self-image of helper and receiver. At least three motives seem necessary in understanding the dynamics of the helping relationship[6] — power motivation (n-Power), affiliation motivation (n-Affiliation), and achievement motivation (n-Achievement). These motives are important because they determine how the helper and receiver will orient themselves to one another and to their task.

The helper's and the receiver's power motivation determine how much they will be concerned with influencing and controlling one another. By asking for and/or receiving help offered, the receivers place themselves in a dependent position, where they often feel weaker and more vulnerable to the source of help. The helper, at the same time, must deal with tendencies to feel superior, thereby letting the satisfactions of power and control overshadow the sometimes elusive goal of acting in the receiver's best interest. If the helper and receiver are unable to resolve power struggles and bring about a situation of power equalization, the relationship can degenerate into rebellion and passivity by the receiver or rejection by the helper ("She doesn't appreciate what I am trying to do for her"). One empirical example of the detrimental effects of a helper's overconcern with power can be seen in Prakash's[7] study of effective and ineffective organization change agents. He found that ineffective change agents were more concerned with their personal goals and with their political position within the organization than were the effective change agents who were more concerned about task accomplishment.

The helper's and receiver's affiliation motivation determines how much they will be concerned with the factors of intimacy and understanding. To be helpful, the helper must know his/her receivers and understand how they perceive their problem. The intimacy required for effective understanding is difficult to achieve in situations where the helpers have impossible demands on their time, even though a lack of intimacy can leave the helper and receiver in two different worlds, speaking two different languages. Too great a concern with affiliation by the helper and the receiver, on the other hand, can produce pressure toward conformity and mutual sympathy, which may cause the helper to lose perspective of the receiver's problem and the receiver to lose respect for the helper's expertise.

The achievement motivation of the helper and receiver of help influences how concerned they will be about accomplishing their task or solving their problem. A major question here is: How is the goal of helping relationship defined? Does the helper decide what is good for the receiver or does the receiver retain the power to decide what help he wants? In the first case, the receiver is likely to have little motivation to accomplish the helper's task; and in the second, the helper's motivation is likely to be reduced. Only when the interpersonal issues of influence and intimacy have been resolved does it appear possible that the helper and receiver can agree on a goal to which they are mutually committed. Even if this is accomplished, a problem still remains of what are often strong desires to achieve the goal of the helping relationship. Help is often so late in coming that both helper and receiver feel a compulsion to accomplish *something*. The result is usually assistance programs designed to eliminate the receiver's immediate desperation rather than programs of education designed to help the receivers diagnose the causes of the problem and learn to solve the problem themselves.

There is an interaction among motives in any helping relationship. It is possible for the helper and receiver to be so highly power motivated that they become preoccupied with controlling one another at the expense of understanding one another and/or accomplishing their task. Similarly, as we have suggested, high achievement motivation can cause the helper and receiver to orient themselves to

---

[6] These motives have been treated in detail in three other chapters dealing with motivation. Motives other than these three, for example, security, can also influence the helping relationship.

[7] S. Prakash, "Some Characteristics of an Effective Organization Development Agent" (unpublished Master's thesis, Sloan School of Management, Massachusetts Institute of Technology, 1968).

accomplishing the task without attending to the interpersonal processes of influence and understanding necessary if the receivers of help are to learn to solve the problem on their own. In a case like this, the offer of "Here, let me help you" by the helper is often his cue to push the receiver aside and do the task himself, leaving the receiver in an unresolved state of ignorance about how to solve the problem. And finally, high affiliation motivation can lead to concerns about intimacy and understanding that preclude attempts to influence others and accomplish tasks.

The implication of this analysis for helping relationships is that moderate levels of achievement, affiliation, and power motivation in the helper and receiver are optimal for effective help to take place.[8] The dynamics of the helping relationship are such that influence, intimacy and understanding, and a concern for task accomplishment are all necessary for effective help to take place; yet excess concern in any one area can lead to the deterioration of an effective helping relationship.

The self-image and attitudes of the helper and receiver are also important defining variables in a helping relationship. Receivers must see themselves as capable of improvement and willing to receive help. If this is not so, a major portion of helping activity must center on building self-confidence and optimism before learning can take place. Helpers, on the other hand, must see themselves as capable of helping and yet, at the same time, must not feel that they are the "know-it-all" expert. This latter point is related to the issues of influence and intimacy discussed earlier. The helper must be willing to influence and at the same time have empathy with the feelings of the person being helped.

## C. The Environment and Psychological Climate

It is a truism in contemporary social psychology that behavior is a function of both the person and the environment. While one could imagine many environmental variables that could influence the process of helping — such as comfort of surroundings, freedom from distraction, and so on — we have limited ourselves for the present time to a consideration of those environmental factors that are related to influence, intimacy and understanding, and task accomplishment. Atkinson and Feather have argued that the tendency (T) to act in these three ways can be predicted by the strength of the individual's motivation (M) for power, affiliation, and achievement; times the individual's perceived probability (P) that action in terms of one or more of these motives will be rewarded; times the incentive value (I) of power, affiliation, and achievement rewards he expects to get. Thus, the individuals act to maximize their satisfaction following the formula $T = M \times P \times I$ for three motives: power, affiliation, and achievement. While M refers to the individual's motivation, P and I refer to the individual's perception of the environment.[9]

This analysis has important implications for predictions about effective helping; for if the environment tends to reward one motive disproportionately, it can alter the behavior of an otherwise moderately motivated helper and receiver. One example of this occurs in the Peace Corps, where volunteers who might otherwise establish very effective relationships with host-country nationals become bogged down in issues of power and control because the host-country people (and sometimes the volunteers themselves) perceive the Peace Corps to be a political agent of U.S. foreign policy.

## D. Feedback

The last element of the model is the information feedback that occurs during the helping process. Two aspects of information feedback are important here. First, there is the source that controls

[8] See David A. Kolb and Richard Boyatzis, "On the Dynamics of the Helping Relationship" (Working Paper 372-69, Sloan School of Management, Massachusetts Institute of Technology, 1969), for empirical validation of this hypothesis. *Readings.*

[9] (a) J. Atkinson, *An Introduction to Motivation* (Princeton, N.J.: D. Van Nostrand Co., Inc., 1964).
(b) J. Atkinson and N. T. Feather, *A Theory of Achievement Motivation* (New York: John Wiley & Sons, Inc., 1966).

information. Feedback can be controlled by the task, as in the case of programmed instruction, or by the receiver of help, as in self-research methods,[10] or by the helper, as in traditional teaching methods.

The second aspect of information feedback is the characteristics of the information itself, whether it is accurate or distorted, intense or mild, positive or negative, and so on. This second aspect of feedback has been the subject of a great deal of theoretical speculation, especially among students of sensitivity training. For example, Schein and Bennis suggest[11] the following criteria for valid, helpful feedback:

1. The feedback should be based on publicly observed behavior.
2. It should be contiguous in time to the experience it refers to.
3. It should be modified through all the data sources (i.e., group members) available.

A major question about the characteristics of helpful feedback is concerned with whether this feedback should be positive (pleasant for the receiver to hear) or negative (unpleasant). While there are those who feel that negative feedback is sometimes helpful in that it serves to unfreeze the receiver's self-satisfied concept and increase motivation to change,[12] most learning theorists have concluded that in the long run, reward is more effective than punishment. One example of reward-centered feedback is found in the programmed instruction technique of "error-free learning." Rogers, too, places heavy emphasis on the importance of positive feedback to the receiver in his concept of unconditional positive regard.[13] "I find that the more acceptance and liking I feel toward this individual, the more I will be creating a relationship which he can use. By acceptance I mean a warm regard for him as a person of unconditional self-worth — of value no matter what his condition, or his feelings. . . . This acceptance of each fluctuating aspect of this other person makes it for him a relationship of warmth and safety, and the safety of being liked and prized as a person seems a highly important element in a helping relationship." To support his conclusion, Rogers cites psychotherapy research by Halkides[14] which showed that therapists who demonstrated a high degree of unconditional positive regard for their clients were more successful than those who did not.

The exercise in this unit is designed to give you an opportunity to practice your skills in giving and receiving help and to observe the psychological dynamics of the helping relationship.

## IV. PROCEDURE FOR GROUP MEETING

### A. Tower Building Game (Time Allotted: 2 Hours)

For this exercise, the class should divide into four-person teams. The simulation you will experience is called the Tower Building Game. As you will see, it is purposefully structured in a somewhat extreme fashion to maximize your opportunity to learn about leadership and the helping relationship.

---

[10] (a) David A. Kolb, Sara Winter, and David E. Berlew, "Self-directed Change: Two Studies," *Journal of Applied Behavioral Science*, Vol. 4 (1968), 435–473. (b) Ralph Schwitzgebel, "A Simple Behavioral System for Recording and Implementing Change in Natural Settings" (unpublished doctoral thesis, Harvard University, 1964).

[11] Edgar H. Schein and Warren G. Bennis, *Personal and Organizational Change Through Group Methods* (New York: John Wiley & Sons, Inc., 1965).

[12] Warren G. Bennis, Edgar H. Schein, David E. Berlew, and Fred Steele, *Interpersonal Dynamics* (Homewood, Ill.: Dorsey Press, 1964).

[13] Rogers, *On Becoming a Person*, p. 34.

[14] G. Halkides, "An Experimental Study of Four Conditions Necessary for Therapeutic Change" (unpublished doctoral dissertation, University of Chicago, 1958).

*Step 1.* The basic game will be played four times. In this way, each member of a four-person team will have the opportunity to be a manager, an observer, and a subordinate (twice). The basic structure is as follows:

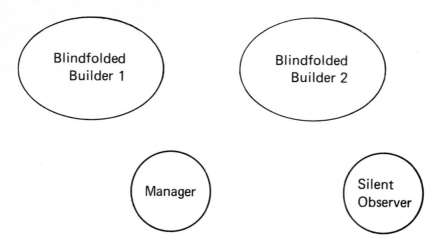

*As soon as the order of rotation has been decided, the first two builders should don their blindfolds and leave them on until their production periods have been completed.*

**Observer's Role**

Observers should begin immediately to record their observations using the Observer's Guide to the Tower Building Game on page 287 as a guide. These data will be an important part of the discussion after the entire game is completed.

*Step 2.* There are two production rounds during each phase of the game. Round 1 has no time limit; it is untimed. Round 2 is timed—there is a limit of 2 minutes. Each builder's task is to construct as high a tower as they can using their *nondominant hand only* (left hand only for right-handers, and vice versa) while totally blindfolded.

*Managers can talk to their builders, but they should not personally touch them or any of the building materials.*

*Step 3.* Goal Setting and Scoring Procedure

At the start of each of the two rounds, the manager should indicate to the observer the goal that has been set for each builder individually. The observer will record these on the Tower Building Record Form on page 287.

The *score* for each person will be determined by how accurately this goal meets the actual size of the tower. In other words, if the goal is 8 blocks and the person stacks 10 blocks, the final score is only 8. If, on the other hand, the goal is 8 blocks and the person stacks only 7 blocks, the score is 0. If at any time any part of the tower should collapse, the round is over and the score is 0. *Blocks must be stacked singly*, one on top of the other, with no double block foundations.

*Step 4. Total group meeting after first cycle of tower building* (30 minutes). The meeting is important because everyone can gain ideas about how to improve the helping process during subsequent cycles of the Tower Building Game.

After each group has completed the first two production periods (one untimed and one timed), the entire class should reconvene for 30 minutes to analyze the process of helping which occurred during the first cycle of the tower building game.

# OBSERVER'S GUIDE TO THE TOWER BUILDING GAME

## A. Tower Building Record Form

| Name of Manager | | | | |
|---|---|---|---|---|
| Builder 1 | | Builder 2 | | Timed rounds for 2 minutes |
| Untimed Round | Timed Round | Untimed Round | Timed Round | |
| GOAL | | | | |
| SCORE | | | | |

TOTAL BUILDER 1 =          TOTAL BUILDER 2 =

## B. Particular Points to Observe

1.  Definition of the Task
    a. Where along the assistance-education task continuum did the manager (helper) appear to lean? the subordinates (helpees)? Jot down behavior that was exhibited in this regard.

2.  Relationship Between Helper and Receivers
    a. In what behavioral ways did the helper's/receiver's n-Aff, n-Power, and n-Ach manifest themselves? With what consequences?

3.  Feedback
    a. In what way was feedback given/received? With what effect?

4.  General Observation
    a. In what way did the helpers and receivers behave that facilitated/hindered an effective helping relationship?

One way to proceed in the meeting is to place the following chart on the blackboard and have the members of each four-person team share their reactions. The observers should give their observations first, then the subordinates (receivers), and finally the manager (helper).

### ANALYSIS OF THE SUPERVISORY HELPING RELATIONSHIP

| Subordinate's Actions that: | | Supervisor's Actions that: | |
|---|---|---|---|
| Helped | Hindered | Helped | Hindered |
| 1 | 1 | 1 | 1 |
| 2 | 2 | 2 | 2 |
| 3 | 3 | 3 | 3 |
| 4 | 4 | 4 | 4 |
| 5 | 5 | 5 | 5 |

This total group meeting is often viewed as an unnecessary disruption. Many people, however, gain significant insight during this discussion which helps them directly during subsequent rounds of the game. Although the specifics are impossible to predict beforehand, the major learnings often come from the insight that the receiver (the person who needs the help) can behave in ways that facilitate or hinder his/her ability to get help.

At another level, this half-hour total group meeting is still another example of the helping relationship process in that the group will be trying to help each individual benefit more from the remainder of the exercise. When the listing of forces that helped/hindered and subsequent discussion has been completed, members should return to their quartets for the three remaining cycles of the Tower Building Game.

*Step 5.    Completing the Tower Building Game.* Each four-person team should now complete the remaining three cycles of the Tower Building Game.

B. Discussion of Tower Building Game (Time Allotted: 30–60 Minutes)

The discussion of the game is probably best conducted, at least initially, within the same four-person teams to make most productive use of the data generated and recorded by the observers.

1.    Observers should begin the discussion by sharing their observations of the manager's behavior (helper), the subordinates' behavior (receiver) toward the manager, and the nature of the helping relationship that developed. Others should *listen* and strive to hear/understand what is being said.

*Note: In sharing your observations, you are in effect involved in another helping relationship — you as observer are the helper and the manager and the subordinate are the receivers.*
After the observer inputs have been made, the manager and subordinates should add their reactions and observations.

2.    In addition to the specific observations you recorded in the Observer's Guide, the following general questions can help you structure your discussions around some themes of importance in better understanding leadership as a helping relationship.
   a. *Information control.* How much information/feedback did managers provide subordinates? At what points in time? With what consequences?

b. Did managers *solicit feedback* from subordinates during the building process? Did subordinates *initiate* (offer) *feedback*? What prevents managers and subordinates from asking for/giving direct feedback in the work setting?

c. *Goal setting.* How were goals set? Who most controlled the process of setting them? What happened after an initial success/failure (during the untimed round)? Did helpers become more controlling? Receivers more dependent?

d. *Differential management.* How were the two builders managed (helped)? The same/differently? If differently, how? With what consequences?

e. *Management turnover.* You each had the chance to be a builder under two different managers. Did you meet any problems in the transition? Did the manager take into account your "experience?" How could manager/subordinates help each other over this transitional period?

## V. SUMMARY

To be effective, a manager must be capable of occupying many roles — leader, teacher, team member, politician, problem solver, and many others. This unit has focused on the key managerial tasks of supervision and employee development. The changing demands of organizational life are making it increasingly imperative that the manager be both a skilled helper and skilled receiver of help. Two of the more important of these changes are worth noting here. First, the knowledge explosion is making human obsolescence a critical problem in nearly all modern organizations. The result is that managers must dedicate time and energy to the continuing development of their staff by helping them acquire the new skills required to stay on top of their changing jobs. At the same time, they must stay on top of their basic job by effectively using help that is available from others. Second, the nature of organizations is itself changing. Bureaucratic organization structures with highly programmed static activities are giving way to organizations that emphasize dynamic systems which are formed to accomplish a new task or solve an emerging problem that the organization faces, and are disbanded when the problem or task is no longer important. The manager of these temporary groups must be a highly effective consultant in defining the group's role in accomplishing tasks and in bringing the appropriate resources to bear on a problem. Then the group itself becomes a consultant to various parts of the organization and a receiver of help from those agencies whose resources it needs to accomplish its mission.

In the Introduction, the formula $T = M \times P \times I$ was discussed, where M referred to an individual's motivation, while P and I referred to perceptions of the environment, or the psychological climate. The concept of climate has relevance for managers and the helping process at two levels. First, it has relevance to the extent that the reward system within an organization reinforces a manager's efforts at employee development. Many organizations pay lip service to this aspect of a manager's role but, in fact, communicate a different message by a reward system that emphasizes short-term productivity over employee development goals. The long-run success and adaptability of an organization depends on the establishment of an organization climate that is conducive to the maintenance of mutual managerial helping relationships throughout the organization. Second, as discussed earlier, managers sometimes feel they must be clairvoyant (or at least omniscient!) in order to be an effective helper who is capable of understanding another's needs, motives, or problems. True, certain skills are needed to be an effective helper — developing trust, listening accurately, and so on. These same skills, however, will help managers to develop a climate within their work group which will facilitate the helping process: people will feel safer seeking help and be more willing to accept help when it is offered. Effective management and effective helping are closely intertwined.

## VI. SELF-EVALUATION AND COMPLETING THE LEARNING LOOP

A. What questions do you now have as a result of your learning experiences from this unit? Jot these down below.

B. From these questions, what *key concepts* can you extrapolate for further learning? Write these concepts below.

C. How can you now go about finding answers to the questions you raised above? Below are some suggested ways to continue your learning process by beginning new learning loops:

1. Look up the key concepts from your questions above in the Yellow Pages of Learning Experiences at the back of the book. Find a few suggested readings or exercises to facilitate the learning of these key concepts.

2. If you don't find the key concepts in the Yellow Pages related specifically to your questions, perhaps there are other concepts listed in the index that might lead you to relevant learning resources at this time. Look for concepts similar to those you identified in B above.

3. In the event that you don't find the Yellow Pages directory useful for your present learning goals, discuss your questions with other students, faculty, or persons outside your learning environment. Discuss further learning possibilities with them.

# chapter 11

## leadership: the effective exercise of power and influence

*Photo by Mike Sands, courtesy of Case Western Reserve University*

## I. OBJECTIVES

    A.   To learn about four styles of power and influence.

    B.   To practice using these styles under two different situations.

    C.   To get feedback on which styles you may tend inappropriately to overuse or underuse.

## II. PREMEETING PREPARATION

Read the Introduction.

*Note:* The exercises provided in this unit will be built around a fishbowl arrangement—one group does the exercise while a second group observes and then provides feedback. In situations where one is fortunate enough to have audio tape recorders available, observers and the fishbowl arrangement need not be used. Each group could listen to and score their own tape after the exercise.

Finally, it has been our experience that issues of power and influence have more reality when something of real value is at stake. Consequently, we have recommended that participants put up a small amount of real money in each exercise. For a variety of reasons, this option may not be feasible in your group. In those cases, an effort should be made to substitute an incentive of real value into each of the games.

## III. INTRODUCTION

Power and influence have rather negative connotations for many people. They conjure up unpleasant images such as the misuse of the power of the presidency, the high-pressure tactics of some salespeople, and the destructive behavior exhibited by military dictators. These negative connotations have, until recently, made it very difficult to examine the role of power and look objectively at its potential positive as well as negative consequences.

The power and status differences that exist between supervisors and subordinates are *real* and *natural.* They cannot be ignored or wished away. Indeed, in its simplest, most basic form, your role as a manager is to *make a difference* in the behavior of your subordinates. Your responsibility as a manager is to behave in ways that (hopefully) add to your subordinates' ability to do their jobs effectively and efficiently. If your subordinates can perform as well or better by themselves—as if you did not exist—then (a) the managerial role is irrelevant and ought to be eliminated, (b) you do not fit the demands of the role, or (c) you have successfully worked yourself out of the job and ought to be moving on to a new role. The issue is not, therefore, whether or not managers have power, but how they choose to exercise the power demanded by the role and with what consequences. One does not "make a difference" without exercising power and influence somewhere, somehow, sometime.

Traditionally, managers have relied almost exclusively upon the power inherent in their position. "I'm the boss. I have the right and responsibility to tell you what to do and if you don't perform, I retain the ultimate power of reward and punishment" would be the extreme form of this condition. Increasingly, however, managers are finding their positional power being eroded; union contracts, governmental equal employment opportunity regulations, and a shifting value structure among younger employees are all forces contributing to this erosion. Finally, those in staff positions and consultant roles recognize that they have little, if any, positional power in the first place.

Given the erosion/weakening of formal or positional power, what is the manager to do to continue to make a difference? Recent work by Berlew and Harrison has shed considerable light on this dilemma. Effective managers, in their view, will need to develop an expanded range of *personal* power and influence behavior and skills and be able to match these skills to situational requirements. There will be times, in other words, when the exercise of "raw" positional power will (a) not be feasible or complete, (b) will be inappropriate to the task at hand, or (c) will create negative consequences (i.e., resistance and/or rebellion). Under these conditions, one or some combination of personal power and influence behaviors will be essential. Berlew and Harrison[1] have identified four typical patterns of behavior reflecting the exercise of power and influence. These will be described as four pure types for the purposes of conceptual clarity, recognizing that few people, if any, ever use (or should use) only one style exclusively.

---

[1] The ideas used here are part of a series of training programs developed by Berlew and Harrison on positive power and influence. For more detail on the actual program, contact Situation Management Systems, Inc., 25 New Chardon Street, Box 9166, Boston, Massachusetts 02114.

*Assertive Persuasion*

The essential quality of *assertive persuasion* (AP) as an influence style is the use of facts, logic, rational argument, and persuasive reasoning. While the influencer may argue forcefully with great élan and spirit, the power of assertive persuasion does not come from an emotional source. Facts and logic are, by definition, emotionally neutral. A person may react to a fact emotionally and thereby be persuaded to behave in a certain way. The feelings of the person using assertive persuasion are, in the pure form, meant to be kept out of their argument. The facts are supposed to speak for themselves.

People using assertive persuasion to persuade others are usually highly verbal and articulate. They are forward with their ideas, proposals, and suggestions and can support their proposals with rational reasons. They tend to listen selectively to others' attempts at assertive persuasion, hoping to find a weak spot so that they can effectively reason against others' proposals.

*Reward and Punishment*

*Reward and punishment* (R&P) is the use of pressures and incentives to control others' behavior. Rewards may be offered for compliance; and punishment or deprivation may be threatened for noncompliance. Naked power may be used, or more indirect and veiled pressures may be exerted through the use of status, prestige, and formal authority.

This influence style is characterized by "contingency management": letting others know clearly what they must do to get what they want and avoid negative consequences through bargaining, negotiating, making offers, and threats. The use of the word "if" often signals the use of this style.

Both reward and punishment and assertive persuasion involve agreeing and disagreeing with others. The difference is that in assertive persuasion one agrees or disagrees with another's proposal because it is more or less effective, correct, accurate, or true. In using reward and punishment, on the other hand, the judgment of right or wrong is an evaluation based on a moral or social standard, a regulation, or an arbitrary performance standard. The person making the evaluation sets herself/himself up as the judge rather than appealing to a common and shared standard of rationality.

People using reward and punishment are very comfortable, generally, in situations of conflict. They are comfortable giving clear feedback—both positive and negative—and are very direct about prescribing their goals and expectations. Very often, however, the reward or punishment—the second part of an "if" statement—is left implicit or vaguely defined.

As you reflect on the descriptions above, it will hopefully be clearer that any individual, regardless of formal position, can effectively utilize many reward and punishment behaviors. Anyone, theoretically, can make evaluative statements involving praise and criticism. Similarly, if a meeting were dragging, anyone could prescribe a goal and expectation ("We've got to finish our work by six o'clock"). The crunch is most clear around "incentives and pressures." The ability to follow through on (a) an evaluation and/or (b) a prescribed goal or expectation is dependent on one's access to and control of meaningful rewards and punishments (incentives and pressures). Many managers recognize that subordinates can/do exercise significant incentives and pressures. By withholding support, dragging their heels, carrying out orders they know to be inappropriate ("I'm safe because I'm doing exactly what my boss told me to do!"), and other forms of subtle "sabotage," subordinates are demonstrating that bosses are not the only ones who have reward and punishment power.

*Participation and Trust*

Unlike assertive persuasion and reward and punishment, where influence is exerted by *pushing* others to accept ideas or to behave in desirable ways, the use of the *participation and trust* (P&T) influence style *pulls* others toward what is desired or required by *involving them*. By actively listening to and involving others, an influencer using participation and trust increases the commitment of others to the target objective or task. Follow-up and close supervision, therefore, become less critical.

People who use participation and trust are generally rather patient and have developed the capacity to be very effective listeners. They are very good at reflecting back to people (paraphrasing) both the content and feelings of what the person has said. They build on others' ideas and are quick to credit others for their contributions.

In addition to the above, people who use participation and trust as an influence style are readily able to admit their own areas of uncertainty and mistakes. By openly acknowledging their own limitations and taking a nondefensive attitude toward feedback, they help others to feel more accepted for what they are.

On the surface, participation and trust may appear to some to be a rather weak and wishy-washy style of influence in contrast, for example, to the toughness of assertive persuasion or reward and punishment. It is not. It can be very powerful by building the trust and commitment needed to implement actions and with it a willingness to be influenced. As with the other influence styles, participation and trust can be used to manipulate others. The manager who tries to involve subordinates in a consensus decision-making process when the manager already has the solution is treading on thin ice. If there is a best way to go, the assertive persuasion or reward and punishment mode of influence is probably more appropriate in this situation.

### Common Vision

This influence style aims to identify a *common vision* of the future for a group and to strengthen the group members' belief that through their collective efforts, the vision can become a reality. The appeals are to the emotions and values of others, activating their personal commitment to private hopes and ideals, and channeling that energy into work toward a common purpose. Common vision also has an intellectual component achieved by clear articulation of goals and the means to achieve them. The well-known speeches by Martin Luther King, Jr., and John F. Kennedy are classic examples of the effective use of common vision.

Within the more day-to-day world of organizations, there are numerous opportunities for the effective use of common vision. Many an organizational meeting becomes an exercise in competing assertions (AP). In such situations the ability to help the group pull together around a common goal can provide a much-needed spirit of collaboration and inspiration—"What we can accomplish *if* we work together."

People who use common vision are generally very emotionally expressive. They are aware of what they feel (it is *hard* to create enthusiasm if you yourself feel bored) and are willing and able to project and communicate their feelings articulately. They talk in emotionally vivid imagery and metaphors. They are often called charismatic.

### The Value Issues — Positive Versus Negative Power

None of the styles described above is inherently right or wrong, good or bad. All are important, relevant, and can be used in a variety of ways. The important distinction has to do with how the exercise of power and influence is experienced—what is its impact? Assertive persuasion, reward and punishment, participation and trust, and common vision can be used in a way that results in other people feeling stronger. They can also be used to make people feel weaker—to feel like pawns in the hands of someone else. Common vision, for example, will result in people feeling weaker if it is used to raise people's hopes and expectations but nothing is ever realized or gained. People will thus feel "had" and become cynical to further influence attempts. On the other hand, we recognize that there are some situations where it is extremely difficult to exercise needed influence and leave people feeling stronger. Firing someone is not a pleasant experience and the dismissed person is bound to feel badly.

The need to exercise power and influence is an inherent part of the managerial role. Effective managers develop the skills needed to have a positive vs. a negative effect, whenever the situation allows that potential. During the upcoming class session you will have an opportunity to explore each of these styles in more depth and practice ways of using power positively.

*THE WIZARD OF ID reprinted by permission of Johnny Hart and Field Enterprises, Inc.*

## IV. PROCEDURE FOR GROUP MEETING

*Notes:*

1.  Two very different simulations are used in this session; one that stresses a win–win collaborative situation and one that leans toward a competitive, win–lose situation. In this way, individuals will be able to explore their own and others' influence styles under two different (but typical) situations.

2.  While the two simulations described take place in a group context, we recognize that a considerable number of situations in which managers exercise power and influence are dyadic in nature, one-on-one. Using the group context allows participants to see a wider range of power and influence behaviors and to see how various styles interact with one another.

3.  Both of these simulations have proven to be more productive learning experiences when real money (or some other equivalent incentive) is at stake. It is suggested, therefore, that individuals be requested to put up $1–$2. Whether or not any of the money is returned ought to be a function of their performance in the various simulations; i.e., some will "profit" and others will "lose" as a result of these simulations.

A. Simulation 1: The Michael Anthony[2] Game (Time Allotted: 60 minutes)

For this exercise, the class should split into groups of five or six persons. One group will do the Michael Anthony Game while another group act as observers — in a fishbowl arrangement. The observers should use the Observer Rating Form (on p. 299) and should, in addition to observing the total group, be responsible for observing one particular member of the inner group.

[2] Michael Anthony was a character in the once-popular TV program "The Millionaire." Michael Anthony represented an anonymous benefactor who would give a person $1,000,000 if certain conditions were met. This simulation is designed to replicate those conditions.

*Step 1.* Each person playing the Michael Anthony Game should take out $1 and place it in the center of the group.

*Step 2.* Your group will have 30 minutes to decide by group consensus which *two* of your members are to receive this money. The following conditions must be adhered to:

   a. No more than *two* persons can receive this money.

   b. One of these two persons must receive at least 75 percent of the total, the other person can receive no more than 25 percent of the total.

   c. These persons must use the money for their own individual and personal satisfaction. They cannot, for example, offer to buy everyone drinks, or offer to split it up/return it to the group in any other form in the future.

   d. The group must be able to state an agreed-upon set of criteria and rationale for their choice within the allotted time.

*Failure to adhere to these conditions will result in the forfeiture of all the money to the instructor/session coordinator. This is a real exercise, not a game.*

*Step 3.* *Observers' feedback to partners* (time: 10 minutes). Observers should meet with their partners and share their observations. The following guidelines will help to focus this feedback.

   a. What styles did your partner use most often? Least often? Most effectively? Least effectively?

   b. How did your partner react to styles used by others?

   c. How did others react to the styles used by your partner?

*Step 4.* *Inner group discussion* (time: 20 minutes). After the individual feedback has been given, the inner group which played the game should reconvene and share their own impressions.

*Note:* It is important that this discussion *not* become a rehashing of the group's decision or lack of decision. The objective is to sharpen everyone's understanding of how the various power and influence styles can be used effectively/ineffectively in an essentially win–lose situation.

The following guidelines will help to focus this discussion.

   a. Can you identify examples of where/when in your group's efforts each of the four styles—assertive persuasion, reward and punishment, participation and trust, and common vision—could have been and/or were used effectively?

   b. How would you characterize the climate of this group? How did various styles contribute to the development and/or reinforcement of the climate?

   c. What kind of limits would have been more helpful to the group? How could the various styles have been applied to help create this climate?

   d. Since each of you has received individual feedback only from your partners so far, the group should take some time to share reactions as to what styles they saw each other using and with what consequences.

B. Simulation 2: Consensus Seeking (Time Allotted: 60 Minutes)

While the Michael Anthony Game has inherent win–lose qualities, this next simulation is designed to be more collaborative in nature. Group performance should improve as a result of effective use of all the group's resources.

**OBSERVER SHEET**
**POWER AND INFLUENCE BEHAVIORS**

*Persons in the Group*\*

| *Power and Influence Behaviors* | | | | | | |
|---|---|---|---|---|---|---|
| 1. *Assertive persuasion* (AP) Logic, facts, rationality, ideas, proposals, reasons for and against | | | | | | |
| 2. *Reward and punishment* (R&P) Evaluations, use of incentives and pressures, bargains, stating own personal goals and expectations | | | | | | |
| 3. *Participation and trust* (P&T) Active listening, recognizing others' contributions, involving others and getting their contributions, disclosing own areas of uncertainty | | | | | | |
| 4. *Common vision* (CV) Building a sense of group spirit, a *we* feeling, creating a superordinate group goal, shared identity | | | | | | |

\*List the names of members of the group you are observing. Place a check mark each time you see a particular power and influence behavior exhibited. Pay attention to your partner's behavior.

For this exercise, the inner group from the Michael Anthony Game should sit on the outside of the fishbowl and become the observers; i.e., the inner and outer groups from simulation 1 should switch roles.

*Step 1.*   Each person playing this game should give the game coordinator/instructor $1.[3]

*Step 2.*   Listed below you will find ten traits of an Ideal Man. In January 1976, *Psychology Today* polled its female readership[4] to discover their views of the Ideal Man. Fourteen thousand women responded.

*Your task as a group is to rank the importance (from 1 = most to 10 = least) of these ten traits as they were ranked by the 14,000 women, i.e., to predict how 14,000 women would describe their ideal man.*

### Payoff System

Since there is a "right answer," the money that has been collected will be distributed at the end of the exercise according to how close each group's consensus ranking comes to the actual ranking *(the lower the absolute difference, the closer is the group's score).* The recommended payoff distribution is as follows:

    a. Winning group (closest to actual ranking) gets 60 percent of total money in pool.

    b. Second-place group (next closest to actual ranking) gets 25 percent of total money in pool.

    c. Third-place group (third closest to actual ranking) gets 15 percent of total money in pool.

    d. Any remaining groups finish "out of the money"—no payoff.

*Step 3.*   Your group now has 30 minutes to come up with a consensus rank order of each of the following traits (1 = most important and 10 = least important).

——— Intelligent

——— Physically strong

——— Successful at work

——— Aggressive

——— Stands up for beliefs

——— Fights to protect family

——— Able to love

——— Warm

——— Skilled lover

——— Sexually faithful

[3] Any monies forfeited during the Michael Anthony Game can be added to the pool of money available for this exercise.

[4] The typical female reader of *Psychology Today* is younger, more affluent, less religious, better educated, and more liberal than the population at large. The results, therefore, are not typical of the average American female.

Observers should remain silent and use the Observer Sheet on page 299 to record their observations.

Step 4.    *Determine the winners.* In the solutions on page 467 you will find the actual ranking of the ten traits. To compute your group score, simply take the absolute difference (irrespective of plus or minus) between your ranking and the actual ranking. The lower the absolute difference, the better your group score. The instructor will distribute winnings to the top three groups.

Step 5    *Observers' feedback to partners* (time: 10 minutes). Observers should meet with their partners and share their observations. The following guidelines will help to focus this feedback.

   a. What styles did your partner use most often? Least often? Most effectively? Least effectively?

   b. How did your partner react to styles used by others?

   c. How did others react to the styles used by your partner?

Step 6.    *Inner group discussion* (time: 20 minutes). After the individual feedback has been given, the inner group that played the game should reconvene and share their own impressions.

*Note:* It is important that this discussion *not* become a rehashing of the group's decision or lack of decision. The objective is to sharpen everyone's understanding of how the various power and influence styles can be used effectively/ineffectively in an essentially win–win situation.

The following guidelines will help to focus this discussion.

   a. Can you identify examples of where/when in your group's efforts each of the four styles—assertive persuasion, reward and punishment, participation and trust, and common vision—could have been and/or were used effectively?

   b. How would you characterize the climate of this group? How did various styles contribute to the development and/or reinforcement of the climate?

   c. What kind of limits would have been more helpful to the group? How could the various styles have been applied to help create this climate?

   d. Since each of you has received individual feedback only from your partners so far, the group should take some time to share reactions as to what styles they saw each other using and with what consequences.

C. Discussion of Both Simulations (Time Allotted: 30–45 Minutes)

A total group discussion of both simulations is of value to generalize the experiences. The following questions should be addressed to help guide these discussions.

   1.    Which influence styles were most frequently used in both simulations? Least frequently used?

   2.    Which styles/combination of styles seemed most productive in the "win–lose" Michael Anthony Game? In the more collaborative "win–win" ranking situation? Which styles were least productive or most dysfunctional?

   3.    Timing is an important variable in the effective use of power and influence. When, in both situations, were various styles most/least effective?

## VI. SELF-EVALUATION AND COMPLETING THE LEARNING LOOP

A. What questions do you now have as a result of your learning experiences from this unit? Jot these down below.

B. From these questions, what *key concepts* can you extrapolate for further learning? Write these concepts below.

C. What are some ways you can now go about finding answers to the questions you raised above? Below are some suggested ways to continue your learning process by beginning new learning loops:

1. Look up the key concepts from your questions above in the Yellow Pages of Learning Experiences at the back of the book. Find a few suggested readings or exercises to facilitate the learning of these key concepts.

2. If you don't find the key concepts in the Yellow Pages related specifically to your questions, perhaps there are other concepts listed in the index that might lead you to relevant learning resources at this time. Look for concepts similar to those you identified in B above.

3. In the event that you don't find the Yellow Pages directory useful for your present learning goals, discuss your questions with other students, faculty, or persons outside your learning environment. Discuss further learning possibilities with them.

# chapter 12

## managing work team effectiveness

*Photo by Sybil Shelton*

## I. OBJECTIVES

    A.    To learn about the task-related factors that influence team effectiveness.

    B.    To sharpen the ability to see the impact of those factors upon team functioning.

    C.    To practice using this model to enhance a team's effectiveness.

## II. PREMEETING PREPARATION

    Read Sections III and IV.

## III. INTRODUCTION

Increasing organizational complexity and the knowledge/information explosion guarantee that the existence of teams and the need for effective teamwork will remain organizational realities. Particularly as one moves up the organizational hierarchy, tasks become less structured and problem solutions become less programmable or routine. Whenever a task requires that two or more people coordinate their efforts to maximize effectiveness, a team exists, by definition.

Many skeptics of teams or managers whose personal style leads them to operate autonomously often raise the question: Are teams more or less effective than individuals? Given the situation described above, one sees that this question is irrelevant. Given that a team situation exists, as defined by the nature of the task, the only rational question to address is: What factors make a team more or less effective? This unit addresses that question directly.[1]

### Task-Related Factors Influencing Team Effectiveness — The GRPI Model

There are four categories of work or task-related issues which all teams must deal with successfully if they are to operate effectively — goal issues, role issues, procedural issues, and interpersonal issues.

### A. Goal Issues (What is the Team Trying to Accomplish?)

To be an effectively functioning team, individual members must have a shared, agreed-upon common definition of the team's mission — its reason for existence as a team. Goal priority conflicts must be understood, and be clearly resolved. In the absence of these conditions, it would not be surprising to find people working very hard but pulling in different directions.

To many people, these seem like trivial issues. "Of course we all agree," they will say quickly. Seldom, however, does this agreement develop naturally, nor is it an easy task. Part of the difficulty stems from the fact that most managers really wear two hats. They are both the leaders of one team (their subordinates) and a member of a second team (that of their boss). Each of these "two" teams has different, although hopefully related, goals and objectives.

### B. Role Issues (Who Should Be Doing What to Help This Team Reach Its Goals?)

Formal, written job descriptions can, at best, be counted upon only partially to cope with role problems. To use a sports analogy, they can tell you only whether you are a center or a forward but cannot specify how you should behave on a day-to-day basis. The way you function as a center (if that were your formal role) varies with (a) the qualities of those on your team playing forward, (b) the nature of the opposition, (c) the score of the game, and so on.

One particular source of role problems on a team is ambiguity. People are simply not clear about what they expect of one another, and often they are hesitant to ask for clarity ("If I ask someone what they expect of me, they will think I don't know my job!")

---

[1] Much of the conceptual material discussed in this unit is adapted from work done by Plovnick, Fry, and Rubin. (See "New Developments in O.D. Technology: Programmed Team Development" by Mark Plovnick, Ronald Fry, and Irwin Rubin, *Training and Development Journal*, April 1975.

Beyond the problem of ambiguity, three forms of role conflict are frequently observed. Self-other conflicts arise because what someone else expects of me does not fit my expectation of myself. Two or more other team members can have expectations of me which, although they are unambiguous, are incompatible, thereby creating an other–other conflict. Finally, the sum total of everyone's expectations can result in an overload conflict—there just are not enough hours in the day to fulfill all the expectations.

## C. Procedural Issues (How Should We Function?)

Within the procedural area are a host of "how to" kinds of issues: How will decisions be made? How will conflicts be resolved? How will information be shared? What kinds of meetings will we have? When? What norms do we need to reinforce/extinguish?

Team meetings, as a microcosm of team functioning, are notoriously ineffective, for reasons related to procedure. Some people sit in the meeting waiting for the boss's decision; others share opinions as if they were being consulted; others argue assertively for one or another proposal as if a consensus decision-making procedure were in operation; and still others are just plain confused or bored.

## D. Interpersonal Issues (Feelings People Have Toward Each Other)

One hears many references, particularly in poorly functioning teams, to "personality clashes," "bad chemistry," and the like. The negative consequences of poor feelings between team members are not hard to recognize. When the team is meeting, all may look smooth on the surface but under the table or at the water cooler, hostile barbs fill the air. The extent to which people trust, support, respect, and feel comfortable with one another can certainly influence the effectiveness of teamwork.

### A Summary Example

Let us examine one final example that will serve to clarify the points made above. A surgical team within a hospital must and most often (fortunately) can perform an operation as a highly effective and efficient team. During the surgical situation itself, goals are very clear and unambiguous, e.g., successful removal of the gallbladder. Roles are specifiable and learnable before the fact. Remove one scrub nurse and substitute another and little if any difference will be noticed. The decision-making procedure is appropriately hierarchically determined. (Who among us wants a long consensus decision!) While team members may have feelings toward one another, the crisis-oriented, compressed nature of this specific task situation keeps these feelings out of the way. Now consider the situation when the patient is on the ward, recovering from the surgery and being prepared for discharge. The task situation has changed dramatically. The goal is much less clearly measurable, roles are more broadly defined, and the hierarchical decision procedure of the operating room may need to shift dramatically. Teamwork of a different form and quality will be required because the nature of the work has changed. Both "teams" are influenced by goals, roles, procedures, and interpersonal relations issues. Because of the nature of the work, however, one team will find it easier to cope with these issues than will the other team—in spite of the fact that the people involved could be identical.

The classroom simulation is designed to enable everyone to test the validity and usefulness of this categorization framework. Try to be consciously aware of this framework in the team meetings you will have and observe. Its application should enable you to have more effective team meetings.

*Reprinted by permission of the Chicago Tribune-New York News Syndicate*

## IV. PROCEDURE FOR GROUP MEETING

### A. Background of Universal Wicket, Inc.

For the purposes of this exercise, the total group should assume they are an organization entitled Universal Wicket, Inc., a 53-year-old specialized company engaged in manufacturing and selling recreational supplies. During its history it has failed to show a profit only during the years 1932–1934. It began by producing croquet sets, and in recent years has diversified into closely allied lines, including aboveground swimming pools. Its largest seller at the present time is the 108-gram professional-model flying saucer. During the fiscal year just concluded, Universal Wicket showed an operating loss of over $500,000 on sales of just over $26,000,000. The cash on hand has decreased, but not markedly. Current cash account is about $1 million; weekly payroll is $150,000. The stockholders and board members, as well as management and labor, are deeply concerned about the operating loss. Most people in the organization feel that immediate remedial action is required.

The company president not only feels this pressure but he also feels a definite commitment to get the company on the upward track again. He knows that the situation cannot continue as it is now, and has called on the various departmental vice presidents to meet with managers in their departments preparatory to a later meeting at which decisions will be reached about the future of the company.

He and the executive vice president, who serves as V.P.–Finance and who works closely with him on overall company affairs, have been given as much latitude as they need by the board of directors. They can deal with the various problems and formulate any new policies they wish.

In addition to the president and executive vice president, Universal Wicket has the following functional groups, each headed by a vice president.

1. Research
2. Production
3. Personnel
4. Sales
5. Marketing

Brief thumbnail sketches of the present situation in each of the five major departments of Universal Wicket follow: *Each department will have to be creative and imaginative in the additional assumptions they make about their own and other departments in the organization. The only constraint is that all assumptions be consistent with the general descriptions provided.*

*Marketing Department Situation*

1.  This is a sophisticated market research group that has developed team skills at staying ahead of the competition in developing new markets.

2.  The competition has cut into sales through lower prices on merchandise first introduced to the market by Universal.

3.  The department, which is also in charge of advertising, has not been able to decide on places where future advertising dollars would be best spent.

*Sales Department Situation*

1.  The Sales Department includes 50 field representatives, almost evenly divided between people who formerly sold other items (appliances, clothing, and the like) and people who taught recreation before joining Universal.

2.  Sales to department stores have decreased as more former recreational personnel have joined the sales force.

3.  Sales to schools and institutions have increased as former recreational personnel have joined the company.

*Production Department Situation*

1.  During the past fiscal year, production was up 20 percent over the preceding year.

2.  Labor costs, however, rose by 24 percent during the year, largely as a result of increased overtime and time lost through mechanical failure.

3.  The rate of rejection of finished products increased by 14 percent from retailers and 19 percent from sales personnel.

*Personnel Department Situation*

1.  Through the efforts of its Personnel Department, Universal Wicket has developed the reputation of being an excellent place to work.

2.  Competition from other organizations and a slight increase in turnover have put added strain on the department in its efforts to recruit top-quality people.

3.  The department has recently begun to experiment with some new management development programs; not enough time has passed to evaluate the results.

*Research Department Situation*

1.  During the past two years the Research Department has developed more patents than any company in the recreational field.

2.  Only three of a total of 56 patents have reached the production stage.

3.  Only one of those three items has been put on sale, with sales results thus far inconclusive and unexciting.

The following memo was sent to all vice presidents:

TO:        All Vice Presidents
FROM:      Mr. A. Pex, President, Mr. J. Jones,
           Executive Vice President
SUBJECT: Profit Situation

As you are all undoubtedly aware, company profits took a substantial turn for the worse during the past year. This is a matter of serious concern and Mr. Jones and I would like, therefore, to meet with all of you to discuss this problem. It would be helpful if before the meeting, each of you would:

1. Meet with your department heads and prepare an assessment of the strengths and weaknesses you see within your respective departments—i.e., areas where fat could be eliminated, sources of inefficiency, hidden assets we are not using, and so on.

2. Give some thought to the company as a whole and what we might be able to do to improve our position.

We must come out of this meeting with decisions concerning what we plan to do in response to this problem.

B. Group Meeting: Specific Instructions

*Step 1.*  The group should:
   a. Elect a president, who should then choose an executive vice president. (See the following Instructions to President and Executive Vice President.)
   b. The rest of the class should form themselves into the five functional groups (of at least three members each, if possible).
   c. Each functional group chooses one of its members as vice president. (See the following Instructions to Vice Presidents and Their Department Members.)

*Step 2.*  At this point the various groups (see the following instructions) prepare for the meeting. (*Note:* You should try to leave yourself *20 minutes* to prepare for the executive committee, so gauge your time accordingly.)

*Instructions to President and Executive Vice President*

In response to your memo, your functional vice presidents will arrive shortly to discuss plans for improving the company's profit picture. The two of you should use the time until they arrive to plan a format for this meeting and do whatever else you feel you must to prepare yourselves. Midway through this meeting there will be a 10-minute break wherein each of the vice presidents will reconvene with his own group. *The meeting must end 1 hour after you begin.*

Twenty minutes from now, all vice presidents will be meeting with the president and executive vice president to develop a plan for improving the company's profit picture. To facilitate observation and save time, department members will be able to *observe* (no interaction) this meeting. An Observer Form has been provided for this purpose (p. 315). This will eliminate the need for each vice president to fill in his group as to what has transpired in the meeting. There will be a short break (10 minutes) midway through the meeting. After the break, the vice presidents should return to the meeting, which will continue until the *1 hour* allotted for it is over. Then the entire group will discuss the exercise.

*Step 3.*      While the president, executive vice president, and departmental vice presidents are meeting, the remainder of the group should act as observers. After the conclusion of the board meeting, the observers will be able to feed back their impressions of what helped/hindered the team effectiveness of the board.

*Step 4.*      *Discussion.* It is suggested that you try to handle the discussion of this exercise as a total group. The reason for this is that the total group participated in and observed the exercise, and the totality of reactions and observations will be important.

     It would also be helpful if, on each function discussed, the observers should share their observations initially. Then the members of the board meeting should add their comments and reactions.

     If, however, you find that structure completely unwieldy, split up into two subgroups. Each subgroup should contain at least one member of each of the functional departments (who also acted as observers). The executive committee (president, executive vice president, and departmental vice presidents) should also split up, to ensure representation of the diverse experiences and observations. The following are meant to serve as a guide and stimulus to your discussion:

a. What were some frequently observed examples of goal, role, procedure, and interpersonal behavior which help/hinder the board's effectiveness as a team?

b. Many interpersonal behaviors are often the symptomatic result of issues stemming from the other three areas (versus causal problems in and of themselves). Can you identify examples of apparent interpersonal problems that were really caused by unresolved issues in goals, roles, or procedures?

c. What transpired during the "coffee break?" How did this influence the board's decision making?

d. What kinds of concerns were discussed in the meetings of vice presidents and their departments prior to the board meeting? How did these factors influence the organization's ability to make a decision?

e. How did the group go about deciding what was an important problem and what problems were less important?

f. How did the total group decide to elect a president? Upon what basis was the executive vice president selected? Upon what basis and by what method were department vice presidents selected?

g. To what extent did department vice presidents feel the issue of split loyalty — commitment to their own group versus commitment to the organization? What were the effects of split loyalty?

## OBSERVER RATING FORM

| In the spaces below, write down *behavioral* examples of these kinds of issues that you observed which helped or hindered the accomplishment of the task. | Next to your observations, write down any *consequences* you saw. What was the result of the behavior in terms of the team's ability to get its work done? |
|---|---|
| G. Things to do with goals | |
| R. Things to do with roles | |
| P. Things to do with procedures (i.e., decision making) or group process | |
| I. Things to do with personality or inter-personal communication | |

## V. SUMMARY

The introduction of the GRPI model expands our understanding of the complex dynamics of team functioning. They can be viewed as content issues with which any work team must deal if they are to function effectively. The process dimensions discussed in an earlier unit ("Group Dynamics") run through each of the GRPI issues. Task-oriented and maintenance-oriented behaviors are important to a team and will influence *how* the team deals with the need to clarify goals, define roles, and so on. Either one — process *or* content — in the absence of the other creates an incomplete picture.

Two important assumptions that underlie the GRPI framework need to be emphasized. First is the issue of symptoms versus causes. Interpersonal issues are treated, within the GRPI framework, more as symptoms of poor team performance rather than as causes of poor team performance. Unresolved goal conflicts or role conflicts will, for example, often pop up as "personality clashes" or examples of "bad chemistry."

Second, the GRPI framework is a hierarchical model. The issues are listed and described in a recommended sequence. Rationally speaking, issues of roles (who should be doing what?) cannot be successfully resolved until such time as the "what" (goals) issue has been resolved. Similarly, effectively designing team procedures (how?) requires resolution of who and what. Many a team meeting, for example, could be enhanced if a few moments were taken at the start of the meeting to go through at least the GRP sequence.

Finally, although many of the obstacles to effective team functioning lie within the team's boundary, few teams can operate in a completely autonomous fashion. As you probably experienced in this class simulation, while the executive committee was a team, it had to interface with five other teams (the various departments). Each of these departmental teams was related to and influenced by their interactions with the other four departments. Any single team, therefore, is influenced by its wider organizational environment, and the board has an added set of interface problems with the extra-organizational environment. These complex issues of intergroup (interteam) relationships, and the relationship between an organization and its environments, are the subject of the following units.

## VI. SELF-EVALUATION AND COMPLETING THE LEARNING LOOP

A. What questions do you now have as a result of your learning experiences from this unit? Jot these down below.

B. From these questions, what *key concepts* can you extrapolate for further learning? Write these concepts below.

C. How can you now go about finding answers to the questions you raised above? Below are some suggested ways to continue your learning process by beginning new learning loops:

1. Look up the key concepts from your questions above in the Yellow Pages of Learning Experiences at the back of the book. Find a few suggested readings or exercises to facilitate the learning of these key concepts.

2. If you don't find the key concepts in the Yellow Pages related specifically to your questions, perhaps there are other concepts listed in the index that might lead you to relevant learning resources at this time. Look for concepts similar to those you identified in B above.

3. In the event that you don't find the Yellow Pages directory useful for your present learning goals, discuss your questions with other students, faculty, or persons outside your learning environment. Discuss further learning possibilities with them.

# chapter 13

## managing conflict among groups

Photo by Mike Sands, courtesy of Case Western Reserve University

## I. OBJECTIVES

    A.    To increase understanding of the problem of suboptimization in organizations, particularly where group goals take precedence over total organizational goals.

    B.    To examine strategies for reducing the negative effects of conflict on the effectiveness of intergroup relations.

    C.    To explore ways of establishing collaborative, as opposed to competitive, intergroup relations.

## II. PREMEETING PREPARATION

    A.    Read the Introduction.

# III. INTRODUCTION

Although the assumption is often made that our behavior is strictly an individual matter—that personality factors alone are responsible for specific actions—there is a growing body of research that points to membership in groups and the relationships between groups as major determinants of behavior, particularly when groups are in competition or conflict. The work of Sherif, for instance, has shown how easily behavior may be changed by putting individuals in a competitive, limited contact situation with another group, consisting of people like themselves.[1] By emphasizing competition rather than collaboration or understanding, the experimenters were able to observe that individuals' behavior became increasingly hostile toward members of the rival group.

Many other studies[2] have since confirmed and added to the body of knowledge about the effects of group membership on individual behavior. Researchers have noted strong tendencies to believe whatever others in a strong reference group believe, even when it contradicts one's visual perceptions. Groups that we belong to, particularly the ones we value most, tend to affirm us in ways we cannot always do for ourselves. By accepting us they let us know that we are "okay," and erase a lot of the doubts we may have had about our identity. But with that acceptance often comes a series of pressures, subtle and/or overt, to conform to a set of values or behaviors that the group deems acceptable.

In organizations, there are different functional groups, professional specialties, geographical groupings, power levels, race, sex, and social class distinctions. Any or all of these can serve as focal points for the creation of strong reference groups that provide their members with a sense of acceptance and identity in exchange for group loyalty and commitment. To the individual, these reference groups are often the most immediate and tangible sources of a sense of belonging to the organization. Because of this, these groups are a vehicle for gaining commitment to organizational goals and motivation to work.

Yet, group loyalty and commitment lead group members to value their own priorities, goals, and points of view more highly than other, "out" groups. This difference in views often leads to a we–they competitive atmosphere between groups, which further strengthens internal group loyalty and out-group hostility in a cycle of increasing intensity. Organizations often find this to be a major stumbling block in optimizing productivity and reaching organization goals. The people in production may see the marketing department as making inordinate demands on them for changes in products with insufficient lead time. Marketing, on the other hand, may see production as intractible, a group that does not understand the necessity of meeting the competition from other companies. As a result of the conflict, the energy of both groups is being expended in defense of their own position as well as attacking the position of the other group, all at the expense of organizational goals.

Is this competition between groups always bad? Not necessarily. There are numerous examples in our society of the advantages of intergroup competition. In the sports world, one team is always competing against another. This phenomenon produces much excitement for audiences, since they have an emotional identification with one or the other team and feel actively involved in the battle. The competitive nature of the encounter produces excitement for the players and motivates or induces them to exert maximum effort to reap the rewards of winning. In the business world, companies compete with one another for a larger share of the consumer dollar. Competition between organizations often increases the excellence of the product.

These situations where competition between groups is productive have several distinguishing characteristics. First, they involve entities (groups) that are not part of the same formal organizational structure. The Giants and the Colts are a part of the NFL, but they represent independent and autonomous operating organizations. Deliberate intergroup competition has been used by many government contracting agencies within the framework of parallel projects. The same task (usually a feasibility

[1] M. Sherif, *Intergroup Relations and Leadership* (New York: John Wiley & Sons, Inc., 1962).
[2] For example D. Cartwright and A. Zander, *Group Dynamics Research and Theory* (New York: Harper & Row, Publishers, 1968).

study) is given in two or more different companies with the understanding that the best proposal will win the follow-up contract. The assumption underlying this strategy is that the higher quality of the final product resulting from such a competitive structure will justify the duplication of effort and expenditure of funds. A second distinguishing characteristic is that seldom do any of these competing organizations (groups) find it necessary to work together to solve a common problem or to reach a common goal. Indeed, when they must come together, as in the case of two nations to resolve an international dispute or a group of baseball owners to elect a new commissioner, the competitive element that proved so beneficial in their other activities often gets in the way when they must collaborate. Finally, the prize for which these groups are competing is a scarce resource of relatively fixed amount —there will be only one recipient of the government proposal or there can be only one winner of the Super Bowl. The reward system is such, in other words, as to create a zero-sum, win–lose situation: for me to win, you must lose.

There are, then, two distinct kinds of competitiveness as far as organizations are concerned, each with its own sets of consequences. Competitiveness internal to an organization usually results in energy being expended at the expense of the overall mission of the organization. Competition between organizations is the essence of the marketplace.

The purpose of this exercise is to simulate a set of organizational relationships among groups. As you go through the exercise you should try to be aware of your feelings about your group and other groups; there will be time after the exercise to reflect on your feelings individually and to discuss them with your group and the entire class.

## IV. PROCEDURE FOR GROUP MEETING[3]

### The Task

Throughout its 40-year history, the Nadir Corporation has been run by George Nadir, founder, president, and majority stockholder. Nadir rules with a heavy hand and takes part in all company decisions. He adjudicates disputes between the two major divisions of the company, marketing and manufacturing, insisting at all times that the divisions communicate through him on major issues.

Nadir's surprise sale of his stock to Apogee, Inc., has made Nadir Corp. a wholly owned subsidiary which must now operate without "the old man." Not being willing to impose a new president on Nadir without first finding out what the company's needs and executive resources are, Apogee has sent their executive vice president for acquisitions, Brian Cleary, to meet with Nadir personnel to get a clearer picture of what should be done—whether, for instance, a new president should come from the outside or from within, and just what kind of manager s/he should be. Mr. Cleary has sent the memo on page 322 to members of the manufacturing and marketing departments.

One half of you will represent manufacturing (group A). The manufacturing division is about evenly divided between managers who began their careers as engineers and managers who operated the facilities starting as hourly workers. Marketing (group B) is managed totally by college graduates, with about half having started as engineers, the other half coming to the company from liberal arts backgrounds.

For the purpose of this exercise, no further specific information about the Nadir Company is necessary. Information about the products made by Nadir should have no influence on the task you are asked to accomplish. (Note, if your total group size exceeds 18 people, you may want to run two separate, but simultaneous sessions.)

---

[3] The intergroup exercise used in this unit is similar to many that have been developed previously. The original concept should probably be credited to Sherif, *Intergroup Relations and Leadership*, but has been further developed by many others—notably, Robert Blake.

Apogee Corporation
Inter-Office Memo

TO: Manufacturing Department
Marketing Department
FROM: Brian Cleary, Executive Vice President
RE: Criteria for choosing new president, Nadir Corporation

You are requested to hold a department meeting for the purpose of establishing criteria for choosing a new president for Nadir Corporation. Please prepare a brief report listing five criteria, in short phrases, that you think should be used in the choice. Please rank-order them in terms of their importance to the Nadir Corporation.

When you have prepared your reports, we will have a joint meeting of the two departments to evaluate them.

*Step 1* (10 minutes). The total group will be the Nadir Corporation, with half representing marketing, half manufacturing. Assign or divide into the groups on whatever basis seems most appropriate, keeping the same number of members in each group. The group leader or instructor will act as Brian Cleary, the EVP, and coordinate the simulation and discussion.

*Step 2* (30 minutes). Marketing and manufacturing meet separately to prepare their response to Cleary's memo, listing their criteria for choosing a new president of the Nadir Corporation. Short phrases should be used, and there should be no more than five criteria listed by each group. They should be rank-ordered in terms of importance to the company. *Each group member* should make a clear, legible copy of the group report for use in the next step.

*Step 3* (20 minutes). To evaluate the two reports, Cleary has asked individuals in marketing to pair off with someone in engineering. During this period you will be paired with a member of the other team. The pairings may be done as you wish. You will be expected to provide a copy of your group's criteria report for your discussion partner to review.

Your task as a two-person team will be to decide which set of criteria is better in its entirety and by how much. You must allot 100 points between the two, but cannot allot them 50-50. There must be a preference indicated, whether by 52-48 or by 90-10. Concentrate on the content of the list rather than peripheral things such as style or elegance of wording.

At the end of 20 minutes (the instructor or leader should let you know when the time is up) give your numerical results to the instructor or leader and return to your original group. S/he will tabulate them and announce which report is best.

*Step 4* (20 minutes). Back in your original groups, discuss the preceding hour's events, focusing on:

a. How this group operated during the time in which you were generating the criteria report.

1. What was the predominant leadership style? What were its effects?

2. What were the effects of time and task pressures on group interaction?

3. How were conflicts handled? Decisions made?

b. The state of this group now.

    1. What is the climate in this group right now? Is it different from when you were doing the task?

    2. How willing would you be to give or receive help from someone in the other group right now? How easy would it be for you to work with the other group now (e. g., to implement the winning criteria list)?

    3. What effect did winning or losing have on your group?

*Step 5* (30 minutes). Reconvene as a class. Read the summary (pp. 323–325) and, using it as a guide, discuss:

a. What happened within the groups during the task? Were the summary predictions correct? How did they vary from the reality?

b. What happened between the two groups?

c. In the group discussion (step 4), what was the winning group's discussion like? Were the summary predictions valid?

d. What was the climate in the losing group? Were the summary predictions valid for them?

e. What conclusions can you draw about the effect of intergroup competition on group behavior? On your behavior as an individual group member?

f. How might the EVP's memo be rewritten to reduce conflict?

*Optional*
*Step 6* (20 minutes; if time permits). Meet once again with your partner from the other group for purposes of giving each other feedback on your influence styles. Discuss:

a. Your perception of your partner's influence style during the interaction and your reasons for it.

b. Your partner's perception of your influence style and the reasons for it.

c. How these perceptions agree or conflict with your own perception of your influence style.

(Refer to your experience in the unit, "Leadership: the Effective Exercise of Power and Influence," and compare your style then and now. Do you perceive changes in your style of influencing others?)

## V. SUMMARY

Schein, in *Organizational Psychology*,[4] provides a brief but lucid description of intergroup problems in organizations. This summary draws heavily upon his ideas. The simulation you have just experienced has been replicated many times with a variety of groups.[5] Because the results have been surprisingly constant, it is now possible to predict, with relative certainty, what will generally happen as a consequence of intergroup competition. These predictions are summarized here.

### A. What Happens *Within* Groups?

The members of each of two competing groups begin to close ranks and quickly experience increased feelings of group loyalty and pride. Each group sees itself as the best and the other group as

---

[4] Edgar H. Schein, *Organizational Psychology* (Englewood Cliffs, N.J.: Prentice-Hall, Inc., 1965), pp. 80–86.
[5] The most systematic research in organizational settings is reported in Robert R. Blake, H. A. Shepard, and Jane S. Mouton, *Managing Intergroup Conflict in Industry* (Houston, Tex.: Gulf Publishing Company, 1964).

the enemy. Under the pressure of time and task deadlines, the group willingly accepts more structure and autocratic leadership. The group climate is characterized by work, as opposed to play or fight; task, as opposed to maintenance. Conformity is stressed and there is little tolerance for individual deviation.

### B. What Happens *Between* Groups?

Whatever interaction there was between the members of the two groups before the competition decreases and becomes more hostile. Whatever communication there is becomes very selective, each group hearing only comments that confirm its stereotype of the other and support its own position.

### C. What Happens to the *Winners?*

The winning group climate can be called "fat and happy." Tension is released; there is little desire to get on to work. People would prefer to play and rest on their laurels. There is little desire to explore earlier conflicts and possibly learn from them.

Generally, the winners not only retain their prior cohesion, but become more cohesive. The exception is when the group really does not feel as if it won or when the decision is close and they did not win decisively. Under these conditions, winners often act like losers.

### D. What Happens to the *Losers?*

The members deal initially with having lost in one of two ways. Some groups deny reality — "We didn't really lose. It was a moral victory." Other groups seek a scapegoat, someone other than themselves to blame for the defeat. Rules, for instance, are often seen as at fault.

A losing group is, however also a "lean and hungry" group. Tension increases, old conflicts are reexamined, and the group really digs in and learns a lot about itself in preparation for the next task.

### E. What Happens to *Negotiators* Between Groups?

The negotiator often experiences significant role conflict between being a good judge and a good group member. Judges often find it difficult to ignore loyalties to their own groups and be completely neutral. If theirs happens to be a loser, they experience much difficulty reentering, and often bear the brunt of much of the scapegoating behavior described (often in a jocular fashion).

People seldom realize how much responsibility a person feels when he is asked to represent his group and the tension that results from being put in such a position. In addition, it is often unclear just how free a representative really is to be himself as opposed to being what the group expects him to be. How flexible is he to deviate from the group's mandate in response to changes in the situation? Finally, if his group loses, the representative often feels guilty and responsible.

We have, in this unit, explored some of the dysfunctional consequences of intergroup competition and conflict, and it would be a simple step to assume that all conflict between groups in an organization is bad. More recent studies[6] have pointed to a different view of conflict — that too little expressed conflict between groups can be as dysfunctional as too much.

Brown maintains that conflict will exist between groups by their very nature, and that the task of the manager is not necessarily to eliminate conflict but to maintain it at a level appropriate to the task. Too much conflict can lead to defensiveness and an inability to work collaboratively toward organization goals. Too little conflict can stifle ideas and innovation. Relative differences in power between

[6] L. Dave Brown, "Managing Conflict Among Groups," *Readings.*

groups, for instance, often lead to too little conflict being expressed as the "low-power" group finds the expression of such views to the "high-power" group much too risky.

The manager who wishes to manage conflict productively needs to develop skills in diagnosing dysfunctional situations at both extremes in terms of attitudes, behaviors, and structures that are needed to increase or decrease the level of conflict. Many conflicts in society (race, sex, age) require the effective manager to be aware of those larger conflicts, assessing as clearly as possible the extent to which his/her organization reinforces them, and working to change those attitudes, behaviors, and structures that institutionalize them.

As we have seen in the exercise, intergroup conflict is easy to induce. Getting the conflicts in the open and managing them effectively is another matter. Generally, it has been found that intergroup conflict, once it begins, is extremely hard to reduce.[7] The strategy of locating a common enemy or a superordinate goal is useful, but much work must be done to overcome the negative consequences that have already developed before such strategies become feasible. Educational techniques[8] exist and are being used with considerable success to help organizations deal with intergroup conflict that has dysfunctional consequences.

Given the difficulties of reducing intergroup competition, strategies for eliminating it in the first place may be desirable. Shein suggests four steps that have proved to be effective in helping organizations avoid the dysfunctional consequences of intergroup conflict.

1.  Relatively *greater emphasis is given to total organizational effectiveness* and the role of departments in contributing to it; departments are measured and rewarded on the basis of their *contribution to the total effort* rather than on their individual effectiveness.

2.  *High interaction* and *frequent communication* are stimulated between groups to work on problems of intergroup coordination and help; organizational *rewards given partly on the basis of help* that groups give each other.

3.  There is frequent *rotation of members* among groups or departments to stimulate high degrees of mutual understanding and empathy for one another's problems.

4.  *Win-lose situations are avoided;* groups should never be put into the position of competing for the same organizational reward; emphasis is always placed on pooling resources to maximize organizational effectiveness; rewards are shared equally with all the groups or departments.

[7] The reality of this is nowhere clearer than in our efforts to combat years of racial prejudice and discrimination.
[8] See Blake et al., *Managing Intergroup Conflict in Industry;* for discussion on this point and various publications of the National Training Laboratories, Washington, D.C.

## VI. SELF-EVALUATION AND COMPLETING THE LEARNING LOOP

A. What questions do you now have as a result of your learning experiences from this unit? Jot these down below.

B. From these questions, what *key concepts* can you extrapolate for further learning? Write these concepts below.

C. How can you now go about finding answers to the questions you raised above? Below are some suggested ways to continue your learning process by beginning new learning loops:

1. Look up the key concepts from your questions above in the Yellow Pages of Learning Experiences at the back of the book. Find a few suggested readings or exercises to facilitate the learning of these key concepts.

2. If you don't find the key concepts in the Yellow Pages related specifically to your questions, perhaps there are other concepts listed in the index that might lead you to relevant learning resources at this time. Look for concepts similar to those you identified in B above.

3. In the event that you don't find the Yellow Pages directory useful for your present learning goals now, discuss your questions with other students, faculty, or persons outside your learning environment. Discuss further learning possibilities with them.

# PART III

# ORGANIZATIONS AS SYSTEMS

# chapter 14

## organization design: organization structure and communication networks

*Photo by Sybil Shelton*

## I. OBJECTIVES

A.  To understand the concepts of formal and informal organizational structures and communication networks.

B.  To understand the effects of the organizational structures and communication networks that have developed thus far in this learning organization.

C.  To test ways of changing the nature of an organization's structure and patterns of communication to facilitate present goal achievement and future adaptability.

## II. PREMEETING PREPARATION

Read the Introduction.

## III. INTRODUCTION

Suppose that you are the manager of a group of six subordinates. You are given the task of communicating to your group the following diagram:

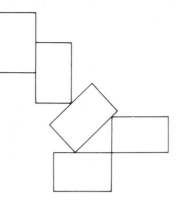

One approach would be for you to face *away* from the group (so that all they can see is your back) and verbally (use no pictures) try to convey your message. The group must remain silent—no questions allowed of you or each other. This approach would approximate many organizational structures of the following form:

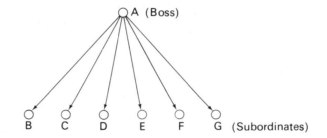

This has been called the closed, one-way communication network. A can communicate with B, C, D, and the rest, but they "cannot" communicate with each other and seldom do they communicate with A (short of saying "yes").

A second approach would be for you to face your group, verbally try to convey your message, and allow (and encourage) them to ask questions of you and each other. This approach would approximate a substantially different organizational structure, which could be represented as follows:

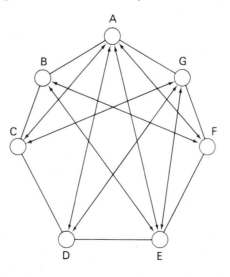

This has been called the open, two-way communications network. Full and open communication is encouraged between each and every group member.

In experimental investigations with these two (pure and extreme) networks, the following effects have been observed.[1] For the given task, the closed network is considerably faster than the open network — the boss finishes sending the message sooner in the closed network. The closed network is considerably less efficient, however, in terms of accuracy — more of the members get the wrong message. In a series of related experiments, the open group has been found to be more adaptable to changes in task requirements.

With respect to morale, the members of the open network are more satisfied and feel more involved in the task. In the closed network, only man A (the boss) feels satisfied and involved. In the open network, every member has the opportunity to assume a position of leadership. The open network, therefore, provides a training ground for the development of future managerial talent. These very simple experiments demonstrate clear relationships between the structure of a group (or organization) and the content of the communication, and demonstrate the process by which information is communicated in a way that influences people's feelings of satisfaction, involvement, commitment, and future capability to assume leadership positions.

*Organization Structure and Design*

Present-day organizational theorists consider organization structure and design in terms of a contingency approach that argues that there is no one best way to structure an organization. The form the organization takes — its structure — should fit the function to be fulfilled — the organization's purpose or mission. Galbraith's research provides the practicing manager with some contingency design principles that make this concept operational.

Any organization must address two basic questions. The first is: How will our major tasks be subdivided? The second question relates to differentiation: Will the organization be differentiated by functions (e.g., marketing, finance, engineering, etc.)? Will it be differentiated by project or profit centers? Or is a combination of the two required? Should the organization, as many high-technology companies have done, adopt a matrix form of organization, which differentiates on both functional and project lines and requires collaborative decisions between managers of both, as shown below:

| | Design Dept. | Estim. Dept. | Elect. Eng. | Mech. Eng. | Production | Finance | Quality Control | Marketing |
|---|---|---|---|---|---|---|---|---|
| Project Mgr. A → | | | | | | | | |
| Project Mgr. B → | | | | | | | | |
| Project Mgr. C → | | | | | | | | |
| Project Mgr. D → | | | | | | | | |
| Project Mgr. E → | | | | | | | | |

It is easy to see that in such a complex differentiation, communication and decision-making patterns and procedures must be much more open and collaborative than in organizations with simpler

[1] See, for example: (a) P. Lawrence and J. Lorsch, *Developing Organizations: Diagnosis and Action* (Reading, Mass.: Addison-Wesley Publishing Co., Inc., 1969). (b) Jay R. Galbraith, *Organization Design* (Reading, Mass.: Addison-Wesley Publishing Co., Inc., 1977). (c) Jay R. Galbraith, "Organization Design: An Information Processing View," *Readings.*

configurations. This is but one example of a way organizations go about differentiating themselves: All complex organizations must subdivide their total tasks somehow.

Once the differentiation decision is made, the organization must then confront the issue of integration. Differentiated outputs must be coordinated—the pieces must be put back together—to achieve the organization's basic purpose. Herein lies the basic dilemma of organization structure and design. The more complex the overall task, the higher the level of differentiation required. The greater the required differentiation, the more complex and essential is the problem of integration.

The central issue in this dilemma according to Galbraith is information processing. Routine programmable tasks require very little exchange of information or decision making during task execution, i.e., little on-line information processing. The more complex and nonroutine the task, the more information needs to be processed on-line. A complex, non-routine R&D department must therefore be structured very differently from a production department, where an assembly line may be warranted.[2]

*Formal Integration Mechanisms*

To handle their information-processing needs, organizations rely on a series of formal integrating mechanisms, three of which will be discussed here.[3]

1. *Formal rule.* All organizations have formal rules and procedures, operating manuals, or policy books. The purpose of these, from an organizational structure and design point of view, is to eliminate the need for on-line information processing and decision making. When a situation or problem comes up, the individual employee refers to the policy book and finds the right answer. Carried to an inappropriate extreme, use of formal rules and procedures as a way of coping with needed integration results in our stereotyped image of the ossified bureaucracy. Rules proliferate, policy manuals abound and are continuously updated, and "nothing happens unless it is written in the rules."

2. *Formal hierarchy.* A major reason, from an organization structure and design point of view, for the existence of the formal hierarchy is to deal with exceptions. Given that it is not possible to develop rules for every task situation, people (bosses) are needed to process certain information and make certain decisions about exceptions to the rules. If the same exception occurs frequently enough, it may result in a new rule or policy.

   As task complexity increases, the hierarchy also tends to become overloaded. "I'm overloaded with day-to-day fires and have no time for longer-range issues such as employee development and planning," is a common lament of the "over-exceptioned" manager. When this condition develops, the organization must look to a third integrative mechanism.

3. *Formal targets or goals.* Through the use of specific subunit goals, budget limits, completion dates, and so on, subunits are able to work on their differentiated tasks with less continuous information processing and decision making. The pieces come together—assuming everyone meets their agreed-upon targets as expected. Some tasks, however, do not lend themselves easily to such mechanisms. It is harder for the R&D department, for example, to agree to "be creative" by X date than it is for the production department to agree to Y units by X date. This is *not* because the employees in

---

[2] Thomas J. Allen, "Communications in the Research and Development Laboratory," *Technology Review*, Vol. 70, No. 1 (October–November 1967), pp. 31–37. *Readings.*
[3] See Galbraith for more detail on these three and other mechanisms.

these departments are dramatically different personalities, although this is a typical assumption. Rather, the nature of their tasks is different.

### Reward Systems

Organization structure and design also involves the nature of reward systems. For example, if the reward system is such that rules have absolutely no area of flexibility and individual discretion on a manager's part, one would expect many exceptions. Issues get bumped upstairs with great frequency. If mistakes are intolerable and severely punished, the hierarchy is likely to become overloaded very quickly, and rules and procedures will grow like Topsy.

In addition to specific subunit goals, budgets, and so on, the organization must also ensure that the formal reward system positively reinforces needed behaviors. In many organizations, you can hear: "Always ask for twice what you need because they will cut your budget in half anyway" or "If we set a realistic goal and meet it, they'd expect us to do it faster next time" or "I know it can't be done that fast, but if that's what they want to hear, that's what I'll tell them and then I'll try to blame the other shift for the delay." Such comments are a sign that the organization's reward system is acting as a counterforce to integration from the use of formal targets or goals.

### The Informal Organizational Structure

The points discussed above focus upon the formal organizational structures. An organization chart, for example, specifies the nature of the formal organizational structure and the path that should be taken for the transmission of information through the organization. The actual path taken often departs markedly from this formal structure. In fact, informal networks often develop because the formal network is not satisfying key individual needs. Brown discusses this distinction between formal versus informal organizations in terms of primary and secondary groups and points out:

> There is, therefore, no abrupt point of distinction between primary and secondary groups. But the contrast remains a valid one; the secondary group tends to be organized for a formal purpose (in the case of a factory, for the production of goods), its structure is more or less rationally designed towards that end, and its members are not all intimately known to each other. The primary group may have a specific practical goal, and when in pursuit of that goal will organize itself logically to that end, but essentially it is based on social satisfaction and personal choice, and, quite apart from any practical goal, it seeks to maintain itself as a unity.[4]

Further on, in a discussion of "things people should observe if they are trying to understand the behavior of people in organizations," Brown suggests:

> It is useful, therefore, to distinguish between those actions which are fundamentally technical, those which are sociotechnical[5] and those which are purely social. . . . Clearly technical and sociotechnical behavior is an aspect of formal organizations, whereas social behavior belongs to the informal structure of the factory.[6]

[4] J. A. C. Brown, *The Social Psychology of Industry* (New York: Penguin Books, 1954), pp. 128–129.
[5] "Sociotechnical" refers to social groupings that are determined by the technology used for the task. Offshore-platform oil well personnel, for instance, have a different social system than on-shore oil well people, as the technology requires them to be together for long periods of time, sharing in eating, sleeping, and recreation.
[6] Brown, *The Social Psychology of Industry*, p. 131.

The importance of understanding the distinctions between formal versus informal organizations and the problems that can arise if the two are not understood is at no time clearer than when one attempts to introduce a technical change into an organization and encounters great resistance. Such was the case in Trist's study of an attempt to change the process by which coal was mined.[7] The anticipated production increases from the new method were not being realized, and upon investigation it was observed that the new technology substantially altered the social system that had developed within this mine. The point here is that whereas a formal organization chart can be redrawn to account for the effects of a technological change, the informal social system, which does not appear on an organization chart, is also influenced by the technological change. Both must be taken into account.

*Informal Integrative Mechanisms*

We have already discussed several integrative mechanisms which are a part of the formal organizational structure. At this point, we need to explore the integrative mechanisms which are a part of the informal organizational structure.

1. *Informal rules—norms.* The informal counterpart to the formal use of rules in an organization is the concept of norms. A norm is an unwritten, informal "rule" that governs individual behavior in an organization. All social systems develop norms; they are an inherent consequence of social interaction. Consequently, the existence of norms is neither inherently good nor bad. The diagnostic question is whether or not the norms that arise function to positively support/reinforce or inhibit the organization's primary formal function. Let us examine how norms influence the organization's primary formal mission or function. Imagine an R&D group whose primary function is the generation of new, creative ideas. This group has a formal leader, a boss.

   One might observe in such a group that ideas are freely exchanged and critically examined, with one exception. The boss's ideas tend to go unchallenged. When the boss states an opinion, the group behaves as if it were a decision, a fact. Now, if the boss possesses a unique technical expertise, one could argue that this is a functional norm. However, it is possible that, for a variety of reasons, people have come to believe that some form of punishment will befall anyone who does not agree with the boss—the "yes-man" syndrome. This norm would be potentially dysfunctional to the group's efforts to fulfill its primary formal function.

   Let us carry the example one step further. A new person joins the group. As the "new kid on the block," s/he does not yet know all the rules of the game—the norms. The person, at some point, may vigorously try to persuade the boss that his/her idea has some serious flaws. A norm has been violated. There is some anxious laughter in the group, some uneasy shuffling around in chairs. After the meeting, an old-timer pulls the newcomer aside for a "Dutch uncle" talk. "Look, friend, let me tell you something for your own benefit. In this group, you never take on the boss the way you did today. It's a no-no, a taboo." Unless an organization is willing to consciously examine its norms—a norm in itself—it runs the risk of having this element of the informal structure act counter to the organization's primary formal function. Norms will develop in all social systems. The issue is one of diagnosing their appropriateness to the task of the organization and instituting new norms where necessary.

2. *The informal hierarchy—status differentials.* An important source of status in any organization is one's position in the formal hierarchy. Bosses are differentiated from subor-

[7] E. Trist as reported in Warren G. Bennis et al., *The Planning of Change,* 2nd ed. (New York: Holt, Rinehart and Winston, Inc., 1969), pp. 269–281.

dinates in terms of the formal power associated with their position — power to control certain rewards, to make certain decisions, to resolve certain exceptions to formal rules, and so on. In many organizations, one finds other less formal dimensions along which people differentiate one another. Any element of difference can be a source of status and power. For example, in many organizations, a comment made by a male will be treated much more seriously than if the same comment were made by a female — a sex differentiation. An age/seniority differentiation is also common: "These young turks are really something. They think a college education gave them all the answers!" The perceived status of one's educational background can also act as a source of differentiation. Many organizations find themselves to be heavily dependent on a particular task function: "We're a marketing-oriented company" or "We're an R&D-oriented company." The perceived consequence may be: "When push comes to shove, the top positions always go to people from Marketing." The impact of these status differences can be positive or negative in terms of the organization's primary formal function. Again, the critical issue is one of appropriateness to the organization's primary formal function. Differentiated subunit tasks must be integrated — coordination is essential. Age/seniority, sex, educational background may have little to do with the issue at hand. Integrative decisions influenced by the informal hierarchy may, therefore, ultimately be dysfunctional to the accomplishment of the organization's primary formal functions.

3. *Informal goals — individual needs and goals.* The degree to which individual goals and organizational goals can be integrated has and will continue to be a major source of concern to organizational theorists and practicing managers. Many approaches exist and are being implemented to maximize the degree of overlap, such as goal-setting procedures, management by objectives, participative performance appraisal systems, and flexible and adaptive formal reward systems. The less the agreement between formal targets and goals (a formal integrative mechanism) and individual needs and goals, the more difficult it will be to achieve the needed integration of formally differentiated subtasks to ensure fulfillment of the organization's primary formal function.

Examples of these informal goals are not easy to see because they tend to be defined as "antiorganizational" and therefore operate under the table. Such comments as "She always has a hidden agenda" or "He's always trying to build his own little empire" are indicative of the tension between formal organizational goals and informal individual goals. In the specific context of group decision making, this tension has been discussed more fully as an example of self-oriented behaviors.[8]

A very typical example of this dilemma can be seen operating on many assembly lines. A formal goal or target has been set — X units per hour per employee. This becomes the group norm or standard. Along comes a capable individual who wants to get ahead (perhaps an achievement need). Efforts on this person's part to better the formal standard are met with group pressures to get back in line — the group punishes rate busters. Here individual needs to belong to the group (an affiliative need) may take precedence over the formal goal of increasing productivity.

*Mapping Organizational Structures*

The usefulness of mapping the formal and informal aspects of an organizational structure is demonstrated in Allen's research[9] on the process of communication in research and development laboratories. Allen finds that, in addition to the formal organization structure, the informal structure,

[8] For more details on this concept, see Chapter 8, Group Dynamics.
[9] Allen, "Communications in the Research and Development Laboratory." *Readings.*

as represented by patterns of friendship and extraorganizational social encounters, has an important effect on the flow of technical ideas. Scientists were found to discuss technical ideas with many of the same people with whom they interacted on a social basis.

Allen's research also uncovered the existence within research and development laboratories of people he called "technological gatekeepers." These few people, much like the opinion leaders identified in early research on voting behavior, were mentioned very frequently as sources of critical information. These gatekeepers act as a link between the organization and the outside environment, as evidenced by their attendance at professional meetings and reading of professional and technical periodicals. Knowledge of who these gatekeepers are and of the nature of the existing sociotechnical and social networks within an organization can serve as important inputs into many organizational decisions. One would not, for example, want to make an architectural decision that would act to break up an effective informal communication group by moving its members apart from one another.[10]

The interdependence of formal and informal structures is often complex and difficult to map. However, in the process one may gain surprising insights into the real communications process of a group or organization. The purpose of this unit is to diagnose and explore the impact of the organizational structure, both formal and informal, as it currently exists in this learning organization — the group you are taking this course with.

## IV. PROCEDURE FOR GROUP MEETING

### A. The First Part (Time Allotted: 60-90 Minutes)

This unit will be somewhat different from the others in this book. In other units, a formal structure has been recommended in the way of specific steps, specific times, and so on. To do likewise in this case would be to run counter to a primary function of the unit — to have you diagnose and explore the existing structure. Consequently, the approach to the first part of this class will be as follows.

1. We will describe the primary formal function of the first part of the class, the overall output you will be asked to achieve.

2. You will then have the responsibility to decide how you are going to go about accomplishing this overall task. In other words, you will have to confront the differentiation issue: How, if at all, will the total task be subdivided?

3. In the process of implementing your differentiation decision, you will then experience the need for various integrative mechanisms, both formal and informal.

4. After you have completed the above, a series of questions will be provided (an element of a formal integrative mechanism) to guide your discussion of the exercise.

*Your Primary Formal Function*

During the first part of this class, your primary formal function is to come up with the following:

1. A statement of this learning organization's (the course) primary formal function.

2. A description of how this overall task, as you have described it above, has been dif-

[10] The architecture of an organization is an important element of its formal structure. For more detail on this element see Fred I. Steele, *Physical Settings and Organization Development* (Reading, Mass: Addison-Wesley, 1973).

ferentiated: What are the subunit (individual, small group, total class) tasks that must be accomplished if the overall function is to be achieved?

3. With respect to formal integrative mechanisms, describe and define specific examples that exist in this organization of:

   a. Formal rules or procedures.

   b. Formal hierarchy.

   c. Formal targets and goals.

   d. Formal rewards or punishments.

4. With respect to informal integrative mechanisms, describe and define specific examples that exist in this organization of:

   a. Informal rules — norms.

   b. Informal hierarchy — status differences.

   c. Informal goals — individual needs and goals.

*How you go about fulfilling this primary formal function is entirely up to you.* However, it will be useful, in order to discuss the exercise during the second part, for the entire group to be able to see the end product(s). Plan for this by using the blackboard or large pieces of newsprint paper.

B. The Second Part (Time Allotted: 60 Minutes)

During the second part, there will be two phases: (1) a discussion of the *content* of your output from part 1, and (2) a discussion of the *process* you used to complete your tasks during part 1.

*Content Discussion Guidelines*

1. In what way, if any, could this organization's overall task, as you defined it, be differentiated differently; i.e., is there a different way to define subunit tasks (e.g., group papers versus individual papers)?

2. Evaluate the effectiveness of the formal integrative mechanisms you described; i.e., in what ways do they seem to facilitate needed integration of differentiated subunit tasks? In what way could they/should they be changed to enhance the achievement of this organization's primary formal function?

3. Evaluate the effectiveness of the informal integrative mechanisms you described; i.e., which norms seem to be helpful/dysfunctional? Which status differences seem to be helpful/dysfunctional?

4. To what extent are the formal and informal structures operating harmoniously? In conflict?

5. If they are in conflict, in what way could they be altered to become more mutually integrative?

*Process Discussion Guidelines*

1. What structure did the group adopt for the first part of today's exercise (total group, subgroups)? Diagram that structure.

2. If you did split into subgroups, upon what basis (what criteria) did people form one group or another? Formal task reasons? Informal personal/social reasons? Be specific.

3. What were the effects of the structure you decided upon on this organization's ability to perform the task? On people's feelings of satisfaction, involvement, commitment?

4. What integration dilemmas did this structure require? How was needed integration achieved?


## V. SUMMARY

Many groups find this unit difficult. One reason for this is that the lack of structure provided by the unit instructions places a heavy responsibility upon group members. We have not tested the hypothesis empirically, but prior research (discussed in the Introduction) would suggest that groups that had developed a more open two-way communications structure would find it easier to adapt to this "new task" (and provide their own structure) than would groups whose structure had been more closed or one-way.

To summarize, let us look at one individual's analysis of his group in this exercise. In his analysis, he identifies the formal structure that he feels is appropriate for a "learning organization" and compares the actual informal structure to it.

> I would like to discuss the organization within our class. I believe the formal and informal structures are in great conflict with one another as a result of differences in procedures and objectives, resulting in competition, dissatisfaction, and a severe hindering of the learning process.

> I conceive of the formal structure of the class as something that can be represented as:

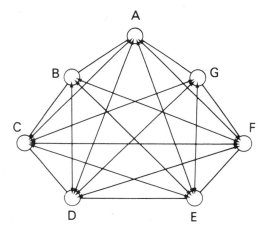

In this structure, each member of the class communicates with every other member of the class without having to go, indirectly, through a third member. There is no leader; all share equally in the task of leadership. This structure implies a number of distinct characteristics.

1. Every member fully participates in the group process (i.e., communication and task accomplishment). Also, each member participates equally in the process. Thus, each member shares all his ideas and is able to learn from the ideas of all the other members. The group is then enabled to work with the maximum number of ideas, and learning becomes the best that the group is capable of.

2. Every member is equally responsible for the progress and accomplishments of the group. This reinforces characteristic 1.

3. Learning is a group process. There is no leader or teacher whose ideas and contributions are superior to the rest of the group, who instructs or "lectures" the other members. The members learn as much, or as little, as they can from the pooled ideas of all. Learning is thus not passive, but depends on active participation in the group process.

4. The group shares a common sense of direction. It pursues one subject or goal at a time, even though the goal may shift frequently.

It is clear that, to have these characteristics, the members must be open and honest with one another, at least in the matter of sharing their ideas, and probably also in the areas of individual goals, feelings, and attitudes with respect to the group and each of its members. Before such honesty can occur, the members must learn to trust each other. However, trust requires knowledge of the other persons, so honesty and trust must develop together, i.e., a small commitment of trust expressed in honesty concerning some limited areas, followed by further development of trust and honesty if the initial step results in reciprocative action by the other members. As honesty and trust develop, such things as agreement on a common goal and the mutual acceptance of responsibility to reach that goal become possible.

The structure that has developed in this class also implies definite characteristics.[11]

1. There is an unequal distribution of both participation and responsibility. The groups tend to filter out many individual ideas, preferring to work on certain ones by themselves, passing on only some of the total (perhaps the least interesting ones?). They may be responsible and participate equally, as a unit, with other units, but this lessens individual involvement relative to units with smaller numbers of members.

2. Learning becomes segmented. As different units hold back various ideas from the group, each unit works on a different combination of ideas, so that various units learn different things. This has the effect of reducing the learning possible for each individual.

3. A multiplicity of goals occurs. Each unit is learning different things, experiencing different ideas, so each unit tends to develop and pursue goals that are different from every other unit. There is no common direction, unless, by chance, all the groups happen to move in the same direction.

It is clear that this structure is in opposition to the formal structure. The primary reason for the development of this structure is a lack of the two basic prerequisites to the formal structure: truth and honesty. Two or more people can trust each other more than the other members of the class, leading to the foundation of a subgroup. Some individuals do not trust anyone else very much or have not been successful in developing trust (no reciprocal response), and so they form individual units. As units begin to form, goals begin to diverge and the development of separate units is reinforced and accelerated. Thus, the group cannot attain an optimum learning process, because ideas are not fully shared. Group members will choose suboptimization rather than risk fully trusting one another.

Thus, learning is hindered, and competition and dissatisfaction result. Competition arises from the interaction of units as they pursue divergent goals. For example, one unit may pursue goals implied by the formal structure. As the class begins to move in that direction,

[11] The student perceived the structure within his class to be a series of subgroups or cliques. Within a given subgroup, communication was direct and two-way. Communication between subgroups was much less direct and more one-way in nature.

requirements of trust and honesty arise. This movement diverges from the goals of other units. It even threatens their existence. They respond by attempting to change the direction of the class toward the pursuit of their goal. Competition becomes intense as all the units attempt to move in their own direction. The final result is that no goal is ever reached, except perhaps the goal of reaching no goal. Thus, each unit becomes dissatisfied and frustrated by the failure to reach its own goals. This reinforces each unit's solidarity and moves each further into itself, additionally reducing potential learning. The frustration and competition further undermine any basis for trust or honesty, making it even more difficult to operate in the formal structure, while reinforcing the informal characteristics.

There are class members whose goal is the formal structure as it is conceived of here. The only way to reach the objectives of that structure is to break up the informal structure as it now exists. Bavelas points out, and it is clear in itself, how inefficient and dissatisfying such a structure as our informal one is; some people participate more than others and communication is hindered and heavily filtered. Brown argues against disintegrating the informal structure, pointing out the needs that it satisfies. I do not disagree with him, but I argue that our formal structure is very much like the informal structure that he describes, or it could be. That is, the large group could satisfy the same basic needs as the small ones now do. I would like to see our informal structure become similar to, and complement, the formal one. I believe this can happen if those pursuing the formal ideal will practice reciprocal trust and honesty with each other, thus showing the class how to respond to honesty; they might even explain the technique. Also, they should extend trust to the other class members and be honest with them, especially as to how to see the destructive effects of subgroups. Perhaps, the class will respond. If so, growing trust and honesty will destroy the basis of the present informal structure and allow modifications in the desired direction. Of course, it should be recognized that I am advocating the pursuit of my goals. If the class will not accept these, competition will prevent their attainment.

## VI. SELF-EVALUATION AND COMPLETING THE LEARNING LOOP

A. What questions do you now have as a result of your learning experiences from this unit? Jot these down below.

B. From these questions, what *key concepts* can you extrapolate for further learning? Write these concepts below.

C. How can you now go about finding answers to the questions you raised above? Below are some suggested ways to continue your learning process by beginning new learning loops:

1. Look up the key concepts from your questions above in the Yellow Pages of Learning Experiences at the back of the book. Find a few suggested readings or exercises to facilitate the learning of these key concepts.

2. If you don't find the key concepts in the Yellow Pages related specifically to your questions, perhaps there are other concepts listed in the index that might lead you to relevant learning resources at this time. Look for concepts similar to those you identified in B above.

3. In the event that you don't find the Yellow Pages directory useful for your present learning goals, discuss your questions with other students, faculty, or persons outside your learning environment. Discuss further learning possibilities with them.

# chapter 15

## the organization as an open system

*Photo by Mike Sands, courtesy of Case Western Reserve University*

## I. OBJECTIVES

A. To explore implications of the open-systems view of organizations.

B. To identify and analyze your own personal theory of organizational functioning.

C. To explore relationships between theories of organization and managerial action.

## II. PRE-MEETING PREPARATION (TIME ALLOTTED: 1–1½ HOURS)

A. Form subgroups. Since this exercise involves building and comparing personal theories about how organizations function, it is useful if group members build their theories in reference to the same organization or type of organization. Prior to the group meeting for this unit, we therefore recommend that the total group divide into subgroups of about four to six persons who share a common interest in building their theory about a particular organization (e.g., Acme Products, the City Hospital, Fraternity) or a particular type of organization (e.g., printing companies, hospitals, sororities). Such a common reference point will make it easier within the subgroup to examine different individual ways of seeing the organization as a system. In addition, comparison among the subgroups will allow examination of how different types of organizations operate.

B. Read the Introduction.

C. Complete the Premeeting Preparation Assignment described on pages 349–360.

D. Gather materials—several pairs of scissors, magic markers, and a sheet of newsprint for each group member.

(*Note:* An alternate approach that in some cases is more productive is for the whole group to focus on a single organization that they have in common, e.g., the university they are attending or the company they work for. In this case, the four to six person groups can be formed on any basis the group desires.)

## III. INTRODUCTION

There is hardly a manager in present-day organizations who does not on occasion sit back and yearn for the "good old days." Running an organization seemed so much simpler then. And for many, it seemed more satisfying. Executives felt freer to make independent decisions and were able to pursue the organization's objectives more single-mindedly. Particularly in the early days of the industrial revolution in America, natural resources were plentiful, labor was cheap and abundant, the market for goods was captive and growing, pollution in such a vast land was of little concern, and government control of free enterprise was nonexistent. Managers were free to set up and run their businesses as they saw fit. Their main problems were inside the organization—in developing production technology and organizing to get work done efficiently. It is little wonder that in this context the early theories of management and organization reflected a primary concern with internal organizational functioning. The classical theories of management addressed the problem of how to organize clearly and efficiently without consideration of environmental problems. Quite reasonably, the theories were developed to cope with the major problems of concern to managers, and the environment for business was, at least from our present-day perspective, relatively benign and free of problems.

Today the situation is quite different. While the problems of internal organizational functioning have become more and more complex, advances in technology, management science, and organizational behavior have kept pace with these problems by providing new techniques and systems for solving them. Tools such as computer-based information systems, sophisticated planning and control techniques, such as PERT (program evaluation review technique) and zero-base budgeting, matrix organization structures and MBO (management by objectives), have given us the capability to manage the internal operations of amazingly complex technological and human systems. In modern organizations, the truly perplexing and difficult problems lie in the organization's relationships with its environment. In our shrinking world, organizations are finding themselves increasingly dependent upon, and responsible for, social justice, consumer protection, environmental protection, community development, economic policy, energy policy, and international political and monetary affairs. All of these are having more and more influence on the achievement of many organizations' primary mission.

### Organizations as Open Systems

This dramatic increase in the interdependency of organizations with their environment has increased the need for organization and management theories that describe how organizations adapt and survive in their environment. Perhaps the most promising theoretical approach to date comes from general systems theory. This approach, which began in biology, has identified common organizational characteristics in all living systems—from the single cell to society. From this perspective, the central characteristic of living systems at all levels is that they are open to their environment—they take in matter/energy and information from the environment, transform it in some systematic way, and return it to the environment by means of information or matter/energy output. In a factory the raw materials and human labor are the input, the patterned activities of production are the transformation of matter/energy, and the finished product is the output. Maintaining the system requires continued inputs which in social systems depends in turn on the product or output. Thus, in a successful system the outputs furnish new matter/energy for the initiation of a new cycle. The auto manufacturer sells the firm's products and by so doing obtains the means of securing new raw materials, compensating the labor force, and refining production technology, thereby assuring the continuation and growth of the organization. In addition, systems require an information return in the form of negative feedback, which allows the system to correct deviations from its goals. For the manufacturer this information takes the form of sales figures, return of poor-quality products, return on investment, and so on.

With this overview of open-systems theory, let us now examine the basic components of an open system (see Figure 15-1).

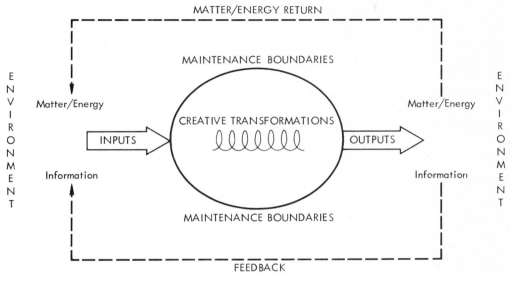

**Figure 15-1**   Components of an Open System

1. *Definition of "system."* First, we must understand what is meant by the concept "system." Basically, a system is a set of units or elements that are actively interrelated and operate in a regular fashion as a total entity. The importance of this definition is that it focuses on processes of relationship and interdependence among structural components rather than on their constant attributes.

2. *Closed vs. open systems.* Theoretically, a closed system has totally impermeable boundaries and receives no matter/energy or information from the environment and exports no matter/energy or information to the environment. No such systems exist in nature. Thus, systems are only relatively open or closed, depending on the extent of a continuing flow of matter/energy and information between the system and the environment.

3. *Inputs.* Inputs in organizational systems are matter/energy in the form of raw materials, human labor, power, and so on, and information in the form of data about the environment, knowledge of production techniques, and so on. Organizational systems have input subsystems to cope with the input process, e.g., personnel departments to hire and train workers, supply departments for production materials, and market research groups for analyzing market data.

4. *Creative transformations.* Through work processes of various kinds, inputs are transformed into outputs by means of transformation subsystems — energy is transformed, products are created and produced, information is analyzed, people are trained, services are organized. The basic tendency in systems is for these transformation subsystems (as well as input and output subsystems) to become more differentiated and specialized, requiring successively higher levels of integration and coordination to hold the system together.

5. *Outputs.* System outputs include products, knowledge, or services useful to the system's

survival and waste. In organizations, these outputs are managed by output subsystems, such as sales or pollution control.

6. *Maintenance boundaries.* Systems develop maintenance boundaries to control input and output processes and define the system's identity. In some cases these boundaries are physical, such as a fence around a plant to keep out unauthorized personnel or to prevent pilferage. Boundaries are also symbolic, as in the case of bookkeeping systems for transferring money into and out of the organization. More intangible are cultural/psychological boundaries, such as norms for membership and inclusion in the system. Systems vary in how permeable their boundaries are — on how open or closed they are. Prisons, for example, are relatively closed organizational systems physically, symbolically, and culturally, while a community organization such as the YMCA is more open.

7. *Matter/energy returns.* According to the second law of thermodynamics, all systems have a tendency toward entropy or maximum disorganization and disorder. Thus, to survive, systems must achieve a steady state by taking in inputs of higher complexity than their outputs. In this way the system acquires energy for the transformation process, for internal repair and for reserves to ensure a comfortable survival margin. For example, an organization buys coal, transforms it to ashes, and uses the energy released to produce products that are sold, thus providing resources for the acquisition of other resources the system needs and profits for the organization.

8. *Feedback.* In order to control its activities and maintain a steady state, a system needs feedback from its environment to alert it to deviations from its course (called *negative feedback*). A thermostat controlling room temperature is a simple example of this negative feedback process. In complex organizations and environments, identifying and analyzing the information needed to control systems processes is much more multifaceted and complex. Without adequate negative feedback controls, no system will survive.

9. *The environment.* In general systems theory the environment of a system includes the suprasystem or systems of which it is a part. The body is the suprasystem of the heart, defining relationships among the heart and other organs. Organizational suprasystems include the community and the wider society of which it is a part. These suprasystems define the organization's physical, economic, political, and social relationships with other subsystems of the society.

*Using the Open-Systems Perspective to Build Your Personal Organizational Theory*

The open-systems view of organizations is not so much a theory as it is a perspective or a vantage point from which one can build a theory of how particular organizations function. Since general systems theory is of necessity formulated at a high level of abstraction in order to encompass living systems at all levels from single cells to society, it needs to be translated to a more concrete level in order to be useful for a particular manager in a particular organization. The value of the open-systems approach is that its perspective rises above that of a particular job or function to encompass a systematic framework for interrelating specific components of an organization. That is, it can help managers rise above priorities and prejudices of their jobs and departments and to see how their work fits into the total picture of the organization's adaptation to the environment.

The exercise that follows is designed to help you build your own personal theory of organizational functioning by translating the abstract concepts of systems thinking into the particular case of your own experience in organizations. It is designed to help you systematically to review your thinking about your organizational experience and to explore the action implications of your theory.

All managers have a personal theory of organizations that they use to make sense of their organizational lives. For some it is very explicit and systematic; for others it is more implicit or "intuitive." No theory is absolutely more correct/better than any other theory. The value of a theory depends on the user's style and what the theory is used for. Theories are guides to perception and action. It is important, therefore, that we understand our personal theories and how they influence our behavior. Many people, for example, do not realize how situation-specific their theories are. When they enter a new situation, they apply their old theory and are chagrined to find out that something is wrong. The more firmly entrenched their theory is, the more likely they are to blame others for their failure ("They just don't accept my leadership") rather than to modify their theory.

Just as our perceptions of other individuals are subject to a series of potential biases or limiting filters, our theory of organization is subject to a similar set of potential distortions. The basic dilemma is that we all must have a theory to organize our experience and action. In the absence of some theory, however narrow or implicit, the world becomes a jumble of chaotic possibilities. Kuhn points out with respect to the scientific theories:

> In the absence of a paradigm (theory) or some candidate for a paradigm, all of the facts that could possibly pertain to the development of a given science are likely to seem equally relevant. As a result, early fact gathering is a far more nearly random activity than the one that subsequent scientific development makes familiar.[1]

As soon as a theory becomes formalized and accepted, however, the other horn of the dilemma begins to operate. Facts that are outside the boundary of the theory are either not examined at all or are examined with a biased eye. The basic theory, in other words, becomes very resistant to change.

Argyris and Schön describe this phenomenon as the "self-sealing" nature of most theories.[2] In part to reduce uncertainty and anxiety, our personal theories are often designed to create a self-fulfilling prophecy. They are untestable. We need, therefore, to build into our theories what Argyris and Schön call a "double-loop-learning" capacity. We need to act and at the same time test the appropriateness of our actions in order to revise our personal theories when experience dictates a need for such revision.

This is by no means an easy task. In the upcoming class session you will have an opportunity to sharpen your understanding of your own personal theory of organizational functioning. By sharing and discussing your view with others, you can gain a better grasp of the assumptions and values on which it is based.

[1] T. S. Kuhn, *The Structure of Scientific Revolutions* (Chicago: University of Chicago Press, 1970), p. 15.
[2] C. Argyris and D. Schön, *Theory in Practice: Increasing Professional Effectiveness* (San Francisco: Jossey-Bass, Inc., 1974); and C. Argyris, "Double Loop Learning in Organizations," *Harvard Business Review*, September–October 1977. *Readings.*

## PREMEETING PREPARATION ASSIGNMENT

Your task before the class meeting is to analyze the organization or type or organization that your sub group decided to focus on in step A of the premeeting preparation. The forms provided in this assignment will help you to construct your own personal theory or model of how the organization you chose functions. A personal organizational theory or model is simply a representation or picture of the components of an organization and how they function together. This "picture" can be crude and simple or very detailed and complex. It can be accurate or inaccurate. The purpose of the exercise in this unit is to help you refine and increase the accuracy of your organizational model by systematically analyzing the organization using the general framework provided by open systems theory, and by sharing your analysis with others in order to broaden your view and correct misperceptions you may have about the organization or type of organization in question.[3]

The preparation assignment has three main parts — 1) defining the boundaries of the organization you are examining, 2) analyzing the organization's environment, and 3) analyzing the organization's internal functioning.

---

[3] The readings book contains two articles that discuss the use of open systems theory for describing organizations. You may want to read these articles before building your model. The articles are Clark and Krone, "Toward an Overall View of Organization Development in the Seventies" and Nadler and Tushman, "A Congruence Model for Diagnosing Organizational Behavior".

The first step in creating your organizational theory is to focus sharply on the organizational entity you want your theory to describe. For many individuals this represents the single organization they are currently working and living in. For some their focus is on the immediate locale or departmental environment. For others the focus includes a broad network of organizations. The important task here is to define just what portion of your organizational experience you want your theory to explain. It may be useful to pick an organization of moderate size to avoid making the analysis too complex and time consuming. (You may want to create this description with other members of the subgroup you formed in step A of the premeeting preparation.)

Complete the following:
The organization my theory seeks to explain includes:

_____

_____

_____

_____

_____

What is the organization's mission (its primary function or long term goal)?

_____

_____

_____

_____

Is the organization a part of a larger system? (For example, a company may be owned by a larger corporation, or a state university will be a part of state government and the looser system of higher education in the U.S.).
List the larger system or systems that your organization is a part of:

_____

_____

_____

_____

This step involves identifying the environmental entities that interact with the organization and are critical to its survival. These entities can be organized groups or organizations (e.g., unions); clusters of people (e.g., customers or the labor market); individuals; bodies of knowledge (e.g., the body of research on chemistry); governments, or even more abstract entities such as changing values of young people. These entities can be loosely grouped into three types — those that provide *inputs* to the organization (e.g., suppliers); those that consume *outputs* from the organization (e.g., customers); and those that *maintain* the boundaries of the organization by defining what it can and cannot do (e.g., regulatory agencies). These are somewhat arbitrary categories however since the organization will engage in transactions with each of the entities critical to its survival which involve both *giving* something and *getting* something in return. For example, a manufacturer will give money to get coal from a supplier (input) and get money from customers for giving them its products (output). The form on page 353 provides space for you to list the significant entities that you see transacting with your organization. After listing each significant entity, specify in the space provided the nature of the transaction the organization makes with that entity — what the organization gives and what it gets in return.

## Part III: Analyzing the Organization's Internal Functioning

In this portion of the analysis of your organization you will be building a model of how the organization functions internally to transform inputs into outputs and maintain its boundaries. The forms provided will assist you in examing three aspects of internal organizational functioning.

A. The way that the organization is *differentiated* — that is how the organization divides itself into specialized subgroups to accomplish its major tasks.

B. The way the organization is *integrated* — that is the way the organization draws together and coordinates the work of various specialized subgroups.

C. The important *creative transformations* that the organization must perform to survive and be effective — that is the tasks and processes that the organization must manage and control to cope with its environment and achieve its mission.

## A. Organizational Differentiation

The form on page 355 provides space to list the major formal and informal groups in the organization. Formal groups are often easy to identify because they appear on organizational charts and are often clearly defined by physical location, task, etc. As anyone who has looked at an organization knows, formal groups can often be identified at several levels of detail (e.g., division, department, section, work group, etc.). For this analysis it is best to use major groupings without going into subsections of those groups.

Informal groups are more difficult to identify and require a more intimate knowledge of the organization you are analyzing. Nonetheless, in many organizations informal groups such as a Black caucus, a regular luncheon meeting of key executives, or a group of friends often perform significant functions for the organization.

When you have completed your list of major groups, list each group's major task or tasks and the major environmental entities that the group carries on transactions with (if any).

## B. Organizational Integration

The next step is to analyze how the work of these different groups gets coordinated to make the organization function smoothly as a unit. The form on page 357 is designed to assist you in this analysis. In the circles provided put the name of the major formal and informal groups you identified in the differentiation analysis. Then draw lines connecting groups that coordinate their activities with one another. Write on the line *how* that coordination takes place. In describing how integration takes place you may want to refer to the previous chapter on Organization Design and the article by Jay Galbraith in the readings book — "Organization Design: An Information Processing View." For example, if marketing and sales coordinate their work via the formal hierarchy with a common supervisor you might write on the line connecting marketing and sales "common boss." On the other hand, marketing might coordinate with research via task forces, committees or informal liason; some groups may not coordinate with others at all.

## C. Key Creative Transformations

The last task in building your model is to identify the key processes that the organization must manage to survive and be effective. To do this you will need to examine the model you have created thus far, and examine your own experience with the organization to identify those aspects of the organization's operation that are central to its operation — either because they are necessary for its survival or because they are problematical for the organization at this time. To assist in this examination we have listed on pages 359 and 361 a variety of factors that can be important to an organization's functioning. On these pages circle those issues that are critical management issues for your organization, and briefly note in each circled box why it is critical. For example, in a rapidly growing organization SIZE may be a critical issue to manage. You would circle that box and write "to manage rapid growth." If you identify key management issues not listed on these pages relabel an unused box, circle it, and note why it is critical.

# COMPONENTS OF THE ORGANIZATION'S ENVIRONMENT

| Significant Groups or Entities | Nature of Transactions | |
| --- | --- | --- |
| | What the organization GIVES | What the organization GETS |
| *Input Entities* | | |
| | | |
| | | |
| | | |
| | | |
| | | |
| *Output Entities* | | |
| | | |
| | | |
| | | |
| | | |
| | | |
| *Maintenance Entities* | | |
| | | |
| | | |
| | | |
| | | |

# ANALYSIS OF ORGANIZATIONAL DIFFERENTIATION

| Major Organizational Groups | Primary Task(s) | Environmental Relationship(s) |
|---|---|---|
| *Formal* | | |
| 1 | | |
| 2 | | |
| 3 | | |
| 4 | | |
| 5 | | |
| 6 | | |
| 7 | | |
| 8 | | |
| 9 | | |
| 10 | | |
| *Informal* | | |
| 11 | | |
| 12 | | |
| 13 | | |
| 14 | | |
| 15 | | |
| 16 | | |

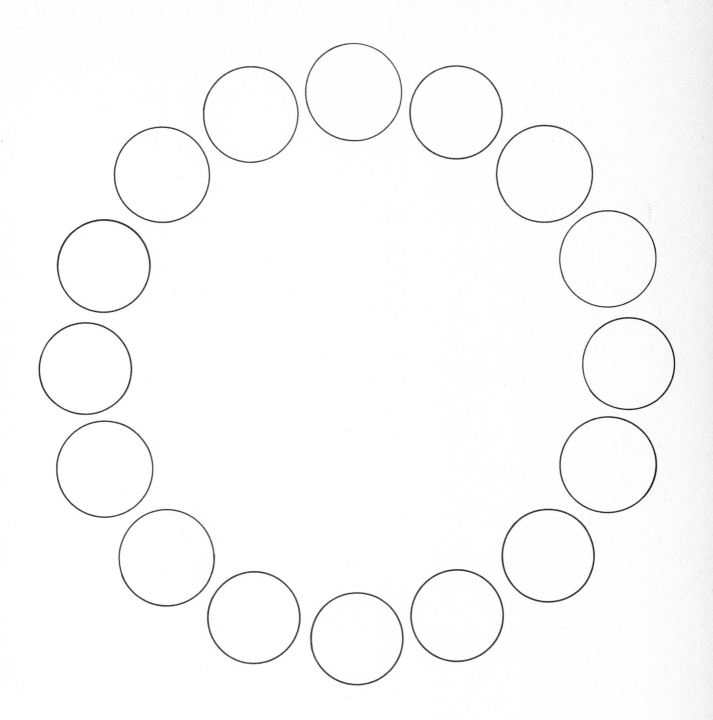

| 1<br>ARCHITECTURAL/PHYSICAL<br>FACILITIES | 2<br>CAPITAL | 3<br>CAREER DEVELOPMENT |
|---|---|---|
| 4<br>CLIQUES AND INTEREST<br>GROUPS | 5<br>COMMUNITY RELATIONSHIPS | 6<br>COMPENSATION/BENEFITS |
| 7<br>CONFLICT | 8<br>CONTROL PROCESS | 9<br>COSTS |
| 10<br>CULTURE/VALUES/BELIEFS | 11<br>DECISION-MAKING METHODS | 12<br>EFFICIENCY, WASTE |
| 13<br>FORMAL AUTHORITY<br>STRUCTURE | 14<br>FORMAL INFORMATION<br>SYSTEM | 15<br>FORMAL REWARD SYSTEM |
| 16<br>GOVERNMENT RELATIONSHIPS | 17<br>INFLUENCE STYLES | 18<br>INFORMAL COMMUNICATION |
| 19<br>INFORMAL REWARDS | 20<br>INTERGROUP RELATIONSHIPS | 21<br>INTERPERSONAL<br>RELATIONSHIPS |
| 22<br>JOB/ROLE DEFINITIONS | 23<br>JOB SATISFACTION<br>OF EMPLOYEES | 24<br>MANAGEMENT STYLE |

| | | |
|---|---|---|
| 25<br>MARKET RELATIONSHIPS | 26<br>MORALE/EMPLOYEE<br>ATTITUDES | 27<br>MOTIVATION |
| 28<br>ORGANIZATION CHART | 29<br>ORGANIZATION<br>CLIMATE/NORMS | 30<br>PERFORMANCE APPRAISAL |
| 31<br>PERSONALITY<br>CHARACTERISTICS | 32<br>PLANNING PROCESS | 33<br>POLICY AND PROCEDURES |
| 34<br>PROBLEM/OPPORTUNITY<br>IDENTIFICATION PROCESS | 35<br>PROBLEM SOLUTION<br>PROCESS | 36<br>PROFITS |
| 37<br>RETURN ON INVESTMENT | 38<br>SCHEDULING | 39<br>SELECTION PROCEDURES |
| 40<br>SYSTEM GOALS | 41<br>TEAM FUNCTIONING | 42<br>TECHNOLOGY |
| 43<br>TIME DEMANDS | 44<br>TRAINING/EDUCATION | 45<br>TURNOVER/ABSENTEEISM |
| 46<br>UNIONS/WORKER<br>ORGANIZATIONS | 47<br>WORK FLOW | 48<br>SIZE |

## IV. PROCEDURE FOR GROUP MEETING

*Step 1:* *Subgroup meetings to compare and refine individual models* (time: 45 minutes). The groups formed in step A of the premeeting preparation should meet together to share the models they created in the prework assignments. Each person in turn should share his or her model with the others and solicit their reactions. The group may want to pool the individual models to form a consensus model of how their common organization or type of organization functions. This will facilitate discussion and evaluation of the organization's health and effectiveness in step 2.

*Step 2:* *Each subgroup joins with another subgroup to compare models and evaluate the organization's health and effectiveness* (time: 1 hour 15 minutes). Before beginning everyone should read the summary below with special emphasis on the ten criteria for organizational health and effectiveness described at the end of the summary. There are two tasks for the combined subgroups. First they should briefly describe to one another the models they have built for their respective organizations. In this sharing process they should explore how their organizations are different and what seems to account for these differences (different mission, environments, technologies, for example).

The next step is to use your analysis to evaluate the health and effectivenss of the organizations using the ten criteria outlined in the summary. Your first clue about an organization's health and effectiveness may well come from how difficult *you* found it to build the organizational models. Some organizations have clear missions and clear structures with key management issues well defined. Others seem disorganized and confusing i.e., the organization itself lacks a clear model of how it functions or should function to be maximally effective. The group should examine each criterion in turn rating their organizations on how well it meets these criteria. For example in criterion 1, does the organization recognize and deal effectively with the important entities in its environment, or does it have a more closed view focusing only on customers or financial returns?

## V. SUMMARY

As authors and practitioners in the field, we quite obviously have developed our own personal theories of organizations. Our selection of topics for inclusion in this text has been, in some way, influenced by these theories. It seems appropriate at this point, therefore, that we make explicit certain aspects of our own personal theory of organizations.

*Organizational Health and Open-Systems Approach to Organizations*

It is increasingly clear that there is no longer "one best way" to organize and manage. The appropriate organization structure and management depends on the demands of the organization's environment, the tasks it must accomplish, and the people who are its members. Modern organizations must, in other words, be viewed as open systems. In this view, organization effectiveness is governed by three major factors—the individuals who make up the organization, the organization itself, and the environment the organization exists in. Effective management of the interfaces between these factors—between the individual and the organization and between the organization and its environment—is central to organizational success. Figure 15-2 illustrates this model of organizations.

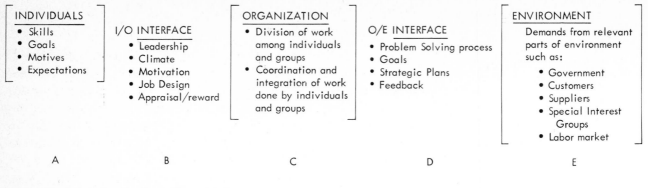

| INDIVIDUALS | I/O INTERFACE | ORGANIZATION | O/E INTERFACE | ENVIRONMENT |
|---|---|---|---|---|
| • Skills<br>• Goals<br>• Motives<br>• Expectations | • Leadership<br>• Climate<br>• Motivation<br>• Job Design<br>• Appraisal/reward | • Division of work among individuals and groups<br>• Coordination and integration of work done by individuals and groups | • Problem Solving process<br>• Goals<br>• Strategic Plans<br>• Feedback | Demands from relevant parts of environment such as:<br>• Government<br>• Customers<br>• Suppliers<br>• Special Interest Groups<br>• Labor market |
| A | B | C | D | E |

*Note: The letters A – E refer to the text below.

**Figure 15–2**   The Open System View of Organizations*

A.   The major input resources to an organization are its human resources. People bring to their jobs a diversity of skills, needs, goals, and expectations. They are socialized into the organization through its personnel recruitment, hiring procedures, and job experiences.

B.   The interface between the individual and the organization is critical to the full utilization of human resources. The individual and the organization establish a "psychological contract." The individual member expects to make certain contributions to the organization and to receive certain rewards in return. The organization expects to provide certain rewards to the individual in return for certain contributions. It is at this interface between the individual and the organization that issues such as leadership, organizational climate, job motivation, job design, and the appraisal/reward process become important.

C.   The organization itself provides the major transformation or throughput function. Individual and group tasks are identified and assigned according to the demands of the organization's technology; this leads to division of labor or specialization. However, specialization creates an equally important requirement to integrate the work of individuals and the various groups in which they work. It is here that such variables as job clarity, delegation of work and responsibility, decision making, communications, and conflict management become important.

D.   An organization exists to act upon the environment, to have certain transactions with the environment. The desired nature or effect of these transactions defines the mission and goals of the organization. Feedback from the environment is required to determine the quality of these transactions, or how effectively the organization is performing its mission. This critical interface between the organization and its environment is defined by the problem-solving process that determines the organization's goals and strategic plans, and the feedback procedures which the organization uses to measure its impact on the environment.

E.   The environment impacts on the organization in many ways. For example, within many organizations today, governmental agencies are demanding changes in employment practices. This demand clearly has an influence on the individuals who are brought into the organization (A); the way individuals respond to leadership and climate (B); and upon the appropriate form of organization (C). Special interest groups (e.g., environmental protectionists) can and do have an impact on organizational goals (E) and the human resources available to the organization (A).

The open-systems model helps to describe an *effective* organization. An effective organization is one which is able to accomplish the following. It attracts skilled and motivated individuals (A) and manages them in such a way as to increase their skills and motivation (B). It separates tasks and allocates them to appropriate individuals and groups (C) without producing gaps and overlaps, i.e., the authority structure produces clear assignment of authority and responsibility. It develops effective formal and informal work units (C). It effectively coordinates the work of different individuals and groups (C). It has an effective problem-solving procedure for setting and reviewing goals and plans (D). It has clearly defined and well-communicated goals and plans which reflect the organization's basic mission and which are based on a careful analysis of the demands of relevant parts of the environment (E), and it obtains and uses feedback from the environment to evaluate effectiveness (D). More specifically, the following characteristics of organizational health or effectiveness can be identified.[4] These dimensions are much like the "vital signs" (e.g., temperature, pulse rate, blood pressure) a physician would diagnose. Their main value is that they signal a potential problem somewhere in the system, although they do not, in and of themselves, represent a complete diagnosis of specific organization problems.

1.  The organization and its parts see themselves as interacting with each other *and* with a *larger* environment. The organization is an "open system."

2.  The total organization, the significant subparts, and individuals manage their work against *goals* and *plans* for achievement of these goals.

3.  Form follows function (the problem, or task, or project, determines how the human resources are organized).

4.  Decisions are made by and near the sources of information regardless of where these sources are located on the organization chart.

5.  There is a minimum amount of inappropriate win/lose activities between individuals and groups. Constant effort exists at all levels to treat conflict and conflict situations as *problems* subject to problem-solving methods.

6.  There is a shared value, and management strategy to support it, of trying to help each person (or unit) in the organization maintain his (or its) integrity and uniqueness in an interdependent environment.

7.  Communication laterally and vertically is *relatively* undistorted. People are generally open and confronting. They share all the relevant facts, including feelings.

8.  There is high "conflict" (clash of ideas) about tasks and projects, and relatively little energy is spent in clashing over *interpersonal* difficulties, because they have been generally worked through.

9.  The reward system is such that managers and supervisors are rewarded (and punished) comparably for all of the following:

    a. Short-term profit or production performance.

    b. Growth and development of their subordinates.

    c. Creating a viable working group.

10. The organization and its members operate in an "action–research" way. General practice is to build in *feedback mechanisms* so that individuals and groups can learn from their own experience.

[4] Adapted from Richard Beckhard, *Organization Development: Strategies and Models* (Reading, Mass.: Addison-Wesley Publishing Co., Inc., 1969), pp. 10–11.

## VI. SELF-EVALUATION AND COMPLETING THE LEARNING LOOP

A. What questions do you now have as a result of your learning experiences from this unit? Jot these down below.

B. From these questions, what *key concepts* can you extrapolate for further learning? Write these concepts below.

C. How can you now go about finding answers to the questions you raised above? Below are some suggested ways to continue your learning process by beginning new learning loops:

1. Look up the key concepts from your questions above in the Yellow Pages of Learning Experiences at the back of the book. Find a few suggested readings or exercises to facilitate the learning of these key concepts.

2. If you don't find the key concepts in the Yellow Pages related specifically to your questions, perhaps there are other concepts listed in the index that might lead you to relevant learning resources at this time. Look for concepts similar to those you identified in B above.

3. In the event that you don't find the Yellow Pages directory useful for your present learning goals, discuss your questions with other students, faculty, or persons outside your learning environment. Discuss further learning possibilities with them.

# PART IV

## DEVELOPMENT AND CHANGE

# chapter 16

## planned change and organization development

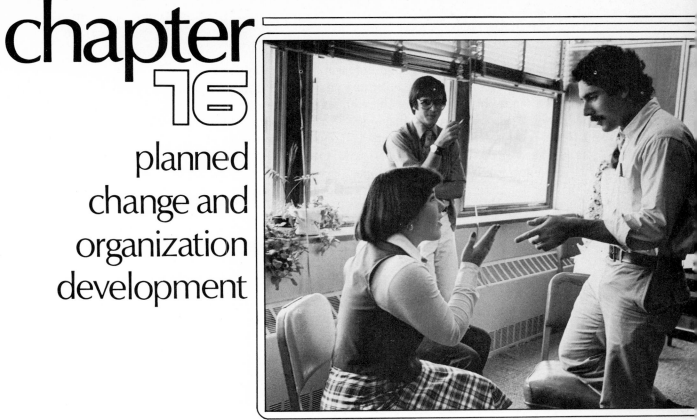

*Photo by Sybil Shelton*

## I. OBJECTIVES

A. To increase understanding of the process of planning and introducing changes in a system.

B. To identify sources of resistance to change.

C. To practice organizational consulting skills.

## II. PREMEETING PREPARATION

Read the entire unit.

## III. INTRODUCTION

Change is becoming a way of life, and managers' jobs today are more and more preoccupied with coping with change thrust upon them, initiating change and improvement, and managing the process of implementing change. In planning for these changes, administrators and managers too often tend to move immediately from a superficial diagnosis of a problem to the action steps. Yet more effective results and fewer tensions in the system will occur if a more thorough diagnosis is made of the situation to be changed and the change process is managed systematically. Kolb and Frohman have developed a sequence for initiating and managing change that is a simple, seven-stage process (see Figure 16-1).[1]

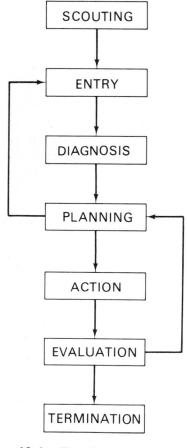

**Figure 16-1**  The Process of Planned Change

The model emphasizes two important facets in the management of change:

1.   It is a sequential process, with each step equally important.
2.   Much of the success of the change effort will depend on the manager's relationship to those who will be impacted most by the change.

[1] This model of the planned change process was generated through the collaborative efforts of Frohman and Kolb. For a more detailed description, see David A. Kolb and Alan L. Frohman, "An Organization Development Approach to Consulting," *Sloan Management Review*, Vol. 12 (1970), pp. 51-65.

As with most models of behavior, the steps may blur into one another, but the articulation and recognition of them can help steer a clearer course through a change effort. The central issues for the change manager are summarized below for each stage of the change process.

## A. Scouting

Although many managers feel they have an adequate knowledge of their own system, it is beneficial in the beginning to test that assumption. At this stage the manager is determining readiness for change, identifying obvious obstacles, and observing what is going on. This stage involves a passive diagnosis of the situation to size up costs and benefits of intervention (Is it worth "rocking the boat?") The key task is to find the entry points for initiating a change, those individuals whose permission is needed, key informal leaders in the system, and so on.

## B. Entry

Once the entry point(s) has been chosen, the manager and system to be changed through the entry-point representative(s) begin to negotiate a "contract" which will define if and how the succeeding stages of the planned change process will be carried out. "Contract" is used here in quotation marks because this process implies more than a legal document agreed upon at the outset of a project. The emphasis here is on a continuing process of sharing the expectations of the change manager and system and agreeing on the contributions to be made by both parties. It is important to emphasize the continuing process of contract renegotiation, because as the planned change process enters succeeding stages, the nature of the problem may change and the resources needed for its solution may increase or decrease. Another aspect of the continuing negotiation process is represented by the feedback loop that reenters the entry stage from the planning stage (see Figure 16-1). As the diagnosis and planning stages proceed, the entry point into the system may have to shift or expand to include those parts of the system which are affected by and/or are responsible for the problem. For example, the personnel department of a company might begin work on the problem of high turnover among first-level management. Diagnosis of the problem may well reveal that the reasons for this turnover lie in poor morale in the line operations. Since responsibility for the ultimate solution of this problem lies with the line managers, the entry contract must be expanded to include these managers in the change process.

The main issue around which the contract negotiation process centers is power—gaining the influence necessary to implement the new program or method of operating. There are four primary sources of this power:

1. The legitimately constituted authority of the system (e.g., the president says one should do this).
2. Expert power (e.g., the prestige of a consultant, or the compelling logic of a solution).
3. Coercive power.
4. Trust-based power (the informal influence that flows from collaborative problem definition and solutions).

While in most change projects power from all four of these sources is brought to bear in implementation of the change, the power derived from collaborative problem definition is often especially critical to the success of those planned change efforts where the system's formal power structure and experts are seen as part of the problem to be solved.

## C. Diagnosis

Diagnosis, as much as possible, should be a collaborative effort involving as many of the affected parts of the system as possible. It focuses on three elements: the perceived problem, the goals of the group or organization, and the resources available.

1. Problem definition: The first step in defining the specific problem is to identify the subpart(s) of the system where the problem is located and identify the relationship between that subpart and other parts of the system. This is necessary in order to anticipate the effect of change in one part of the system on other aspects of the system's functioning. If more and/or different problems surface as the diagnosis progresses, the group can assign priorities and focus attention on the most important problem or the problem that must be solved before other problems can be attacked.

2. Goal definition: At this point goals do not need to be as precise and measurable as they should be later. It is usually sufficient to simply articulate in broad outline the state you would like the organization or group to reach as a result of the change effort. Broadly stated, goals can give direction to your planning effort without overly constraining it.

3. Resource identification: Since people in the system will be involved in implementing the change (indeed, they are the major resources in many cases), their abilities, motivation, and commitment must be used if the change effort is to proceed properly. As these are identified, the manager will also want to ask: "What resources from outside our system do we need to use in order to reach our goal?"

## D. Planning

The results of the diagnostic phase form the starting point for the planning phase. Depending on the findings, these results may require a renegotiation of the entry contract. During the planning phase, the entry contract should be expanded to include those members of the system who will be responsible for implementing the change and/or will be immediately affected by it.

The first planning step is to define the objectives to be achieved by the change. Once clear-cut objectives have been established, alternative solutions or change strategies should be generated. Following this, some attempt should be made to simulate the consequences of each of the alternatives. Often this is done simply by thinking through the implications of each change strategy, but more sophisticated simulation methods, such as computer simulation, can be used. The final change strategy is then chosen from the alternatives available.

Intervention plans can be classified on two dimensions: the source of power used to implement the intervention (formal power, expert power, coercive power, and trust-based power) and the organizational subsystem to which the intervention is addressed. The six organizational subsystems are defined below.

1. The *people subsystem.* Two general types of interventions can be used in this subsystem: manpower flow interventions and education. The manpower flow interventions affect the selection, placement, rotation, and retention of organization members. Educational programs have been designed to change motives, skills, and values. Some common educational interventions include seminars, university programs, T groups, data collection and feedback, role playing, and on-the-job training.

2. The *authority subsystem.* The authority subsystem has a formal and an informal aspect. Changes can be made in formal authority relationships—in job titles and

responsibilities, in the span of control, in the number of organizational levels, in the location of decision points. In addition, informal leadership patterns can be the object of change interventions. For example, a team-building program may be designed to base leadership more on team members' expertise than on organizational titles.

3. The *information subsystem*. This subsystem also has a formal and an informal aspect. The formal information system of the organization can be redesigned to give priority and visibility to the most important information and to provide mechanisms for getting information to the right place at the right time. Much of the organization's information, however, is carried by the informal system, which is often faster than the formal system. Many work team development programs focus in part on this process, using interventions designed to improve the quality of communications among organization members.

4. The *task subsystem*. The two identifiable parts of this subsystem are the human satisfactions offered by the job and the technology on which the job is based. Job enlargement, an increasingly important area of organizational development, has done much to redesign jobs to obtain a better match between the job holder's motives and the satisfactions provided by his job. Several schemes have been developed for classifying technology and exploring the implications of each classification for the organization of the firm and for the individual holding the job.[2] Likewise, the impact of technological change on the organization has been studied in detail, although little has been done to plan systematic technological changes with a consideration for their impact on other organizational subsystems or on the total development of the organization.

5. The *policy/culture subsystem*. As the name implies, this subsystem has a formal, explicit aspect and an informal, implicit aspect. The policy subsystem is made up of rules concerning working hours, promotion, the formal reward system, and work procedures. The culture subsystem consists of the norms and values of the organization—what type of behavior is rewarded, how conflict is handled, what is expected among peers. Perhaps the most common focus of organization change is on the formal policy system. Less common and more difficult are attempts to change the culture or climate of an organization. The Blake Grid OD program is perhaps the most systematic and comprehensive approach to cultural change.[3]

6. The *environmental subsystem*. The environment can be divided, somewhat arbitrarily, into the internal physical environment and the external environment. One important component of the internal environment is architecture. The spatial relationships of organization members, for example, can have a great impact on the information subsystem.[4] The external environment has many characteristics that affect the organization: rapidity of change, uncertainty, quality and quantity of labor supply, financial and material resources, political and legal structures, market, and so on. An organization chooses its environment when it begins operation. It can subsequently redefine certain elements of its environment. For example, an organization initially conceived to serve a specific market can redefine its objective and self-image to that of a growth company in a wider market, thereby relating more to uncertain rather than stable aspects of its environment. This redefinition will have implications for all the other organizational subsystems.

---

[2] See Jay R. Galbraith, "Organization Design: An Information Processing View," *Readings;* also J. Thompson, *Organizations in Action* (New York: McGraw-Hill Book Company, 1967); and J. Woodward, *Industrial Organization: Theory and Practice* (New York: Oxford University Press, 1965).

[3] Robert R. Blake and J. Mouton, *Building a Dynamic Corporation Through Grid Organization Development* (Reading, Mass.: Addison-Wesley Publishing Co., Inc., 1969).

[4] For a systematic treatment of the impact of architectural and physical settings, see Fred I. Steele, *Physical Settings and Organization Development* (Reading Mass.: Addison-Wesley Publishing Co., Inc., 1973).

The four sources of power and the six organizational subsystems can be combined to form a checklist to be used by the manager when planning or executing any action intervention. An example of such a checklist is shown here as Table 16-1. The primary purpose of the checklist is to remind the manager that a change in one subsystem will affect other organizational subsystems. The list can be useful for selecting the best leverage point and for identifying the other subsystems most likely to be affected by the intervention. It may be easier, for example, to redefine jobs than to change motives, an indication that the manager should at least start with the task subsystem rather than the people subsystem. In addition, the manager must plan the intervention in such a way that both aspects of the subsystems are kept in harmony: educational programs and manpower flow interventions must be compatible; the formal and informal authority systems must be mutually supportive; the design of a formal information system must take into account the existing informal flow of information; a program that will redesign jobs must consider the human satisfaction factor as well as the existing technology; policy changes are doomed to subversion if they are not supported by cultural changes; and a close relationship must be maintained between the internal and the external environment.

Table 16-1.  Planning Checklist

| Subsystem | Problem Definition | Proposed Solutions | Possible Effects on Other Subsystems |
|---|---|---|---|
| 1.  People | | 1.<br>2.<br>3. | 1.<br>2.<br>3. |
| 2.  Authority | | 1.<br>2.<br>3. | 1.<br>2.<br>3. |
| 3.  Information | | 1.<br>2.<br>3. | 1.<br>2.<br>3. |
| 4.  Task | | 1.<br>2.<br>3. | 1.<br>2.<br>3. |
| 5.  Policy/Culture | | 1.<br>2.<br>3. | 1.<br>2.<br>3. |
| 6.  Environmental | | 1.<br>2.<br>3. | 1.<br>2.<br>3. |

The checklist can also be useful for identifying the sources of power available for bringing about change and for determining which source, or combination of sources, is the most appropriate for the type of intervention planned. Certain combinations may not be enough to implement even the most optimal plan. The lack of trust-based power, for example, could doom the intervention to failure, as in the case of a consultant who was hired by the head office to do work in the field offices. Perceived as a representative of the head office, with which most of the field offices had great difficulty working, he was unable to develop trust-based power. His intervention in the people subsystem of the offices, which depended on using this power source, therefore met with little success. The consultant's own "post mortem" noted that his inability to establish trust with each field office prevented him from operating effectively.

## E. Action

The action phase of a planned change effort can encompass a wide range of activities, from management training, to creation of new information systems, to changes in organization structure, to changes in architectural and spatial relationships. No matter what the changes are, there is likely to be some *resistance to change*.[5] This resistance, when it occurs, is often treated as an irrational negative force to be overcome by whatever means; yet, in some cases, resistance to change can be functional for the survival of a system.[6] If an organization tried every new scheme, product, or process that came along, it would soon wander aimlessly, flounder, and die. The positive function of resistance to change is to ensure that plans for change and their ultimate consequences are thought through carefully. The failure of most plans for change lies in the change's *unanticipated consequences*. In industry, these failures often take the form of technical changes (e.g., a new information system, a new production process) which fail to anticipate and plan for the social changes that the technical changes cause (e.g., increases and decreases in power at different levels of the organization in the information system example or new working relationships and/or more or less meaningful work in the new production process example). The result is that managers and administrators are annoyed at the stupidity of those subordinates who resent this very logical improvement. Yet the subordinates often are not resisting the logic of the improvement (and hence logical arguments for the change do not help), but are resisting the social changes that management has not recognized and planned for.

Another cause of resistance to change can be the sudden imposition of changes in someone's environment without that person's prior knowledge of, or participation in, the change. To have an important part of one's environment suddenly changed by forces outside one's knowledge and control can cause great anxiety, even panic. The human response to this experience is hostility toward the source of change and resistance to the new method. The process of growth and maturation is one of gaining mastery over one's environment. Management, by imposed change, serves to arrest this process by denying subordinates the opportunity to live in an environment they can understand and control. People who spend their lives in organizations managed by imposed change can become helpless, passive victims of the system, cursed by management for their stupidity and lack of initiative.

These dysfunctional aspects of resistance to change can be alleviated by careful preparation for the action phase. If system members can be involved at the appropriate stages of the scouting, entry, diagnosis, and planning phases, the plan for change can be made more intelligent and more appropriate to the system's needs, both technological and social.

## F. Evaluation

The tradition in the scientific evaluation of change projects has been to separate the evaluation phase from the action phase. To ensure unbiased results, an independent researcher is often hired to evaluate the change efforts. While this approach has some benefit from the standpoint of scientific objectivity, it has some cost in terms of the effective implementation of change. It should be clear in this model that the evaluation phase is an integrated part of the change process.

The evaluation of the action strategy is conducted in terms of the specific objectives defined during the planning phase as well as interim task goals designed to determine if the change is progressing as desired. Members of the system therefore know on what dimensions they are being evaluated. The potential bias created by this knowledge can be overcome by careful choice of objective evaluation indices that cannot be manipulated. For example, the goal of an action intervention may be

---

[5] Paul Lawrence, "How to Deal with Resistance to Change," *Harvard Business Review*, May–June 1954, pp. 49–57.

[6] As we have seen in the Intergroup Relations chapter, too little conflict or resistance can be as serious a problem as too much.

to increase the quantity of patentable products produced by a research group. The validity of the results obtained from using the number of patents as the evaluation index will not be affected by the group's knowledge of the intervention goal, whereas the use of self-evaluation ratings of creativity might.

To develop within the system the ability to use the information generated for self-analysis, the group or organization should monitor the progress of the action phase and evaluate the data itself. The results of the evaluation stage determine whether the change project moves to the institutionalization stage or returns to the planning stage for further action planning and perhaps to the entry stage for further contract negotiation among the participants.

### G. Institutionalization

If the steps so far outlined have been followed, a great deal of effort will have gone into the change, excitement about reaching change goals will have been high, and the natural tendency will be to experience a letdown once the change has been implemented. Institutionalization should not mean a rehardening of the organization's arteries, but a new way of working that combines stability and flexibility. If the change is seen as "complete," those arteries will harden. If it is seen as "continuous," there will be mechanisms in place for continuing to flex and change as situations demand. Some of these conditions necessary for the maintenance of change are as follows:[7]

1. Management must pay conscious attention to the "continuous transition."
2. Explicit processes or procedures for setting priorities for improvement should be instituted.
3. There should by systematic and continual processes of feedback.
4. The reward system should reward people for time and energy spent on these processes.

## IV. PROCEDURE FOR GROUP MEETING

### A. The Acquisition Game

This exercise is designed to simulate some of the organizational processes that occur when two companies merge. During the exercise, the group will divide into two corporations—the Enterprise Corporation, which manufactures spacecraft, and the Merger Corporation, a conglomerate that has just acquired the Enterprise Corporation. The exercise focuses on a visit by a management consulting team from the Merger Corporation to the production facility of the Enterprise Corporation. The two corporations have agreed that Merger Corporation would visit Enterprise, observe their production process, and help Enterprise improve its operations by implementing new managerial and production systems.

Step 1.   *Choose a game coordinator.* The group should first choose someone to act as Game Coordinator. S/he will act as leader and timekeeper for the exercise, the government inspector and buyer of Enterprise's product, and the postgame discussion leader. (The instructor often plays this role.)

Step 2.   *Form the Enterprise and Merger Corporations.* The group should divide itself

[7] Richard Beckhard and Reuben Harris, *Organizational Transitions; Managing Complex Change* (Reading, Mass.: Addison-Wesley Publishing Co., Inc., 1977).

approximately in half to form the two corporations. (If there are more than 20 people in the total group, it will be easier if the group subdivides so that the game is run in two parallel sections with two game coordinators, two Merger Corporations, and so on.) The Game Coordinator should flip a coin to determine which group is the Merger Corporation and which is the Enterprise Corporation. (See the instructions to Merger Corporation and to Enterprise Corporation in the following sections.)

*Step 3.* *Timetable and overview of game procedure.* The procedural steps in the exercise are summarized in Table 16-2. The Game Coordinator may want to copy this summary on a blackboard so that the procedure is visible to everyone.

Table 16-2.   Timetable for the Acquisition Game

| Step | Activity | | Time |
|------|----------|---|------|
| A | Read Procedure Overview; elect Game Coordinator; form corporations | | 10 min |
| B | *Merger Corporation*<br>—Develop plan for helping Enterprise improve<br><br>—Observe Enterprise's management and production process | *Enterprise Corporation*<br>—Organize management and production process<br><br>—Build spacecraft mock-ups<br>—Buy materials<br>—Prepare to produce | 20 min |
| C | Continue observation | Produce spacecraft | 5 min |
| D | Coordinator evaluates, buys, and computes profit | | 2½ min |
| E | Merger Corporation implements new Management/Production System | | 30 min |
| F | Merger observes | Enterprise Production Period 2 | 5 min |
| G | Coordinator evaluates, buys, and computes profit | | 2½ min |
| H | Game Coordinator leads analysis of the Change Process — Discussion | | 45 min |
| | Total time | | 120 min |

*Step 4.* *Instructions for the game coordinator.* While the two corporations are preparing for the first production period, you should read the instructions for the total unit. Your most important tasks are to:

a. Keep the time schedule described in Table 16-2.

b. Sell materials to Enterprise Corporation during Production Periods 1 and 2.

c. Inspect and buy materials from Enterprise Corporation during Production Periods 1 and 2 (see Quality Control Points on blueprints).

d. Record and average numerical responses for each team on the analysis scale, and lead the discussion following.

## B. Instructions for the Enterprise Corporation

Your previous successful experience in the aerospace industry has just won you a government contract to produce as many Enterprise Spacecraft as your production facilities will allow during the next 2 months (represented in this exercise by the two 5-minute production periods). The government has given you a set of blueprints for the spacecraft as well as a number of quality control points (see p. 387). You must buy raw materials from the Game Coordinator as determined by the price schedule in Table 16-3. Your profit is determined by the number of spacecraft you sell to the government at a price of $5,000,000 each minus the cost of materials (other factors, such as overhead, materials, and waste, have been eliminated for simplicity). Only completed vehicles of acceptable quality can be sold. No materials can be returned.

Table 16-3. Materials' Costs of Enterprise Spacecraft

| Number of Sets Purchased | Cost per Set |
|---|---|
| 0–4 | $4,500,000 |
| 5–9 | 4,400,000 |
| 10–14 | 4,300,000 |
| 15–19 | 4,200,000 |
| 20–24 | 4,100,000 |
| 25–29 | 4,000,000 |
| 30–34 | 3,900,000 |
| 35–39 | 3,800,000 |
| 40–44 | 3,750,000 |
| 45–49 | 3,700,000 |
| 50–100 | 3,650,000 |
| Over 100 | 3,600,000 |

In the 20-minute preparation time, you can organize your members in any way you wish to make purchasing and production decisions. During this time, the corporation is allowed two free sets of materials *for each member* to use in any way the corporation wishes to establish production techniques and time estimates. Any additional materials used during this time must be purchased at full cost. These materials cannot be used during the production periods.

Your agreement with Merger Corporation is that they may observe your activities during this time, but that they are not to interfere in any way.

When you have decided how many units you want to produce, tell the Game Coordinator how many sets of materials you want to buy and record that information on the Enterprise Corporation Accounting Form (p. 379).

## C. Instructions for the Merger Corporation

Your task during the first 20 minutes is to decide how best to work with Enterprise Corporation after the first production period to help them increase their profit during Production Period 2. You can organize yourself in any way you want to do this (e.g., you can choose one or two members to act as consultants and feed information and ideas to them; work one-to-one with members of the Enterprise Corporation; or any other model you may choose).

During the 30 minutes before Production Period 2 begins, help the Enterprise Corporation in any way you see fit. *Once the second production period begins,* however, Merger Corporation is only allowed to observe. During round 2, Enterprise Corporation can have no more members than the

## ENTERPRISE CORPORATION ACCOUNTING FORM

| | Material Sets Purchased | Cost per Set | Number of Units Sold at $5,000,000 per Unit | Profit or Loss |
|---|---|---|---|---|
| Production Period 1 | | | | |
| Production Period 2 | | | | |

number they had during round 1. Personnel transfers are, however, legitimate. In other words, the total number of people in Enterprise during round 2 must be the same, but specific people can be shifted from Merger Corporation to *replace* someone in Enterprise.

### D. Analysis of the Change Process

Merger Corporation has just attempted to effect an improvement in the way Enterprise Corporation produces spaceships. On the whole, how successful do you think they were? Draw a circle around the number that most closely represents your opinion:

| 1 | 2 | 3 | 4 | 5 | 6 | 7 |

Completely
unsuccessful

Completely
successful

(The game coordinator will record and average scores for both corporations before proceeding with the discussion.)

Before beginning the discussion of the exercise, take a few minutes to respond to the following questions with short, written phrases. When you have done this, the game coordinator will lead the discussion in which you may share the written responses.

1. Scouting:
   a. How did Merger go about scouting Enterprise?

   _____

   b. How effective was it? Be specific.

   _____

2. Entry:
   a. Was the psychological contract clarified? _____
   b. Was a feeling of collaboration established? How?

   _____

3. Diagnosis:
   a. Was the problem defined adequately? _____

   _____

   b. Were broad goals defined? _____

   _____

   c. Were resources identified and used? _____

   _____

   d. How involved was Enterprise in the diagnosis? _____

   _____

4.	Planning:

a. Were the proper subsystems identified and changed?

_____

b. Which subsystem(s) was worked on, and with what effect? _____

_____

5.	Action:

a. Where did resistance appear? What seemed to cause it?

_____

b. How was it dealt with? _____

6.	Evaluation:

a. Were Merger's objectives met? _____

b. Were evaluation questions asked (e.g., "Is this being helpful to you?") _____

_____

7.	Institutionalization (and flexibility):

a. Would Enterprise improve if a third round were held?

_____

b. What was done to ensure continued improvement?

_____

_____

## DIRECTIONS FOR MAKING THE SPACESHIP ENTERPRISE

The following are directions for making the spaceship. After each step, there is a picture showing what to do and another picture showing what it should look like. Make sure you check this before going on to the next step. There are eleven steps.

1. You should have a piece of paper that has one blank side, and one side that looks like this:

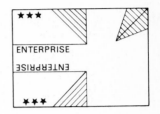

2. Turn the paper over so that the *blank side* is facing up and the lettering "ENTERPRISE" is on the left-hand underneath side.

   It should now look like this:

   "ENTERPRISE" lettering on this end

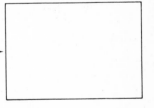

3. Fold corner A to B at the bottom of the paper.

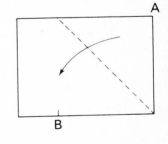

   It should now look like this:

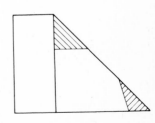

4.  Fold corner C to D.

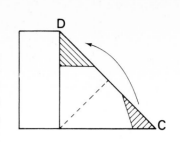

It should now look like this:

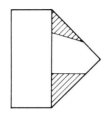

5.  Fold E to F.

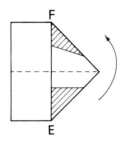

It should now look like this:

6.  Fold on GH by starting with the part with the stars (* * *) on it and folding down so that the fold comes along the printed solid line. *There are 3 thicknesses of paper — make sure you only fold the first layer.*

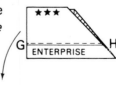

It should now look like this:

7. Make a fold (up direction) about 1 inch from the bottom along JK.

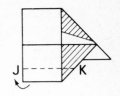

It should now look like this:

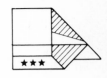

8. Turn the spaceship over and round so that L is on the left side.

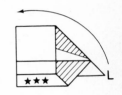

It should now look like this:

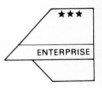

9. Fold on MN by starting with the part with the stars (* * *) on it and folding down so that the fold comes along the printed solid line. *There are two thicknesses of paper — make sure you only fold the top one.*

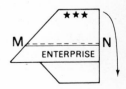

It should now look like this. *Make sure this sticks up in the center.*

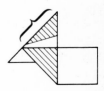

10. Make a fold (up direction) about 1 inch from the bottom along OP.

It should now look like this:

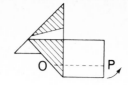

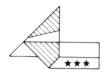

*Read all of step 11 and then go back and do it part by part.*

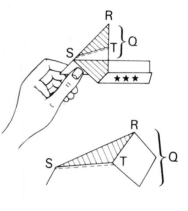

a. Hold spaceship in hand.
b. Open up Q with finger and flatten the lined area (//////) by bringing central point R toward the main body of the plane.
c. Fold along ST to keep it flat.
d. Make wings level so that plane can fly.

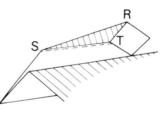

*Finished plane should look like this:*

side view   top view   back view

### QUALITY CONTROL INSPECTION POINTS FOR THE SPACESHIP ENTERPRISE

1. Printed lines should be in the position shown on the diagram.
2. The wingtips must be turned up just enough to let the stars show.
3. The "pilot's cabin" (step 11) must be puffed out noticeably. Skinny cabins crowd the astronauts.
4. The two wings must be level and even with each other — i.e., the entire wing deck should be at the same level. The Game Coordinator will buy only those spacecraft which meet the above quality control points.

## V. SUMMARY

The dynamic changing environment to which most of today's organizations must adapt has added a new dimension to the classic managerial functions of planning, organizing, motivating, directing, and controlling. Today's managers must also manage the process of change—they must be able to diagnose problems and to plan and implement changes in such a way that they are accepted and carried out by the system being worked with. To be successful, a change must have two characteristics. It must be a *high-quality solution* to the system's problem in terms of its technical and logical soundness, and it must be *acceptable* to the members of the system. Unfortunately, the quality of a solution and the acceptability of a solution do not always go together. The acceptability of a change is often determined less by the quality of the problem solution and more by the *process* through which the change is introduced.[8] For example, changes that are imposed by administrative decree are often actively or passively resisted because the members of the system are not aware of the problem that the change is intended to solve. On the other hand, involvement of system members in the total process of diagnosing the problem, planning alternative solutions, and implementing a chosen alternative is more likely to produce solutions that will be acceptable to the system.

While the quality and acceptability of solutions must be developed internally, the demands of the environment on the organization increase the complexity of the task in the management of change. As organizations have become more open and interdependent with their environment, government regulations, special interest groups, and other organizations are intervening in what were once the sole provinces of management—personnel policies, safety, product quality, etc.—and forcing changes that often work hardships on the organization or individuals within it. The managers' task thus becomes even more complex in that they must often initiate a change in response to the demands from outside, making the planned, orderly process a necessity.

In initiating a change in the status quo of a relationship, a program, a procedure, a communications pattern, an organization, or a way of work, the person wishing to initiate the change can improve the change effort by:[9]

1. Diagnosing the present condition, including the need for change.
2. Setting goals and defining the new state or condition after the change.
3. Defining the transition state between the present and future.
4. Developing strategies and action plans for managing this transition.
5. Evaluating the change effort.
6. Stabilizing the new condition and establishing a balance between stability and flexibility.

[8] Alfred J. Marrow, David G. Bowers, and Stanley E. Seashore, *Management by Participation* (New York: Harper & Row, Publishers, 1967).
[9] Beckhard and Harris, *Organizational Transitions*.

# VI. SELF-EVALUATION AND COMPLETING THE LEARNING LOOP

A. What questions do you now have as a result of your learning experiences from this unit? Jot these down below.

B. From these questions, what *key concepts* can you extrapolate for further learning? Write these concepts below.

C. How can you now go about finding answers to the questions you raised above? Below are some suggested ways to continue your learning process by beginning new learning loops:

1. Look up the key concepts from your questions above in the Yellow Pages of Learning Experiences at the back of the book. Find a few suggested readings or exercises to facilitate the learning of these key concepts.

2. If you don't find the key concepts in the Yellow Pages related specifically to your questions, perhaps there are other concepts listed in the index that might lead you to relevant learning resources at this time. Look for concepts similar to those you identified in B above.

3. In the event that you don't find the Yellow Pages directory useful for your present learning goals, discuss your questions with other students, faculty, or persons outside your learning environment. Discuss further learning possibilities with them.

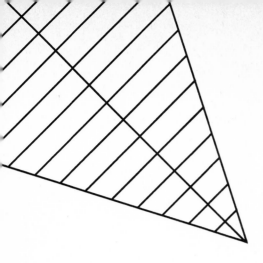

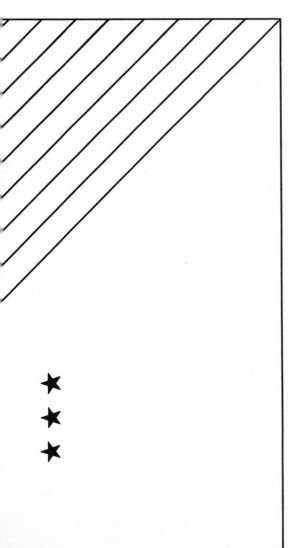

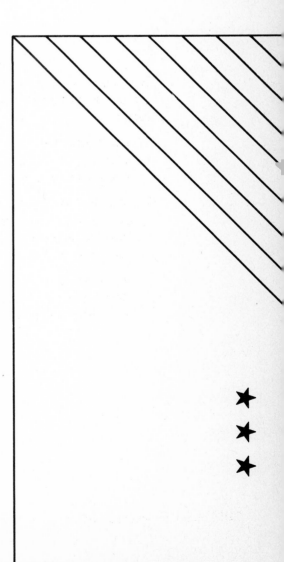

ENTERPRISE

ENTERPRISE

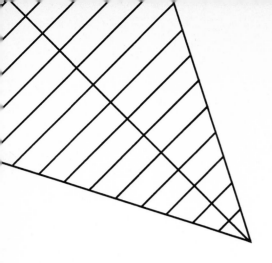

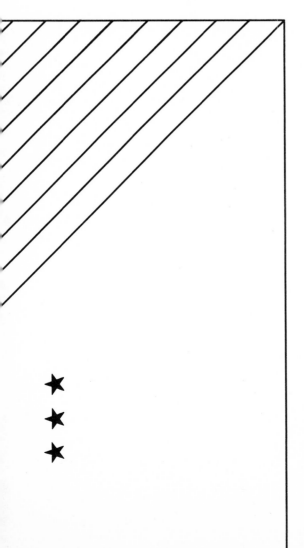

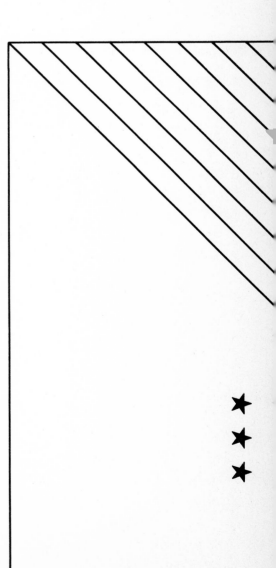

ENTERPRISE

ENTERPRISE

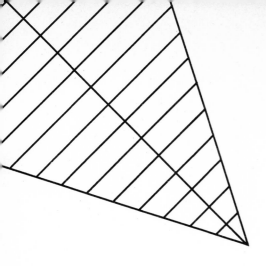

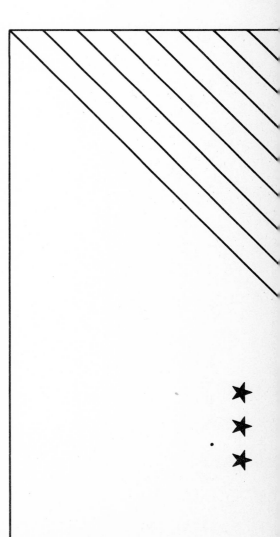

ENTERPRISE

ENTERPRISE

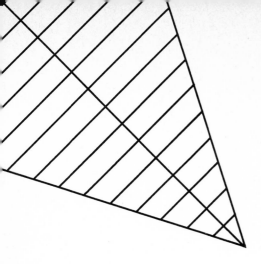

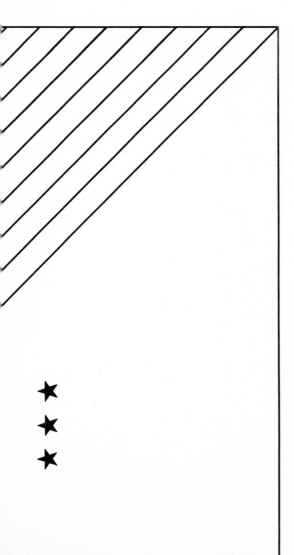

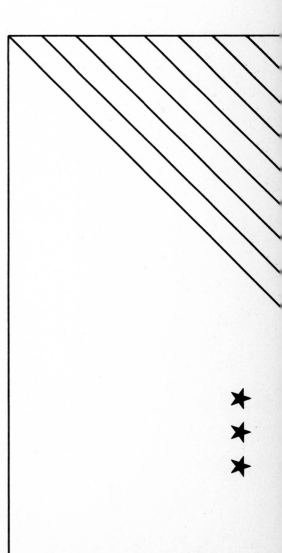

ENTERPRISE

ENTERPRISE

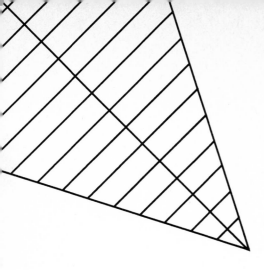

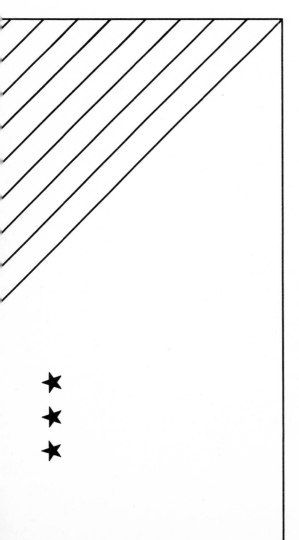

**ENTERPRISE**

**ENTERPRISE**

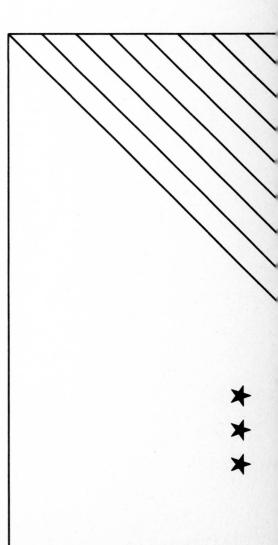

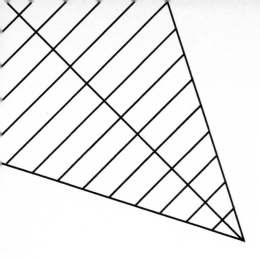

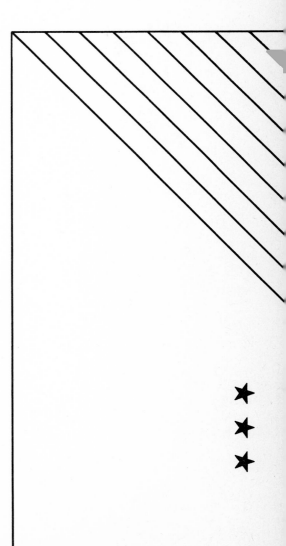

ENTERPRISE

ENTERPRISE

★
★
★

★
★
★

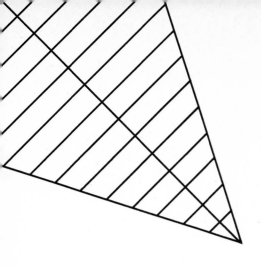

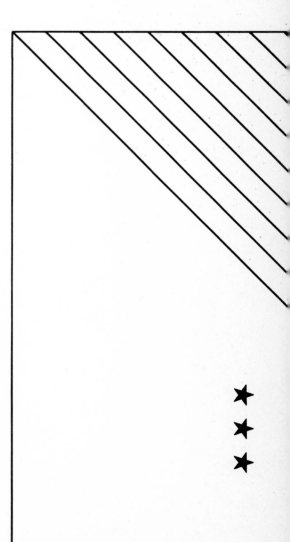

ENTERPRISE

ENTERPRISE

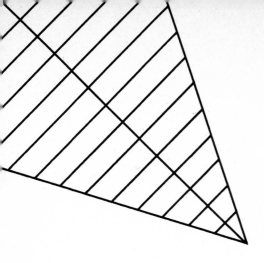

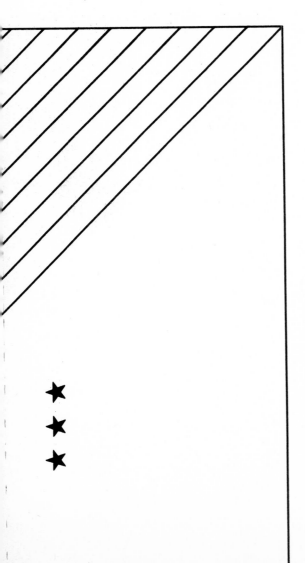

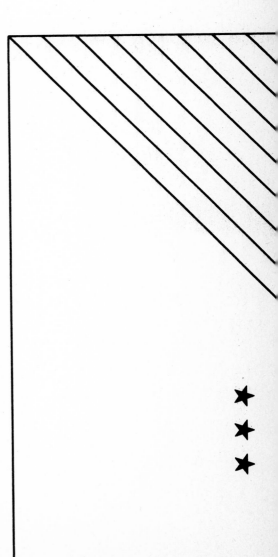

ENTERPRISE

ENTERPRISE

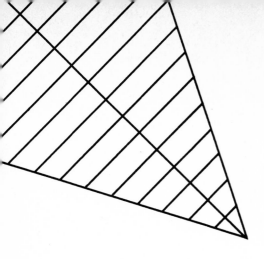

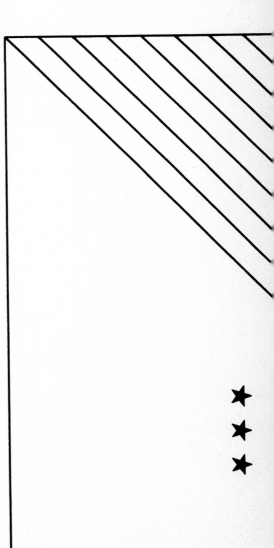

ENTERPRISE

ENTERPRISE

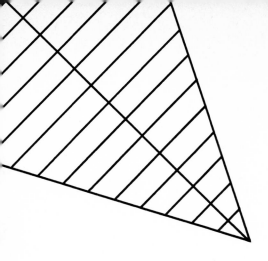

ENTERPRISE

ENTERPRISE

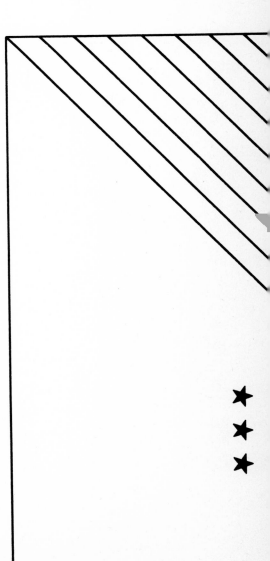

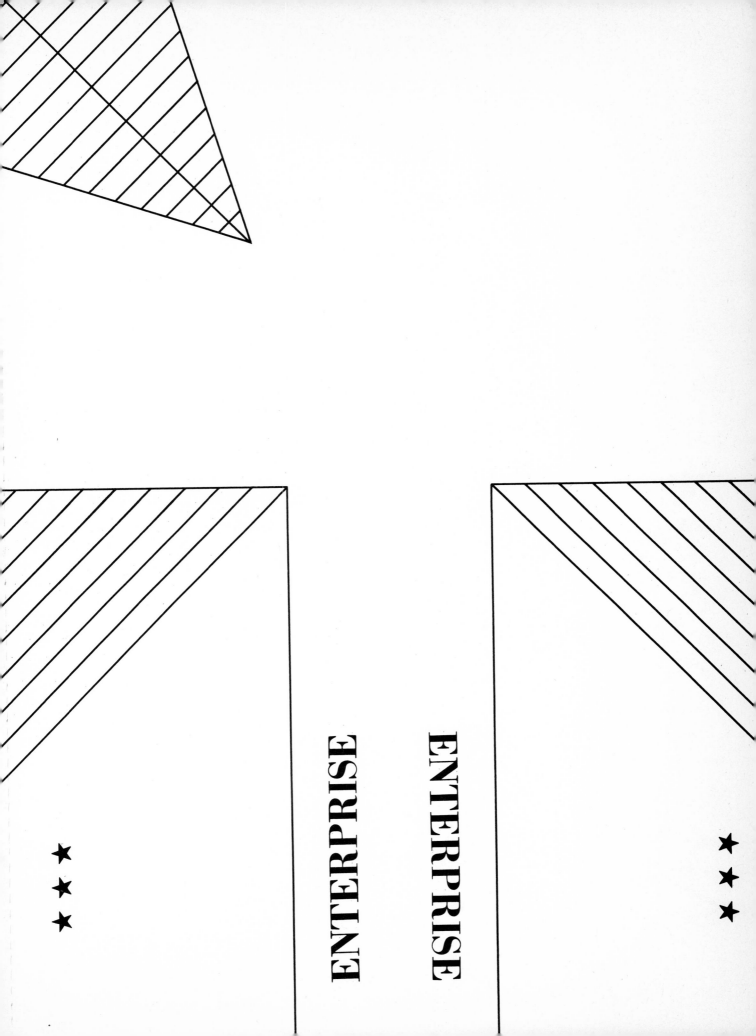

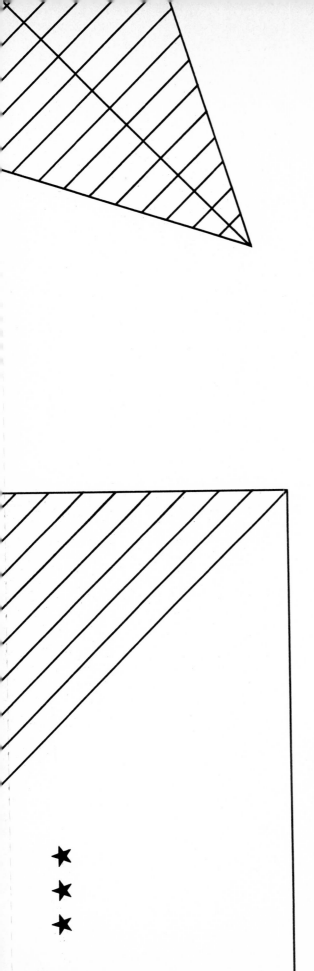

ENTERPRISE

ENTERPRISE

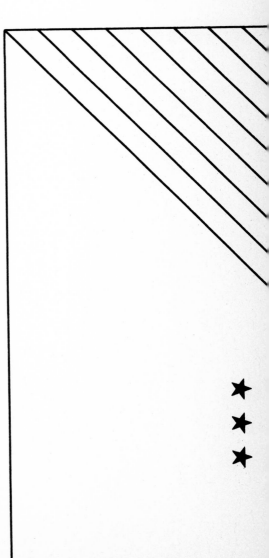

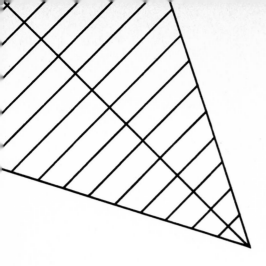

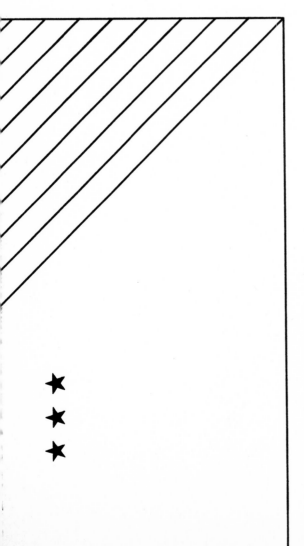

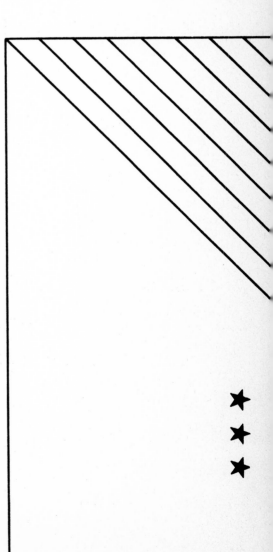

ENTERPRISE

ENTERPRISE

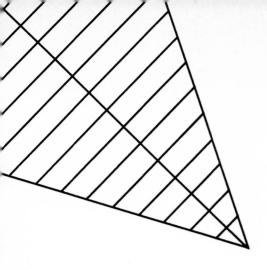

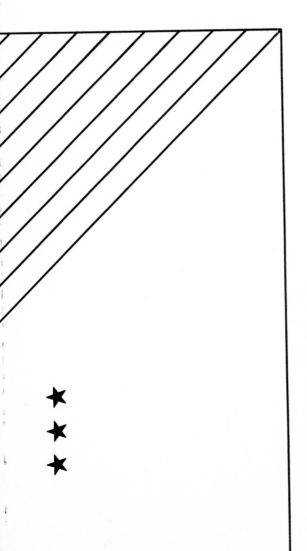

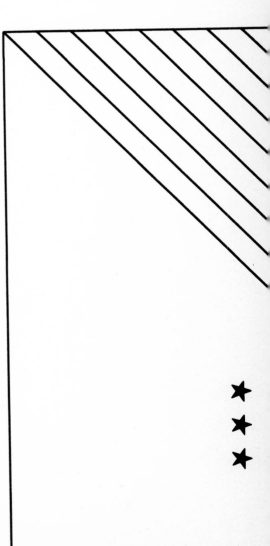

ENTERPRISE

ENTERPRISE

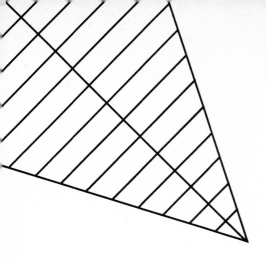

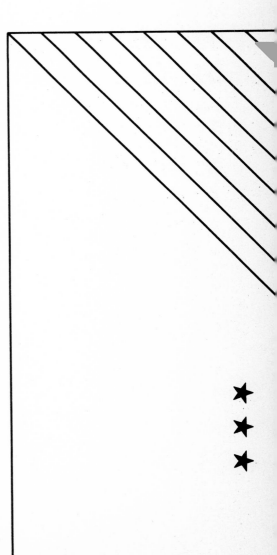

ENTERPRISE

ENTERPRISE

★
★ ★
★

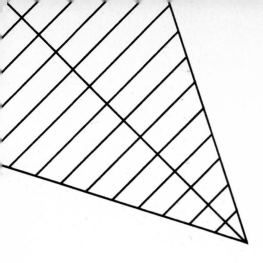

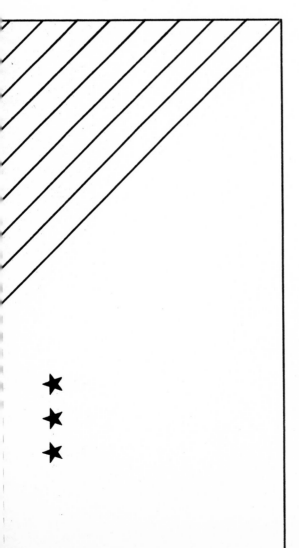

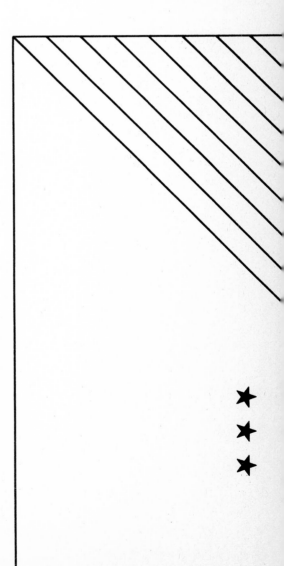

ENTERPRISE

ENTERPRISE

# chapter 11

## personal growth and career development

*Photos supplied by David Wilder*

### I. OBJECTIVES

    A.    Documentation and assessment of your personal history.

    B.    To get help and feedback in identifying personal trends in your life.

    C.    To speculate on what your future will be like if those trends continue.

    D.    To set goals for the changes you would like to make in order to have the future you want.

### II. PREMEETING PREPARATION

    A.    Read the entire unit.

    B.    Write your autobiography, with critical incidents included. (*Note:* This unit will take considerably more time for preclass preparation than others, and you should plan to spend four to six hours before class in the preparation of your autobiography).

    To provide some structure to your autobiography, you should first reflect on your life thus far, to see if any natural divisions occur. Some may be situational (e.g., "The High School Years"), others more introspective and less dependent on institutions (e.g., "A Time of Growth"). As you think of these divisions, write them down. They will be the chapter headings for your personal history.

    A narrative autobiography, has some limitations built into it. One tends to skim over the surface of life events and never look at anything in sufficient detail. In order to develop that level of detail without writing volumes, it is necessary to focus on one "critical incident" (at least) per chapter.

A critical incident is an event that stands out in your memory from a particular time or phase. It does not usually drag on for a long time, although a long time may have been spent building up to it. It allows you to look at your own actions in a specific situation and draw some inferences from that action. You may, for instance, be describing your high school years in terms of the things that, in retrospect, seem of major importance — grades, athletics, romance — but find just writing about your concerns broadly lacks a certain flesh-and-blood quality. Recalling and writing about an incident that illustrates how meaningful something was helps solve that problem. It might have been a time when you unexpectedly became a hero, or even a goat. Whatever the incident, you will want to be specific about when and where it happened, what the situation was, how you felt, who was involved, what you did, and what the results were. Each critical incident that you wish to include should be described in about 100 words.

The final product, your autobiography, will be a mixture of the "broad-stroke" narrative and the critical incidents that illuminate it, as when a movie camera gives a panoramic view of the scenery, then zooms in for a close-up. From this combination you should gain a little clearer insight into yourself (no "Eurekas," but maybe a couple "a-has") that you will be asked to share with two other group members. You should have the autobiography completed before the class session begins.

Autobiography of: _____

Chapter title: _____

## CRITICAL INCIDENT

Below, write out the critical incident. Remember that there are many specifics to include. The specifics in a well-written critical incident are:

when and where
what the situation was
how you felt

who was involved
what you did
the result — and why

Autobiography of: _____

Chapter title: _____

## CRITICAL INCIDENT

Below, write out the critical incident. Remember there are many specifics to include. The specifics in a well-written critical incident are:

when and where
what the situation was
how you felt

who was involved
what you did
the result — and why

Autobiography of: _____

Chapter title: _____

## CRITICAL INCIDENT

Below, write out the critical incident. Remember there are many specifics to include. The specifics in a well-written critical incident are:

when and where
what the situation was
how you felt

who was involved
what you did
the result — and why

Autobiography of: _____

Chapter title: _____

# CRITICAL INCIDENT

Below, write out the critical incident. Remember there are many specifics to include. The specifics in a well-written critical incident are:

when and where
what the situation was
how you felt

who was involved
what you did
the result — and why

Autobiography of: _____

Chapter title: _____

# CRITICAL INCIDENT

Below, write out the critical incident. Remember there are many specifics to include. The specifics in a well-written critical incident are:

when and where
what the situation was
how you felt

who was involved
what you did
the result -- and why

Autiobiography of: _____

Chapter title: _____

## CRITICAL INCIDENT

Below, write out the critical incident. Remember there are many specifics to include. The specifics in a well-written critical incident are:

when and where
what the situation was
how you felt

who was involved
what you did
the result — and why

Autobiography of: _____

Chapter title: _____

# CRITICAL INCIDENT

Below, write out the critical incident. Remember there are many specifics to include. The specifics in a well-written critical incident are:

when and where
what the situation was
how you felt

who was involved
what you did
the result — and why

Autobiography of: _____

Chapter title: _____

# CRITICAL INCIDENT

Below, write out the critical incident. Remember there are many specifics to include. The specifics in a well-written critical incident are:

when and where
what the situation was
how you felt

who was involved
what you did
the result — and why

## III. INTRODUCTION

One of managers' most important tasks is management of the personal growth and career development of their subordinates. In addition, managers have the very personal responsibility for their own career planning. While in an earlier time, career planning was often handled in large part by the firm one joined and belonged to for life, today's rapidly changing work environment and increasing job mobility have vastly increased the future alternatives and potentialities for almost any executive. Recent reports of labor statistics indicate that Americans will, on the average, change jobs seven times and careers three times during their actual working life. This increasing pattern of career change has great implications for how organizations and educational systems manage career development. At present, social responses to these changes have lagged far behind. Organization and educational systems remain structured to respond to traditional stable notions of career development that are no longer appropriate. Although today the career paths of many men and women may pass through two, three, or four distinct phases — each of which requires major new learning of knowledge, skills, and attitudes — education and training programs remain primarily oriented to the early stages of life. In most educational institutions, adult and continuing education are low-status, low-priority activities done half-heartedly in the name of community service. The provision of midcareer educational programs has been left primarily to private industry. While this is, in some cases, as it should be and some of these programs are of quite high quality, all too often the implicit price for admission is a further commitment to the organization and to one's previous career path. Changing careers is made harder. For example, selection criteria for midcareer programs often include previous experience in that career, and tax laws allow deductions for job-related training but not for changing jobs.

The failure to provide avenues for career change produces great losses in social productivity and in human satisfaction. Organizations do not benefit by locking their employees into careers that long ago ceased to be rewarding and challenging. Society loses the creativity and productivity of those who are barred from entry into new careers in midlife. This is particularly true for the female half of the population. Traditional adult developmental patterns for women have included a phase where marriage and family kept them from the job market in their early career. Although social norms are changing, entry into careers in midlife when family demands are less pressing still remains most difficult for women.

While organization and educational system changes are essential to ensure access to education and learning throughout our life span, it is equally important that men and women in our society gain a greater awareness and insight into the problems and possibilities of adult development.

We are becoming more and more responsible for managing our own lives and careers. In earlier times, personal identity and continuity were sustained in relatively stable environments of expectation and demand. Career and life style were ascribed, not chosen. Once on a life path, personal choice was primarily a process of affirming expectations. In today's "future-shock" world, environmental complexity and change have denied us this easy route to personal identity. Now, more than ever, identity and continuity are forged through personal choices. These choices go beyond the computational selection of one alternative over another according to some predetermined values. They require the selection of the basic values themselves. In addition to asking, "What is the right thing to do?" we now ask, "What do I believe is right?" In addition to, "Who am I?" we ask, "Who do I want to be?"

To cope with these increasing challenges for career self-management we all need to develop our skills for planning and guiding the direction of our lives. Several themes seem important for effective career self-management.

1.  *A focus on life rather than occupation.* Career development and life planning should start from a holistic analysis of the person's life space and examine the relationship among work, family, leisure, spiritual/development needs, and so on. The term *career* therefore is used in its broadest sense — the self-mediated progress through time of transactions between person and environment. If career planning places work/income

in a central focus (this fits for many but not all people), other life interests are placed in an *a priori* peripheral and compensatory role. Such a bias precludes a fundamental reassessment of one's life and life-style and places in a secondary position the primary problem experienced by many individuals—that of integrating the many diverse elements of their lives.

2. *Career as a here-and-now issue.* An individual's goals and interpretations of his/her own personal history represent attempts to make sense and meaning of his/her present existential life situation. Major tasks in coping with change are the reinterpretation of personal history and the readjustment of goal images in the context of emerging life circumstances. In this sense, previous accomplishments and developed abilities and life goals are as much determined by life experiences as they are causes of these experiences.

3. *Emphasis on choice as well as planning.* Implicit in the above is an emphasis on immediate personal choice in the context of longer-range planning. Individuals need to manage their choice-making process. This can be accomplished by increasing awareness of choice making and control over the choice-making process by shortening the time lag between choices and consequences (e.g., seeing a first job choice in terms of its immediate consequences as well as a long-term determining decision).

   Planning and goal setting are but one mode for achieving personal continuity and direction. Many achievement-oriented individuals prefer this mode. But for others this mode is antithetical to their life style (e.g., some find their sense of meaning in the context of the here and now; for them goals are merely abstractions).

4. *Emphasis on the learning process as opposed to outcomes.* The problem of managing and adapting to change as a central task of adult development in contemporary society is, at its most fundamental level, one aspect of the process by which people learn.[1] Learning as a central focus implies that individuals need to examine not only the "content of the self"—abilities, interests, aspirations, and needs—but also the "self as process"—the process by which one makes choices among various alternatives. When one focuses only on the contexts or outcomes, where you are going and what you want to accomplish becomes more important than how you are getting there. As a result, we may still be ill-prepared to cope with a future set of career and life choices.

The following exercise is designed to assist you with your personal career self-management process. The purpose of the autobiography you prepare is to generate data for self-assessment of your skills and accomplishments, your weaknesses, your aspirations, satisfactions, values. It provides a starting point for developing your vision of the future, setting goals and taking action to achieve them.

## IV. PROCEDURE FOR GROUP MEETING

*Step 1.* (30 minutes). Form groups of three people, choosing two others you feel comfortable working with. Share your autobiographies with one another. For each autobiography note on the following form the trends or themes you see in the stories. Examples of themes or trends might be: "can't stand failure," "seldom mentions others," "always does what authorities expect," or "would rather play than work." The themes should emerge as you listen and/or read.

[1] See Donald M. Wolfe and David A. Kolb, "Career Development, Personal Growth, and Experiential Learning," *Readings.*

| Self | Partner 1 | Partner 2 |
|------|-----------|-----------|
|      |           |           |
|      |           |           |
|      |           |           |
|      |           |           |
|      |           |           |
|      |           |           |
|      |           |           |
|      |           |           |

Step 2. *Individual work to analyze trends* (20 minutes). You and your partners have identified trends and themes in all your biographies. Some identified by or for you have seemed positive, some not so positive. The crucial issue for this session, however, is how well you are managing those trends and themes in your present life.

This is not intended as parlor psychotherapy. We are not dealing here with the causes of these themes and trends, but with the surface manifestations of them in your life. The goal is not catharsis, but objective identification of habits and behaviors that are increasing or decreasing your chances of being what you want to be.

There are some themes that you are managing better than others. You may, for instance, have picked up a strong achievement theme in your autobiography. The question of whether you are managing that theme well or not is essentially one of whether you are in control of your achievement need, or if it is controlling you. Steady progress toward identified goals is usually an indication that you are in control. On the other hand, a constant need to compete with others, even where such competition is inappropriate and unnecessary, would indicate that this theme is not being well managed.

In the space below, write the themes or trends identified in your autobiography by yourself and your partners in the left column. In the second column make note of the incidents or words that describe the theme's role in your life. In the right column enter your conclusions, either "managed" or "uncontrolled."

| Themes or Trends | Key Words, Phrases, or Incidents | Being Managed? |
|---|---|---|
|  |  |  |

Step 3.   *Individual and trio work: scenario projection* (20 minutes). The principal benefit of looking at themes and trends in your life so far is the opportunity to project into the future what your life or career will be like. During this time period you should work alone for the first five minutes on a short written scenario in outline form of what you think your life will be like ten years from now if the trends and themes continue as they have been.

This scenario should not deal with what you would like your life to be, but what you can realistically expect it to be if no changes are made in your patterns. It will be used in the next step to help determine the kinds of changes you would like to make and goals for change you would like to set for yourself.

At the end of the five minutes, share your scenario aloud with your two partners of the previous step, and get their verbal feedback on the realism of your scenario. After their feedback, make any changes that you feel would make it more realistic.

Step 4.   *Individual work: setting change goals* (20 minutes). Up to this point you have been focusing on your history and what it might mean for your future if you make no basic changes in the habits and behaviors that have been typical of you until now. Now it is time to think about the kinds of changes you would like to make in those patterns and set some specific goals for change.

The increased likelihood of change resulting from the setting and articulating of goals is well documented. Kay, French, and Myer, for instance, found that improvement needs among managers were accomplished only about one-fourth of the time when they were not translated into goals in performance appraisal interviews. When they were made into clearly stated goals, the likelihood of accomplishment increased to about two-thirds.[2] It is not enough just to think about how you would like to change. It is necessary to translate those visions into concrete goals.

To facilitate that process, take 20 minutes to work by yourself, completing the following sentence: "Five years from now, I will be satisfied if. . . ." Do this at least five times, then rank-order your goal statements in the space provided to the right. This will help establish the personal importance of each of the goals for you.

### GOAL STATEMENTS

"Five years from now, I will be satisfied if":

Value Ranking

a. _____  ____

b. _____  ____

c. _____  ____

d. _____  ____

e. _____  ____

f. _____  ____

Step 5.  *Trio work: developing action strategies* (30 minutes). Having made your goal statements and ranked them for their value to you, you will need to think about and work on some strategies for getting where you want to go. In your three-person group, discuss each of your number 1 priority goals first, making suggestions to each other about some of the ways you might go about moving toward your goal. Make notes on the suggestions about your possible strategies and list them below when you feel you have some actions you can make work.

For goal valued number 1, I will do the following:

a. _____

b. _____

c. _____

Repeat the process for the other goals, as long as time permits.

For goal valued number 2, I will do the following:

a. _____

b. _____

c. _____

For goal valued number 3, I will do the following:

a. _____

b. _____

c. _____

[2] E. Kay, J. R. P. French, Jr., and H. H. Myer, "A Study of the Performance Appraisal Interview" (Management Development and Employee Relations Services, General Electric Co. New York, 1962).

For goal valued number 4, I will do the following:

a. _____

b. _____

c. _____

For goal valued number 5, I will do the following:

a. _____

b. _____

c. _____

For goal value number 6, I will do the following:

a. _____

b. _____

c. _____

## V. SUMMARY

The product of your work in this unit is a set of prioritized goals and strategies for achieving them based on an assessment of your life history. Goal setting is a critical aspect of personal growth and career development. The ability to conceptualize life goals and to imagine future alternatives for living can free us from the inertia of the past by providing future targets that serve as guides for planning and decision making.

Research results from several areas—management, psychotherapy, and attitude change—all confirm the importance of goal setting for personal growth and achievement of one's goals.[3] Commitment to clearly stated goals leads to achievement of those goals. Yet achieving commitment is not as easy as it sounds. There are several factors that make it difficult:

1. Reluctance to give up the alternative goals not chosen: To choose one goal is to implicitly reject others. Unless one clearly believes in the importance of the goal and its superior value, other goals will, as time passes, dominate and overshadow the initial decision.

2. Fear of failure: Without goals and ideals, one never risks failure. Making a commitment to a future state involves a risk to one's self-esteem if the goal is not achieved. This fear of failure makes it difficult to totally commit oneself to a goal.

3. Lack of self-knowledge: It is difficult to choose goals and make future plans when one is not certain who s/he is and what s/he values. Confusion about oneself leads to confusion about what one's future self should be.

4. Lack of knowledge about the environment: Lack of awareness of the opportunities available in the environment can also produce confusion and an inability to define goals that one can become committed to. An important part of the goal-setting process is researching the resources and opportunities afforded by the environment and using the information gained to discover new goals and redefine old ones.

5. Insecurity and low self-confidence: If one's circumstances or life style lead her/him to feel as though s/he is a hopeless victim of circumstances, s/he will have difficulty in planning her/his future and becoming committed to future goals. To achieve goals

[3] David A. Kolb and Richard E. Boyatzis, "Goal-Setting and Self-Directed Behavior Change." *Readings*.

implies a sense of self-control and control over one's environment. To become committed to a goal, one must feel as though s/he has the ability to achieve it.

There are, however, some things that can be done to increase commitment to goals:

1. Explicit examination of the value of the chosen goal and comparison with rejected alternatives: By explicitly considering alternative opportunities that may arise, one can avoid being swayed in a weak moment by an unconsidered alternative. One especially useful technique here is linking short-term goals with long-term objectives. Awareness that a particularly difficult short-term goal is linked to a long-term objective can avoid its rejection for a more immediately gratifying but useless short-term pleasure.

2. Committing oneself to a continuing process of self-evaluation and goal setting: One cannot in one sitting plan his/her future life. The world is changing far too rapidly for any of us to anticipate the future clearly, and our goals change as our experience increases. The risk of missing unforeseen alternatives by working blindly toward obsolete goals can be minimized by continued reassessment of goals. By seeking feedback from others about oneself and by using these data for continuing self-evaluation, one can achieve a more accurate self-image and a clearer conception of one's values.

3. Support from others: Commitment to goals is best achieved in a supportive atmosphere. Others significant in one's life are invaluable for building self-confidence, helping to clarify thinking about the future, and getting helpful feedback about behavior. Personal growth cannot occur alone. It is through interactions with others that we discover ourselves and first experience our ideals.

4. Future visions and here-and-now awareness: Planning for the future implies a continuing awareness of ways we can pro-actively shape our own futures. The goal-setting process means that I acknowledge that what I do at this moment in time will affect what I am able to do or be at some time in the future.

Reprinted courtesy of Mell Lazarus and Field Newspaper Syndicate

## VI. SELF-EVALUATION AND COMPLETING THE LEARNING LOOP

A. What questions do you now have as a result of your learning experiences from this unit? Jot these down below.

B. From these questions, what *key concepts* can you extrapolate for further learning? Write these concepts below.

C. How can you now go about finding answers to the questions you raised above? Below are some suggested ways to continue your learning process by beginning new learning loops:

1. Look up the key concepts from your questions above in the Yellow Pages of Learning Experiences at the back of the book. Find a few suggested readings or exercises to facilitate the learning of these key concepts.

2. If you don't find the key concepts in the Yellow Pages related specifically to your questions, perhaps there are other concepts listed in the index that might lead you to relevant learning resources at this time. Look for concepts similar to those you identified in B above.

3. In the event that you don't find the Yellow Pages directory useful for your present learning goals, discuss your questions with other students, faculty, or persons outside your learning environment. Discuss further learning possibilities with them.

# solutions

**G. B. A. CONSTRUCTION COMPANY CASE — ACTUAL OUTCOMES**

**New President**

1. Manager II was selected to be the new president of the G. B. A. Co. The major points in his favor were as follows:

    a. A high n-Achievement, combined with a moderate n-Affiliation, was felt to be critical in developing the teamwork needed among the top management group.

    b. His ability and commitment to developing younger people would set a tone for the company that would help it develop the human resources needed to continue its rapid growth.

    c. He seemed strong enough and had enough of a history with G. B. A. Jr. to "help" G. B. A. keep his fingers out of the daily operations.

2. Manager I was also a strong candidate. His age and autocratic style were his major drawbacks. There was an underlying feeling that with more experience and "polish," he could be a strong candidate the next time around. For now, his strengths were best utilized as a division manager.

3. Manager III was not a serious contender. In a nutshell, he was too much like G. B. A., Jr.

4. The Assistant to the President was a hard candidate to exclude for a variety of reasons. Chief among these was a concern that if his loyalty were not rewarded, he might subsequently leave the company. These fears proved valid. Although he was included in a new compensation program which was developed (one of the supporting changes introduced), this was not enough to satisfy his hurt feelings.

The major structural changes actually considered concerned the nature and form of reward systems, particularly as they related to the top management group. In addition to some relatively standard industrial stock option plans, a group incentive scheme was also examined.

To create the kind of teamwork at the top needed to help the G. B. A. Construction Company move through its next phase of development, top managers would need to wear two hats. On the one hand, they had major divisional responsibilities (e.g., their functional hats) which must be maintained. On the other hand, they also needed, upon occasion, to wear their executive hats, i.e., to be concerned about the entire G. B. A. Construction Company, not solely their own divisions. A group incentive scheme was developed to reward top managers for collaborative behavior designed to build the overall company. In addition team development activities for this top team were initiated (see Chapter 12).

## LEADERSHIP AND DECISION-MAKING CASES

| Case | ANALYSIS | | | | | | | | PROBLEM TYPE | FEASIBLE SET |
|---|---|---|---|---|---|---|---|---|---|---|
| | A Quality? | B Leader's Information? | C Structured? | D Acceptance? | E Prior Probability of Acceptance? | F Goal Congruence? | G Subordinate Conflict? | H Subordinate Information? | | |
| 1 | Yes | No | No | No | — | Yes | — | Yes* | 14, Group | C11, G11 |
| 2 | Yes | No | No | Yes | No | No | — | Yes* | 18, Individual | C1, G1 |
| 3 | Yes | No | No | Yes | No | Yes | — | Yes* | 16, Group | G11 |
| 4 | Yes | No | Yes | Yes | No | No | — | No* | 8 or 9, Individual | C1, G1 |
| 5 | Yes | Yes | — | No | — | Yes | — | No | 4, Group | A1, A11, C1, C11, G11 |

*The question pertaining to this attribute is asked in the decision tree but is irrelevant to the decision.

## IDEAL MAN RANKING PROBLEM

### Survey Results

| Rank | Trait | *Percent Women Saying Trait Is Very Important or Essential to Ideal* |
|------|-------|-----------------------------------------------------------------------|
| 4 | Intelligent | 84 |
| 10 | Physically strong | 21 |
| 7 | Successful at work | 66 |
| 9 | Aggressive | 28 |
| 2 | Stands up for beliefs | 92 |
| 5 | Fights to protect family | 72 |
| 1 | Able to love | 96 |
| 3 | Warm | 89 |
| 8 | Skilled lover | 48 |
| 6 | Sexually faithful | 67 |

*Source:* Carol Travis, "Men and Women Report Their Views on Masculinity," *Psycology Today,* January 1976, p. 37.

# THE YELLOW PAGES OF LEARNING EXPERIENCES

# I. PURPOSE

This section of the book[1] is intended as an aid to those students who would like to continue their learning beyond the classroom and the readings. It is a way of completing the learning loop (see the chapter, "Learning and Problem Solving") by moving into the active experimentation stage, experimenting with approaches to new questions that have been raised by the experiences of each chapter.

The directory is divided into two major parts:

1. An index of key words and concepts related to organizational psychology.
2. The listings of suggested experiments, readings, films, and experiences, under the following four headings:
   (I) Individuals, I-1 through I-50
   (G) Groups, G-51 through G-65
   (O) Organizations, O-66 through O-82
   (C) Culture and Environment, C-83 through C-90

These categories are meant to help you identify the relevant focus of your questions. A question raised by the motivation chapters, for example, may have implications for your own motivation, its effect on groups, its relationship to organization climate, or the effect of achievement motivation on the economic growth of a culture. It is up to you to choose your own level of learning and to look up appropriate entries in the directory.

# II. USE

At the end of each chapter in the book there are two questions related to key concepts in the chapter *from your perspective*. After writing down those key concepts, take the key words in your statements and look for them in the index. If the exact words are not there, think of similar words, other ways of expressing the concepts. There should be some representation of your questions somewhere in the index.

If your concerns are about *conflict resolution* or *interpersonal competition*, for example, pertinent resources may be found somewhere in the four categories of learning resources: Individual suggestions, 1 through 50; Group suggestions, 51 through 65; Organization suggestions, 66 through 82; and Culture and Environment suggestions, 83 through 90. Not all of the index words have listings in each of the four categories, so it will be up to you to match the key concept with a learning resource in the appropriate category for your learning goal. Learning in a group situation may have precedence over the exact key word, for example, so you would find a group exercise to approximate the particular concept you have in mind.

In effect, the directory of learning resources is conveniently arranged to meet many kinds of learning needs, and your use of it will no doubt vary from unit to unit. Wherever possible, books have been listed by their paperback editions to minimize cost, and information as to how to obtain films is included.

# III. ATTITUDE

The way in which you approach the use of this directory will determine how much learning you can gain from it. The books and films are not unusual listings for students who are used to reading

---

[1] This section in the second edition was developed in collaboration with Margaret Fox.

bibliographies, but the exercises are not the usual fare. It will take a commitment on your part to the process of experimentation to learn from these experiences, but you should find your ability to learn from everyday situations considerably enhanced as you make use of the directory.

The ultimate goal of these suggestions is *to increase your ability to learn from everything you do or observe*. Hopefully, the process can be started here, knowing that in the study and understanding of human behavior there is no such thing as "time out."

### IV. FEEDBACK

In order to improve the Yellow Pages directory and more adequately meet the needs of students using the book, the authors need feedback from you on your use of the directory. Any information on the success/failure of particular segments, or the entire directory concept, would be helpful. Any suggestions for additions and improvements will, of course, be welcomed.

The following index of key concepts highlight some of the major areas of learning about individuals in organizations and about organizational processes and structures. These key words will refer you to the entries in each of the four categories—Individuals (I-1 to 1-50), Groups (G-51 to G-65), Organizations (O-66 to O-82), and Culture and Environment (C-83 to C-90)—that are appropriate to the concept.

**Empathy (Cont.)**
    Cult. & Env. 85, 90
**Excellence**
    Ind. 2, 4, 38
    Grp. 55, 63
    Org. 70, 78
    Cult. & Env. 88, 89
**Expectations**
    Ind. 6, 15, 19, 27, 38
    Grp. 52, 57
    Org. 66, 76, 78
    Cult. & Env. 84
**Experience**
    Ind. 3, 5, 36, 49
    Grp. 54, 65
    Org. 66, 75
    Cult. & Env. 87, 90
**Fantasy**
    Ind. 4, 13, 15, 20, 24, 45
    Cult. & Env. 84, 88, 90
**Feedback**
    Ind. 11, 18, 40, 46, 50
    Grp. 54, 55, 59
    Org. 68, 76
    Cult. & Env. 88, 90
**Feelings**
    Ind. 3, 10, 13, 16, 42, 44, 49
    Grp. 54, 59, 62
    Org. 74, 75
    Cult. & Env. 90
**Future**
    Ind. 6, 15, 20, 23, 24
    Org. 78, 81, 82
    Cult. & Env. 84, 87
**Goals**
    Ind. 15, 20, 23, 50
    Grp. 55, 57, 64
    Org. 74, 78, 81
    Cult. & Env. 84, 90
**Goal Setting**
    Ind. 14, 20, 43, 50
    Grp. 63, 64
    Org. 74, 78, 81
**Group Process**
    Ind. 30
    Grp. 52, 53, 54, 57, 60–64
    Org. 69, 71
    Cult. & Env. 84, 86, 87, 90
**Growth**
    Ind. 4, 5, 6, 13, 19, 38, 49
    Grp. 54, 59
    Org. 71, 74, 75
    Cult. & Env. 84, 86–90
**Helping**
    Ind. 36, 37, 47
    Grp. 55, 59

**Helping (Cont.)**
    Org. 74, 75, 79
    Cult. & Env. 90
**Impressions**
    Ind. 8, 29, 32, 48
    Grp. 56, 58
    Org. 76, 77
**Independence**
    Ind. 14, 23, 40, 43
    Grp. 59
    Org. 78, 79, 82
    Cult. & Env. 88, 90
**Individuality**
    Ind. 2, 3, 5, 6, 16, 19
    Grp. 58, 59
    Org. 66, 73, 75
    Cult. & Env. 83, 84, 86, 90
**Influence**
    Ind. 28, 38, 40, 41
    Grp. 60, 61, 63, 64
    Org. 72, 78, 79
    Cult. & Env. 83, 84, 86, 90
**Interaction**
    Ind. 8, 11, 19, 28, 31, 37, 41, 42
    44, 49
    Grp. 51, 54, 56, 61
    Org. 67, 72
    Cult. & Env. 87, 90
**Interdependence**
    Ind. 28, 31, 37, 40, 41
    Grp. 51, 56, 59
    Org. 67, 72
    Cult. & Env. 89, 90
**Language**
    Ind. 8, 26, 32, 44
    Grp. 56
    Cult. & Env. 85
**Leadership**
    Ind. 27, 40
    Grp. 55, 56, 57, 61
    Org. 71, 73, 78
    Cult. & Env. 83, 85
**Learning**
    Ind. 5, 12, 13, 16, 25, 33–35, 39
    Grp. 55, 58, 65
    Org. 74
    Cult. & Env. 89, 90
**Listening**
    Ind. 11, 16, 22, 47, 48
    Grp. 55, 61, 64
    Org. 72
    Cult. & Env. 85, 90
**Management**
    Ind. 9, 23, 27, 43, 47
    Grp. 55, 57, 59, 61
    Org. 67, 70–73, 79

**Management (Cont.)**
    Cult. & Env. 87
**Motivation**
    Ind. 11, 13, 14, 22, 31, 36, 38
    Grp. 57, 59, 60, 61
    Org. 71, 72, 74, 76, 78
    Cult. & Env. 87–90
**Needs**
    Ind. 14, 22, 28, 42, 44, 47
    Grp. 60, 61, 62
    Org. 66, 70, 72, 74, 78, 81
**Nonverbal**
    Ind. 26, 31, 40, 42, 44, 47
    Grp. 54, 56
    Org. 77
    Cult. & Env. 90
**Norms**
    Ind. 19, 26
    Grp. 56, 62, 63
    Org. 66, 74, 77, 78
    Cult. & Env. 85, 87, 89
**Observation**
    Ind. 1, 29, 30, 39
    Grp. 53, 58, 61
    Org. 69, 72, 76, 77
    Cult. & Env. 84, 87
**Organization**
    Ind. 9, 23, 46
    Grp. 53, 56, 57, 61, 63
    Org. 66–70, 72, 74, 76, 78
    Cult. & Env. 84, 89
**Perception**
    Ind. 1, 5, 8, 18, 24, 29, 33, 39,
    41, 48
    Grp. 52, 56, 58
    Org. 76, 77
    Cult. & Env. 84, 85
**Planning**
    Ind. 6, 14, 15, 20, 23
    Grp. 64
    Org. 67–69, 79–82
    Cult. & Env. 83
**Play**
    Ind. 4, 16, 21
    Grp. 55, 63, 65
    Cult. & Env. 89, 90
**Power**
    Ind. 11, 14, 21, 22, 27, 41
    Grp. 55, 57, 61
    Org. 68, 72, 74–76, 78
    Cult. & Env. 83, 88, 90
**Prejudice**
    Ind. 22, 29, 48
    Grp. 52, 58, 62
    Org. 68, 72, 78
    Cult. & Env. 85

## PART II
## LEARNING EXPERIENCES

## I. LEARNING ABOUT INDIVIDUALS

The exercises and references in this section are mainly concerned with learning about behavior, your own as well as others', at the individual level. Some require interaction with other people, but the majority of these learning resources may be used individually.

The relevance to organization behavior of some of the suggested activities may seem remote at first, but the individual must be seen as the basic unit of any organization. What helps us understand ourselves and other individuals also helps us in understanding collections of people in groups and organizations.

The following resources (I–1 through I–39) can be used by you individually, although you may want to share your learning experiences with another person or several persons.

**I-1.** How many F's do you see in the following paragraph?

FINISHED FILES ARE THE RESULT OF YEARS OF SCIENTIFIC STUDY COMBINED WITH THE EXPERIENCE OF MANY YEARS:

Answer: There are six F's. How many did you find? Which ones did you miss?

**I-2.** Construct something with modeling clay. Spend about two minutes building it and then destroying it. Experience what it feels like to destroy something you create.

a) Build another object, creating it until you reach a point where you decide you can't destroy what you build. Then destroy it. How much time did you put into creating it?

b) How valuable are your products? By what standards? What does the quality of what you build or the amount of effort put into building it have to do with how you feel about destroying it?

c) There is considerable attention these days on the process of job enlargement in organizations. What are the pros/cons of having people "feel" personal ownership in a whole product vs. being responsible for only one small piece (as on the typical assembly line)?

**I-3.** Put yourself in a situation which, from past experience, you know you would not enjoy and might even avoid and/or know you would enjoy and frequently seek out from time to time.

a) Record how you feel as you think about approaching the situation, in the situation itself, immediately after, and some longer period after.

b) Keep track of what, if anything, you say to others before, during, and after the experience concerning what it was like.

c) If the situation brings about a negative experience, write a story about how the situation could have been a positive one — what you would have to change in the situation. How much of the negative experience is dependent on external forces outside your control? What are they?

d) How much personal responsibility do you feel for the experience, good or bad?

**I-4.** Create the most beautiful thing you can.

**I-5.** Sensory awareness may often be enhanced through sensory deprivation. Using blindfolds, earplugs, nose clamps, and heavy gloves, deprive yourself of one of your senses one at a time.

a) In what ways did your remaining senses change?

b) Did other senses compensate for the loss? How?

c) Vary the experiences — e.g., while blindfolded, peel an orange, listen as you separate the sections, smell the newly released aroma, taste the sweetness of the pulp. Describe it to someone.

**I-6.** *Adult Development*
Current research suggests that contrary to Freudian assumptions, growth and development continue beyond childhood. For portraits of the dramatic changes in adult life, see:

a) Gail Sheehy, *Passages* (New York: E. P. Dutton, 1974).

b) Daniel Levinson, "The Mid-Life Transition: A Period in Adult Psycho-Social Development, *Psychiatry*, Vol. 40 (1977), pp. 99–112.

**I-7.** *Congruency Exercise*
Write ten to fifteen spontaneous completions to the statement "I believe _____." Categorize these responses into one of the following:
Something I believe/value which:
   i) I've never shared with anyone publicly
   ii) I've shared publicly with a few people
   iii) I've shared publicly with many people

a) For each of the responses, if possible, list several behaviors in which you have engaged that you feel are congruent with one of these values. List behaviors that are incongruent with one/some of these values.

b) This activity can help you become more aware of blind/hidden aspects of your self-image, can provide insights into conflicts within yourself, and provide clues as to how these conflicts become manifest in your interpersonal relationships.

**I-8.** Within a language, certain words have a dramatic impact upon the nature of human interactions. Consider the following:

A child tells his mother that he has spilled his milk on the floor.

a) In what way would the subsequent interaction be different if the mother responded with "How?," with "Why?" What implications do these words have — what implicit meanings?

b) Make a list of words that have value implications (e.g., "should," "ought").

According to some of the general semanticists, one way we hide our specific feelings from ourselves is through the use of general verbs. Try to speak for extended periods of time without using any of the forms of the verb "to be" (is, are, was, etc.).

a) How much difficulty did you have in doing this?

b) Did the experience force greater concreteness? How?

Think of how you address the people you know (e.g., formally, by first name, nickname, etc.) and how they address you.

a) What do these communications tell you about your relationships with these people?

b) See Roger Brown, *Social Psychology* (New York: The Free Press, 1965), Chapter 2, for conceptual help.

**I-9.** Rearrange the furniture in your room or, the next time you clean it, pay attention to the organization of your things, where you place certain objects, etc.

a) Where, in relation to windows and doors, do you feel most comfortable? Where do you place furniture such as a desk, sofa, bed, or a chair in your room? Try a new arrangement that helps you organize your personal life more efficiently.

b) What objects did you find behind furniture, under rugs, etc.? How did you feel about finding them again?

c) Managing one's own life or space is, in some ways, similar to managing a group. How flexible vs. structured are you? What differences, if any, are there in your "managerial" approaches?

**I-10.** Notice your own and others' behavior when entering a relatively empty restaurant.

a) Do you head for a corner? Center of the room?

b) Is it important for you to have a wall at your back? To choose a booth rather than a table?

c) Describe your feelings when such a choice has to be made whether you are alone or with a friend.

**I-11.** Experiment with a tape recorder and get feedback on your voice and style of communication.

a) Analyze your speech for affect level, logical ideas, precision of meaning, etc.

b) Analyze the word content for *n*-Ach, *n*-Pow, and *n*-Aff.

You can talk into a recorder while alone or try to record several live interactions. When real situations are used, you can check after the fact to see if you said what you thought you were saying. In addition, you can check your listening — what do you hear now that you didn't hear the first time?

**I-12.** Line up your books and magazines in order of preference.

a) What kinds of books do you like best/least? How do these books and magazines differ from each other in size, appearance, and content?

b) How do you arrange your books and magazines? Which ones do you want other people to know you have/don't have? What "image" do you project to others by your books and magazines? Analyze the books and magazines of another person in this way.

c) What aspects of these books do you most remember? What do you "know" as a result of reading them? Is it content knowledge? What feelings did you have while reading them?

**I-13.** Analysis of your own dreams is a good way to better understand your hidden feelings, motives, and desires, but since dreams are constructed so as to "hide" feelings and motives by symbols and distortions, it is more useful to record several dreams and to pull together recurring themes for analysis.

a) Before you go to sleep at night, tell yourself to "dream" several times and then "will" yourself to remember your dreams when you wake up. A conscious effort such as this often proves useful for remembering.

b) When you awake, try to write down the feeling tone of the dream even if you can't remember the sequence of events or the details. In writing, allude to parts that are unclear or

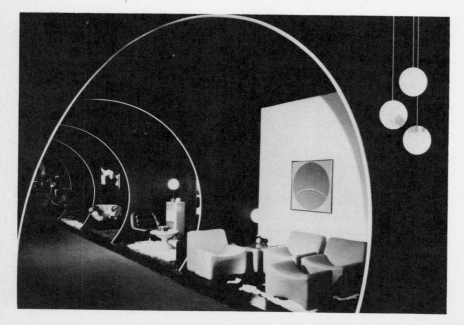

"blank." Concentrate for the next ten minutes on reconstructing the dream until you are satisfied with it as a "whole" dream. Throughout the day, think about the dream several times to pick up any parts you may have left out or failed to remember earlier. (With practice, this will become easier.)

c) Look for recurring themes, significant persons, the affect level (what emotions are being expressed in the dream?), and pay attention to your reactions to the dreams and their meaning to you as you remember them.

d) One way to increase recall and to understand meaning in dreams is to use the "role play" method of Gestalt therapy. Attempt to get back into the dream by acting out your own actions, perceptions, and movements. Then continue by role playing all the other things, animate or not, in your dreams (since even inanimate things are results of your own fantasies, they all have personal meanings). You should find your recall becoming clearer and your understanding of feelings deeper.

**I-14.** Career choice reflects personal values and personality traits. One way that motives and needs often become manifest is by a person's choice of career. What career are you in now/considering at this time?

a) What careers seem appealing/disagreeable to you? Write a list of those you would consider and those you would reject.

   i. What factors in those careers that appeal to you reveal your need for affiliation with other people, your need for achievement and independence, your need for power and control over situations and other people?

   ii. What factors in the careers that you would reject reveal your needs and motives?

b) What factors in the careers that appeal to you reflect your style of goal setting; short- or long-term, individual or joint decision making?

c) Almost all career choices involve some kinds of conflicting feelings (job vs. family; commitment vs. comfort, etc.). List, in the order of their importance, the conflicts you feel.

d) Can you think of career paths that might help you manage these conflicts? What changes in you and your relationships will be necessary in order to manage them?

e) The following short story may be helpful in understanding how a career choice affects an individual's life:

"The Trap of Solid Gold," in *The End of the Tiger,* John D. Mac-Donald (Greenwich, Conn.: Fawcett Books, 1965). To all outward appearances, his career is going well. His income is high. The problem is that the company's demands force him into a life style he can't afford.

**I-15.** Think of changes going on in the world at this moment. What trends do you see in motion that will affect your present career choices?

a) Write a scenario about the immediate environment you will be living in ten years from now. How is it different/similar to the present?

b) What does this forecast tell you about career choices?

c) How do you feel about the possibility of changing careers several times during your lifetime (many people will!)? What do these feelings tell you about your own resistance to/comfort with the process of change?

d) See the Open Systems Planning Model (O-81) for a personal career development tool.

**I-16.** Play a musical instrument you have never played before, but with which you can make sounds. Express your feelings with the sounds.

a) How does the strangeness of the instrument affect your expressions?

Are you able to express a full range of emotions — e.g., anger to tranquility?

b) Does trying the instrument as a means of expression make you want to learn to play it? In what way is this different from taking lessons?

c) Does the absence of a teacher affect your feelings? Your ability to learn? Can you learn to play a song on your own?

**I-17.** For a fascinating theory of how the mind works, see Edward de Bono, *The Mechanism of Mind* (New York: Pelican Books, 1971). De Bono describes different styles of thinking and why "lateral" creative thinking is difficult. Also see William Gordon, *Synectics* (New York: Collier Books, 1962).

**I-18.** *Self-Perception*
Make a list of the ways you would predict how others see you. Check it out with them.

a) How accurate do you think they were in describing you? To what do you attribute the differences, if any, in people's perceptions of you?

b) A film on perception, *Eye of the Beholder,* may be helpful to you. A crime seems to have been committed, but eyewitnesses disagree due to previous stereotypes. (Available from Harvard Business School, Audio-Visual Dept., Boston, Mass. 02163.)

**I-19.** *Personal Change and Growth*
Develop a list of behavioral habits/patterns/attitudes you think you exhibit which you believe have become expectations that others hold of you. These can cover a variety of factors — e.g., supporting a particular sports team, playing a particular role in groups (friendly helper), lending people your car, etc.

a) As an experiment, try to alter one of these patterns in some significant way. Monitor your own reactions/feelings and the reactions/feelings of those whose expectations you have "violated."

b) Consider these data in light of their relationship to concepts like roles, expectations, norms, resistance to change, personal growth.

**I-20.** Write a scenario about a day in your life ten years from now.
a) What do you want to be able to say about yourself?
b) What trends are in motion in your life now that will facilitate/hinder your reaching these statements/goals?
c) What trends are in motion in society that will affect your future goals? How?
d) What do you need to do now in order to achieve your future goals?

**I-21.** Play in a stream of running water. Create dams, divert the stream's path, make bridges and waterfalls.
a) What do you enjoy most about this kind of activity? Is it the freedom of playing as a child? The power of changing or building part of the environment? The sound and feel of running water?
b) Does it feel like a "waste of time"? Why or why not?
c) Hard-driving, aggressive, achievement-oriented people often have considerable difficulty with leisure time/play activities. Are these inborn characteristics or socially induced?
d) In what ways do organizations contribute to/help one cope with the work vs. leisure conflict many people experience?

**I-22.** Listen carefully to the words of some songs you consider your favorites.
a) What can you infer about your own motives, values, needs, and present concerns? What emotions do these songs elicit in you?
Analyze the themes contained in the "top forty." Does this give you any insight into the values and concerns of the youth subculture?
a) How are these songs in accord or discord with the values of society?
b) Find out why people of other subcultures dislike the music typically liked by youth, what kinds of

emotions, stereotypes, attitudes it evokes, etc.

**I-23.** *Time Management Exercise*
Keep a log for several days of how you spend your time. The more frequent the entries — e.g., every 1 to 2 hours — the better will be your data base for subsequent analysis and reflection.
a) Examine these data in terms of initiation by self vs. others, wanted vs. had to do, present-oriented demands vs. potentially growth-producing activities, useful vs. wasteful with time (after-the-fact).
b) How congruent is your daily living or life style with your self-image? Which do you intend to modify?
c) In what way is your personal time management style related to/different from your style of managing other people?

**I-24.** *Who Am I Exercise*
On ten separate sheets of paper answer the question "Who Am I?" as quickly as possible. Then go back and rank order each of these statements — i.e., give a number 10 to the statement you would be *most* willing to discard and so on until you reach number 1, the statement you would be *least* willing to discard.
a) Reflection and analysis of these rank-order statements can provide clues to the cognitive map you use in thinking about yourself — e.g., did you use role descriptions, adjectives, verbs (action-oriented), etc.?
b) With a partner (friend, spouse), this exercise can yield insights into the hidden and blind parts of your self-images (Johari Window), by asking them to make a similar set of rank-ordered cards about you and sharing them with you.
c) After doing this exercise, try writing a scenario about yourself ten years in the future (see I-15, I-20). Does the "Who Am I?" data change your perception of your future? In what ways?

**I-25.** *Tough and Tender Learning,* David Nyberg (Palo Alto, Cal.: National Press Books, 1971). Written by a creative teacher, this book emphasizes

the differences between teaching and learning, with particular emphasis on developing individual learning styles.

**I-26.** *The Silent Language,* E. T. Hall (Greenwich, Conn.: Fawcett Premier Books, 1959). A general treatment of the ways in which nonverbal behavior communicates cultural norms and values.

**I-27.** *Leadership Style Questionnaire*
*Source:* Adapted from M. Scott Myers, *Every Employee a Manager* (New York: McGraw-Hill Book Company, 1970).

This instrument is designed to help you better understand the assumptions you make about people and human nature. There are ten pairs of statements. Assign a weight from 0 to 10 to *each statement* to show the relative strength of your belief in the statements *in each pair.* The points assigned for each pair must in each case total 10. Be as honest with yourself as you can and resist the natural tendency to respond as you would "like to think things are." This instrument is not a "test." There are no right or wrong answers. It is designed to be a stimulus for personal reflection and discussion.

1. It's only human nature for people to do as little work as they can get away with. ____ (a)
   When people avoid work, it's usually because their work has been deprived of its meaning. ____ (b)
                                                                    10

2. If employees have access to any information they want, they tend to have better attitudes and behave more responsibly. ____ (c)
   If employees have access to more information than they need to do their immediate tasks, they will usually misuse it. ____ (d)
                                                                    10

3. One problem in asking for the ideas of employees is that their perspective is too limited for their suggestions to be of much practical value. ____ (e)
   Asking employees for their ideas broadens their perspective and re-

sults in the development of useful suggestions. ____ ( f )
10

4. If people don't use much imagination and ingenuity on the job, it's probably because relatively few people have much of either. ____ ( g )
   Most people are imaginative and creative but may not show it because of limitations imposed by supervision and the job. ____ ( h )
   10

5. People tend to raise their standards if they are accountable for their own behavior and for correcting their own mistakes. ____ ( i )
   People tend to lower their standards if they are not punished for their misbehavior and mistakes. ____ ( j )
   10

6. It's better to give people both good and bad news because most employees want the whole story, no matter how painful. ____ ( k )
   It's better to withhold unfavorable news about business because most employees really want to hear only the good news. ____ ( l )
   10

7. Because a supervisor is entitled to more respect than those below him in the organization, it weakens his prestige to admit that a subordinate was right and he was wrong. ____ ( m )
   Because people at all levels are entitled to equal respect, a supervisor's prestige is increased when he supports this principle by admitting that a subordinate was right and he was wrong. ____ ( n )
   10

8. If you give people enough money, they are less likely to be concerned with such intangibles as responsibility and recognition. ____ ( o )
   If you give people interesting and challenging work, they are less likely to complain about such things as pay and supplemental benefits. ____ ( p )
   10

9. If people are allowed to set their own goals and standards of performance, they tend to set them higher than the boss would. ____ ( q )
   If people are allowed to set their own goals and standards of performance, they tend to set them lower than the boss would. ____ ( r )
   10

10. The more knowledge and freedom a person has regarding his job, the more controls are needed to keep him in line. ____ ( s )
    The more knowledge and freedom a person has regarding his job, the fewer controls are needed to ensure satisfactory job performance. ____ ( t )
    10

The theory behind this instrument is discussed in detail below. To get your scores, add up the points you assigned to the following:

Theory X score = sum of (a), (d), (e), (g), (j), (l), (m), (o), (r), and (s).

Theory Y score = sum of (b), (c), (f), (h), (i), (k), (n), (p), (q), and (t).

*Assumptions About People and Human Nature — Personal Values*

One of the forces that operates to shape leadership style is the basic assumption we hold about people and human nature. McGregor described two ends of a continuum of such assumptions, labeling them Theory X (traditional assumptions) and Theory Y (emerging assumptions). These two sets of assumptions are summarized below.

The Personal Analysis of Leadership Style Questionnaire is designed to help you assess the extent of your own Theory X vs. Theory Y assumptions about people. Understanding these assumptions is of crucial importance because of the potential that exists for self-fulfilling prophecies. In other words, if you believe people are lazy, irresponsible, etc. (Theory X assumptions), you will manage them in a way that is consistent with these assumptions — e.g., watch over their shoulders all the time. This behavior can cause your subordinates to feel that they really have no responsibility in their job, which could lead them to work hard only when you are watching them closely. A self-fulfilling prophecy has thus begun and will be continually reinforced.

McGregor's conceptualization also highlights the inherent complexity of human behavior. People are not motivated by a single driving force. Instead, people seek many satisfactions and these needs are dynamic, changing as people grow and develop. This fact reinforces the need for flexible, adaptive behavior on a manager's part for differential leadership styles.

| Theory X Assumptions *(traditional)* | Theory Y Assumptions *(emerging)* |
|---|---|
| *Source:* Douglas McGregor, *The Human Side of Enterprise* (New York: McGraw-Hill Book Company, 1960). | |
| 1. People are naturally lazy; they prefer to do nothing. | 1. People are naturally active; they set goals and enjoy striving. |
| 2. People work mostly for money and status rewards. | 2. People seek many satisfactions in work: pride in achievement; enjoyment of process; sense of contribution; pleasure in association; stimulation of new challenges, etc. |

3. The main force keeping people productive in their work is fear of being demoted or fired.

4. People remain children grown larger; they are naturally dependent on leaders.

5. People expect and depend on direction from above; they do not want to think for themselves.

6. People need to be told, shown, and trained in proper methods of work.

7. People need supervisors who will watch them closely enough to be able to praise good work and reprimand errors.

8. People have little concern beyond their immediate, material interests.

9. People need specific instruction on what to do and how to do it; larger policy issues are none of their business.

10. People appreciate being treated with courtesy.

11. People are naturally compartmentalized; work demands are entirely different from leisure activities.

12. People naturally resist change; they prefer to stay in the old ruts.

13. Jobs are primary and must be done; people are selected, trained, and fitted to predefined jobs.

14. People are formed by heredity, childhood and youth; as adults they remain static; old dogs don't learn new tricks.

15. People need to be "inspired" (pep talk) or pushed or driven.

---

3. The main force keeping people productive in their work is desire to achieve their personal and social goals.

4. People normally mature beyond childhood; they aspire to independence, self-fulfillment, responsibility.

5. People close to the situation see and feel what is needed and are capable of self-direction.

6. People who understand and care about what they are doing can devise and improve their own methods of doing work.

7. People need a sense that they are respected as capable of assuming responsibility and self-correction.

8. People seek to give meaning to their lives by identifying with nations, communities, churches, unions, companies, causes.

9. People need ever-increasing understanding; they need to grasp the meaning of the activities in which they are engaged; they have cognitive hunger as extensive as the universe.

10. People crave genuine respect from their fellow men.

11. People are naturally integrated; when work and play are too sharply separated both deteriorate; "The only reason a wise man can give for preferring leisure to work is the better quality of the work he can do during leisure."

12. People naturally tire of monotonous routine and enjoy new experiences; in some degree everyone is creative.

13. People are primary and seek self-realization; jobs must be designed, modified, and fitted to people.

14. People constantly grow; it is never too late to learn; they enjoy learning and increasing their understanding and capability.

15. People need to be released and encouraged and assisted.

---

**I-28.** Domestic pets interact with your personality traits. Describe the relationship you have with a pet and how it differs from your relationships with other members of the group you live with.
a) How does your pet respond when you are friendly/angry/involved with another person or task?
b) For a week, keep a diary recording the behaviors of your pet. Assess what you think are your pet's needs and what your own needs are in relation to the animal. Whose needs get met the most and how?
c) Do you relate to/manage your pets in ways similar to your style with other people? What characteristics of you/them affect these relationships?

**I-29.** Observe a stranger on a bus or subway. Watch his/her movements, expressions, mannerisms, dress, etc.
a) What can you infer about this person — social status, race, religion, occupation, marital status, nationality, etc.?
b) What stereotypes come to mind about this person's personal habits, work habits, family life, attitude about sex, crime, responsibility?
c) If possible, interview the person. Specifically, check the validity of your stereotypes.

**I-30.** Watch a favorite talk show on T.V.
a) Observe the reactions of guests to the questions they are asked. What things do they say or do to "avoid" the issues? Why do you think they are avoiding them?
b) How does a public audience affect an individual on television? What kinds of things do you think the M.C. wants to ask but doesn't?
c) Compare your analysis to your own reactions to "being on stage." How does an audience influence your behavior? How do you prepare yourself psychologically to "walk on stage"?

**I-31.** *Games People Play,* Eric Berne (New York: Grove Press, 1961, also in paperback). This book can help to

enhance your understanding of the behavioral effects of different motives, the dynamic way in which motives interact, and the impact of self-fulfilling prophecies.

**I-32.** *Spatial Language*

Visit the office of an executive in an organization. Examine the way his/her office is laid out.

a) How does the arrangement of the furniture affect you? Does the desk act as a "barrier" to communication? How accessible is this person to you in this room?

b) Is the office conducive to thinking and reflecting or doing things?

c) How formal or informal can you be in this room?

d) If you can, interview the person to see if he/she had any goals in mind in arranging the office. Find out how they feel about working in the office, talking with others, just relaxing and reflecting.

e) For conceptual help see *Physical Settings and Organization Development,* Fred I. Steele (Reading, Mass.: Addison-Wesley Publishing Co., 1973).

**I-33.** "Learning how to learn" has been postulated as the cornerstone to self-renewal and adaptation for individuals and organizations. To learn something is to "know" it. A crucial step, therefore, in learning how to learn is to understand our own definitions of knowledge.

a) What does it mean to you to "know something"?

b) Do you feel your knowledge base has increased if you "know," for example, that being dependent on someone else makes you angry? What difference, if any, would it make if no one else/many other people "know" the same things as you or feel the same way you do?

c) What can you do to expand your definition of knowledge? Would

you have to change your learning style? How?

d) Predict the patterns your friends or family will score on the Learning-Style Inventory (see page 23). Show them your predictions and explain to them the basis for your predictions. What "traits" give you clues as to their learning styles? How accurate were you in your predictions?

**I-34.** *Contrary Imaginations,* Liam Hudson (New York: Schocken Books, 1966). The learning styles of groups of boys are divided into two broad categories: a) *convergers,* who do well in structured situations, and b) *divergers,* who prefer situations that are more open ended and who show higher creativity.

**I-35.** *The Teachings of Don Juan: A Yaqui Way of Knowledge* and *A Separate Reality: Further Conversations with Don Juan,* Carlos Castaneda (New York: Pocket Books, 1972). Personal and fascinating accounts of a young

anthropologist's apprenticeship to a Yaqui Indian's world of "nonordinary reality." Castaneda struggles to grasp a system of knowledge totally different from his familiar concepts of Western civilization.

**I-36.** The following books describing the inner experiences of people who became mentally ill or "schizophrenic" give insight into the disruptive effects of socialization on individuals and how inner conflicts can lead to total ineffectual behavior and distrust of human relationships.

*I Never Promised You a Rose Garden,* Hannah Green (New York: Signet, 1964). A very moving account of a young girl's struggle to find her way out of the world of mental illness. Many insights can be gained as to how personalities develop, how various motives manifest themselves in fantasies, dreams, and behavior. The helping relationship with her doctor is enlightening and encouraging.

*The Bell Jar,* Sylvia Plath (New York: Signet, 1971). Six months in a young creative woman's life in which she descends into sickness. A good account of how the inner world and the outer world of a person collide.

**I-37.** *I'm OK – You're OK,* Thomas A. Harris (New York: Harper & Row, Publishers, 1969, also in paperback). Harris outlines his theory of Transactional Analysis, a system of "script" writing between parents and children. Offers insight into how we develop (internalize) the Parent, Child, and Adult in ourselves.

**I-38.** Think of the ways in which a person's childhood influences his behavior today – his values, goals, achievements, motives, etc. Some biographies and novels which illustrate the impact of early years on later life are:

*Cheaper by the Dozen,* Gilbreath and Cary (New York: Bantam Books).

*To Kill a Mockingbird,* Harper Lee (New York: Popular Library, 1963).

*Hitler: A Study in Tyranny,* H. R. Trevor-Roper, (New York: Torchbooks).

*A Puritan in Babylon,* W. A. White (New York: Capricorn Books, 1965).

*The Education of Henry Adams,* H. Adams (Boston: Houghton-Mifflin Co.).

**I-39.** Look at the squares below and count how many squares you see.

a) Ask somebody else to count the squares. Do you perceive the same number of squares? Share how you arrived at your answers.

b) What feelings do you have when you can't perceive the same number as somebody else? How are your problem-solving methods the same or different?

c) How does your problem-solving method correspond to your learning style?

Learning resources I-40 to I-50 call for interaction with a partner in order to benefit from the exercises.

**I-40.** With a friend, mirror each other's movements and behavior. One person is the mirror, the other the viewer. The mirror follows the viewer's actions. Do this for five to ten minutes.

a) Switch roles for another five to ten minutes.

b) For the next five minutes mirror each other at the same time.

c) In discussing your experiences, pay particular attention to issues of shifts in control, the nature and quality of the sharing process, the ways in which you competed vs. collaborated.

d) Leadership and followership go hand-in-hand. How did it feel when your partner would not/could not easily follow your lead? As "leader," did you exercise power in a way which made your follower feel like an Origin or a Pawn? With what consequences?

**I-41.** *Role Reversal Game*
Arrange with another person (friend, spouse, child) to switch roles for about one hour. You behave like the other person and he/she behaves like you.

a) Pay attention to the feelings you have about losing the status of your normal role, your feelings about playing the role of the other person, about experiencing your normal role from another point of view.

b) Discuss with your partner such interpersonal processes as: styles of influence, decision making and conflict resolution, perception, control, dependency, and the psychological contract.

**I-42.** *Boundary Game*
With another person, discover where both of your "psychological boundaries" are — where proximity to the other person "violates" the space around you that you feel is your space. Do this nonverbally once.

a) What feelings and reactions do you have when the other person "enters" your territory? What expectations do you have of him/her when this happens? What kind of "contract" do you establish?

b) How does your partner react when you enter his/her space?

c) In conversing with another person, what is your "effective communication distance" (the distance at which you usually stand to converse with another person)?

d) What are the different reactions you get from violating another person's space?
  i. in encounter with the same sex
  ii. in encounter with the opposite sex
  iii. in encounters where there are clear status differences

e) In what ways do boundary issues manifest themselves in organizations? Office locations, lunch facilities, etc.? With what consequences?

**I-43.** Interview a "successful" entrepreneur and somebody who failed in business.

a) How does each spend his/her time? What things do they enjoy?

b) What frustrations or obstacles did each encounter in their business and how were they met? What kinds of risks did they take?

c) What part did interaction with other people play in the success or failure of the business? What part did self-directed achievement play?

d) In what ways do their experiences influence your desires to become/not become an entrepreneur? Your feelings about entrepreneurs? How do you regard "failure" in business after the interview?

e) For conceptual help, see *The Achieving Society,* David C. McClelland (New York: The Free Press, 1961). McClelland explores the relationship between the entrepreneurial spirit (achievement motivation) in a culture — as found in its literature — and the probability of a subsequent economic growth.

f) Achievement Motive Exercises can be obtained from Education Ventures, Inc., 209 Court St., Middletown, Connecticut 06457.

**I-44.** Communicate nonverbally with another person for about ten minutes.

a) What facial expressions, body expressions, gestures did you use?

b) What was the "language" of your partner?

c) What feelings, motives, thoughts could you communicate nonverbally? What was difficult for you to communicate in this way?

**I-45.** Draw or paint a picture of yourself or create a self-descriptive collage.

a) Show your picture or collage to a partner and describe yourself.

b) How do colors and designs reveal your personality? What words do you use in expressing yourself? What kinds of expressions?

c) How difficult is it to communicate thoughts and feelings about yourself?

d) The U.S. Navy, for example, is struggling with the pros/cons of allowing sailors to "express themselves" — i.e., hair style, pictures by their beds, etc. What could you tell the Navy — as an "expert" in organizational psychology — that would help them make the best decision about this issue?

**I-46.** Let someone be a consultant to you for this exercise. Ask him/her to describe your room in terms of an organization.

a) What things in your room tell about your feelings, your personality, your activities, your ideas? How does your room reflect your personality?

b) How does color and design reveal personal information about you?

c) How does the organization of the room reflect your personality? What kind of "image" does this organization (or lack of) give to your consultant? What kind of advice do you get?

d) Analyze the room of a partner or a friend in the same way.

**I-47.** *Empathy Triads*

(*Empathy:* "The projection of one's own personality into the personality of another in order to understand him better." *Webster's New World Dictionary.*)

With a partner spend about ten minutes playing the role of an empathic friend or consultant and then for another ten minutes play the role of a person receiving empathy from a friend or consultant. A third person may observe and help process the interaction.

a) What did you say or didn't you say that was most helpful? Least helpful? What did your helper say to you or didn't he/she say that was helpful? What facial and behavioral cues did you use in giving empathy?

b) Did you find "Why" questions or "How" questions to be most helpful in giving empathy?

c) Can you define the kinds of techniques that seem to be most effective in giving empathy to another person?

d) How empathic do you feel you are capable of being, for what kind of people, in what kind of situations?

e) What functional role, if any, does empathy play in organizational life? Why should/should not a manager try to increase his empathic skills?

f) Why should/should not an organization try to be empathic with the needs of others — e.g., the underprivileged, the handicapped, etc.?

**I-48.** *Operation Empathy*

Think of someone who is very different from yourself (for example, a corporation president might feel that a hippie is his "opposite"). Jot down the ways in which you think this person is different from/similar to yourself. Then seek out such a person and try to find out how this person sees the world — try to "get into his/her shoes." (If you do this in a triad, the third person may observe the interaction and provide useful feedback.)

a) How empathic did you feel toward this person? What were your first impressions, perceptions, projections, stereotypes of this person that changed during or after the interaction?

b) Which impressions, stereotypes, etc., remained the same?

c) How different/similar do you feel this person is to you now?

d) What barriers did you find that made it difficult for you to be empathic to this person? Did you discuss these with him/her? Why or why not?

**I-49.** There are many books available with suggested activities for enhancing your awareness of how you communicate to another individual, for increasing your sensitivity to another's feelings, how to build trust, etc. Some of these (available in paperback) are:

*What to Do Till the Messiah Comes* and *Below the Mind,* Bernard Gunther (New York: Collier Books, 1971).

*Gestalt Therapy,* F. Perls, R. Hefferline, P. Goodman (New York: Delta, 1951).

*Joy: Experiencing Human Awareness,* W. Schutz (New York: Grove Press, 1967).

*Supervisory and Executive Development: A Manual for Role Playing,* Maier, *et al.* (New York: John Wiley & Sons, Inc., 1964).

**I-50.** Find a dart game and a partner. Play a few rounds.

a) Did you set any goals for the number of points you wanted to score each round? How did you react to reaching or not reaching your goals?

b) What can you learn from your risk-taking posture according to how near or far you stand from the dart board?

c) What difference does another person make in your behavior, the goals you set, your reactions to success or failure?

d) While playing, announce your goal before each dart throw. Give yourself your announced goal points if you make it or better it. If you miss your goal, score zero. Does this affect your risk taking? Concentration? Use of feedback on performance?

e) Of what use are the insights of this game to organizations — e.g., goal setting, feedback, interpersonal competition, etc.?

## G. LEARNING ABOUT GROUPS

Although groups are made up of individuals, they tend to develop in ways that are more than just the sum of the parts. Individuals take different roles in groups, and the group itself will establish implicit patterns of interaction over periods of time.

In organizations, the problem of intergroup competition and conflict often leads to decisions that are less than optimal and, to a high degree, resistant to change. Change is often feared for possibly upsetting the equilibrium between groups and giving one group more power.

The following learning resources will add to your knowledge of group dynamics as well as your own relationship to groups.

**G-51.** *Intergroup Relations*
All of us belong to multiple groups because we are members of many systems. One way to better understand the nature of intergroup relationships is to draw a map of our own multiple group connections. This can be called a role-set analysis. (For a related approach at the organizational level, see O-66).
a) Make a list of all the groups of which you feel you are a mem-

ber — e.g., fathers, husbands, students, members of a political party, fans of a particular sports team.

b) To what extent is your membership in each of these groups central (very important) or peripheral (relatively minor) to you?

c) Which of your group memberships create a conflict for you? What is the nature of the conflict? Do the people in your most central group

tend to share other roles and groupings with you?

d) How do these conflicts affect your relationships with others within your most central group? In your more peripheral group?

**G-52.** *Intergroup Conflicts*
Intergroup conflict is one of the most pervasive of all organizational phenomena. Think of a group membership which is important to you. It could be

a fraternity, a particular department in a company, or residence in a particular location.

a) Identify another group with which you and your group feel some conflict or competition.

b) How do you think that other group sees your group and the people in it in terms of strengths and weaknesses, likes and dislikes, etc.?

c) Interview several members of the other group to find out how they do, in fact, see your group.

d) Which of your predictions was verified? Which were not? To what do you attribute any misperceptions? How sure are you that the people you interviewed were being absolutely honest about their perceptions of your group?

**G-53.** Observe a dinner discussion (at home or in a restaurant).

a) What kinds of things are discussed, not discussed here? By whom?

b) What does the arrangement of people at the table tell you? What roles do people play?

c) How does conflict at the dinner table get expressed? Resolved?

**G-54.** *Sociometric Game*
Creating human sculptures and arranging people in seats are some concrete ways of making affiliation with others explicit. Such an activity helps to highlight group issues such as inclusion, exclusion, trust, distrust, and closeness vs. distance. When a group is having difficulty determining which people distrust others and which people feel close to others, the following exercise can help to illustrate the reality of affiliation or lack of affiliation in a group.

a) Ask members in the group to place themselves in relation to the center of the room depending on how close or distant they feel to the rest of the group members. They should also try to place themselves near those individuals they feel closest to. Concentric circles or "rings" of people may be defined in this way.

b) Process how it feels to be in the position you have chosen. Find out how others feel about you being in that position.

c) Another exercise is to have each member of the group place each of the other members around him according to how he feels about them. The other members of the group become his "sculpture." Each person should have a chance to do this if time permits.

**G-55.** *Tinkertoy Game* (for either a small or large group)
As the leader or teacher of a group of people, experiment with two distinct styles of leadership: nondirective and democratic vs. directive and authoritarian. Pass out several pieces of a Tinkertoy set to each person seated around a table and put the remaining pieces in the center of the table.

a) In the first round, tell people they may choose six pieces to construct an object with. When everybody has the pieces they want, tell them to begin building until each person completes something.

b) In the second round, tell them to find a stick and a square piece, then to take a yellow round piece and attach it to the other end of the stick, and so on, giving *specific* directions for completing a six-to eight-piece model (they all will look alike if built as directed).

c) Process the two rounds and compare motivation and feelings toward the leader, creativity, etc.; compliance and defiance to directions given, task performance, etc.

**G-56.** Go to the ZOO.

a) Which animals remind you of yourself, of other people you know? Why?

b) What animals do you feel afraid of, puzzled by, humored by, etc.?

c) What behaviors of animals resemble human beings? How do groups of animals express cooperation, conflict? Can you distinguish the leader, the outcast, or the scapegoat? How do animals enforce group norms?

d) Engage a monkey's attention nonverbally. Try to get him to imitate you. What cues did he pick up from you? Imitate him imitating you. How does he react? How does this relate to interpersonal behavior?

e) Experiences such as visiting a zoo/farm or reading Desmond Morris' book, *The Human Zoo* (New York: Dell Publishing Co., 1969) can highlight such concepts as leadership, group norms, status/power, motivation, and interpersonal behavior, particularly as they relate to our biological heritage and development from lower animals.

**G-57.** *Master-Slave Game* (for a group of about ten to twelve people)

Perception of power is a vital factor in any group or organization's leadership. The execution of power by leaders depends to a great extent on the perception of power by the subordinates in a group, their need to give others power, and their inability to designate power to themselves. The following game illustrates how groups vary in leadership dynamics depending on these variables.

Divide into two teams. Each group of Slaves has the task of selecting two Masters for their group who will exercise "absolute power" over the group during the game.

a) Masters should meet for about five minutes alone (in pairs) and each group of Slaves should meet for about five minutes together before the game begins.

b) Each team meets in a separate room for twenty minutes with their Masters. Groups should not be aware of what is going on in the other group.

c) Both groups then reconvene to discuss what happened, what issues came up, how power was exercised. The Masters should explain to everybody what their "plans" were (strategies, for example) and the Slaves should reveal what went on in the pre-game meeting.

d) How were the two teams different/similar in the twenty-minute period? What differences in perception and execution of power were there?

e) Most groups in formal organizations have *designated* leaders. How could these leaders (Masters) behave to mitigate the suspicions, resentment, hostilities, etc., that often develop? How could subordinates (Slaves) behave to improve the relationships between the "have" and the "have nots"?

**G-58.** *Lemon Exercise*

The following game highlights the concepts of stereotyping, first impressions, individual vs. group traits, and differentiation in a group.

a) Gather a group of ten to twelve people and show them a lemon. Ask people to describe the lemon by writing characteristics down on a piece of paper.

b) Next, give everyone a lemon and ask them to "get to know" their lemon. In a few minutes, ask everyone to put their lemons in the middle of the floor, scramble them, and then identify their own lemon.

c) Next, ask everyone to get even more familiar with their own lemon. The final task will be to identify their lemon with their eyes closed (have people label their lemon with a marker first).

d) Discuss how people found their lemons (a majority of people will be able to do this), and what cues or traits they used to identify their lemons. Compare final methods of identification with the initial descriptions or impressions of the lemon held up to the whole group.

**G-59.** *Blindfold Game* (for three people)

In managing people, there are obviously many styles of helping. The following exercise will help you better understand your own personal helping style, how you feel about being a helper or a helpee, and the effect your style has on another individual.

a) One person dons a blindfold (A), one is his helper (B), and a third person acts as a silent observer (C). A should wear the blindfold for about twenty to thirty minutes and try to be as active as possible — e.g., eating a meal, taking a walk, etc. Just sitting still will be of no value.

b) B is A's helper while C is the silent observer. As the helper in this exercise, pay attention to how comfortable you feel "helping" A, how dependent or independent you want him to be with you, the ways you go about helping A to do what he wants to do (or whoever decides what he will do).

c) Switch roles until everybody has a chance to be blindfolded. Discuss the issues of responsibility for another person, what "help" really means in a concrete situation, how it feels to be dependent and to give and receive support and empathy. What other feelings are elicited by the exercise? Did anybody feel resentment or hostility at helping or being helped?

d) In what areas and in what ways is a manager a helper? What are the personal (in both parties) and organizational barriers (e.g., reward systems) to the development of effective helping relationships?

**G-60.** *The Benefactor Game* (for six to ten people)

Gather together a group of people. The following exercise will highlight various aspects of a group decision-making process: competition vs. collaboration, task-oriented vs. maintenance-oriented vs. self-oriented behavior and motives, styles of group decision making, conflict resolution, and interpersonal influence. This exercise is *for real and is not just a game.*

a) Place in an envelope a sum of money large enough to be meaningful to any one of the members of the group. Someone in the group must *in fact* receive this money — so do not expect it back. Place the envelope on a table in front of the group. The instructions to the group are as follows:

A sympathetic benefactor has decided to leave a sum of money to one of your members. For a variety of reasons, however, he decided not to choose the recipient himself. You, therefore, have the following task: Decide by *group consensus* which member of your group is to be the recipient of the money. The following conditions must be adhered to:

1. One, and only one, person can receive the money.

2. He must use the money for his *own personal satisfaction,* he *cannot,* for example, offer to buy everyone drinks, or offer to split it up in some other way later.

3. The group must be able to state the criteria and rationale for their final choice.

4. It will be the recipient's to keep and cannot be given back to the benefactor or his or her representative after the decision.

*Failure to adhere to these conditions within the allotted time of thirty minutes will result in forfeiture of the money. This is a real exercise — not a game.*

**G-61.** Meetings are a good way to observe groups in the decision-making process. Even though you may not know all the facts about the issues on the agenda, you will be able to observe some basic dynamics in any decision-making group. Often at a meeting where there are set limits (a time schedule, an agenda, etc.) power strategies and interpersonal dynamics make themselves apparent even to an outside observer. Sit in on a group that has to make a decision, a committee meeting, or a voting membership meeting of some small organization.
a) What is the style of leadership in this meeting? How are "agenda items" presented for discussion and decision making?
b) Who has the most influence in this group? How is it exerted? Who has the least influence on the decision-making process?
c) What kinds of roles do people play in this meeting? What needs make themselves apparent? What are the main concerns of the group members?

d) If the group makes a decision, what effects does it have on the group members and their relationship to each other? If no decision is made, what are the consequences?

**G-62.** Often group norms are implicit rather than explicit, and may even be difficult to define explicitly. Individuals, of course, are influenced by group norms even when they are not aware of what norms are. When you are aware of group norms, it is easier to understand your own behavior in terms of a group context. Describe the three most salient norms that operate in the group that is most important to you.
a) What are the feelings and assumptions behind them? How do these norms get communicated to others?
b) What happens to people who violate these norms? How does the group "police" itself? How does it feel to "go against" the group norms?
c) Has the group ever systematically examined their norms and tested their present relevance?
d) How do new norms develop and old norms get discarded? Understanding this process can help you consciously manage the process of change — both individually and in a group.

**G-63.** Paint a mural with some friends. This joint project will highlight several facets of group dynamics: decision making, teamwork, influencing, task-oriented vs. self-oriented behavior.
a) Whose ideas get executed? How is this done?
b) How does talent or inspiration translate into work? What definition of work is generated by this project?
c) How does the finished mural compare to the original conception of it? What changes were made along the way to alter the original plan? How were these decisions made? How would you improve the teamwork of the group if you were to paint another mural?
d) With others in a group or organization to which you belong, create a mural or collage that is representative of that group or organization. Discuss together the following questions:
i) What new insights do you have about the group?
ii) What did the group learn about its norms, climate, values?

**G-64.** *Modified Delphi Technique*
The Delphi Technique is usable as a means of reaching group consensus when prioritizing a list of items or any other task which requires the group to come to a mutually agreeable rank ordering.

It was originally used as a method for future forecasting aiming for agreement among experts on the likelihood of certain events. In the modified form below, it is still usable for forecasting and planning, but is also adaptable to more immediate tasks.
a) Display the lists of items to be ranked so that all may see them. To the right of the items, construct a matrix with the names of participants across the top.
b) Ask participants to rank order the items on a separate sheet of paper. It is important that they be written so that participants do not adjust their ratings due to group pressure.
c) Collect the rankings and enter them in the appropriate places in the matrix, determining the mean and range:

| | Jim | Peg | Irv | Deb | Dave | Cheryl | Bill | Mean | Range |
|---|---|---|---|---|---|---|---|---|---|
| Item 1 | 4 | 4 | 3 | 4 | 3 | 4 | 4 | 3.7 | 3–4 |
| Item 2 | 2 | 1 | 1 | 2 | 1 | 1 | 2 | 1.4 | 1–2 |
| Item 3 | 1 | 2 | 2 | 1 | 4 | 3 | 3 | 2.3 | 1–4 |
| Item 4 | 3 | 3 | 4 | 3 | 2 | 2 | 1 | 2.5 | 1–4 |

*Source:* We are indebted to Charles Case, Cleveland State University, for this modification of the Delphi Technique.

d) *Discussion:* The purpose of the discussion is to:
1. bring out the reasons for the extremes in those items with the largest range.
2. to attempt to reduce that range by discussing criteria used by individuals and attempting to get new agreement on the best criteria for rating the items.

e) If consensus is apparent, the group may want to move toward it at this point without going through another round. If there is still some disagreement, repeat the ranking process.

f) If two cycles of ranking do not reduce the range enough to reach consensus, stop and discuss the process issues that may be interfering with decision making.

**G-65.** *Serious Games,* Clark C. Abt (New York: Viking Press, 1970). The author, whose company specializes in simulations for learning and problem solving, has provided both theory and examples of the usefulness of experiential learning for groups.

---

# O. LEARNING ABOUT ORGANIZATIONS

This section is concerned with organizations — collections of individuals who come together to carry out transactions with the environment that would be impossible to do separately. They are also composed of groups of people who are often in conflict with other groups within the organization, usually as a result of competition for resources, influence, and recognition.

The study of individuals and groups yields an awareness of a high level of complexity. The study of organizations is even more complex. The exercises and references in this section are intended to help with thinking and learning about organizations, and ways of acting on them to precipitate planned change.

**O-66.** *Socialization*

Socialization experiences take place continually and in a variety of contexts. Each of us has had numerous experiences with socialization already: as a child in the family, every new grade or class we enter in school, new jobs we take, new group experiences, etc. Seldom, however, do we think explicitly about this recurring process.

a) Think of a recent new group, organization, or class you have joined.
b) Using the framework at the right, try to articulate the "contract" as it existed at the point of entry.
c) Review your entries and consider the following:
1. In what ways did you and the organization communicate these expectations to each other?
2. In what areas can you identify the greatest matching? The greatest mismatches?

| INDIVIDUAL (You) | | ORGANIZATION or GROUP | |
|---|---|---|---|
| Expect to Get | Expect to Contribute | Expect to Get | Expect to Contribute |
| | | | |

3. How were mismatches handled at entry? During your life with the organization? With what consequences or satisfactions (in terms of productivity, satisfaction, etc.)?

d) Think about the many organizations of which you have been, are, or will be a member.
1. Is there a pattern to what you expect to get/give?
2. Is there a pattern to what you

think the organization will expect to get from/give to you?

3. To what extent are any patterns related to your individual needs? Your theory of organizations?

## 0-67. *Responsibility Charting*

A recent technique that has proven useful in clarifying roles and responsibilities in project management is *responsibility charting*. The first step is to construct a grid with the tasks that must be done on the left side, and the people most likely to be involved listed across the top:

The chart is used to indicate each person's responsibilities for each decision or task that must be done. There are four levels of involvement possible for each person in each task or decision:

1. *Responsibility ("R")*. The person with this designation under his/her name would be responsible for action to make sure decisions are carried out.

2. *Approval required, or the right to veto ("A–V")*. This item must be reviewed by the person(s) designated, who will *either approve or reject it.*

3. *Support ("S")*. Provides logistical support and resources for this task or decision.

4. *Inform ("I")*. Must be informed of decisions, but cannot influence them.

Each item is considered and responsibility (R) is assigned. It is essential that there be only one R for any one horizontal line. A consensus must be reached or an authoritarian decision made on who has responsibility. If there is lack of agreement, it is often

because the task is defined too broadly. At that point the group should attempt to draw another horizontal line or two and break down the task into components, assigning R for each.

## 0-68. *Pecking Orders*

Pecking orders in an organization can tell you a lot about the nature of the organization: its hierarchy of power and affiliation between members, the kinds of status that are important to individuals, etc. Visit several different types of organizations — e.g., a supermarket, a hospital, a police station, etc. In each case, try to develop a picture of the "pecking order" or status hierarchy which exists.

a) Pay attention to the multiple ways in which this pecking order is communicated — e.g., forms of dress, locations of work space, forms of address. What can you infer about the degree of openness vs. closedness, flexibility vs. rigidity, assumptions about people, etc., of these various types of organizations?

b) Interview several people in these organizations and try to check the accuracy of your own diagnosis.

c) In what ways do aspects of the "pecking order" in an organization vary as a function of the task — e.g., military organization vs. a volunteer welfare organization?

## 0-69. *Force Field Analysis*

There are several diagnostic tools available in diagnosing and planning for change. Application of these tools should increase the skills of the administrator in bringing about effective improvement in organizations, groups, and individual relationships. One such

diagnostic tool is called force field analysis. In physics, there is a concept that a body is at rest when the sum of all the forces operating upon it is zero. The body will move in a direction determined by the unbalancing forces. This concept can be applied to situations involving human factors, for example, the production level of work teams in a factory, which often is constant (within small limits) around a certain level. The level stays reasonably constant because the forces tending to *raise* the level are just counteracted by forces tending to *lower* the level.

This kind of analysis can be applied to a wide range of situations involving human behavior. For example, suppose you are a member of a group and another member remains silent and uncommunicative. In an effort to understand his behavior better, you might make up a Force Field Diagram. Some *increasing* forces might be:

A. Pressure from other group members.

B. Rewards given for amount of participation.

C. Relevant topics he knows about.

Some *restraining* forces might be:

D. Desire to avoid hurting other members.

E. Fear of retaliation if he does talk.

F. Anxiety about exposing himself.

There could be any number of forces, of course, and of varying intensities. As long as the total strength of the *restraining forces* exceeds that of the *increasing forces,* the group member will reduce the amount of talking he does. He will maintain his rate of talking if the forces match exactly, and increase his rate if the *increasing forces* outweigh the *restraining.*

There are two different strategies one could employ in an attempt to help the person in the illustration above talk more. One is to increase the strength of the increasing forces — e.g., apply more pressure. This may temporarily raise the present rate of talking. The problem with this strategy is that it tends to increase the tension in the system, causing new restraining forces to appear. As a result, this approach

| Sue | Bob | John | Beth | Dick | Ralph | Jim | |
|-----|-----|------|------|------|-------|-----|------|
| I | A–V | R | A–V | S | | I | Task$_1$ |
| A–V | | | R | A–V | A–V | I | Task$_2$ |
| | S | S | I | R | | A–V | Task$_3$ |
| S | A–V | | I | R | | S | Task$_4$ |
| R | | S | | A–V | | I | Task$_5$ |

Source: Richard Beckhard and Reuben Harris, *Organizational Transitions* (Reading, Mass.: Addison-Wesley Publishing Co., Inc., 1977).

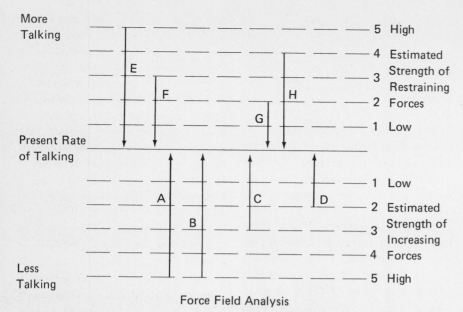

More Talking

Present Rate of Talking

Less Talking

5 High
4 Estimated
3 Strength of
   Restraining
2 Forces
1 Low

1 Low
2 Estimated
3 Strength of
   Increasing
4 Forces
5 High

Force Field Analysis

may result in changes which are temporary in nature.

A second approach is to eliminate or reduce the strength of the restraining forces. In this way, the rate of talking rises to a new, higher level without any resulting increase in tension. To understand why this second approach is less frequently used, we must understand certain characteristics of the forces people generally see operating. Most forces fall into one of three categories:

1. Self — having to do with myself as a person
2. Others — other people than myself
3. The environment — nature of facilities, time available

In diagnosing a problem, most people, if they see themselves at all related to the problem, see themselves as increasing forces while others and environment are the restraining forces. One reason for this is that they may implicitly be aware of the effects of the two change strategies outlined above. In other words, if I recognize the part I might be playing (my attitudes or my behavior) in *holding back* problems, I may be the one who has to change! In the example presented above, my tendency to dominate may be the most powerful force keeping others (restraining) from talking — and in order to help them talk more, I will have to be less dominant.

Force field analysis can be a powerful diagnostic tool in helping to uncover possible problem areas in planning a change effort. From the change agents' point of view, it can help them to diagnose a system's readiness, capability, and potential for change. It can help them to understand their own motives and goals for being involved.

**O-70.** *Organizational Decision Making*

Many organizations claim they operate to "maximize" performance or growth. Simon (1947), on the other hand, argues that man is not a maximizer, but a satisficer (he will settle for results that satisfy without being optimal).

a) Think of several organizational decisions you have been part of.

b) Were they optimizing or satisficing decisions?

c) What are the forces (individual, group, organizational) which operate to create satisficing decisions? Maximizing decisions?

d) Can an organization ever make an optimizing decision? Under what conditions?

**O-71.** Management literature that may add further understanding of organization theory are listed below:

*Managing With People,* J. Fordyce, R. Weil (Reading, Mass.: Addi-

son-Wesley Publishing Co., 1971). A practical handbook for managers of all types with suggestions for long-range development as well as immediate results.

*Parkinson's Law,* C. Northcote Parkinson (New York: Ballantine Books, 1957). An antidote to the deadly seriousness of management literature. Probably nearer the truth, also.

*Supervisory and Executive Development: A Manual for Role Playing,* N. R. F. Maier, *et al.* (New York: John Wiley & Sons, Inc., 1964). A good source for understanding the dynamics behind group effectiveness.

*Up the Organization,* R. Townsend (New York: Fawcett Books, 1970). A successful manager describes his use of "Theory Y" assumptions and leadership to revitalize an ailing company.

**O-72.** A good understanding of how "top management" operates in an organization can be gained by sitting in on a political meeting (town, city, state, or federal) and observing intergroup dynamics of a political organization structure such as group loyalty, intergroup conflict and resolution of conflict, power strategies, influencing, decision making, and policy-making tactics. Observe the communication channels that are both overt and covert (implicit).

a) Which groups in the meeting are in conflict with which other groups? What issues are most salient to each group? What determines group loyalty and group factions — around what political issues?

b) What behaviors communicate power-motivated individuals, affiliation motivation, achievement motivation? What individuals appear to be self-oriented, task-oriented, maintenance-oriented?

c) What is the organizational climate of this meeting? Which people are ready to fight, eager to cooperate, most likely to conform or be influenced by others? Who holds the most persuasive power?

The Republicans in Nominating Convention in Their Wigwam at Chicago, May, 1860.

workers, and, if possible, talking to inmates.

a) How comfortable do you feel being around people who are diagnosed as mentally ill? How comfortable are you talking to nurses, attendants, doctors about the institution?

b) What rules do you observe? What are the behavioral norms for patients, for the attendants, nurses, and doctors? What kinds of structures exist that seem to encourage mental health or mental illness? What kinds of "authority" issues do you think are necessary or unnecessary? In what ways do you feel patients may be dehumanized?

c) Find out how doctors set goals in helping patients terminate their illness. How do they determine prognosis of patients? What are the motivations of those persons in a helping role? Try to predict what their learning styles might be. How open/closed do you feel they are to their own personal growth and change.

d) If possible, interview one of the members after the meeting and find out what his/her motivations were, whether this person's needs were met by the decisions made, how he/she viewed the process of the meeting.

e) How would you, as an organizational psychologist, go about trying to improve the functioning of such a complex organization? Consider changes you would make at the level of the individual, small subgroup, organization, and environment (e.g., constituency, relationship to other political structures, etc.).

**O-73.** The fiction of management and business can be a good source of learning. Although most novelists have dealt with themes of interpersonal relations, some writers have made management a major theme. Some popular fiction recommended for your enjoyment are:

*The Boss is Crazy Too,* Mel Lazarus (New York: Dell, 1963). Imagine a publishing company in which the president can become wealthy by driving it into bankruptcy.

*The John Putnam Thatcher Mysteries* by Emma Lathen (New York: Popular Library). Thatcher, vice-president of a Wall Street investment bank, continually encounters murder while about his business. Fine inside insights into the irrational workings of a supposedly rational organization.

John D. MacDonald, a Harvard MBA, has written some sixty-five novels (Fawcett Books), many about business. Recommended:

*The Crossroads* (about family business).

*Slam the Big Door* (land development).

*Pale Gray for Guilt* (a swindler is swindled in an amazingly clever financial transaction).

*Rich Man, Poor Man,* Irwin Shaw (New York: Dell Publishing, 1969). A bright young man goes through a number of successful careers as an entrepreneur, manager, and politician.

**O-74.** Understanding how architecture and spatial arrangements within an organization affects personal interaction can give you insights into the organization's assumptions about people, the group norms that exist, the hierarchy of status, and the kind of work climate that exists. Visit a state or private mental hospital and try to "analyze" the organizational climate by observing a patient ward, talking to

**O-75.** The climate of an organization has a dramatic impact on the individuals who are part of it. In some cases, our family and educational organizations contribute to a person's inability to cope with their environment, a situation we have labelled "mental illness." Some popular books which offer insight into how culture, environment, and organizations may initiate and sustain such effects are:

*The Politics of Experience,* R. D. Laing (New York: Ballantine Books, 1967). A maverick British psychiatrist looks at the damage we do to each other through our institutions and attitudes; particularly the way his profession perceives mental illness.

*Myth of Mental Illness* and *The Manufacture of Madness,* Thomas S. Szasz, M.D. (New York: Dell Publishing Co., 1970). Szasz challenges the underlying assumptions of mental illness and presents the concept of mental illness as a misused part of a strategic struggle for power.

*One Flew Over the Cuckoo's Nest,* Ken Kesey (New York: Signet

Books, 1963). A novel about a ward in a mental hospital in which the authority ("Big Nurse") is so dedicated to running a smooth ward that she punishes anyone who shows signs of recovery.

## O-76. *Organizational Diagnosis*
Just as we have cognitive maps which influence our perceptions of other people, we also have our own theory of organizations which may "filter" our perceptions of an organization's climate and structure. These implicit theories consist of a set of key variables, concepts, and a map of the relationships among them.
a) Walk into an organization and write down your immediate conclusions about its climate. Take time after-

ward to check those conclusions with people at several levels in the organization. Are your conclusions supported or disconfirmed? Now go back and write down the data you used to come to the initial conclusions. What do they tell you about your filters?
b) Think of an organization you are presently working with, have worked with recently, or one you'd like to work with (either full-time or in some consulting, training, or other part-time capacity):
   1. If someone who is unfamiliar with this organization asks you to describe it briefly, how would you respond?
c) Suppose you have been asked by an appropriate person in this organization to do an organizational diagnosis in order to understand it as a preliminary step to helping it change.
   1. What data would you collect (categories or variables, *not* method) to use in the diagnosis? Why?
d) Now go over your responses to b and c above and try to consider the following:
   1. What is your cognitive map of organizations? What key variables or categories of variables do you use in describing an organization?
   2. How would the variables you examined in your diagnosis relate to each other? Which variables are causally related? What does this map tell you about how *you* would go about making organizations more effective?
   3. How do your own motives (*n*-Ach, *n*-Aff, etc.) influence your own theory of organizations?

(See the chapter "The Organization as an Open System.")

## O-77.
A simple comparative study of organization climates can help you understand the implications that architecture, furniture arrangements, personnel systems, and group norms have for the joining-up process in an organi-

zation. You may want to "pretend" you are seeking employment in order to establish what the criteria for joining up in an organization are.
a) What does it feel like to approach the building or office when you enter the organization? Compare this process of walking into a bank, hospital, courthouse, police station, etc., with some informal operation such as a small restaurant, store, or volunteer organization.
b) What aspects of the physical structures induce feelings of acceptance or informality? Feelings of distrust or defensiveness? How are you greeted? What effects do the spatial arrangements have on you? How do they relate to the behavioral norms of the employees?
c) What can you infer about what it is like to work in these organizations from the style and manner of communication of the personnel? From the employees? What are the prevalent attitudes of the employees about the management of the organization?
d) What mixed messages do you get about what it is like to work in each of the organizations you visit?

## O-78. *Political and Military Organizations*
Although they tend to have different goals (control, defense) than profit-making or helping organizations, governmental and military organizations share the same problems. The following books provide insights into organization behavior by chronicling patterns of organizations under stress.
*Papillon,* Henri Charriere (New York: Pocket Books). A description of life in the ultimately controlled organization — a prison. Both prisoners and guards have their own cultures and organization structures, interfacing in the overall organization in some surprising ways.
*Inside the Third Reich,* Albert Speer (New York: Avon Books). From his position as an insider, Speer provides detailed accounts of how this "organization" was built, functioned, and was eventually defeat-

ed. In addition to an excellent analysis of Hitler's style of leadership, important insights can be gained into such concepts as: organization structure (project vs. functional vs. matrix organization), centralization vs. decentralization and organizational decision making, patterns of organizational communication, planned organizational change, resistance to change, individual vs. organizational goals.

*The Caine Mutiny,* Herman Wouk (New York: Doubleday Anchor Books). A good description of what happens when an organizational task under the leadership of a strict authoritarian figure becomes a focus for rebellion — leading to organizational breakdown. See also *The Arnheiter Affair,* Neil Sheehan (New York: Dell).

*Patton,* Ladislas Farago (New York: Dell Books). An excellent portrayal of a general's impact on the military organization — his leadership style, military goals and personal values and needs in conflict with the military organization.

*Power,* Adolf A. Berle (New York: Harcourt, Brace and World). A lengthy treatise on the realities of political power from one who has both participated in government and observed as an academician.

*Rules for Radicals,* Saul D. Alinsky (Vintage Books). The master organizer of mass political action has set down his laws for forcing change. Although they would seldom be part of an organizational planned change effort, they do provide stimulation for thinking about the effective use of power.

## O-79. *Planned Change*

Argyris (1971) has argued that, in all that he does, the effective change agent should strive to accomplish three objectives:

1. to increase the availability of valid information.
2. to increase the possibility of free choice by the client.
3. through 1 and 2, to help the client generate internal commit-

ment among employees and members to those choices.

a) Think of several change agents you have known.
b) To what extent did they seem to operate within the Argyris ideal?
c) What consequences can you see or predict that would occur from not adhering to these criteria — e.g., forcing a solution rather than maximizing free choice?
d) What would a brainwasher in P.O.W. camp say about these criteria?

## O-80. *Planned Change*

The Kolb-Frohman model of planned change (see Planned Change and Organizational Development chapter) is essentially a collaborative model of the change process. Significant change can also occur in a more spontaneous, power-oriented, or forced manner. In these cases, it is usually "planned change" as well, but the planning takes place in a unilateral way.

a) Think of a specific change at the level of the individual (e.g., deciding to get married), group (e.g., change of leadership), organization (e.g., change of work procedure), and environment (e.g., civil rights acts, abortion decisions).
   1. Consider the ways in which the Kolb-Frohman model might have been used — implicitly or explicitly.
   2. Consider the impact on the individual, or organizational or social changes which are spontaneous, power-oriented, and forced rather than collaboratively planned. Which is more permanent? Which has more unanticipated consequences?

## O-81. *Open Systems Planning*

*Source:* Based on an unpublished memo by Richard Beckhard.

Complex organizations are open systems. As such, an effective, proactive organization does not wait to react to the environment, but tries to anticipate, plan for, and influence the nature of the environmental demands placed upon it. One procedure for

such activity is Open Systems Planning.

This procedure may be used productively with any organization of which you are a member, as long as it has an anticipated life of at least a few years. Fraternities, campus organizations, families, and companies are all good places to use the system. The seven phases are:

### Phase One — Identify the Planning Unit

The first step is to identify who the planning unit is and to determine for what level of the system planning is being undertaken. This can range from individual plans for each member of a group to a plan for a group that represents only part of an organizational subunit, to a plan for an organizational subunit or a total system. Generally, it becomes more difficult to draw meaningful action steps from the OSP process when plans are made that members have no authority or responsibility to carry out or when critical members of a unit are not present for unit planning.

### Phase Two — Defining the Mission

The second step in this process is to come to a common definition of the core mission/goal of the system. In forming this mission statement, you should explore all initial differences as fully as possible — i.e., resist the premature conclusion that "It's probably a matter of semantics."

### Phase Three — Present Demands

Once having defined your mission in your own view, the next step is to identify all of the other relevant systems making demands on the present system.

### Phase Four — Present Responses

For each of the demands identified in Phase Three, what is the present pattern or mode of response?

### Phase Five — Projected Future

Looking two to four years ahead, predict the likely demands of these other systems on your group, given normal inertia and trends. In other words, if you took no proactive steps, what would the future look like?

*Phase Six — Ideal Future*

What would we like each demand system to be asking of us two to four years from now?

*Phase Seven — Action Steps*

What short-range — e.g., three to six months — and long-range steps must we take in order to have them demand of us what we would like in Phase Six?

**O-82.** In planning change, Jay W. Forrester contends that we tend to try to provide simple, immediate solutions to only the most obvious parts of the problem, and fail to take into consideration the total system and how it will respond. His following books provide a philosophical framework for large system change, and computer models for anticipated long-range consequences:

*Industrial Dynamics,* Jay W. Forrester (Cambridge, Mass.: Massachusetts Institute of Technology Press, 1961).

*Urban Dynamics,* Jay W. Forrester (Cambridge, Mass.: Massachusetts Institute of Technology Press, 1969).

*World Dynamics,* Jay W. Forrester (Cambridge, Mass.: Wright-Allen Press, 1971).

---

## C. LEARNING ABOUT CULTURE AND ENVIRONMENT

The fourth critical area for organizations is the larger societal system in which they exist. To ignore cultural and environmental factors in making organization decisions is to miss extremely important data. Political, economic, and social change affect every organization.

This section of learning resources can provide a beginning for the manager or student who wishes to expand his/her knowledge of the wider context in which an organization functions and changes.

**C-83.** Change agents who work on larger political systems (Gandhi, Martin Luther King, Jr., Jesse Jackson, etc.) and on organizations from the outside (Ralph Nader, Saul Alinsky) usually have a different approach to initiating change than the manager or organization development consultant.

a) What assumptions does this "cultural" change agent make about the nature of social systems?

b) What are their models of the change process? How do they deal with resistance to change?

c) To what would you attribute the success or failure of such change agents in their major projects (Indian independence, the Montgomery bus boycott, Operation Breadbasket, auto safety, minority employment)?

d) There are numerous examples of national experiments in change, such as civil rights laws, the Equal Rights Amendment, abortion laws and decisions, pollution control, etc. Use the Force Field Analysis (page 337) to analyze the forces that led to one of these changes.

e) Do another Force Field Analysis of the forces that are pushing for success and forces pushing for failure of these changes.

f) A good film on the process of planned change is *A Time for Burning,* William Jersey Organization, New York. The minister of a large urban church attempts to bring about change in the racial attitudes of his parishioners. His heart is in the right place, but his methods are doomed to failure from the beginning.

**C-84.** *Society and the Individual*
There are many current books written

by social analysts that offer insight into the cultural trends and changes that affect the individual's life, his values, goals, and attitudes about change itself. Some popular books dealing with these issues are:

*Pursuit of Loneliness: American Culture at its Breaking Point,* Phillip Slater, Boston: Beacon Press, 1970). An analysis of the relationships between our self-imposed subservience to technology and the quality of life in the United States, why it is destructive, and proposed changes that will alter the values and motives underlying most organizations and institutions existing today.

*The Temporary Society,* Warren Bennis and Phillip Slater (New York: Harper & Row, Publishers, 1968). An insightful analysis of the growing temporality of relationships in Western culture. The short-term "task force" and the matrix organization are organizational correlaries.

*Future Shock,* Alvin Toffler (New York: Bantam Books). The rapidity of technological innovation in the West is leading to a new kind of psychological disorientation, induced by change. It affects individuals and their relationships to work and to others, and the pace is picking up.

*Twelve Angry Men* (United Artists) is a film highlighting group decision making and influence. A jury of twelve men is charged with the responsibility of deciding the guilt or innocence of a young boy charged with the murder of his father. On the first ballot, the vote is eleven guilty and one not guilty. The ensuing seventy minutes dramatizes the process by which each of the other eleven jurors "becomes convinced" of the boy's innocence. When used as a training input, viewers are asked to predict the order in which the jurors will change their minds.

**C-85.** Foreign customs are often strange to us when we don't understand what they mean or how they are similar or different from our own. We have a tendency to defend our own customs when in the company of foreigners until open communication allows us to discover those areas in which we are alike. Go to dinner with a foreign friend.

a) How are your eating customs different, the same? How do your cultural differences affect your ability to communicate?

b) How do you overcome language barriers? What words do you have the most trouble defining?

c) Find out what life is like in an organization in your friend's country. In what ways do cultural differences influence appropriate leadership styles? Styles of decision making? Modes of conflict resolution? The meaning and value of work vs. leisure?

**C-86.** Children are often the best mirrors for viewing cultures, particularly cultures in which there is conflict. These three novels of childhood and adolescence provide some startling insights.

*Lord of the Flies,* William Golding (New York: Capricorn Books, 1955). A group of boys shipwrecked on an island go about organizing their own adultless society with results that reflect contemporary organizations and society.

*A High Wind in Jamaica,* Richard Hughes (New York: Signet Books, 1956). Some children are taken aboard a pirate ship in a routine raid. They adapt quickly to what they think are pirate values, so much so that it is difficult to tell which group is more dangerous.

*The Heart is a Lonely Hunter,* Carson McCullers (New York: Bantam Books, 1940). A young girl growing up in a southern town is faced with conflicting demands, values, and loyalties.

**C-87.** If there are any countercultural organizations (communes, self-help groups, free universities, etc.) in your vicinity you may find a visit to one of these types of organizations valuable in understanding how different values, roles, and attitudes affect the climate and structure of an organization. In many cases, there may appear to be *no* organization in the traditional sense.

a) How does such an organization manage its internal problems — decision-making processes, task division, maintenance, etc?

b) What are the motives or incentives for working or living in such an organization? For leaving one? Try to talk to somebody who has lived or worked in the organization about how it compares with other more traditional structures. How do people relate to each other, work together, resolve conflicts, etc.?

c) What are the underlying values and norms in a countercultural organization and how do they contradict the values of similar but more traditional structures? What are the assumptions about people?

d) See *The Greening of America,* Charles A. Reich (New York: Bantam Books). Reich postulates three levels of consciousness among Americans and forecasts new conflicts that will differ from traditional ones due to the newer sets of values held by the emerging "counterculture."

**C-88.** *Dreams and Deeds,* R. A. Levine (Chicago: University of Chicago Press, 1966). Cross-cultural differences are clearly illustrated in this analysis of the dreams of adolescent boys from two cultures in one country. The group with dreams full of achievement imagery is much more successful than the group with high power imagery.

**C-89.** *The Children of the Dream,* Bruno Bettelheim (Avon Books). In reflecting on the ways organizations socialize new members, it is helpful to look at the ways that societies socialize their children. This study of Israeli kibbutzim focuses on the transfer of values and norms from adults to children, particularly around sharing and interdependence. It also offers insights into the kibbutz as a social system that is intentionally different.

**C-90.** The question of effective helping style is of critical concern to the manager. One source for learning about various ways of helping and their effects on people is found outside management in the area of psychotherapy and humanistic psychology, a rather recent cultural phenomenon. Various schools of psychology have developed helping techniques that transcend the social biases individuals encumber in their process of growing into adulthood. Another current trend in therapy centers is the encounter group, sensitivity group, or self-awareness group method of discovering who oneself really is and how he/she feels about being that self. Some psychological films which illustrate these therapy techniques are:

*Three Approaches to Psychotherapy* (Carl Rogers, Albert Ellis, and Fritz Perls). A good presentation of three contrasting helping styles: non-directive (client-centered), rational therapy, and Gestalt therapy.

*Humanistic Revolution.* Interviews with some of the leaders — Maslow, Perls, May, Watts, Tillich, Rogers, and others.

*Journey into Self.* Classic film of the encounter phenomena, Dr. Carl

Rogers and Dr. Farson co-lead an intensive basic workshop. Academy Award-winning documentary.

*Target Five.* Virginia Satir, eminent family therapist, demonstrates the actualizing relationship to be reached when people/families discard the manipulative relationships that hamper growth and development.

*In the Now.* Dr. James Simkin gives an excellent demonstration of Gestalt therapy principles and techniques with three different subjects.

All of the above films may be obtained on a rental basis for about $30 a day from Psychological Films, Orange, California.

*Dr. Gordon Allport.* An interview with Dr. Allport in which he discusses self-development, personality development, and socialization and existentialism.

*Games People Play.* Eric Berne and Transactional Analysis — theory and practice.

*Nude Marathon.* Paul Bindrim conducts a workshop filmed by the Canadian Broadcasting Corp. for Canadian T.V.

*Rollo May: Human Encounter.* Dr. Rollo May discusses his philosophy and therapy principles.

All of the above films may be obtained on a rental basis from the University of Pennsylvania Film Center.

*Primal Scream.* A documentary film showing progress of patients of primal therapy under the care of Dr. Janov (Primal Institute, Los Angeles, California).